RELIGIOUS FREEDOM
IN THE WORLD

Founded in 1941 by Eleanor Roosevelt and Wendell Willkie, Freedom House is devoted to the promotion of democracy and freedom around the world. Through surveys and special reports, it provides global assessments of the state of political freedom, civil liberties, press freedom, and freedom of belief. It promotes democracy through programs that strengthen civil society in societies in transition from dictatorship to democratic rule. Freedom House also advocates on behalf of freedom by identifying and protesting against abuses of human rights and encouraging the United States and other countries to make the promotion of democracy an integral part of their foreign policies.

Its Center for Religious Freedom, a self-sustaining project within Freedom House, is at the forefront of a national campaign to promote religious freedom worldwide. Since its inception in 1986, the Center has reported on the religious persecution of individuals and groups abroad and undertaken advocacy on their behalf in the media, Congress, the State Department, and the White House. It also sponsors investigative field missions and presses official Washington for overall religious freedom in China, Sudan, Vietnam, Pakistan, Saudi Arabia, Egypt, and elsewhere. The Center is a membership organization that publishes a bimonthly newsletter, periodic reports, and press releases on religious persecution.

Freedom House Board of Trustees

Freedom House Staff

Center for Religious Freedom Staff

Board of Reference for Survey*

Titles are for identification purposes only and do not imply endorsement by organizations.

RELIGIOUS FREEDOM
IN THE WORLD

a global report on freedom and persecution

PAUL MARSHALL, GENERAL EDITOR

BROADMAN
&HOLMAN
PUBLISHERS

Nashville, Tennessee

0-8054-2368-0

Published by Broadman & Holman Publishers,
Nashville, Tennessee

Dewey Decimal Classification: 323
Subject Heading: RELIGIOUS FREEDOM
Library of Congress Card Catalog Number: 00-040405

Library of Congress Cataloging-in-Publication Data
Religious freedom in the world : a global report on freedom and
persecution / Paul Marshall, general editor.
        p. cm.
Includes bibliographical references.
ISBN 0-8054-2368-0 (pb)
1. Freedom of religion. 2. Persecution. 3. Human rights.
I. Marshall, Paul A., 1948–

BL 640.R44   2000
323.44'2'09—dc21

                                                        00-040405
                                                        CIP

2 3 4 5 04 03 02 01 00

CONTENTS

List of Countries vi

Preface vii

Acknowledgments ix

Religious Freedom and American Foreign Policy / Nina Shea 1

The Importance of Religious Freedom / Paul Marshall 9

The Nature of Religious Freedom and
  Religious Persecution / Paul Marshall 14

The Current State of Religious Freedom / Paul Marshall 18

Western Europe: Trends in Religious Liberty / Willy Fautre 28

The Former Soviet Union: Trends in
  Religious Liberty / Michael Bourdeaux 35

Religious Freedom in Latin America / Paul Sigmund 43

Country Profiles 54

Appendix 1: Numbers and Statistics 331

Appendix 2: Criteria for Profiles of Religious Freedom 334

LIST OF COUNTRIES

Argentina	55	Latvia	196
Armenia	57	Lebanon	199
Austria	60	Lithuania	203
Azerbaijan	64	Macedonia	206
Bangladesh	68	Malaysia	209
Belarus	71	Mauritania	213
Belgium	75	Mexico	216
Bhutan	78	Moldova	220
Botswana	81	Mongolia	223
Brazil	83	Morocco	225
Bulgaria	87	Namibia	229
Burma (Myanmar)	91	Nepal	231
Chile	95	Netherlands	234
China	99	Nigeria	238
China-Tibet	106	Norway	242
Colombia	110	Pakistan	244
Cuba	113	Philippines	249
East Timor	117	Poland	252
Egypt	121	Romania	257
El Salvador	126	Russia	260
Estonia	128	Saudi Arabia	265
Finland	131	Singapore	268
France	133	South Africa	272
Georgia	137	Spain	275
Germany	140	Sri Lanka	278
Greece	143	Sudan	282
Guatemala	147	Sweden	289
Hungary	151	Taiwan	292
India	155	Tanzania	295
Indonesia	161	Turkey	297
Iran	167	Turkmenistan	302
Ireland	172	Ukraine	306
Israel	176	United Kingdom	310
Japan	181	United States of America	314
Kazakhstan	184	Uzbekistan	319
Korea, North	187	Vietnam	322
Korea, South	190	Zimbabwe	328
Kyrgyz Republic	193		

PREFACE

The country profiles describe, evaluate, and rate countries containing more than 90 percent of the world's population on a scale from a high of one to a low of seven. They describe the situation of freedom of religion or belief at the beginning of the new millennium. The countries have been selected so that the survey represents each continent, major religion, and area; covers countries with large populations; describes particularly egregious violators of religious freedom; and adequately illustrates variations within regions. It should be emphasized that the numbers are ratings of the situation in *countries*, not of the conduct of *governments*. In some cases, such as in civil war, there may be little religious freedom, but a government may be able to do little about it.

Nor is the survey a catalog of the rights of "religious people." The persecution of all people of any or no religion should be equally as offensive in our eyes as that of believers in any particular religion. Furthermore, since most people in the world profess to be believers of one kind or another, then such a survey would necessarily include most of the world's human rights violations of whatever kind. Rather, the focus here is on the denial to anyone of rights of a particular *kind*, those concerned with practicing one's religion, and the denial of rights for a particular *reason*, because of the religious beliefs of those who are persecuted and/or those who persecute.

Finally, in line with most human rights treaties, this survey covers freedom of "religion or belief." There are beliefs that, functionally, take the place of explicitly religious beliefs, and these, too, should be protected. Atheists and agnostics may also suffer loss of "religion or belief" and, in turn, may deny it to others.

ACKNOWLEDGMENTS

Religious Freedom in the World is a project of Freedom House's Center for Religious Freedom. The Center is deeply grateful to the Homeland Foundation for its support of the survey's research. This book would not have been possible without also the generosity of Frank Batten Jr., The Lynde and Harry Bradley Foundation, and The Carthage Foundation.

The Center is particularly grateful for the advice and input of our Survey Board of Reference, whose members are: Vo Van Ai, Rev. Dr. Michael Bourdeaux, Professor Marshall Breger, Professor Cole Durham, Professor Jean Bethke Elshtain, Professor Robert George, Rabbi Irving Greenberg, Lodi Gyari, Dr. Richard Land, Sovaida Ma'ani, Dick Wilson, and Professor Atilla Yayla.

Willy Fautre, Michael Bourdeaux, and Professor Paul Sigmund kindly agreed to provide essays giving regional overviews of Western Europe, the former Soviet Union, and Latin America. The country profiles were produced by a cooperative process in which initial drafts were reviewed, revised, and edited by a range of people. Consequently, unlike the regional essays, the final products cannot be ascribed to any individual author. However, in most cases, the profiles owe most to those who produced the original drafts. The authors of the draft country reports are: Mick Andersen, Barbara Baker, Michael Bourdeaux, Lisa Campbell, Joanna Chellapermal, Paul Diamond, Martin Dore, Willy Fautre, Robert George, Charles Greybow, Bruce Hardy, Marshall Harris, Krassimir Kanev, Michael Koby, Andrzej Kremplewski, Tina Lambert, Thomas Lansner, Karen Lord, Habib Malik, Mary Beth Markey, Sharon Payt, Suzanna Pearce, Simon Qadri, Christina Regule, Ben Rogers, Robert Royal, Bill Saunders, Daphe Tsimhone, George Zarycky; as well as staff members of the Center for Religious Freedom, including Nina Shea, Joseph Assad, and Paul Marshall.

The materials provided by these people and organizations are included in each profile in the sections headed "Religious Freedom." Also included in each profile is a section headed "Background": each of these sections is a radically shortened (and occasionally updated) version of the overall profile of political rights and civil liberties given in Freedom House's 1998–1999 *Freedom in the World*.

Apart from the members of the Board of Reference, many draft country reports were reviewed by other country authors and by David Estrada, Arne Fjeldstead, Bill Fudge, Dave Garrison, Mary Ann Glendon, Jason Graves, John Graz, the Rev. J. Richard Neuhaus, Michael Novak, Vinay Samuel, Erica Simpson, Jimmy Smith, and Steven Tullberg; as well as by Freedom House staff, including Arch Puddington and Adrian Karatnycky. Willy Fautre provided a valuable list of criteria for religious freedom.

Other assistance was provided by Alexandra Arriaga, Elizabeth Cole, Lisa

Davis, Tom Farr, Lauren Homer, Adam Koziel, Natan Lerner, David Little, James Pellechia, Daniel Pipes, Jane Pratt, Ambassador Robert Seiple, and Larry Uzzell. Other staff of Freedom House's Center for Religious Freedom who worked on producing the report were: Laura Barrett, Sean Domachowski, Eric Munoz, Kristina Robb, Amy Ryback, and Gwynneth Weigel.

Several organizations also gave valuable assistance, including Amnesty International, Boat People S.O.S., the Campaign for a Free Tibet, the Cardinal Kung Foundation, Christian Solidarity International, Christian Solidarity Worldwide, Compass Direct, Human Rights Watch, Human Rights Without Frontiers, the Indian Land Resource Center, the International Buddhist Information Bureau, the Keston Institute, the Organization for Security and Cooperation in Europe, the Vietnam Committee on Human Rights, and the Voice of the Martyrs.

As General Editor, I would like to thank all the above for their work, assistance, and patience.

— PAUL MARSHALL —
General Editor

To receive more information or to become a member of the Center for Religious Freedom, please contact:

Center for Religious Freedom
Freedom House
1319 18th St. NW
Washington, DC 20036
phone: 202-296-5101
fax: 202-296-5078
www.freedomhouse.org/religion

RELIGIOUS FREEDOM AND
AMERICAN FOREIGN POLICY

I was at a restaurant in New York's Chinatown on June 3, 1999, commemorating the tenth anniversary of the massacre of the democracy demonstrators in Tiananmen Square, when we heard the news. Those at my table, the heroic Chinese democracy dissidents Harry Wu, Wei Jing Sheng, and Wang Dan, and the legendary *New York Times* columnist A. M. Rosenthal and his wife, Shirley Lord, all gasped. The Clinton administration had just announced it would renew "Most Favored Nation" (MFN) trade status with China. Whatever one's views on the desirability of conferring U.S. trade benefits on China (and I believe reasonable people are found on both sides of the debate), one had to agree the timing for the announcement could not have been worse.

It signaled to China that the United States had forgotten the incident a decade ago when the People's Liberation Army mowed down or arrested thousands of students and workers who held aloft the statue of the "goddess of liberty," fashioned after our own Statue of Liberty, in a peaceful prodemocracy demonstration that drew its inspiration from the velvet revolutions then sweeping communist Europe. The breathtaking insensitivity of American policy-makers to that infamous date also symbolized the waning importance of religious freedom and human rights in American foreign policy when trade issues were at stake. China was at the time the human rights test case in part because it was the largest single human-rights violator after the fall of the

Soviet Empire and in part because candidate Bill Clinton had himself made it an issue during the 1992 campaign.

During the Cold War, America had taken a firm stand on behalf of political dissidents, samizdat writers, labor unionists, and Soviet Jews, giving these groups critical moral and financial support to put pressure on communist dictatorships from within. For twenty years American political leaders had saved lives and spoken out in defense of human rights activists in South Korea, the Philippines, South Africa, Haiti, and various countries in Latin America. It had put pressure on China itself—during the selection process for the site of the prestigious Olympic Games; at the United Nations, where an American-led effort to censure China in 1995 came within one vote of adoption; and, until 1994, during the annual review of MFN.

For most of the 1990s, however, human rights counted for little in American foreign policy. At congressional hearings, Amnesty International made the observation that the issue of international human rights is an "island off the mainland of American foreign policy." By this it meant that human-rights concerns were being marginalized by the administration, which was increasingly susceptible to trade lobbies intent on pleasing foreign business partners, even when those partners were repressive dictatorships. While many of those charged with human rights advocacy within the Department of State carried out their jobs with dedication, they lacked the clout to make a difference to officials of repressive regimes who correctly saw them as isolated within the United States government.

If human rights policy was an island, then religious freedom in the early and mid-1990s was the drowning man in the life raft, off the island, off the mainland. Even those who cared about human rights—the State Department's human rights bureau and the large human rights groups—suffered from "secular myopia" and rarely addressed situations of religious persecution abroad. In 1996, along with an array of human rights advocates, a representative of Open Doors with Brother Andrew and I met with James Sasser, who was soon to take up his post as the new U.S. ambassador to China. During the previous nine months, the new ambassador had been well briefed on the human rights problems of democracy dissidents, women's groups, and labor, but he was perplexed by our reports of anti-Christian persecution: "What's a house church?" he asked. He had not been briefed about the existence of, much less the persecution suffered by, the fifty million or more house-church Christians, perhaps the most important social force in China today.

By 1997, the results of the U.S. policy failure in China were apparent. A crackdown on Christians who refused to submit to government control in religious matters was in full swing, and the underground churches were calling it the worst period of persecution for them since the Cultural Revolution. Many clergy and preachers were being arrested and sent without trial to labor camps, while others were beaten or given stiff fines. Beijing flouted its contempt of unauthorized Christianity: in October 1997, on the eve of the first American-Chinese presidential summit since Tiananmen, China arrested and jailed the highest ranking Catholic clergyman in China, Bishop James Su Zhimin, who has not been heard from since, and sentenced to a three-year labor-camp term China's most important Protestant leader, Pastor Peter Xu Yongze.

At this time, prodded by Hudson Institute fellow Michael Horowitz, who is himself Jewish, a large coalition of Christian leaders and church groups began to mobilize in horror over the news of mounting anti-Christian persecution abroad and in indignation at the silence of U.S. political leaders. Under pressure to respond, the U.S. State Department took a series of measures. In 1997 and 1998, it impaneled an advisory committee on international religious freedom, which, with its twenty members and meager budget, proved unwieldy and ineffectual. Secretary of State Madeleine Albright sent a series of cables to American embassies overseas requesting greater attentiveness to religious issues in their work and in their reporting. Under a mandate from Congress, in 1997, the State Department's Bureau on Democracy, Human Rights, and Labor issued the first official report on global anti-Christian persecution, finding that the religious rights of Christians were being violated in more than forty countries.

Regarding China, the Clinton administration still appeared reluctant to assert any comprehensive human rights policy for religious persecution. It tried shifting responsibility for human rights to the private sector. It drafted a voluntary business code of conduct, but few American corporations working in China were willing to adopt it. In early 1998, in an agreement with China's leaders, the State Department dispatched three American clergymen to China. The delegation lacked leverage, experience, and backup and seemed designed only, in the words of one State

Department official, to "defuse" church protests at home. The American clerics walked away empty-handed, while conferring a propaganda triumph on the Chinese dictatorship, as the international press made all too clear.

Meanwhile the religious mobilization gained force and rallied in support of legislation on international religious persecution (first introduced in Congress by Rep. Frank Wolf, R-VA). The National Association of Evangelicals, the Southern Baptist Convention, the U.S. Catholic Conference of Bishops, the Presbyterian Church, U.S.A., the Salvation Army, the Anti-Defamation League, the Religious Action Center of Reformed Judaism, and the Campaign for Tibet were only some of the main groups that backed the legislation.

The Clinton administration and a powerful trade lobby launched an energetic counterattack. Secretary Albright opposed the initiative in principle for establishing a "hierarchy of human rights," and, in an address at Catholic University Columbus Law School, seemed to take the discredited view that religious freedom is not a universal or God-given human right but culturally relative: "We must also take into account the perspectives and *values* of others." This she said, moreover, in opposing a bill solely directed at "widespread and ongoing [acts of] abduction, enslavement, killing, imprisonment, forced mass relocation, rape, crucifixion or other forms of torture."

In the summer of 1998, Albright appointed Robert Seiple, the former head of World Vision, as "Special Adviser on International Religious Freedom," in yet another Administration act calculated to show concern and capture leadership of the growing issue without changing underlying policies. Clearly

the appointment was also intended to bolster the administration's argument that no legislation on religious persecution was needed. The national media—with the notable exception of *New York Times* columnist A. M. Rosenthal—was belittling and dismissive of the legislative effort, with the *New York Times* pronouncing the effort dead in a smug, front-page story a few weeks before the final vote. The Act, nonetheless, won overwhelming support in both houses of Congress and was signed into law by the President in October 1998.

Entitled the "International Religious Freedom Act," the law created four mechanisms. Of central significance, the law established the independent U.S. Commission on International Religious Freedom. Comprised of nine voting members and the ambassador-at-large, with a four-year mandate and a three-million-dollar annual budget, the Commission was charged with making policy recommendations to the President regarding religious persecutors. In addition, within the State Department it established an office of ambassador-at-large for international religious freedom to raise the profile of the issue within the department and in foreign capitals. It further mandated the State Department to issue an annual report on the status of religious freedom throughout the world. Finally, it called for the administration to designate a priority identification of the world's most egregious religious persecutors, to be called "countries of particular concern" for which the President was then required to devise appropriate policies within ninety days.

The legislation has made it considerably more difficult for the present or any future administration wholly to ignore religious freedom in American foreign policy. The Commission created by the Act and its other mechanisms were designed to ensure that international religious freedom would be debated and considered by American policy- and opinion-makers on a regular basis. While supporters of the Act had no utopian illusions that it would end religious persecution overnight—or even effect dramatic change in American foreign policy—they believed the legislation to be an important step in sending an unequivocal message to religious persecutors throughout the globe and to officers throughout the American foreign service of a priority policy toward religious freedom. Religious freedom has always been a defining principle for America, and supporters of the legislation intended that this issue not be overlooked in its relationships abroad. Eventually, policy actions determining what America's relationship should be with specific religious persecutors would emerge.

A combination of factors—not the least of which is the sheer scale of its persecution—has made Sudan, then China, the first and primary policy targets under the new law. Our policy makers now anguish over searing reports on how the United Nations and the Clinton administration failed the eight hundred thousand victims of the 1994 genocide in Rwanda, and how the international community should have acted to save thousands of Bosnian Muslims massacred in the UN-declared "safe haven" in 1995. Even as they offer those apologies, however, they fail to recognize or try to stop a religious and ethnic genocide now occurring in Sudan that has destroyed more lives than Bosnia, Kosovo, and Rwanda combined.

Triggered by the government's attempt forcibly to convert and impose Islamic law on the Christian and animist south, a civil war has been raging

in Sudan for seventeen years. In June 1999, Congress officially recognized that conflict as genocide. In south and central Sudan, the homeland of the Christians and African traditional believers, two million people have been killed and five million displaced. More than one hundred thousand Sudanese died from the deliberate starvation policies of the regime in 1998 alone. The situation became ever more urgent when an oil pipeline became operational in August 1999, providing cash-strapped Khartoum with the revenues it needed to subdue the Christian south and insulate the regime from international pressure to carry through on peace negotiations.

Sudan should be an easy human rights case for the administration. It is already on the U.S. list of terrorist nations and thus subject to comprehensive economic and trade sanctions and severed diplomatic relations. The White House launched a cruise missile attack in its capital in 1998. But for whatever reasons—perhaps due to an unwillingness to expend political capital for African lives, or for fear of appearing anti-Muslim, or out of concern for angering China, whose economic and political ties with Sudan are strengthening—the Clinton administration has been largely silent about the genocide in Sudan. The U.S. government's Sudan policy is based on concerns about terrorism, not genocide.

Throughout 1998, many churches and human rights groups protested the crisis. The U.S. Committee for Refugees, Christian Solidarity International, Christian Solidarity Worldwide, and the Family Research Council produced carefully documented reports of massacres, government-induced starvation, scorched-earth policies, and slavery. Freedom

House's Center for Religious Freedom organized a mass E-mail campaign by college students to Congress. The Institute on Religion and Democracy, the American Anti-Slavery Group, the New York Interfaith Alliance, and others mobilized the grass roots. A nationwide network of E-mail updates and Christian media helped get out the word with little help or notice from the mainstream news media. Smith College professor Eric Reeves wrote dozens of articles on the Sudan issue on the nation's op-ed pages. Public awareness on the issue was furthered in fall 1999 by the season's premiere of CBS's popular TV program *Touched by an Angel*, which dramatized religious persecution and slavery in Sudan.

On June 16, 1999, the U.S. House of Representatives adopted with only one dissent a resolution introduced by Representative Don Payne (D-NJ), condemning the government of Sudan for "deliberately and systematically committing genocide." Five days later the new U.S. Commission on International Religious Freedom, an independent panel created by Congress, targeted Sudan as an "egregious and ongoing" religious persecutor. A few months later, on October 6, the administration followed suit and included Sudan in its first designation of "countries of particular concern" for "egregious" religious persecution, though it took no new policy steps to stop it. A "peace envoy" it had quietly appointed for Sudan over the summer appeared to have made no impact.

The Commission presented a set of policy recommendations for Sudan in a meeting with President Clinton on October 19. Foremost, it urged the President to use the bully pulpit of his office to raise public awareness and express American condemnation of Sudan's atrocities. It specifically urged him to meet with Nobel laureate and holocaust survivor Elie Wiesel, who had written him on July 13, 1999, stating he was "haunted by what I know of Sudan," calling it a "genocide" and asking for a meeting "to discuss this urgent matter further." (It was to Dr. Wiesel that President Clinton made a public pledge in April 1999: "I will do my best to make sure that something like [the Rwanda genocide] does not happen again in Africa.")

The Commission also appealed to the President both at the White House meeting and in a follow-up letter to close the gaps in comprehensive economic sanctions against Sudan (imposed by a 1997 Executive Order for terrorism) by denying foreign companies developing Sudan's new oil pipeline access to American capital markets.

The Commission also urged the United States government to increase levels of direct food aid to famine-stricken areas and work to change international relief policy so that it would be politically neutral. Under the UN relief arrangement, "Operation Lifeline Sudan," the U.S. government and the international community gave Khartoum veto power over when, where, and if food aid could be delivered in southern Sudan and allowed it control over UN humanitarian programs for the very people it was trying to exterminate in the Nuba Mountains of central Sudan. The regime had not hesitated in using this power as an instrument of war. It was from the south's famine areas in 1998 that Khartoum had barred international food aid deliveries, and the U.S. and others working under Operation Lifeline Sudan had acquiesced. In that year alone 2.6 million people were brought to the brink of starvation, and more than one hundred thousand in fact did perish. Khartoum continued to veto aid deliveries at various times of acute starvation in 1999 as well. The Vatican news service reported that some seven hundred persons were dying of starvation every day in one area of the south in mid-1999.

The Commission's policy recommendations were reinforced by a large interfaith coalition that pressed for U.S. action to stop the genocide against Sudan's Christians and animists. On November 9, 1999, several hundred leaders of activist religious and rights groups convened in the Senate to set a strategy on Sudan. The international divestment campaign they launched against Talisman Energy, a Canadian company also investing in Khartoum's pipeline that already listed on the New York Stock Exchange, was supported by Secretary Albright. The coalition's conference heard from Senators Sam Brownback (R-KN), Bill Frist (R-TN), and Joseph Lieberman (D-CT) about the Sudan Peace Act that they and Senator Russ Feingold (D-WI) had recently introduced in the Senate. On December 9, 1999, two hundred key mainline Protestant, evangelical, Catholic, and Jewish leaders then united to petition President Clinton, appealing for him to "take a visible, personal stance on the genocide now taking place in Sudan," meet with Elie Wiesel, support the Sudan Peace Act, increase direct food aid, and block American investments of foreign companies in Sudan. They declared: "Either America leads the way towards peace at this crucial historical juncture, or an unspeakable catastrophe evident to all will take its final, dreadful toll in a century already defined too fully by indifference and genocide."

Actions in the fall of 1999 offered encouragement that American policy would change. In late November, the Senate unanimously passed the Sudan Peace Act, which aimed to shift U.S. policy focus toward a greater emphasis on human rights. On November 28, President Clinton signed a bill to permit the U.S. to give food aid directly to those protecting the civilian population in southern Sudan, including the rebel forces. In December the government of Canada, prompted by Secretary Albright's criticisms of Talisman Energy, sent a human rights investigator to Sudan to examine whether Canada should impose its own trade sanctions. Talisman had been forced to announce a buy-back of its stock in order to restore investor confidence after the large teachers' pension fund, TIAA-CREF, CalPERS, the Texas Teachers' Retirement Plan, and others had divested. As reported in the Asia *Wall Street Journal* and the *Financial Times* of London, the Chinese National Petroleum Corporation, working with Goldman Sachs investment firm, had to restructure and downsize by about $7 billion its plan to raise money from American investors through a multibillion-dollar Wall Street IPO (initial public offering) to exclude the Sudan pipeline portion of its operations.

More recently, however, the Clinton administration appears to be responding to pressure from forces within the business and nongovernmental relief sectors that advocate "engaging" Khartoum, not treating it as a pariah. Among the most vocal were the gum arabic importers and the relief group CARE, which risked losing large contracts should the Operation Lifeline Sudan arrangement be changed. This is a perennial foreign policy question: whether to "engage" rogue regimes in the hope of reforming them or isolate such regimes in order to weaken them or force fundamental changes in their policies. Whatever the merits of such debate when governments pursue wrongful policies or even significant persecution, there should be no question as to the proper course with regard to regimes practicing genocide at the levels of Nazi Germany, Pol Pot's Cambodia, Hutu Power's Rwanda—or the present Khartoum regime.

In such cases of genocide, international sanctions are a moral and political imperative. Failure to seek total isolation of the Sudanese government will only increase its power to conduct its genocidal war and insulate the otherwise bankrupt government from pressure to negotiate a just peace.

In mid-December 1999, the administration lifted U.S. trade sanctions against Sudan for gum arabic—America's only import from Sudan—and gave approval to American investments in foreign companies doing business in Sudan, such as a multibillion-dollar Wall Street IPO for Petrochina, a hastily created subsidiary of China's petroleum company that is Khartoum's oil pipeline partner. By the end of 1999, the administration had yet to acknowledge that Khartoum is committing genocide. Secretary Albright told a meeting of nongovernmental groups in the fall that the issue of genocide is "not marketable" to the American people. So far the administration has ignored the millions of deaths, the near unanimous congressional resolution, the appeal from Elie Wiesel, and a petition from two hundred American church and rights leaders. One shudders to remember the lessons from the summer of 1942 when the State Department bungled Gerhard Riegner's urgent cables warning President Roosevelt about the Holocaust.

The final chapter on American pol-icy toward the Sudanese genocide has yet to be written. Regardless of the importance of international business, the fact that our national leaders continue to be haunted by past genocide underscores the salience of human rights to present-day American foreign policy. The debate on Sudan's genocide will continue, and it will, by virtue of the International Religious Freedom Act and a mobilized religious community, eventually force a new Sudan policy—hopefully in time to save lives.

The movement to bring religious freedom to the forefront of American foreign policy has gone far and done much against extraordinary odds. Still, the movement does not yet have the critical mass sufficient to put an end to policies of indifference towards egregious religious persecutors in China and Sudan. In the battle against religious persecution, much of the change that has taken place on the part of government policy makers and the media has been of a lip-service variety.

With such notable exceptions as Abe Rosenthal, the national media continue to treat Christians with patronizing indifference and even outright hostility and tend to view Christians as zealots who partly bring persecution on themselves. Likewise, government leaders now routinely condemn "religious" persecution, but their concern does not often extend beyond an occasional prayer service platitude. This underlying lack of understanding is a continuing barrier to giving full stature to the central American value of religious freedom.

In the end the power to effect fundamental change on behalf of persecuted religious believers abroad rests with America's religious communities. The miracle of democracy—an institution that owes much of its very existence to

Judeo-Christian principles—is that it *will* cause zero-tolerance policies towards religious persecutors if those in the pews are aware of the facts and those in the pulpits speak up about them. Such change will not only help persecuted Christians but will also powerfully serve American national interests, precisely as did firm American policies aiding Soviet Jews and human rights victims of an earlier generation. It will place America on the right side of twenty-first-century history—this be- cause one of the greatest and most revolutionary developments of the coming century will be the spread of faith in general and Christianity in particular. It will be good for America for people of faith to think of us as the friends who protected them when no one else cared.

This book is a further effort to change perceptions and hasten reforms in American policy that are crucial to American interests and the needs of those presently suffering from antireligious persecution.

— NINA SHEA —

An international human rights lawyer for twenty years, Nina Shea is director of the Washington-based Center for Religious Freedom of Freedom House. She is also a member of the U.S. Commission on International Religious Freedom. She is the author of In the Lion's Den: A Shocking Account of Persecution and Martyrdom of Christians Today and How We Should Respond *(Broadman and Holman Publishers, 1997).*

THE IMPORTANCE OF RELIGIOUS FREEDOM

At the end of 1997, the former executive editor of the *New York Times*, A. M. Rosenthal confessed, "Early this year I realized that in decades of reporting, writing, or assigning stories on human rights, I rarely touched on one of the most important. Political human rights, legal, civil, and press rights, emphatically often; but the right to worship where and how God or conscience leads, almost never." While Rosenthal changed dramatically on this core, the pattern he describes is still widespread.

By religious freedom or persecution, I do not mean human rights violations against "religious" persons. After all, since most people in the world claim some sort of religious identity, then most human rights violations of *any* kind are presumably against religious believers. Rather, we are concerned not with all forms of persecution of religious people but with persecution *where the focus or the grounds are themselves religious*—where a person's religion is a component of the persecution or discrimination they suffer. Hence, we do not cover situations such as, for example, Rwanda where, even though most of those who were killed (and who killed) were relatively religious, the genocide was itself ethnically based. People were killed *as Tutsis*, regardless of what their religion was. It must, of course, be added that there are few cases where religion is the only factor: religion is usually intertwined with ethnic, political, territorial, and economic concerns. We could demarcate religious persecution by asking whether some or all of the oppression and discrimination that people suffer would occur if they or their oppressors were of a different religion.

Why should we focus on religious freedom and religious persecution: is suffering or death on such grounds inherently worse than suffering or death on other grounds? Surely not. No, the reason it needs attention is that it is a topic which has been sorely neglected, even in a world where we can say that many human-rights issues are neglected. Until very recently it has been the orphan child of the human rights movement; therefore, it needs our political attention.

The Neglect of Religion

One of the principal reasons religious freedom and religious persecution have been neglected is that religion *itself* has been comparatively neglected as a factor in human affairs. The essential point here is not whether one is personally religious or likes "religion" but whether one realizes that, as an empirical fact, throughout the world religion is a key element of politics and human rights.

One major cause of this comparative neglect is the prevalence in the Western world of what may be called "secular myopia," which can be described as "an inability even to see, much less understand, the role of religion in human life." This myopia is widespread among "the chattering classes." As political analyst Edward Luttwak has written: "Policy makers, diplomats, journalists, and scholars who are ready to overinterpret economic causality, who are apt to dissect social differentiations even more finely, and who will minutely categorize political affiliations, are still in the habit of disregarding the role of religion in explaining politics and even in reporting their concrete modalities" [Edward Luttwak, "The Missing Dimension" in D. Johnston and C. Sampson, eds., *Religion: The Missing Dimension of Statecraft* (Oxford, 1994)].

This secular myopia can have painful consequences. One was U.S. ignorance of the views and power of the Ayatollah Khomini's followers. Luttwak notes that there was *only one* proposal for the CIA to examine "the attitude and activities of the more prominent religious leaders" in Iran and that even this proposal was vetoed as mere "sociology," intelligence-speak for irrelevant academic verbiage. Consequently, as the shah's regime was collapsing about them, U.S. political analysts kept insisting that everything was fine. Following their training, they examined economic variables, class structure, and the military and concluded that since these groups supported the shah, then he was safe. There were, of course, mullahs arousing Islamic sentiment, but analysts had been taught that such religious drives drew only on folk memories, were destined to disappear with "modernization," and were irrelevant to the real structures of political power. Similarly "in Vietnam, every demographic, economic, ethnic, social, and, of course, military aspect of the conflict was subject to detailed scrutiny, but the deep religious cleavages that afflicted South Vietnam were hardly noticed." The "tensions between the dominant Catholic minority (and) a resentful Buddhist majority, were largely ignored until Buddhist monks finally had to re-

sort to flaming self-immolations in public squares, precisely to attract the attention of Americans so greatly attentive to everything else in Vietnam that was impeccably secular" [Luttwak, op. cit.]. Parallel, though less striking, tales can be told of Bosnia, Lebanon, the Philippines, Nicaragua, India, Israel and the Palestinians, Sudan, and Indonesia.

For example, one of the major stories from China in the latter part of 1999 was the sudden, organized appearance of ten thousand members of the Falun Gong movement outside the compound of the Chinese leadership in Beijing, an event that has terrified the Chinese leadership and prompted a further government crackdown. Subsequently, it has been suggested that the group has up to seventy-five million members. But not only had the Chinese leadership apparently missed Falun Gong, so had the media. Generally, Western media have ignored Chinese religion as an important factor in its political future.

This neglect often comes not by ignoring particular trends or events but by redefining them. Americans, in particular, are prone to redefine religion through the nebulous catchall term *ethnic*. For example, distinguished former diplomat Chester Crocker gave an excellent lecture to the Foreign Policy Research Institute on the subject of "How to Think About Ethnic Conflict" (see Foreign Policy Research Institute's *Wire*, vol. 7, no. 10, September 1999). However, even he described the Northern Ireland and India-Pakistan conflicts as "ethnic." But India and Pakistan are separate countries only because of their different religions; and Ireland is divided for the same reason.

Other recent examples include the *Economist's* (September 25, 1999) description of the slaughter of fifty-four

Buddhists in Sri Lanka as perhaps "the first sign of ethnic cleansing" and fights between Christians and Muslims in Nigeria as "cultural" (July 31, 1999). Similarly, the *International Herald Tribune* (July 14, 1999) expresses the fear that an Indian victory in Kashmir would lead to the "ethnic cleansing" of Muslims; while the *New Republic* contrasts the Sudanese conflict between a "predominantly Muslim north and a predominantly Christian south" with a Western dream of a "multiethnic democracy" (July 12, 1999). Many of these depictions seem to take their cue from descriptions of the former Yugoslavia, wherein "Bosnian Muslims" and war between Orthodox, Catholics, and Muslims were routinely described as "ethnic." We have now used the term *ethnic cleansing* to describe the murder of Muslims.

Our press coverage and political analysis often also has an introverted focus on a type of Western Enlightenment culture, as though this constituted the common opinion of humankind, or the common opinion of *reasonable* humankind, or at least the common opinion of Americans. Consequently, movements overseas are assimilated to Western categories. Hence, Islamic or Hindu militants are often described as "right-wing," whatever that might mean. But what is a "right-wing" or "left-wing" view of plans to build a Hindu temple on the site of the Babri mosque in Ayodhya, or a Jewish Third Temple on the site of the Dome of the Rock in Jerusalem? Neither of these schemes has anything to do with categories of left and right; their meaning can only be grasped by understanding their deep-seated religious context. And such understanding is doubly urgent since either of these projects could precipitate war.

When ethnicity fails to subsume religion, a common alternative is to treat it as the sublimation of drives that can *really* be explained by poverty, economic change, or the stresses of modernity. Of course, these factors play a role; no part of human life is sealed off from any other. But all too often what we encounter is *a priori* methodological commitment to treat religion as secondary, as an evanescent and derivative phenomenon that can be explained, but never be used to explain.

Taking Religion Seriously

If we do take religion seriously in international affairs, then we may also learn about a wide range of things, including freedom of all kinds. It was pointed out by religion scholars long before Samuel Huntington's important work on the "Clash of Civilizations" that chronic armed conflict in the world is concentrated on the margins of the traditional religions. The Middle East, the southern Sahara, the Balkans, the Caucasus, Central Asia, and South Asia are where Islam, Christianity, Judaism, Buddhism, and Hinduism intersect. They are also the sites of most wars in the last fifty years. The point is not *why* people fight but *where* they fight. These are not explicitly religious wars. But, since religion shapes culture, people at these boundaries have different histories and different views of human life, and are more likely to oppose one another. Regardless of the varied reasons for conflict, these are the areas where conflict likely occurs. They are religious fault zones and hence sites of political instability.

The Chinese government takes religion seriously; that is one reason it represses it. In 1992, the Chinese press noted that "the church played an important role in the change" in Eastern

Europe and the former Soviet Union and warned "if China does not want such a scene to be repeated in its land, it must strangle the baby while it is still in the manger." "Underground" or "house" church leaders consistently report that the current government crackdown is due to fears prompted by religious events in the former Soviet bloc. Even Chinese government documents actually implementing the crackdown state that one of their purposes is to prevent "the changes that occurred in the former Soviet Union and Eastern Europe" (from "Opinions Concerning the Implementation of the Special Class-Struggle Involving the Suppression of Catholic and Protestant Illegal Activities According to Law," Tong Xiang, Zhejiang province, February 1997).

This also suggests that people interested in democracy should attend more to religion. For example, the attention to China's courageous prodemocracy activists is certainly deserved, but it must be remembered that their following is quite small. Yet there is little attention to China's dissident churches, whose members at a conservative estimate number some fifty million (apart from fifteen million in the official churches) and are growing rapidly. *The Far East Economic Review,* in a 1997 cover story entitled "God Is Back," reported one Beijing official as saying, "If God had the face of a seventy-year-old man, we wouldn't care if he was back. But he has the face of millions of twenty-year-olds, so we are worried." The rapid growth of the only nationwide movements in China not under government control merits *political* attention.

Apart from the important examples of the Balkan conflicts, the rise of the Welfare and Virtue parties in Turkey, the BJP in India, and the growth of radical Islamicism, the following religious trends also merit political reflection and attention:

1. The rapid and alarming upsurge of intolerance (official and unofficial) of minority religions ("cults") in Eastern and Western Europe. (See Willy Fautre's essay.)

2. The pattern of violence and warfare along the sub-Saharan boundary from Nigeria to Ethiopia. This traces a Christian-Muslim divide.

3. The rapid growth of Christianity in Korea (now 25 percent of the population), China (a minimum of sixty-five million, up from one million in 1980), Taiwan, and Indonesia.

4. Tensions in Nigeria and Indonesia. There is widespread religious violence in the north and central regions of Nigeria, with several thousand dead in recent years, and fears that there could be a religious war. In Indonesia, rising religious strife precedes and has some separate dynamics from recent anti-Chinese violence. It threatens to undermine what has been one of the world's best examples of interreligious toleration and cooperation. In both of these regional powers, there is the possibility of instability and violence that could spread far beyond the religious communities themselves.

5. The current exodus of Christians from the Middle East, over a million in the last five years. Currently some 3 percent of Palestinians are Christians compared to an estimated 25 percent fifty years ago. Similar movements have taken place out of Egypt, Syria, Lebanon, Turkey, and Iraq.

6. The emergence of Orthodoxy as a unifying symbol in Russia, the

Balkans, and parts of the former Soviet Union. (See Michael Bourdeaux's essay.)

7. The increasing prominence of religion in the conflicts between India and Pakistan, now enhanced by nuclear weapons.
8. The rapid growth of charismatic Protestantism in Latin America. (See Paul Sigmund's essay.)

I am not making the absurd suggestion that religion, apart from other cultural, ethnic, economic, political, or strategic elements, is the only or the key factor: societies are complex. But I am saying that it is equally absurd to examine a political order *without* attending to the role of religion. We need to deal consistently with religion as an important independent factor, and analyses that ignore religious dynamics

should be inherently suspect. Similarly, discussions of human rights that neglect religious freedom and the role of religion in all human rights should be equally suspect.

In the field of human rights, we must elevate concern for religious freedom. This is not a parochial matter: it is historically the first freedom in the growth of human rights. Such freedom may at times have more to do with the growth of democracy than might a direct focus on political activity itself. A human rights/religious freedom policy is extremely difficult, of course. While all human-rights pressures make realists nervous, religion carries the additional burdens of touching on very deep-seated commitments. But for anyone concerned with freedom and democracy, this is no reason to neglect the matter.

— PAUL MARSHALL —

THE NATURE OF RELIGIOUS FREEDOM AND RELIGIOUS PERSECUTION*

One goal of this survey is to rank countries on a standard scale of religious freedom so that we can compare them with one another, see whether any patterns occur, and eventually discern whether any systematic change occurs over time. Some people have objected to the very idea of rating and ranking countries as necessarily an invidious, even imperialistic, exercise. However, it is a fact that some countries, such as Norway, have more religious freedom than others, such as Sudan. If we cannot say that, then there is little point in any general survey.

What critics may mean is that any attempt to rate countries is very difficult, liable to error, and in need of copious self-criticism. This is certainly correct. In particular, there are two major methodological problems: the use of standardized criteria, and what those criteria should be (for a further discussion of these matters, see Appendix 1: "Notes on Statistics and Numbers").

Clearly, since countries are different, then the facets and problems of religious freedom will be different in each country: Hence, *any* standard set of criteria will be disproportionate. It will highlight things in some countries that may, in practice, be of little relevance. In other countries it may not give adequate place to idiosyncratic features that are of great relevance. There is no "solution" to this problem: it is an inbuilt and inescapable feature of using any universal criteria for *any* particular situations. All we can do is the best we can and be open to refining the criteria as the results come in.

The survey criteria listed in Appendix 2 are developed from the International Covenant on Civil and Political Rights, the United Nations Declaration on the Elimination of All Forms of Intolerance and of Discrimination Based on Religion or Belief, the European Convention on Human Rights, and from a list of criteria developed by Willy Fautre. They are based on the fact that surveying religious freedom is more limited than surveying human rights in general, but also it is different from surveying particular human rights, such as press freedom, which focus only on particular organizations or practices. With freedom of the press, one can look at the intensity of controls on particular media and the weight of penalties applied with those controls. But, unlike press freedom, religious freedom cannot be focused on the freedoms of certain organizations and individuals. Religious freedom cuts across a wide range of human rights.

First, it refers to the freedoms of particular bodies, houses of worship, humanitarian organizations, educational institutions, and so forth. Second, it refers to freedom for particular individual religious practices—prayer, worship, dress, proclamation, diet, and so forth. Third, it refers to human rights in general in so far as they involve particular religious bodies, individuals, and activities. (For an elaboration of these facets of religious freedom, see Appendix 2: "Checklist of Criteria of Religious Freedom.") For example, the freedom to proclaim one's religion or belief is an issue of freedom of speech generally and is parallel to freedom of speech in other areas of life. Similarly, for freedom of the press or freedom of association. This means that we are looking not only at particular "religious rights" but also at *any* human right, insofar as it impacts on freedom of religion or belief. In particular, we need to be aware of any different and unequal treatment of particular religions. This means that the question of adverse discrimination needs specific attention.

There are, of course, many situations where it is not immediately clear whether there is a violation of religious freedom. Some examples, with my own analysis:

- A priest acting alone in Central America is killed because of his human-rights work, and he regards such human-rights work as a necessary consequence of his faith. This is not an instance of religious persecution because any other person of a different faith, or no faith, in the same situation would face the same attack. (Note that this is certainly a human rights violation but not a violation of religious freedom per se.) However, if a church has a pastoral policy that includes such human-rights work, then any limits on this are limits on the believing practice of the church and of its clergy, and so are a violation of religious freedom.
- A European country bans Islamic dress in schools. This is a violation of religious freedom since, while the school may legitimately want to enforce a dress code, that should be outweighed by a right to live according to one's religion. If it were a case of a full covering and veil and the school were worried about

checking someone's identity, say at exam time, then there might be additional legitimate concerns, but a way could be found around them.
- A country bans polygamy or polyandry whereas some religions allow it. This is not a violation of religious freedom since, as far as I know, no religion *requires* polygamy or polyandry.
- A country has a state church or its equivalent but otherwise allows freedom of religion. This is always an instance of religious discrimination and, therefore, a limit on religious freedom; however, its importance may vary greatly. Does the state fund the church in a way that it does not fund other religious bodies? Does the church have political privileges or privileges in areas such as education? (International human-rights documents do not reject a state church per se.)
- A religious group is also a politically separatist group. This can be a very difficult area as states have a legitimate interest in avoiding fragmentation. However, international law also recognizes a "people's right to self-determination." The question of whether the repression of such a group is a violation of religious freedom would depend on whether the group had a religious identity and on the justice of their cause. (Have they been previously repressed, discriminated against, or had their religion violated?) If there has been such a previous threat to the religious identity of the group, then the repression even of a separatist group would be a violation of religious freedom, and any human rights violations in the area are also violations of religious freedom. Consequently, even if religiously

identified groups in Tibet and southern Sudan were separatist, which both sets of groups deny, their repression would still be a violation of religious freedom.

- If a religiously identified separatist or other group is violent, the answer would depend on whether their violence is a legitimate form of self-defense or whether the group is inherently violent or terrorist. In the former case any human rights violations against them would also be violations of religious freedom.
- A family disinherits or ostracizes an (adult) child because the child converts to another religion. This is not a violation of religious freedom since under international standards families can legitimately make such decisions. However, any physical attack on the child would be a violation of religious freedom.
- A family forbids an underage child to convert or marry someone of different religion. International standards allow families to make such decisions.
- In many countries, much law (especially on family and marriage) is divided along confessional lines, with different marriage and divorce rules for different groups. This is not a violation of religious freedom as long as: the groups are treated equally, people can voluntarily change their group, and there are avenues for marriage, and so forth, for those who may not fit in any particular group.
- Are restrictions on the entrance of missionaries or other religious workers a violation of religious freedom? Not necessarily, as there is no universal right to be able to work in a country other than one's

own. It would depend on whether such restrictions discriminated between (and within) religions and whether they had an adverse effect on domestic groups that are denied adequate, trained leadership.

- A decision by a country either to fund or not to fund education by religious groups can be consistent with religious freedom. The question is one of discrimination, that is, whether some groups are denied funds because of their beliefs while others are given funds.

Many more examples clearly could be given of situations where answers to questions of religious freedom are by no means obvious. Nevertheless, from the above, we can suggest some guidelines:

- Are restrictions on religious groups "reasonable"? In the words of many international human-rights documents, are they "subject only to such limitations as are prescribed by law and are necessary to protect public safety, order, health, or morals or the fundamental rights and freedom of others"?
- The question of whether something is a violation of religious freedom (as distinct from a violation of some other human right) depends on whether someone's religion is a factor (usually not the only one) in the treatment they give or receive. To put this another way, would someone of different religious beliefs or no religious beliefs in the same situation mete out or suffer the same treatment? (Of course, groups with different beliefs may, by that fact, also not fall into the same situation.)
- Is there discrimination; is different treatment given to different religious groups?

• Religious freedom can be violated by a government or another religious group even if the violation is not itself for religious motives. The *motive* is not, per se, the issue; the key question is, what is the result? If a government represses churches, mosques, and temples in the same way it represses political parties, newspapers, and other groups, simply because the government wants no other centers of loyalty or authority in the society, then this is still a violation of religious freedom.

Particularly with respect to this latter point, it is vitally important to realize that the fact that something is "political," "economic," or "cultural" does *not* mean that it is not religious (and vice versa). Many things are both "political" *and* "religious": Europe and Latin America have many Christian Democratic parties. China is officially atheist, and Iran is officially Islamic. Or "cultural" and "religious": Tibetan culture and religion are interwoven, as are Mexican or Indian culture and religion. Or "economic" *and* "religious": the Sudanese government's self-proclaimed *jihad* strives for control over oil fields and hydroelectric power stations. In Chiapas, Mexico, Protestants are persecuted by local *caciques* because they refuse to pay extortionate prices for goods to be used in religious ceremonies that they reject. In fact, outside of communist and radical Islamicist settings, it is comparatively rare for someone to be repressed merely for their individual confessional beliefs if these beliefs do not affect some other facet of life. It is usually the very interrelation that leads to perse-cution. Furthermore, religion is usually not merely an additional factor but is also intimately interwoven with other factors. Since religion refers to our ultimate beliefs, it is only to be expected that it is deeply connected to every other area of human life, a fact emphasized by nearly every religion in the world.

We need to take account not only of individual acts but also the religious context in which they occur. This may be illustrated by a comparison with the role of race in South Africa in the period of apartheid. Some blacks were allied with the government, and some whites were fighting for the African National Congress. Nelson Mandela was not imprisoned for his race but because he was accused of terrorism. The government would have imprisoned anyone, of any race, whom it believed to be a terrorist, and it would have imprisoned anyone for terrorism even for a reason unconnected to *apartheid*. The South African troops in Namibia and Angola were not fighting on direct racial grounds but to prevent infiltration. Would we say then that the South African conflict was political not racial, economic not racial, and cultural not racial? Of course not, because we are well aware that it was the policy of *apartheid* and the exclusion of nonwhites from the political process that drove the government's opponents, black and white, to take the steps they did. Racial division lay behind nearly all government policies, hence acts that were not themselves *individually* racially motivated were undertaken to defend a system that was. Similarly, people, regardless of their religion, may be repressed in order to maintain a religious hegemony.

— PAUL MARSHALL —

*A version of this essay was sent to the authors of each of the country profiles before they began.

THE CURRENT STATE OF
RELIGIOUS FREEDOM

The survey does not compare the current situation with the patterns of earlier years. However, each country profile includes, where relevant, a brief history of religious freedom. These histories indicate that, during the mid- to late-1990s, the overall situation of religious freedom in the world has deteriorated. This is particularly so in the larger Asian countries, such as China, India, Pakistan, and Indonesia. Western Europe has also become less religiously free due to widespread hysteria over "cults" (see the essay by Willy Fautre). Some areas, such as Latin America, have improved (see the essay by Paul Sigmund), while others such as Africa, the former Soviet Union (see the essay by Michael Bourdeaux), and the Middle East have remained fairly stable, the latter two at a low level of religious freedom and the last being one of the worst in the world.

The Spread of
Religious Freedom

Religious freedom and religious persecution affect all religious groups. A variety of groups—Christians and animists in Sudan, Baha'is in Iran, Ahmadiyas in Pakistan, Buddhists in Tibet, and Falun Gong in China—are now perhaps the most intensely persecuted, while Christians are the most widely persecuted group. But there is no religious group in the world that does not suffer to some degree because of its beliefs. Religions, whether large, such as Christianity, Islam, Hindu, or Buddhism, or small, such as Baha'i, Jehovah's Witness, or Judaism, all suffer to some degree. In many cases these restrictions come from people who are members of the same general religious group but who are part of a different subgroup. Thus non-Orthodox Christians in Russia, Greece, and Armenia suffer discrimination from the Orthodox, while Shiite Muslims in Pakistan and Afghanistan suffer persecution and even death from some of the dominant Sunni groups.

Religious freedom is also not confined to any one area or continent. There are relatively free countries in every continent (see Figure 1). South Korea, Taiwan, Japan, Brazil, South Africa, Botswana, and Namibia score higher in this survey than do France and Belgium. Latin America also has relatively high scores. There are absolutely no grounds for thinking that religious freedom is an exclusively Western concern or achievement.

Some Westerners and Third World tyrants in China and Vietnam elevate "economic rights," "Asian values," and "cultural relativism" and denigrate civil rights, such as religious freedom, as quasi-luxuries that need be advanced, if at all, only when more basic needs such as food and shelter have been achieved. Proponents of these views should be asked why several Asian countries, such as South Korea and Taiwan, which have a background of poverty and exploitation, and with Confucian traditions as strong as China and Vietnam, both value and successfully defend religious freedom, and why desperately poor African countries can do the same. Religious freedom is desired throughout the world and has been achieved throughout the world. It is a moral travesty of the highest order to pretend that because people are hungry and cold it is legitimate to repress and persecute them as well.

While high levels of religious freedom occur in every area, there are still large regional variations. The Western European and North Atlantic area countries covered in this survey all score from one to three, and thus all show a high level of religious freedom (following Freedom House practice, this survey calls countries with a score of one to three "free," four to five "partly free," and six to seven "not free"). The countries of Latin America also score highly, with only Colombia, Mexico, and Cuba scoring less than three (see Paul Sigmund's essay). A similar pattern occurs in sub-Saharan Africa where Nigeria scores a five and Tanzania scores a four and the other countries surveyed scored higher. However, in the African case, the survey covers relatively few countries, and there are signs that other countries (such as war-torn Angola, Congo, Liberia, or Sierra Leone) would score much less. However, the completed profiles show that several African countries score highly.

The countries of Eastern Europe and the former Soviet Union cover a wide spread, from Estonia, rated a one, to Turkmenistan, rated a seven. There are countries at each level, with those bordering the Baltic (Estonia, Latvia, Lithuania, and Poland) as well as Hungary, Romania, and Ukraine scoring higher. Most countries (ten out of nineteen) are at the intermediate levels of

four and five (see the discussion in Michael Bourdeaux's essay). Other Freedom House surveys indicate that these countries are in transition and are likely to move to higher or lower levels.

Asian countries also show a wide spread, though with more countries at the intermediate and lower levels. East Asian countries (Taiwan, South Korea, Japan, and the Philippines, as well as Mongolia) score higher. The low scores are dominated by communist powers (China, Tibet, North Korea, and Vietnam) and the chaos in East Timor. Apart from these, the only "unfree" countries surveyed are Burma and Bhutan.

The area from northern Africa through the eastern Mediterranean to West Asia tends to have low scores. Israel (excluding the occupied territories) scores a three, and Lebanon, Malaysia, Morocco, and Greece a four, with Egypt and Turkey a five. The others are sixes (Mauritania, Pakistan) and sevens (Saudi Arabia, Sudan, Iran). These findings (as well as those for other areas) are consistent with the general area findings for all political rights and civil liberties contained in *Freedom in the World*.

There is similar variation in the religious background of religious freedom. This is obviously a complex matter, since current regimes may reflect comparatively little of a country's religious background. China, Tibet, and Vietnam all have a largely Buddhist background, but current religious repression comes at the hand of communist regimes who profess to be atheistic materialists. Similarly, Catholic East Timor had, until the fall of 1999, been under Indonesian occupation, and its lack of religious freedom reflected the damage and chaos left in the aftermath of Indonesian military withdrawal. Nevertheless, since the survey usually covers several countries of each religious background, the overall patterns can be revealing (see fig. 2).

Historically Christian countries tend to score the highest in religious freedom, with an average rating of three. This parallels other Freedom House findings, which have found that traditionally Christian countries have tended to score higher on political rights and civil liberties. Of the thirty-four countries that can be rated as religiously "free" (i.e., scoring three or above), twenty-nine of them are traditionally Christian. Conversely, only one of the forty-two traditionally Christian countries surveyed (Cuba) is "not free" (i.e., scoring six or seven). Within Christianity, Protestantism tends to score higher than Catholicism, and both higher than Orthodoxy.

The other religiously "free" countries are Israel and then four countries of largely Buddhist background—Japan, Mongolia, South Korea, and Taiwan. This suggests that a Buddhist tradition also has had a tendency to produce relatively high religious freedom. The Buddhist countries with markedly low scores reflect the communist regimes in China, Tibet, North Korea, and Vietnam. If these are excluded, the remaining countries, except Bhutan and Burma, score relatively high. These patterns are also congruent with the findings of *Freedom in the World*. There is, however, some difference with respect to Hindu countries. Whereas both India and Nepal have relatively free elections, they have tended to score low on civil liberties generally and, in this survey, score even lower on religious freedom. In Nepal the difference is not great, but in India the difference reflects the upsurge in India within recent years of a militant Hinduism coupled with attacks on religious minorities, especially Christians.

The religious areas with the largest current restrictions on religious freedom are the Islamic countries. This parallels problems with democracy and civil liberties, but the negative trend with respect to religion is even stronger. No traditionally Islamic country surveyed is religiously "free" while almost half of those surveyed are "not free." Four countries (Iran, Saudi Arabia, Sudan, and Turkmenistan) score a seven, the lowest category. This situation may soon show some improvement since Indonesia, the country with by far the world's largest Muslim population, is rapidly becoming freer following its 1999 election, and Nigeria, which is about half Muslim, may also be establishing itself as a democracy.

Religious Freedom and Other Human Rights

A comparison of ratings for religious freedom with ratings for political rights and civil liberties allows us to see how the degree of religious freedom in a country compares to its record of human rights in general, and vice versa. In thirty-seven out of the seventy-five countries covered, the score for religious freedom is identical to the score for civil liberties in general. For the rest, except for three countries, the religious freedom score is within one point of the score for civil liberties in general. These other three are within two points. Consequently, freedom of religion correlates very closely with civil liberties in general.

A skeptic may suggest that this might merely reflect methodology—a result of the fact that the criteria for religious freedom in this survey and the criteria for civil liberties in *Religious Freedom in the World* actually overlap considerably. This overlap is real, but it is not merely a methodological accident but a reflection of the simple reality that religious freedom is necessarily a part of civil rights in general. In practical terms this means that restrictions on the press necessarily involve restrictions on the religious press, that restrictions on freedom of association necessarily imply restrictions on religious association, that restrictions on speech necessarily imply restriction on religious speech. Consequently, it is only to be expected that freedom of religion and other freedoms will usually go together. Religion exists not (only) in a transcendent realm but is a fundamental and integral part of all human freedom.

Given the fact that these various dimensions of human freedom *usually* go together, it is also useful to consider situations where differences for religious freedom and for human rights in general are systematic, though small.

Those countries in which the score for religious freedom is less than for civil liberties in general are Austria, Azerbaijan, Bangladesh, Belgium, Bulgaria, Chile, France, Germany, Greece, Hungary, Indonesia, Iran, Latvia, Macedonia, Mauritania, Nigeria, Pakistan, Romania, Sweden, and Spain. While these, along with all the countries surveyed, obviously have idiosyncrasies, nevertheless they also reflect some systematic variations. Many of these countries are Western European ones (Austria, Belgium, France, Germany, Spain, and Sweden) that have both a history and a current practice wherein their reaction to religious nonconformity is more repressive than their response to nonconformity in general. They reflect an attachment to a traditional dominant religion(s) (Austria, Belgium, France, Germany, Spain, Sweden, Bulgaria, Romania, Latvia, Hungary, and Macedonia) and an antipathy to new, unorthodox religions (Austria, Belgium,

France, and Germany). This illustrates two real trends in the world: the increasing Western European phobia of "sects" (described in Willy Fautre's essay on Western Europe) and an Eastern European fear of anything that challenges the hegemony of the dominant religious group.

Another group that has a comparatively lower rating for religious freedom consists of Azerbaijan, Bangladesh, Iran, Mauritania, and Pakistan. All of these countries have governments or opposition groups committed to radical forms of Islam that would relegate other religions to second-class status, or who think that they must accommodate or defer to such militant forms of Islam. Because of this, in many Islamic countries religious freedom lags behind even other freedoms.

Apart from the above two trends, there are the examples of Chile, Nepal, and India (which is two points below). Like the example of the Islamic countries cited, these reflect the influence of a dominant religion (Catholicism or Hinduism) that is currently more wary of the possible consequences of religious competition than it is of human freedom in general. In the case of India, there has recently been a rapid increase in religiously motivated assaults on minority religions.

Finally there are the examples of Indonesia and Nigeria. Their differential scores do not indicate any systematic variance of religious freedom but merely (like India) a process of rapid change. Both have experienced recent major changes, and their scores simply reflect this.

The countries that score higher on religious freedom than they do for civil rights in general are equally varied. However, here too some general patterns emerge. Several of these countries

(Belarus, Estonia, Kazakhstan, Kyrgyzstan, and Ukraine) are remnants of the former Soviet Union. While they vary from comparatively free (Estonia) to comparatively repressive (Belarus), each has found the freedom of its religious institutions easier to achieve, and perhaps less of a threat to power holders, than the freedom of other groups. The rest of this group—Cuba, Egypt, Malaysia, East Timor, Guatemala, Lebanon, Namibia, Vietnam, Singapore, Brazil, and Zimbabwe (the latter two are two points above)—are more idiosyncratic. However, in each case, their religious institutions are comparatively large and are, in fact, the major portion of civil society. Consequently, they may be harder to repress than other bodies. In addition, in most of these instances, the religious bodies have been relatively apolitical and, thus, have not provoked much opposition. The case of Cuba also reflects a slight slackening of religious control, while East Timor has eased due to the United Nations takeover in the fall of 1999.

State Department Reports on Religious Freedom

In September 1999, as required by law under the 1998 *International Religious Freedom Act,* the U. S. State Department released its first annual *Report* on religious freedom worldwide. The *Report* is an impressive piece of work and, by and large, gives a detailed and comprehensive overview of the state of religious freedom in each country in the world. However, the compilation of Freedom House's own survey gives us a basis to evaluate and to point out some weaknesses in the State Department's work.

First, because its material is not standardized and, hence, gives simply an ordered compilation of information about each country, the *Report* makes it difficult to compare one country to another. This has the effect of blurring distinctions so that many countries appear to be equally repressive. The very breadth of the material tends to repress important differences. Indeed, the largest single section on the problems of any individual religious group concerns the situation of Scientologists in Germany. No doubt this is a topic worthy of attention, but does it deserve more attention than the situation of any other group in the world, including Tibetan Buddhists, Iranian Baha'i, and Sudanese Christians?

In other instances the *Report* downplays the severity or significance of restrictions on religious freedom, perhaps in deference to the governments concerned. This appears in reports on Egypt, China, and Saudi Arabia.

• The *Report* says that the Egyptian Coptic Orthodox Church was established in the fifth century, but Egypt has been a major center of Christianity since the first century. It is noteworthy that Egyptian textbooks also omit the first five centuries of Coptic history. The *Report* also merely notes "discrepancies in official and unofficial accounts" of the torture and abuse of more than one thousand Copts in El-Khosheh in 1998, when there is copious detail of these abuses. Finally, it credits Egypt for improvements in permits for church construction and repair. But some of the construction permits were given for churches that had already been built— some in the fourth century.

• While the China section contains numerous details of persecution, it eschews the conclusion that China persecutes believers, stating the weaker conclusion that it "restricts" some religious believers (although the *Report's* executive summary does use the term *persecution*). It even avoids making conclusions as to the situation of the highest ranking member of the Roman Catholic Church in China, Bishop James Su Zhimin, stating only that his whereabouts "remain unclear," though Catholics from his diocese state he was arrested two years ago. The report flags the early release from reeducation camp of seventy-eight-year-old Bishop Zeng Jingmu when, in fact, as the report itself states, he was simply transferred to house arrest and is thus still prevented from carrying out his episcopal duties.

Perhaps most importantly, the *Report* sometimes gives a truncated view of religion. This is not a mere definitional quibble of interest only to academics: it is central to the proper implementation of the entire 1998 *International Religious Freedom Act*. The focus of the act is not human rights violations against "religious" people. After all, as noted above, since most people in the world claim some form of religious identity, the most human rights violations of *any* kind are against religious believers. The act is concerned not with all forms of restrictions or persecution of religious people, *but with persecution where the focus or the grounds are themselves in part religious*—where a person's or community's religion is a component of the persecution or discrimination they suffer. (Therefore it would not address genocide in Rwanda—even though most of those killed had a religious identity—since their death was related to their being

Tutsis.) Hence a truncated view of religion would lead inevitably to a truncated implementation of the act.

The *Report* is aware of the difficulties of defining the role of religion and very carefully and lucidly uses the example of Kosovo to illustrate it ("Introduction," pp. 3–4):

In Kosovo, for example, Serb atrocities were visited predominantly on Kosovar Albanian Muslims. The key question for this report is the extent to which the religion of the victims played a part in Serb behavior. If religion were a significant factor, then the Milosevic regime is responsible for a particular virulent form of religious persecution—alongside its other crimes against humanity—involving prolonged arbitrary detention, torture, mass executions, mass deportations, and rape. By the same token, if religion were not a factor, or constituted an insignificant factor, then religious persecution should not be added to the bill of particulars against the regime.

This is an issue on which people of good will hold strongly differing views. In the Kosovo case, many would argue that the predominant causes of the Serb campaign were political (Milosevic's usual tactic of initiating conflict as a means of retaining power), nationalist (the drive to retain a province central to Serbian identity and power), and ethnic (a determination to cleanse the nation of a non-Serb, unassimilated ethnic minority—the Kosovar Albanians). This view would hold that religion played an insignificant role in the conflict.

. . . By contrast, others argue that the ethnicity of the Kosovar Albanians is inextricably bound to their Muslim heritage, both in their own minds, and more importantly, in the minds of their Serb tormentors.

. . . Serbia is not the only case. In many countries where there is violent persecution against a religious minority, there are also nonreligious factors at work—the ethnicity and separatist policies of the minority, for example. In Sudan, Christians are being persecuted by an Arab regime that is Muslim. In China Tibetan Buddhists who are associated with separatism are being persecuted by an atheist government.

Clearly, as the *Report* says, people of goodwill can have differences about such things. However, it is troubling that at times it contrasts politics, nationalism, and ethnicity to religion, as though concrete acts, events, and movements were necessarily only one or another. In fact, most things human are several of these things at once. A war can be both economic and religious just as a wall can be both thick and tall. Cultures are usually religious, and religions are usually cultural (see section on "The Nature of Religious Freedom"). While the *Report* is often sensitive to these points, at times the tendency to separate religion from other factors leads it astray.

This tendency to minimize religion creates problems with coverage of Sudan. The Sudan section does a very good job of detailing religious persecution in areas under the direct control of the Khartoum regime, and it describes the practice of slavery. However, the

conduct of the war itself—with a death toll higher than that of Rwanda, Bosnia, Kosovo, Chechnya, Algeria, and all the Arab-Israeli wars combined, with up to five million displaced people, and widespread massacre, rape, torture, and forced starvation—is absent. The reason, we must assume, is that the war itself is not understood as "religious." Consequently, the *Report* neglects what may be, in terms of size and intensity, the world's worst situation of religious oppression. This is akin to disregarding race in describing South Africa's military actions and repression of the opponents of apartheid (see section in "The Nature of Religious Freedom").

In contrast to its treatment of Sudan, the *Report* correctly and fully outlines Saddam Hussein's vicious persecution of Shiite Muslims and of Assyrian and Chaldean Christians. However, the grounds for calling these depredations matters of religious freedom or religious persecution are less than they are in the Sudanese war. Clearly Saddam will, without discrimination, kill anyone of any or no religion whom he perceives as a political threat. Religion *per se* is not, apparently, a motive or independent factor for him. Yet the *Report* is correct to detail his depravities, since their result, regardless of motive, is a monumental denial of religious freedom. However, the State Department should have addressed Saddam's ally, Sudan, with the same insight.

Some other examples:

•   In Indonesia, conflict in Ambon between Christians and Muslims, claiming hundreds, perhaps thousands of lives, is related to immigration that has disturbed the "ethnic balance" of the area. But the crucial change has been in the *religious* balance, which is what has precipitated the conflict.

- In Nigeria, the report describes thirty-one followers of Shiite leader Ibrahim El-Zakzaky as having been detained for "political" not "religious beliefs." But, since for El-Zakzaky there "is no government but Islam," here the distinction of "political" and "religious" does not make much sense.
- In Taiwan, in reference to Jehovah's Witness conscientious objectors who have been imprisoned for refusing military service, the *Report* says there "is no indication [they] have been singled out for their beliefs." But their *religious* beliefs in this instance are *precisely* that they must not do military service.
- In Bhutan, the expulsion of Nepalese is described as "political," "economic," and "cultural" rather than "religious." However, it is also noted that the Hinduism of the ethnic Nepalese is one way of identifying them. Surely it is clear that here "religion" permeates "politics," "economics," and "culture."
- In India the caste system is described "as much a cultural and social phenomenon as a religious one"—but all religious phenomena are also always cultural and nearly always social.

Despite these critical comments, it must be reemphasized that the State Department *Report* is an exemplary piece of work and marks a milestone in reporting on religious freedom. It does highlight, however, the need for standardized criteria.

Conclusions

It is clear from the following pages, as well as State Department reports and other surveys, that violations of religious freedom worldwide are massive, widespread, and, in the last five years, growing. This leads to three other conclusions. First, that attention to and action on religious freedom have been comparatively weak. Second, that the important role of religion in conflicts and in political orders has been comparatively neglected. Third, that both of these situations are now beginning to change (on this see Nina Shea's essay), a change that we hope this present survey will accelerate.

— PAUL MARSHALL —

Figure 1. Religious Freedom by Area

Religious Freedom Rating	Former Soviet Union and Eastern Europe	North Africa and West Asia	Western Europe and North Atlantic	Asia	Africa	Latin America
1	Estonia		Finland Ireland Netherlands Norway United States			
2	Lithuania Poland		Austria Sweden United Kingdom	Japan South Korea Taiwan	Botswana Namibia South Africa	Brazil
3	Hungary Latvia Romania Ukraine	Israel	Belgium France Germany Spain	Mongolia Philippines	Zimbabwe	Argentina Chile El Salvador Guatemala
4	Armenia Bulgaria Georgia Kazakhstan Kyrgystan Macedonia Moldova Russia	Greece Lebanon Morocco		Malaysia Singapore Sri Lanka	Tanzania	Colombia Mexico
5	Azerbaijan Belarus	Egypt Turkey		East Timor India Indonesia Nepal	Nigeria	
6	Uzbekistan	Mauritania Pakistan		Bangladesh Bhutan China Vietnam		Cuba
7	Turkmenistan	Iran Saudi Arabia Sudan		Burma North Korea Tibet (China)		

☐ "free"

☐ "partly free"

☐ "unfree"

Figure 2. Religious Freedom by Religious Background

Religious Freedom Rating	Catholic	Protestant	Orthodox	Mixed Christian	Hindu	Buddhism and related religions	Islam	Other	Mixed Muslim/ Christian
1	Ireland	Estonia Finland Netherlands Norway United States							
2	Austria Brazil Lithuania Poland	Botswana Namibia South Africa Sweden United Kingdom				Japan South Korea Taiwan			
3	Argentina Belgium Chile El Salvador France Guatemala Hungary Philippines Spain	Zimbabwe	Romania Ukraine	Germany Latvia		Mongolia		Israel	
4	Colombia Mexico	Tanzania	Armenia Bulgaria Georgia Greece Macedonia Moldova Russia			Singapore Sri Lanka	Kazakhstan Kyrgystan Malaysia Morocco		Lebanon
5	East Timor		Belarus		India Nepal		Azerbaijan Egypt Indonesia Turkey		Nigeria
6	Cuba					Bhutan China Vietnam	Bangladesh Mauritania Pakistan Uzbekistan		
7						Burma North Korea Tibet (China)	Iran Saudi Arabia Sudan Turkmenistan		

WESTERN EUROPE:
TRENDS IN RELIGIOUS LIBERTY

The European continent is multicultural, multilingual, and multireligious. However, this variety of national histories, which is a richness in itself, poses some problems. In many cases specific religions have been closely linked to the building of modern nation-states, and they effectively enjoy a privileged status, legally, politically, and socially. Consequently, most European countries have a two-tiered or multitiered system in which religions have different status and in which citizens of different religions are not treated equally regardless of religion and may suffer discrimination on the basis of their religious or philosophical beliefs.

The clearest gap is between, on the one hand, religions that the state officially recognizes and, therefore, legitimizes with a type of label of quality and, on the other hand, religions that are not recognized. These are exclusively minority religions, also perjoratively called "sects" or "cults," and which do not enjoy the state label of quality. The criteria for distinguishing these various categories of religions are often vague and sometimes nonexistent.

This categorization of religions leads to discriminatory state financing. A number of religions are financed by the state, though unequally, while others are not. In the wide variety of financing systems in force in Western Europe, taxpayers may not be allowed to finance their own religion and may instead be obliged, in various degrees, to finance religions, and sometimes also a secular humanist movement, to which they do not adhere and which may be hostile to their own religion.

This also leads to a very heterogeneous subcategory of unpopular religious groups, often called "cults" and often described as "harmful or even dangerous." Mass homicides and suicides committed by a number of cults in the nineties have triggered an indiscriminate witch-hunt against hundreds of minority religions and their adherents by anticult movements and the media all over Europe and by the parliaments of France, Belgium, Germany, and Austria.

Policies Concerning Sects in European Union Member States

Eleven out of the fifteen European Union member states have decided that "sects" do not require any new institutions or organizations to combat their influence. In these countries' view, existing laws and legal methods can resolve any problems posed by such religious movements. These countries have not, as a result, become refuges for questionable religious movements or experienced any increase in crime or other harmful activities.

However, four other countries have decided on a different course of action. Austria has simply created an information and documentation center about sects and placed it under the authority of the Federal Ministry of the Environment, Youth, and the Family. A brochure containing information about sects has also been widely distributed. This prevention campaign has warned principally about eleven guru-led movements of oriental origin, three psychological groups, two groups claiming to spring from new revelations, three religions of Christian origin, and four other groups under the category "various."

Germany has set up a parliamentary commission, published a report, and placed the Church of Scientology under surveillance. However, no legal action is currently being taken against the movement.

France has set up a commission of parliamentary inquiry, which has published a report containing a list of 172 purportedly dangerous and harmful sects. An observatory of sects was started and later was replaced by a more aggressive Interministerial Mission to Fight Sects. The media have also spawned a widespread climate of suspicion and fear, leading to acts of intolerance and discrimination unheard of before the French government's anti-sect policy. The all-out campaign against sects by the Interministerial Mission has reinforced this pervasive phobia.

Belgium has followed closely on France's heels. It also has a commission of parliamentary inquiry, which published a report listing 189 movements suspected of being harmful sects, created an observatory of sects and an administrative coordination committee against sects, and started a sect prevention campaign (led by Belgium's French community) on television and radio accompanied by a massive distribution of information brochures.

In France and the French-speaking part of Belgium the authorities have, unlike Sweden or Spain, chosen to reject any sort of dialogue with minority religions and favored confrontation, often with the support of anti-sect associations. Neither shows any sign of a change of course.

The European Union and the Council of Europe

On July 13, 1998, the European Parliament rejected a report on cults by Mrs. Maria Bergers and has taken no further initiative. On June 22, 1999, the Council of Europe's Parliamentary Assembly unanimously adopted a recommendation to give priority to the prevention of dangerous sects. However, it also said that "major legislation on sects is undesirable" because any such legislation might contradict the guarantees of freedom of conscience and religion contained in Article 9 of the European Convention on Human Rights. Nonetheless, the Assembly believed that the serious incidents that had occurred in recent years did indicate the need for greater control of groups it referred to as "sects," a term that it did not further define. The Assembly also emphasized that any activities should be carried out in keeping with principles underlying democratic societies. Consequently, it maintained that it was vital to have reliable, objective information that could be used in school curricula and with the children of followers of groups that had a religious, esoteric, or spiritual nature.

Hence, the Assembly called on the governments of member states to:

- support the establishment of national or regional, independent sect information centers;
- include information on the history and philosophy of major schools of thought and religion in the general school curriculum;
- use criminal and civil law procedures against any illegal practices carried out by these groups;
- encourage the setting up of non-governmental organizations to protect victims; but also
- take firm steps against any

discrimination or marginalization of minority groups and encourage a spirit of tolerance and understanding.

The Assembly also requested the Ministerial Committee of the Council of Europe to set up a European Observatory on groups of a religious, esoteric, or spiritual nature in order to facilitate an exchange of information between different national centers. It added that the Council of Europe should also promote the formation of information centers in Central and Eastern European countries.

National Anti-Sect Policies in the Light of the Council of Europe's Report

The French, Belgian, German, and Austrian parliamentary members of the Council of Europe's Assembly have supported the Council's proposals, although these proposals radically contradict the policies in their own countries. For example, the Parliamentary Assembly unanimously condemned:

- the use of the word *sect*;
- any distinction between a sect and a religion;
- any government's involvement in a theological debate about whether groups are religions or not;
- state recognition of only certain religions;
- state supervision of sect observatories;
- spreading information about certain groups before those concerned have had a chance to respond;
- lack of dialogue;
- any discrimination or marginalization of religious minority groups.

However, currently, French, Belgian, German, and Austrian policies are completely founded on a distinction between sects and religions, something the Assembly considers a "pitfall which the authorities must avoid." The text of the Council's report is clear:

The state could agree to adopt the course suggested by certain groups and distinguish between religions—by definition good—and sects—necessarily dangerous—or even between good and bad sects. Once again we do not think that such an approach is acceptable. Under Article 9 of the European Convention on Human Rights, states are prohibited from distinguishing between different beliefs and from creating a scale of beliefs which is, in our view, unacceptable. Merely making such a distinction would constitute a disproportionate violation of the freedom guaranteed by Article 9 of the European Convention of Human Rights because the very basis of this freedom is the absence of distinction between beliefs, which explains the state's duty to maintain neutrality.

Moreover, such an approach is dangerous because if a dispute arose, the debate would focus not on the activities of the groups concerned but on the nature of their beliefs. The first means of defense for some groups is to seek to demonstrate that their beliefs constitute a religion, so that they can then claim to be acting accordingly, even if that entails the commission of illegal acts. In these circumstances, if state authorities agree to enter into an ideological discussion they are obliged to determine the classification of the beliefs concerned and will find themselves in an inextricable situation.

Either they will have to accept that the belief concerned is not a religion and will be accused of violating religious freedom and of persecuting the group concerned. Or alternatively, they will have to consider that the beliefs of the group effectively constitute a religion, and the latter will take advantage of state recognition to justify all its actions, even illegal ones. In both cases, the state authorities will take part in a religious controversy and therefore fail in their duty to remain neutral under the terms of Article 9 of the ECHR. This kind of debate is therefore a trap in which some groups systematically try to ensnare the authorities and which the latter must be at pains to avoid.

When faced with the impossible choice between using the term *religion* or *sect* (a concept with "extremely pejorative connotations"), the Parliamentary Assembly unanimously agreed that diverse beliefs could be encompassed and any negative prejudice avoided by using the more general formula: *religious, spiritual,* or *esoteric groups.*

The Assembly also called on the governments of member states to establish or support "*independent* national or regional information centres on groups of a religious, esoteric or spiritual nature."

Hence, the report in effect condemns the state-dependent Sect Observatories set up by France and Belgium, whatever the name given to these state agencies. France tried to pass an amendment to the recommendation, stipulating that sect information centers should be state controlled, but Sweden opposed this, and the reporter, Mr

Nastase, reminded the Assembly that this point had already been decided. Austria, Germany, and Belgium failed to come to France's rescue, although it was still smarting from the failure of its two other amendments.

The Belgian Anthrosophical Society has taken the state of Belgium to court over the law setting up its Information and Advice Centre to examine harmful sectarian organizations. The society claimed that the administrative coordination body discriminated against Belgians who were not part of an established religion and so contravened the state's duty to remain secular. The case is pending, and its outcome will be important for similar centers in Germany and Austria.

The Assembly also recommended that "the Committee of Ministers take measures to inform and educate young people and the general public." However, it added the guarantee that any information gathered should be reliable and should emanate "neither exclusively from sects themselves nor from associations set up to defend the victims of sects." In addition, the groups and individuals concerned should have the opportunity of expressing themselves "as to the objectivity of such information." This position lends credibility to proposals made by sociologists and religious historians and agencies such as INFORM in Britain that any European Observatory should coordinate all the private centers and should remain free from any political control.

A Belgium sect-prevention brochure appears to violate the report's standards, and following the case brought by the Anthrosophical Society, the French Community of Belgium was ordered to stop the brochure's distribution until the information concerning the Society had been removed. The same criticism can be made about Austria and a number of German Länder, which distribute similar brochures on a massive scale. The French brochure, aimed at high-school students, should also be withdrawn from circulation, as much of the "information" it contains is false and error ridden. Its information comes largely from associations to defend the "victims" of sects, was not shown to the individuals and groups concerned before publication, and was not checked by the French Ministry of Education.

Finally, the Council does allow that, "as a last resort," it may be permissible to "ban certain groups which are known to shelter the perpetrators of criminal activities." However, the suggested conditions for placing such a ban are very restrictive, and in any case there are major questions as to whether such a ban could be effective. Legally, followers could not be stopped from meeting together either in public or in private or from communicating by phone, fax, E-mail, or the Internet.

This last recommendation could also have some unforeseen implications if the Council of Europe continues to reject any distinction between sects and religions. The Catholic Church has at times harboured "perpetrators of criminal activities" when some of its authorities have closed their eyes to pedophilia among some members of its clergy. If it were thought that its teaching concerning celibacy reinforced this problem, then the Catholic Church could be seen as producing sexual delinquents and, if it refused to modify its doctrine, could be banned.

Why a Sect-Hunt in Western Europe?

Nonconventional religious, esoteric, and spiritual movements are expanding throughout Europe. Such groups have always challenged the position of established religions, and it is not surprising that, in return, they have been opposed by established religions. However, the worrying new element in Europe is the active participation of *governmental* institutions in these differences. Moreover, the differences between countries such as France, Belgium, Germany, and Austria, who are targeting sects, and others who have chosen to stay neutral cannot be explained merely by the policy of some governments to separate religion from the state. France and the Netherlands both have such a separation but have very different policies on sects. Sweden has also taken a very liberal attitude, even though its Lutheran church has been closely tied to the state. Anti-sect policies seem to be favored in situations where there exists:

- a historical monopoly by one or two religions;
- increased secularism in the wake of the progress of secular humanism and the regression of established religions;
- the presence of established connections between established religions and/or secular humanism with Parliament, governmental, or social institutions and the media;
- a historical tradition of centralism and a reluctance to accept diversity, whether cultural, linguistic, religious, or ethnic;
- converging interests between historically dominant belief systems, despite their differences or even history of conflict;
- the presence of anti-sect movements.

Just one of these conditions might sometimes be enough to set off an anti-sect movement, but normally it takes a combination. Moreover, the repressive momentum has spread internationally because of converging interests with the dominant belief systems in other states.

The anti-sect movement started in France where militant *laïcité*—one form of secular humanism—has been hostile to religion, especially the Catholic Church, ever since the Revolution. In French-speaking Europe, francophone Belgium and the canton of Geneva have followed hot on France's heels, thanks to the political, social, and media connections of secular humanists. In Germany and Austria the connections have been via established religions. There are already signs that other countries, such as Hungary, are also ready to enter an anti-sect war.

The anti-sect war usually focuses on doctrines, practices, and teachings concerning health and alternative teaching methods. The accusations made about sects usually concern mental instability, bodily harm, sexual abuse, family breakup, indoctrination of children, threats to public order, and fraud. Consequently, in a fight against non-conventional groups, governments can often count not only on the support of the established churches and secular humanism in all its forms, but also the Medical Doctors' Associations, and professionals involved in the market for traditional psychology. Public and denominational schools will also usually defend their own interests when it comes to alternative teaching methods.

The perverse effects of these sect-hunts are clearly visible, even though the main instigators refuse to acknowledge them. They include rumor campaigns, public denunciations, abusive police raids followed by massive separation of children from their parents, loss of jobs or promotions, loss of custody or visiting rights in divorce cases, administrative and fiscal harassment, de-facing of places of worship, assaults, and bomb alerts.

In the wake of this growing pressure for philosophical and religious conformity, some states may be tempted to go beyond sect-hunts and seek to impose a wider conformity. In the future, anyone who is not "ideologically correct" in any area may be exposed to public condemnation.

Conclusions

All European states have agreed to be bound by several international agreements, including the Charter of the United Nations, the (1950) European Convention on Human Rights, the (1966) International Covenant on Civil and Political Rights, and several documents of the Organization for Security and Cooperation in Europe, including the important 1989 Vienna Concluding Document. In addition to these binding instruments, several other important documents outline international standards, including the Universal Declaration of Human Rights, the (1981) UN Declaration on the Elimination of All Forms of Intolerance and Discrimination Based on Religion or Belief, and the (1993) Human Rights Committee General Comment on Article 18 of the Covenant. All of these major human rights conventions, as well as other conventions to which France, Belgium, Germany, and Austria are signatories, include a clause that prohibits discrimination on the basis of religion. For example, Article 14 of the European Convention, provides that "the enjoyment of the rights and freedoms set forth in this Convention shall be secured without discrimination on any ground such as sex, race, color, language, religion, political or other opinion, national or social origin, association with a national minority, property, birth or other status." Similarly, Article 1, section 3 of the Charter of the United Nations provides that there should be no "distinction as to race, sex, language or religion."

OSCE participating states, which include all European countries except Serbia, have pledged not only to prohibit discrimination but also to "take effective measures to prevent and eliminate discrimination against individuals or communities on the grounds of religion or belief in the recognition, exercise and enjoyment of human rights and fundamental freedoms in all fields of civil, political, economic, social and cultural life, and to ensure the effective equality between believers and non-believers."

(Vienna Concluding Document Art. 16.1). These states also have taken upon themselves the affirmative obligation of promoting tolerance. As the 1989 Vienna Concluding Document states, all participating states shall "foster a climate of mutual tolerance and respect between believers of different communities as well as between believers and non-believers" (Vienna Concluding Document Art. 16.2). France, Belgium, Germany, and Austria must be challenged to respect and implement these provisions and fully guarantee their citizens' freedom of religion and belief, especially those whose views seem strange and are unpopular.

— WILLY FAUTRE —

Willy Fautre is the head of Human Rights Without Frontiers in Brussels and editor-in-chief of its Press and Information Service. He is a noted authority on religious freedom around the world and especially in Europe.

THE FORMER SOVIET UNION: TRENDS IN RELIGIOUS LIBERTY

The catastrophic experiment forcibly to impose "state atheism" (*gosateizm*) in the Soviet Union lasted just seventy years. Until Lenin's first decree on the "Separation of Church and State" of January 1918, no government in history had sought to impose a system that rejected all forms of religion. The Roman Empire debased the gods of mythology by decreeing that the ruler should be worshiped, but they never abolished the pantheon. The French Revolution was strongly anticlerical, but Christian worship continued. "State atheism" had its ups and downs for seventy years but continued as the dominant policy in one form or other until 1988. The advent of Mikhail Sergeyevich Gorbachev as General Secretary of the Communist Party put an end to it three years into his rule. It is possible to put a precise date on this: April 29, 1988, the day on which Gorbachev received a group of leading bishops of the Russian Orthodox Church in the Kremlin, the first such meeting that had taken place since Stalin received Metropolitan Sergi in September 1943, and only the second in history. Gorbachev's words truly marked the beginning of a new era:

Not everything has been easy and simple in the sphere of church-state relations. Religious organizations have been affected by the tragic developments that occurred in the period of the cult of personality. Mistakes made in relation to the church and believers in the 1930s and subsequently are being rectified. Believers are Soviet people, workers, patriots, and they have the full right to express their convictions with dignity. Perestroika, democratization and glasnost concern them as well—in full measure and without any restrictions. This is especially true of ethics and morals, a domain where universal norms and customs are so helpful for our common cause.

"Our common cause"—never before anywhere had a communist leader in power pronounced such a phrase. Gorbachev proved to be as good as his word, though of course his own experiment in democracy collapsed three years later. It was not only a shortage of time that prevented the emergence of such a dialogue: the churches themselves quickly became too strong to be tempted in this direction. Gorbachev made two promises: the right to celebrate the millennium of the baptism of Prince Vladimir in Kiev in 988 and the introduction of a new and just law on religion to replace Stalin's 1929 one.

The first was soon implemented, as plans already existed. June 4, the date of the celebration of the conversion of the Eastern Slavs (the ancient land of "Rus") was just five weeks away. But in that short time what might have been a merely local celebration became one of international significance. Guests from around the world came, and they were surprised to find that Russian television, radio, and newspapers led every broadcast and every issue with extensive news of the celebrations. Moscow and Russia received the acclaim that should rightly have belonged to Kiev and Ukraine, but nevertheless it felt as though the USSR had become a Christian country overnight. The apogee was a celebration in the Bolshoi Theater, where the massive forces of the theater itself joined with cathedral and seminary choirs in a symphony of church and state, culminating in a massive peal of church bells—real bells— which a panel rolled back to reveal above the proscenium arch. In retrospect, some aspects of this week seem vastly overdone, but Russia would never be the same again.

Gorbachev's promise of a new law took longer to implement, but when it was promulgated in September 1990, it went beyond almost everyone's expectations in proclaiming total freedom of religion (even, in the version for the Russian Republic, permitting the teaching of religion in state schools: the text for the whole Soviet Union did not go quite this far.) Had this law remained in force for a sensible period of time, it would have been a major step in the painful evolution of Russia towards democracy.

Under the old system every region of the Soviet Union had its local officials responsible for controlling religious activities and reporting back to the Council for Religious Affairs in Moscow. This system was abolished in 1990, but not, as it proved, swept away. Many—perhaps most—of these people remained at their desks or perhaps moved to the local polytechnic to deliver lectures in favor of religion, or at least of the Orthodox Church. They

were awaiting a better day, when their services would once again be needed. That time came with the 1997 law, for which they had agitated in conjunction with the hierarchy of the Russian Orthodox Church.

What had happened during the seven-year interim was basically a revival of all forms of native religion, coupled with an invasion of cults from all over the world. Time might well have shown that the resulting dangers were more perceived than real. However, most reaction was out of all proportion to actual events, but the old atheist guard believed their day had come again. The resulting text was achieved by a secretive process, and *skulduggery* does not seem too strong a word in the context.

It is worth pausing over the preamble of the new law, which is not, we are told by its Russian defenders, part of the law itself but merely the context in which it is set. This text, one convoluted sentence, would fail a test in logic written by a high-school pupil: "Confirming the right of each to freedom of conscience and freedom of creed, and also to equality before the law regardless of his attitudes to religion and his convictions; basing itself on the fact that the Russian Federation is a secular state; recognizing the special contribution of Orthodoxy to the history of Russia and to the establishment and development of Russia's spirituality and culture."

So far, not so very good, but just supportable: the juxtaposition of "secular state" and "the special contribution of Orthodoxy" is bound to lead to misunderstandings somewhere along the line. But then comes a truly astonishing phrase: "respecting Christianity, Islam, Buddhism, Judaism and other religions and creeds which constitute an inseparable part of the historical heritage of Russia's peoples' considering it important to promote the achievement of mutual understanding, tolerance and respect in questions of freedom of conscience and freedom of creed; hereby adopts this federal law."

What is this "Christianity" that is separate from the Russian Orthodox Church? We are not told. And this, we must remind ourselves, is part of the law of the land, not some casual commentary by a careless journalist. We can only assume that, in fact, it means Catholicism and Protestantism, the first of which had a toehold on Russian soil, the second rather more. Representatives of Islam, Buddhism, and Judaism were naturally delighted to find themselves named and protected under the new law. But what are the other "religions and creeds" that constitute an inseparable part of the historical heritage of Russia's peoples?

Confusion is already rife, but the main text goes on to show that there are three tiers of privilege. The Russian Orthodox Church, *de facto* if not *de jure*, and encouraged by this special mention, will arrogate to itself, in the form of the local clergy, the right of deciding, when appealed to by the local state official, which other religions or denominations are to be granted the right of registration. It apparently has first claim on the loyalty of some 148 million people. Any other religion may be considered "traditional" if it was in existence fifteen years before the decree, that is, in 1982— which takes one right back to the end of the Brezhnev years. Hence, the extreme discrimination of those years is perpetuated today. Any group not in existence then must reregister conditionally every year for the next fifteen years to prove its credentials, and in the meantime has virtually no rights: no printing and dis-

tribution of literature, owning property, hiring halls, inviting foreign guests, and much else.

Those familiar with Brezhnev's period of "stagnation" (*zastoi*), as Gorbachev called it, will know that it was a time of widespread discrimination, with a ban on such groups as Methodists (except in Estonia), Lutherans (except in Latvia and Estonia), some groups of Baptists who had separated from the Moscow-dominated All-Union Council, Catholics of Byzantine Rite (the "Uniates" or Greek Catholics of Ukraine), Jehovah's Witnesses, and many others. Some of these had been clearly present even before the Revolution: Lutherans were in Siberia in the seventeenth century and in St. Petersburg from its founding (see the magnificent church, now being restored, on Nevsky Prospekt). The Anglican (Episcopal) Church had owned property in St. Petersburg and Moscow, with flourishing congregations before the Revolution. The subsequent abolition of their chaplaincies would logically mean that they fall foul of the "fifteen-year rule," but, of course, for diplomatic reasons it would be inconceivable to take back the church in Moscow where worship vigorously resumed in 1991.

What are the "other religions and creeds that constitute an inseparable part of the historical heritage of Russia's peoples"? Such a vague, indeed meaningless, phrase may not be susceptible to an obvious interpretation, but one surprising answer is the rise of traditional paganism.

A Perspective from History

Every Soviet leader put his own personal stamp on atheist policy (Lenin's seizure of church property; Stalin's purge of the whole church leadership, moderated during World War II; Khrushchev's renewed physical onslaught; Brezhnev's hunting down of "dissidents"), but the long-term aim of eliminating religion from the face of society always remained. Much of this policy was successful, if the word *face* is emphasized. The effects of the devastation will persist long into the twenty-first century: perhaps it can never be repaired. Every church institution at the local, diocesan, or national level was systematically destroyed. If churches of any denomination continued to exist up to World War II, they were entirely isolated units and therefore all the more vulnerable to persecution. There was no literature, teaching, charitable work, or communal activities outside the four walls of a registered church. The number of the latter did indeed grow following Stalin's concessions during the last decade of his life. Some institutions reemerged after the war, such as eight theological seminaries and two academies, one heavily censored journal, and a politically controlled central administration (the Moscow Patriarchate). The Baptists—the only legal Protestant group—were accorded some similar privileges, but without theological education; the Catholics had two churches and nothing else. Under Khrushchev all these gains came under renewed threat, but his premature removal from office halted the downward spiral, without allowing any restitution of recent losses.

Beneath the surface, however, the elimination of religion had not proceeded as smoothly as the propagandists reported in the Soviet press. Indeed, there was something frenetic and despairing in the tone of the constant assertions in the press that religion was, of course, dying out—but. After the qualifying conjunction, the reader would find diverse accounts illustrating the ways in which survivals of religion persisted long after the destruction of the institutions. In the process it was also revealed that the overlay of Orthodoxy, spread throughout Siberia and the Russian south with the expansion of empire, was thin indeed, and recent researches give evidence of a remarkable revival of pre-Christian religion.

What of the survival of Orthodoxy in the Russian heartland? The evidence is manifold and widespread. No one illustrates it better than Alexander Solzhenitsyn. The meager volume of his published work is suffused with an underlying allegiance to the Orthodox Christian faith. During the long period when his works were banned, he revealed himself as an overt believer. His first publication, the novella *One Day in the Life of Ivan Denisovich* (1962), an account of life in a labor camp, which Khrushchev permitted to be published to back up his anti-Stalin campaign, gives a strong account of how prayer sustained one of the inmates. His second, and last, published work in the Soviet period, a collection of prose poems, contains a remarkable essay that expressed horror at the desecration of Russia's precious Christian architectural heritage, publication of which inspired a new generation to try to do something to preserve the remaining tatters. This extract gives the flavor:

> When you travel the byroads of Central Russia you begin to understand the secret of the pacifying Russian countryside. It's in the churches. They trip up the slopes, ascend the high hills, come down to the broad rivers, like princesses in white and red, they lift their belltowers—graceful, shapely, all different, high over mundane timber and thatch, they nod to

each other from afar, from villages that are cut off and invisible to each other they soar to the same heaven.

But when you get into the village you find that not the living but the dead greeted you from afar. The crosses were knocked off the roof or twisted out of place long ago. The dome has been stripped and there are gaping holes between its rusty ribs. Our forefathers put all their understanding of life into these stones, into these bell-towers.

(The author then peers into the building and sees a youth club meeting.) Ram it in, Vitka, give it a bash, don't be afraid! Film-show at six dancing at eight.

Religious Revival

The revival of religion, especially among the intelligentsia at Moscow and Leningrad even as early as the 1960s, is amply documented. Those writers who have attributed it in some way to Gorbachev's perestroika are seriously in error. What Gorbachev did was to take the lid off a seething cauldron, facilitating the rebirth of religious institutions nationwide and giving voice to the pent-up spiritual aspirations of the Russian people (one meaning of *glasnost*). This is the context in which we must view the events of 1988, when all this suddenly broke the surface.

Apart from this release of a wound-up spring, there was also an influx of foreign missionaries of many denominations and religions. They were encouraged by the 1988 events, by the 1990 legislation, and, especially, by the collapse of the U.S.S.R. at the end of 1991. At this time, too, Russia, Ukraine, and other former constituent republics began to turn urgently to the West for advice and economic support, which soon led to a relaxation of visa restrictions.

This was not to last. The new 1997 law on religion was only one aspect of the gathering spirit of resentment in Russia against the West, underlined by the adoption of the new law by the Duma with a majority of more than three hundred votes. However, if the main intention of the new law was to protect and encourage Orthodoxy over against all other religions (an interpretation based on the first part of the Preamble), then it has signally failed. The revival of all religions, those mentioned in the second part of the Preamble to the 1997 law and many others, is one of the most interesting, significant, but least-known factors in the recent development of Russian society. It deserves to be studied and documented, to be set alongside the endless accounts of economic deprivation in the countryside.

The Keston Institute is halfway through a major field project studying contemporary religion in all of Russia's eighty-nine administrative regions. The picture that is rapidly emerging is a vast canvas stretched out over the world's largest country and filled with the most diversified religious activities. It is a microcosm—almost a macrocosm—of world religion on the threshold of the new millennium. Millions of Russians themselves will find this study a treasure trove of new information. Western scholars of the Russian present as well as would-be missionaries and those who wish to offer fraternal aid to the fellow believers will find this an essential source.

The new law has not even begun to control the explosion of all religions, from Russian Orthodoxy, Protestantism, and Catholicism, through Islam and Buddhism to paganism, with more than a sprinkling of new-age religions and a revival of ancient Russian sects. Nor could it exercise such control, even if the will were there—which it is certainly not in many of the regions. Keston's study brings out the fact that the new laws on religion have very little influence on the main trends, which are a significant factor in the development of Russian society. Wherever one looks there is revival of religion.

Russian Orthodoxy is, of course, a dominant factor, but only in the Russian heartland, which is confined to the territory some three or four hundred miles in all directions from Moscow. North of St. Petersburg, east of the Volga, right across Siberia and the whole of the South and Southeast the picture is very different. For example, there is a major revival of Islam, not only in the well-known example of Chechnya and neighboring Dagestan, but also in Adygeya, the Black Sea region in the South, and especially in Tatarstan, centered on Kazan, an ancient heartland of the Muslim faith. Buddhism is experiencing a major revival not only in the traditional area of the Buryat Mongol Republic, south of Irkutsk in Siberia, but even in Europe itself. Kalmykia was Europe's only Buddhist civilization in tsarist times. In the communist period not only was it eliminated, but the nationality itself was deported to Siberia. Now Buddhism is back on the map as an active force in Europe.

Perhaps most surprising of all is the rise of traditional pre-Christian paganism in many areas where, in tsarist times, the missionary activity of the Russian Orthodox Church did not do much more than introduce a Christian overlay and administration in places where people, especially in rural areas, quietly preserved their ancient customs.

This might not seem so surprising in the tribal areas of Siberia, where reindeer herding and trapping in the forests are still the traditional way of life. But that paganism is in the throes of a major revival in Europe is unexpected. The region in question is the Lower Volga, where the republics of Udmurita, Chuvashia, and Mari El are situated. Particularly in the latter, pagan religion is well on the way not only to dominating the cultural scene but to being encouraged by politicians as a way to reestablish the identity of the local.

However, despite these trends, it is obvious that the Christian church is destined to be visibly and actively present in Russia in a major way in the next millennium. The failed experiment of state atheism destroyed so much, yet what it has left behind shows that human agency, however systematic its efforts over a long period of time, cannot eliminate faith, and that the future of Russia and the future of Orthodoxy will be inseparable. However, this future will now be in a pluralistic society in which the most disparate elements will have to learn to live with one another. Laws favoring one group over another threaten to lead not only to heightened tensions but could even cause disaster by exacerbating ethnic conflict, and Europe today is only too aware of the possible consequences.

A Glance around the Former Soviet Union

The vast territories covered by the newly independent countries of the former Soviet Union present a picture of astonishing diversity that is not susceptible to any generalization. The former imposition of state atheism has, of course, left its mark everywhere, but the speed with which the religious picture has changed in every single new country is astonishing. Religion is acknowledged by the respective governments to be a major factor in these emerging societies.

The group of countries that shows the clearest evidence of progress toward true democracy is, not surprisingly, the Baltic States. Estonia, Latvia, and Lithuania have made rapid strides, despite continuing difficulties, to achieve recognition as members of the "European Community" (in general, if not yet in a political, sense). Of these, Estonia has laws and practices that place it now in the forefront of liberal states, not least in the field of religious liberty. Latvia is showing some tendency to introduce restrictions on the propagation of "new" religions, but it is likely that democratic controls will predominate over authoritarianism. Lithuania exhibits some of the features one would expect in a country where the Roman Catholic Church holds such sway, but there is tolerance for the Lutheran and other minorities.

The countries of the so-called "CIS" exhibit many disturbing features. The Commonwealth of Independent States cannot be said to have achieved any progress towards political unity: probably the reverse since its establishment immediately after the collapse of communism. Economic unity is even further away. Except for Belarus, under its eccentric President Lukashenka, they all fear the possibility of renewed domination by Russia, rather than having any desire to move towards it. Naturally, various countries have made bilateral agreements with their neighbors, but "union" does not go much further than that. Wherever one looks, however, religion, especially Christianity, is a defining feature and is often allied with the newly asserted nationalism. Religious intolerance in one form or another is universally present.

It is surprising, for example, to find that Armenia, in the Trans-Caucasus region, so strongly opposes the propagation of any religion other than the traditional Apostolic Church. To some extent one can understand this. Christianity was its religion, even before the Emperor Constantine adopted it as the religion of the Roman Empire. The twentieth century has been cruel to Armenia: first, the massacres at the hands of the Turks and then long years of Soviet atheist domination. The average Armenian (and the late head of the church, Catholicos Karekin I, an Oxford-educated man of great ecumenical experience) believes that it is now time for the Armenian Church to have its day.

Neighboring Georgia is so torn politically that it is impossible to generalize about it. In the main region around Tbilisi, under President Shevardnadze, the Orthodox Church is dominant but has recently taken major strides against tolerance. It has withdrawn from all ecumenical contact, officially having left the World Council of Churches, and bilateral relations with, for example, the Anglican Church, which were good in the early 1990s, are now being set aside. Minorities, like the long-established Baptist church under Pastor Malkhaz Songulashvili, are feeling the wind of intolerance, however much they wish to assert that they, too, are traditional in Georgia.

Moldova is difficult to evaluate because it is politically and geographically torn between Romania, whose language it shares, and Russia, with the Moscow Patriarchate attempting to hold on to its territory. Its law officially bans proselytism.

Ukraine is a vast and varied land. Not only is it divided between the Orthodox Church in the East and the Greek Catholic Church in the West, but the former is a battlefield between different jurisdictions. In the West the strife between Catholics of the Byzantine Rite and the Latins has now culminated in victory for the former. In addition, there are probably more Protestants, mainly Baptist, in Ukraine than in all the rest of the countries of the CIS combined (not excluding Russia). They are very active and well organized in terms of building churches and reestablishing seminary education. The diversified picture shows many facets of intolerance.

Belarus, too, is a large territory bordering on the Catholic countries of Poland and Lithuania in the West, and Orthodox Russia to the East. The state policy under President Lukashenka is that Orthodoxy must predominate, and one consequence is a high level of intolerance for the strong Catholic minority. Metropolitan Filaret of Minsk, a doughty survivor of the Soviet period, is also a russianizer. This is a country where religious liberty is much under threat.

The six Muslim countries of the CIS all exhibit strongly anti-Western, and anti-proselytizing tendencies. The new 1998 laws on religion in Uzbekistan are probably the toughest introduced by any country in the world in recent years. In 1999, amendments are being introduced to close even the loopholes allowing some degree of flexibility for unregistered communities. The armed conflict between Armenia and Azerbaijan saw major outrages committed against Christian minorities in the latter. In the vast territory of Kazakhstan, the situation is a little better, with Orthodox Russians and Muslim Kazakhs enjoying reasonable relations with each other.

With the exception of the Baltic States, the whole area of the former Soviet Union has failed to implement the kind of religious liberty for which there were such high hopes in 1991 when communism and its atheist policies finally collapsed.

— MICHAEL BORDEAUX —

Michael Bourdeaux was for many years the head of Keston College, which became the Keston Institute in Oxford. Keston is perhaps the major authority on religious freedom issues in Eastern Europe and the former Soviet Union. He is the author of many books and articles. For his work he was awarded the Order of the Grand Duke Gediminos by the government of Lithuania.

RELIGIOUS FREEDOM
IN LATIN AMERICA

It has taken Latin America much longer than other parts of the West to accept religious freedom in theory and to implement it in practice. For most of its history, the right to practice one's religion in accordance with one's conscience was not recognized, and even when that right was guaranteed in constitutions and laws, it was violated in practice. Today all the constitutions of Latin America recognize the right to freedom of worship, and the prospects for religious freedom in Latin America are better now than they have ever been. However, tensions and conflict in the area of religion remain. These tensions have been exacerbated by the recent rapid spread of evangelical Protestantism throughout the region, but religious minorities are more active and self-confident than in the past, and discrimination against Jews and Protestants is rare.

New constitutions have been adopted or old ones substantially amended in almost every Latin American country, and many of them have eliminated or modified the special position of the Catholic Church. Only three countries, Argentina, Bolivia, and Costa Rica, while guaranteeing freedom of worship, distinguish in their constitutions between Catholicism and other religions, and in the first two countries, strong arguments have been made for repeal of those clauses. In two other countries, Chile and Colombia, discussions are underway to modify or generalize the special legal status of Catholicism that results from earlier agreements with the Vatican. Extremists of the left and right who, in the past, favored more authoritarian models of church-state relations no longer contest the norms of liberal democracy regarding freedom of worship. The increasing activism of the worldwide human rights community also gives assurance that violations of religious freedom will be publicized and protested.

Historical Background

The late arrival of religious freedom in Latin America is related to its colonial heritage and to its postcolonial history. That history can be divided into five periods: (1) Iberian colonization, (2) the post-Independence liberal-conservative conflict, (3) the rise of democracy and populism between the 1930s and the 1960s, (4) the cold-war period of military intervention and rule between 1960 and 1990, and (5) the triumph of liberal democracy.

Iberian Colonization

Even before the arrival of the Spaniards, the great pre-Columbian empires, centered in Peru and Mexico, used religion to support their authority and power. It was relatively easy therefore for the European conquerors to replace native religious structures with those of a Catholicism that was closely linked to the Spanish throne. Religious uniformity had characterized the Spanish monarchy after the expulsion of the Muslims, and the papacy, threatened by the spread of Protestantism, was willing to cede vast authority to the Spanish rulers in their colonies. Many of the missionaries who accompanied

43

the conquistadors saw their role as converting the heathen, by force if necessary. "The cross and the sword" were thus closely linked in the Spanish Empire. The monarch had extracted from the papacy the right of patronage, *jus partronatus* or *patronato*, that is, control over the appointment of bishops—elements of which survived in some of the legal systems of Latin America until the second half of the twentieth century. In turn the church received a religious and educational monopoly, control over its own courts, and vast landholdings. The Inquisition was active, and religious dissidence was repressed. Neither in theory nor in practice was there recognition of religious freedom.

Liberal-Conservative Conflict

After independence was achieved in the period between 1810 and 1830, most of the newly independent Latin American states concluded concordats or treaties with the Vatican, often claiming succession to the right of patronage. The Vatican was initially resistant to recognition of Latin American independence because of the opposition of Spain. However, formal relations were established in the 1830s, although the issue of the *patronato* remained to be settled on a case-by-case basis. The problem was complicated by the emergence of a liberal-conservative split in many Latin American republics, with the liberals sharing, to a greater or lesser degree, the anticlericalism of the French Revolution that had inspired them, and the conservatives generally supporting the establishment of Catholicism as the state religion. Issues of control over marriage, education, and cemeteries, plus the large landholdings of the church, complicated the relationship.

Although most constitutions of the nineteenth century recognized Catholicism, the specifics of the relations in each country were fought over throughout the century, with the liberals taking the lead in reducing the influence of the church when they were in power. The formal separation of church and state would take place only in the twentieth century, and legislation regarding the *patronato* was repealed in Bolivia and Argentina only in the 1960s. The provision of the Argentine constitution that the president must be a Catholic, which was related to his earlier role in nominating bishops, and references to the conversion of the Indians and to presidential control over the promulgation of papal legislating were only removed in 1994.

Two examples illustrate the extremes to which the liberal-conservative split on the role of the church could go. In Mexico the 1857 *Reforma* of liberal President Benito Juarez confiscated all church lands except those used directly for worship, abolished clerical judicial privileges, and asserted a general right of the Mexican state to control religious activities. Subsequent legislation suppressed religious orders, broke relations with Rome, secularized cemeteries, and required civil marriage. At the other extreme, Ecuador, under Gabriel Garcia Moreno, president between 1859 and 1874, signed a concordat with Rome that gave the Church complete control of education and made Catholicism a requirement of citizenship. Indeed, in 1873, two years before he was assassinated, Garcia Moreno dedicated Ecuador to the Sacred Heart of Jesus.

The Rise of Democracy and Populism

In the first part of the twentieth century, the general pattern was one of partial separation of church and state, although constitutional provisions recognizing Catholicism often remained. In Mexico the old split between clericals and anticlericals was intensified by the Constitution of 1917 that in effect nationalized all church property, laicized education and marriage, removed the vote from the clergy, strictly controlled religious publications, and forbade all political activity by churchmen. These provisions remained in the Constitution until 1992. Anticlerical legislation was also adopted in Guatemala and Uruguay, but the more common pattern was the adoption of constitutional provisions that guaranteed the free practice of religion to all citizens. In this period, Protestant missionary activity was intensified in Central America, especially in Guatemala. As late as the 1950s, Protestant missionaries in Colombia, one of the most Catholic countries in Latin America, were opposed by fanatical Catholics who burned churches, closed schools, and in 1959 killed more than one hundred Protestants. Also in Colombia, up until 1950, the Liberal and Conservative Parties divided along religious lines. However, the 1958 agreement between the two parties to share power and the advance of ecumenical cooperation in Catholicism have meant that since the 1960s, except for isolated instances, religion in Colombia is no longer a source of conflict.

The period from the 1930s to the 1960s saw the rise of democratic populist parties throughout Latin America. Some were secular social democratic groups like the *Apristas* in Peru and *Accion Democratica* in Venezuela that initially were influenced by Marxism and opposed to any official recognition of Catholicism. However, they did not share the intense anticlericalism of earlier laicist groups. On the other side, beginning in the 1930s and intensifying in the 1950s, Christian Democratic parties were founded in many Latin American countries. These parties broke with the clericalism of the conservatives and specifically endorsed religious freedom, human rights, and democracy. With the Declaration on Religious Freedom, adopted by the Second Vatican Council in 1965, there were no longer obstacles on the Catholic side to cooperation with their former liberal and social democratic opponents, although there remained areas of disagreement, such as divorce and government support for religious instruction in public schools. In the mid-1950s there was a brief flare-up of anticlericalism, organized by the Argentine strongman, Juan Peron, but his attack on the church was one of the factors that contributed to his overthrow in 1955.

The Cold-War Period

With the spread of democracy in Latin America after World War II and the changes on the part of liberals, social democrats, and Catholics, it seemed that religious liberty would become the rule in Latin America. This might have become the case had it not been for the Cuban Revolution and the polarization associated with the extension of the cold war to Latin America.

In Cuba, the Catholic Church, never very strong, eventually took a position opposed to Castro after he moved toward Marxism in 1960, and active Catholics, Protestants, and Jehovah's Witnesses were persecuted as enemies of the state. Church schools were closed, and religion became one of the reasons for the successive waves of Cuban emigration. Elsewhere in Latin America some Catholic intellectuals, clergy, and students were attracted to liberation theology, with its support for cooperation with Marxists in the establishment of revolutionary socialism.

On the other side, the military governments, that had taken over in many countries in response to the perceived threat of Communism, attempted, usually unsuccessfully, to enlist the support of the Catholic Church for their crusade against Marxism in the interests of national security. Christians who were politically active on the left or defended human rights were tortured or "disappeared." Conservative Catholics and many evangelicals either supported the military because of their opposition to Marxism or became politically apathetic.

In Central America, Christian-Marxist alliances were established in Nicaragua and El Salvador. After the Sandinistas came to power in Nicaragua, a process of polarization took place among Christians, with the government giving support to leftist Christian groups but restricting the official Catholic Church hierarchy and opposition Protestant groups, especially on the Atlantic coast. Military regimes elsewhere often encouraged the spread of more conservative versions of Protestantism and allowed the establishment of private schools and universities by church and business groups in order to compete with the public institutions that had been influenced by the left. The churches, like the societies in which they were working, were deeply divided along ideological lines.

The Triumph of Liberal Democracy

By the late 1970s the military began to surrender power. By the 1990s every country in Latin America, except for Cuba, had a civilian constitutional government based on competitive elections, governing under constitutions that guaranteed political and civil rights, including the right to freedom of religion. During the military period, the Organization of American States Human Rights Commission had become active, and nongovernmental human rights organizations emerged in many countries in response to the military repression. New constitutions, which included guarantees of religious freedom, were adopted in Brazil (1988), Ecuador (1989), Colombia (1991), Paraguay (1992), and Argentina (1994). Mexico amended its constitution in 1992 to remove the anticlerical clauses, and there was discussion in Bolivia of amending article 3 of the 1967 constitution that, although it guarantees the public exercise of all religions, gives official recognition to the "Roman Catholic, Apostolic religion." In Paraguay and Colombia, the new constitutions omitted the previous provisions that had given special privileges to Catholicism.

Especially during the period of military rule, Protestantism, especially of the evangelical, pentecostal, and fundamentalist kind, began to make spectacular advances in many parts of Latin America. These advances were often related to the shift in the 1960–1990 period from a largely rural to a predominately urban population. The migration to the cities made many Latin Americans amenable to conversion to evangelical religions, which offered spiritual direction, the support of small communities, and strong moral teachings and practice that emphasized hard work, abstention from alcohol, and family responsibility. In addition, in Central America and Colombia, there was U.S. financial support and proselytism through American television evangelists. However, it should be emphasized that, contrary to some critics both on the left and in the Catholic hierarchy, the bulk of the expansion and organization of the evangelicals has been carried on by Latin Americans, and evangelical Protestantism now has strong indigenous roots.

It has also already made a political impact, despite the widespread belief that evangelicals tend to be apolitical. The vice president of Peru during Alberto Fujimori's first term was an evangelical, and at the outset Fujimori received public support from evangelical pastors. Jose Serrano, the president of Guatemala until his removal after an unsuccessful "self-coup" in June 1993, was an evangelical Protestant, and General Efrain Rios Montt, president of Guatemala in 1982–1983, before the transition to democracy, was a member of a California-based group, the Church of the Word. Rios Montt was so active in promoting its members and doctrines in his administration that he was removed by other military figures after seventeen months in power. His party won the most seats in the August 1994 congressional elections and became the second-largest party in Guatemala. In 1999, it became the largest party. In the El Salvador elections in March 1994, there were two evangelical parties, and one of them won a congressional seat. The Brazilian constitutional convention that wrote the 1988 constitution included a highly visible evangelical group of fifty deputies, and about half that number continue as members of the Brazilian Congress.

There is considerable debate about the actual number of Protestants in Latin America. Everyone agrees that, in terms of percentage, Guatemala has the largest Protestant community, with estimates of up to 30 percent. El Salvador and Chile are estimated to be about 15–20 percent Protestant, with somewhat lower percentages in Brazil, Costa Rica, and Nicaragua. However, some

critics argue that the figures are inflated since they are based on conversions and do not track the numbers who actually *continue* to attend services or who move back and forth between Catholicism and evangelical Protestantism. Overall perhaps 10 percent of the population is Protestant, mainly evangelical, and that percentage is increasing.

While the conspiracy theories of the left, portraying evangelicals as agents of American imperialism, are heard less frequently today, the Catholic Church continues to be concerned about the advances of what the Catholic bishops at their 1992 Conference in Santo Domingo called "the sects." Referring to the challenge posed by "proselytizing . . . sectarian, Christian groups who hinder the sound ecumenical path," the bishops accused them of hostility to Catholicism and of resorting "to defamation and to material inducements," adding that "although they are only weakly committed to the temporal realm, they tend to become involved in politics with a view to taking power" (National Conference of Catholic Bishops, *New Evangelization, Human Development, Christian Culture: Conclusions of the Fourth General Conference of Latin American Bishops*, Washington, D.C. 1993, 95–97).

The spread of Protestantism has led to other problems in Latin America. In some rural areas there are deep divisions between Catholics and evangelicals. Issues such as participation in traditional folk festivals with a heavily Catholic flavor—for example, processions and fiestas in honor of the town's patron saint—have caused problems, especially in Chiapas in Mexico. Mormon missionaries have been harassed, in one case a Mormon missionary in Bolivia was murdered, and, in the past, leftist revolutionaries in Chile bombed Mormon temples. While David Martin (*Tongues of Fire: The Explosion of Protestantism in Latin America*, Oxford, 1990) overstates the situation in predicting the kind of conflicts associated with the Reformation in Europe, there is no question that it is not easy to shift from a heavily Catholic culture to one that is more religiously plural—and secular. This is especially so since Catholic practice is relatively low, estimated at between 5 percent and 25 percent depending on the country.

In the early 1990s, the previous two exceptions to the general advance of religious freedom in Latin America, Mexico and Cuba, took steps to bring their legal systems in line with the rest of the continent. As noted earlier, the 1917 constitution of Mexico nationalized church property, abolished religious orders, forbade church garb, and excluded the church from education. These provisions were circumvented through a variety of devices, but it was not until 1992 that Mexico amended the anticlerical, indeed antireligious, provisions of the 1917 constitution. Now the churches, if they are officially registered as "religious associations," can own property and operate educational institutions—although the property must be used only for "religious" purposes. Members of the clergy can now vote, but they may not run for, or hold, public office unless they have given up their church positions five years previously. The churches may not own or operate radio or television stations or carry out political activities and, in order to be registered, they must have been active in Mexico for at least five years.

While the Catholic Church has been tolerated in Cuba, its schools have been closed (although there is still a Catholic seminary in Havana), and government and party youth programs are regularly scheduled on Sunday mornings, the time of religious services. It had also been announced as public policy that religious believers were excluded from government, education, and professions such as psychology. In 1992, however, the rubber-stamp Cuba People's National Assembly amended the constitution to guarantee religious freedom and to prohibit any form of religious discrimination. However, it did not change the article stating that no constitutional liberty may be exercised "contrary to the Cuban people's decision to build socialism and communism." In 1997, just prior to the pope's visit to the island, Cubans were permitted to celebrate Christmas for the first time since the 1970s, and the papal visit in January 1998 gave Catholicism unprecedented visibility. The Catholic Church continues to enjoy more freedom than in the past, as long as it is not linked to the increasingly visible opposition groups. Public celebration in 1999 also gave great visibility to Protestant groups, perhaps as a counterbalance to Catholicism.

While, with the exception of Cuba, religious freedom prevails in Latin America, many problems remain. First, there are issues of the relation of religious doctrine to public policy, especially in the area of sex and marriage. Catholic opposition to divorce has meant that laws allowing the dissolution of marriage were adopted later in Latin America than elsewhere and, as late as the 1960s, five countries still prohibited divorce. Today only Chile does so, and there is active discussion of a divorce law in that country—although many Chileans prefer the current mechanism of fraudulent annulment to a presumably more restrictive law on divorce. The Catholic Church opposed government-supported contraception programs in Latin America in the 1960s, but it now tolerates them as preferable to the alternative of wholesale abortion. The legalization of abortion has not become a public issue in Latin America, and both Catholics and evangelicals are strongly opposed to any change in the current legislation outlawing it.

Second, there is the question of the financial relationship of the government to the churches. Three constitutions, those of Argentina, Bolivia, and Costa Rica, refer to state support for Catholicism. Some direct state subsidies go to the Catholic Church in Argentina, Colombia, Bolivia, and Venezuela. In the 1994 budget of Argentina, $11 million was assigned to Catholic bishops and seminarians. In addition, since 1979, Argentine bishops have received a state salary equivalent to 80 percent of the salary of a federal judge, and some commentators have linked this to the lack of public opposition by the Argentine hierarchy to the violation of human rights during the "dirty war" of the 1970s. Elsewhere in Latin America, government support is given to church-owned schools, hospitals, and charitable institutions, and church property used for religious purposes is exempt from taxation. In some countries instruction in Catholicism is given in public schools, while other countries do not allow it.

Third, there are issues concerning government permits for religious activities. In Venezuela the assignment by the government of areas of missionary activity has caused serious Catholic-Protestant disagreement. Departments of Religious Affairs in many countries attempt to regulate, and perhaps control, religious bodies. (In Argentina and Bolivia, for example, the Department of Religious Affairs is located in the foreign ministry, which is officially entitled the Ministry of Foreign Affairs and Worship.) In Central America efforts

have also been made to revoke the visas of members of the Unification Church of Reverend Moon, and Venezuela has withdrawn permission for them to operate in that country.

Fourth, evangelicals are beginning to press for chaplaincies in the armed forces and hospitals, which heretofore have been exclusively Catholic. In 1993, Colombia adopted a Religious Liberty Law that authorized Protestant chaplaincies in the armed forces, the police, and state-run hospitals, as well as offering parental choice on religious instruction in public schools.

Fifth, there are cases of religious discrimination in the military, education, and the civil service. Officers in the Chilean navy are expected to attend mass regularly and to produce documentation on the religious practice of their families. As noted earlier, in Cuba until the 1990s believers could not secure positions in fields such as education or psychology, or advancement in government. The Communist Party was closed to believers as well, although that prohibition was formally removed in 1991.

Sixth, there have been occasional instances of outright religious conflict and persecution in Colombia, Guatemala, and Mexico, often involving Indian villages. Much more serious cases of the persecution of Protestants took place in Colombia in the 1950s, and the persecution of the Catholic clergy in Argentina in the mid 1950s, and in Mexico in the 1920s, is well known.

Sparked by the dramatic increase in religious pluralism, the spread of constitutional democracy, and the growth of global communication and concern for human rights, there has been a striking increase in religious freedom in Latin America in the post-cold-war period. As for the future, the movement towards greater religious freedom in

Latin America seems irreversible. Anomalous situations or survivals from earlier regimes will gradually be harmonized with the legal and political requirements of liberal constitutional democracy. Tensions will continue, and support for religious freedom will be subjected to strains from competing pressures to use the instruments of law and the state in favor of one or another religious group. Yet, as the promotion of human rights and democracy becomes more widespread in the Americas and the world, the right to preach freely and practice one's religion has become the norm rather than the exception on the Latin American scene.

Constitutional Provisions on Church and State in Latin America

Argentina: Political Constitution of the Argentine Nation (1853, as amended 1994)

Article 2. The federal government supports the Roman Catholic Apostolic, Religion.

Article 14. All the inhabitants of the Nation enjoy the following rights in conformity with the laws that govern their exercise; to work and exercise every legal industry; to sail and trade; to petition the authorities; to enter, stay, and leave the Argentinean territory; to publish their ideas through the press without previous censorship; to use and dispose of their property; to associate for useful purposes; to profess their religion freely; to teach and learn.

Article 73. The regular clergy cannot be members of the Congress, nor can provincial governors while in office.

Bolivia: Political Constitution of the State (1967)

Article 3. The State recognizes and supports the Roman Catholic, Apostolic, religion. It guarantees the public exercise of all other religions. The relationship with the Catholic Church will be governed by concordats between the Bolivian State and the Holy See.

Brazil: Federal Republic of Brazil, Constitution (1988)

Article 5. VI. Freedom of conscience and belief is inviolable, assuring the free exercise of religious groups and guaranteeing, by law, the protection of places of worship and liturgy.

VII. The provision of chaplains in civil and military prisons is assured by law.

VIII. No one will be deprived of rights due to religious belief or philosophical or political convictions, unless he claims them in order to exempt himself from legal obligations enforced on all and refuses to fulfill the alternative duty, established by law.

Article 210. 1. Optional religious education shall be available during normal school hours in public elementary schools.

Article 213. Public funds shall be provided for public schools, but they may be allocated to community, religious, or charitable schools, provided that they (1) attest to their non-profit status and invest their financial surpluses in education.

Chile: Political Constitution of the Republic of Chile (1980)

Article 19. The Constitution guarantees for every person:

6) Freedom of conscience, the manifestation of all beliefs, and the free exercise of all religions not contrary to morality, good customs, or public order. Religious communities can build and maintain churches and their facilities in

accordance with the safety and hygiene conditions established by the laws and regulations. The churches, religious communities, and institutions of any denomination will have the rights regarding their property, that are granted by the laws currently in effect. Church buildings and their facilities exclusively devoted to worship will be exempt from any kind of taxes.

Colombia: Political Constitution of Colombia (1991)

Article 18. Freedom of conscience is guaranteed. No one will be adversely affected because of his convictions or beliefs or forced to reveal them or forced to act against his conscience.

Article 19. Freedom of worship is guaranteed. Every person has the right to profess his religion freely and to spread it in individual or collective form. All religious confessions and churches are equally free before the law.

Costa Rica: Constitution of the Republic of Costa Rica (1992)

Article 75. The Roman Catholic, Apostolic religion is that of the state, which contributes to its support, without preventing the free exercise in the Republic of other religions that are not opposed to universal morals or good customs.

Cuba: Constitution of the Republic of Cuba (1976, as amended 1992)

Article 8. The State recognizes, respects, and guarantees religious freedom. In the Republic of Cuba, religious institutions are separate from the State. The different creeds and religions enjoy equal consideration.

Article 42. Discrimination based on race, skin color, sex, national origin, religious belief, or of any other kind offending human dignity, is prohibited, and punishable by law.

Article 55. The State, which recognizes, respects, and guarantees freedom of conscience and religion, simultaneously recognizes, respects, and guarantees the freedom of all citizens to change religious creeds, or to have no religion, and to profess the religion of their choice, based on respect for the law. The law regulates the State's relations with religious institutions.

Article 62. None of the freedoms recognized for citizens may be exercised contrary to the stipulations of the Constitution and the laws, or contrary to the existence and goals of the socialist State, or contrary to the Cuban people's decision to construct socialism and communism. The violation of this principle is punishable.

Ecuador: Constitution of the Republic (1989)

Article 19. Without affecting other rights needed for the clear moral and material development that derives from the nature of the person, the State guarantees:

6) Liberty of conscience and of religion, in individual or collective form, in public or private. Persons will practice the religion they profess freely with only the limitations that the law prescribes to protect security, public morality, or the fundamental rights of the rest of the people.

Mexico: Political Constitution of the United States of Mexico (1917, as amended 1992)

Article 3,1. As guaranteed by article 24 on religious freedom, (public) education will be secular, and therefore will remain free of any religious doctrine.

Article 24. Every man is free to profess the religious belief that he prefers and to practice its ceremonies, devotions, and acts of worship, provided that they do not constitute a crime or offense punishable by law. The Congress cannot adopt laws that establish or prohibit any religion. Religious acts of public worship will ordinarily be celebrated in churches. Those that on special occasions are carried out outside of churches will be subject to legal regulation.

Article 27, 11. Religious associations which are constituted in accordance with article 130 and its implementing law will be able to acquire, possess, or administer in exclusivity the property that is indispensable for their purposes, subject to the requirements and limitations that the law establishes.

Article 130. The historical principle of the separation of church and state provides the orienting principle of the provisions of this article. Churches and other religious groups are subject to the law. It is the exclusive right of the federal Congress to legislate on public worship, churches, and religious groups. The implementing legislation regarding public order will carry out and apply the following provisions:

a) Churches and religious groups will receive legal recognition as religious associations as soon as they have been registered. The law will regulate these associations and establish the conditions and requirements for their registration.

b) The authorities will not intervene in the internal life of religious associations.

c) Mexican citizens can exercise the ministry of any religion. Both Mexicans and foreigners must satisfy the requirements of the law in order to do so.

d) The regulations will provide that religious ministers may not hold public office. As citizens they have the right to vote but they may not be candidates. Those who have ceased to be ministers of religion for the period and in the manner provided by law may run for office.

e) Ministers may not organize for political purposes or campaign for or against any candidate, party, or political organization. Nor may they, in public meetings, acts of worship, or religious preaching, oppose the laws or institutions of the country, or attack in any way its patriotic symbols. The establishment of any kind of political group whose title contains any word or indication relating to any religious creed is strictly prohibited. Meetings of a political nature may not be held in a church.

Panama: Political Constitution of the Republic of Panama (1972)

Article 35. The profession of all religions is free as is the exercise of all other worship groups, without any limitation other than respect for Christian morals and for public order. It is recognized that the Catholic religion is that of the majority of Panamanians.

Article 36. Religious associations have legal capacity, and order and administer their properties within the limits established by the law in the same way as other juridical persons.

Paraguay: Constitution of the Republic of Paraguay (1992)

Article 24. Religious liberty, freedom of worship, and ideological liberty are recognized without other limits than those established in this Constitution and the law. No confession shall have official status. The relationship of the State with the Catholic Church is based on independence, cooperation, and autonomy. The independence and autonomy of the churches and religious confessions are recognized without any limitations other than those imposed in this Constitution and the laws. No one can be harassed, investigated, or forced to testify concerning his beliefs or his ideology.

Peru: Political Constitution of Peru (1993)

Article 2. Every person has the right:

3) To freedom of conscience and of religion, in individual or associated form. There is no persecution due to ideas or beliefs. . . . The public exercise of all creeds is free, whenever it does not offend morality or threaten public order.

18) To the privacy of political, philosophical, religious, or any other beliefs, as well as to the maintenance of professional secrecy.

Venezuela: Constitution of the Republic of Venezuela (1961)

Article 65. Every person has the right to profess his religious faith and to worship, privately or publicly, whenever it is not contrary to public order or good morals. Religion will be subject to the supreme inspection of the National Executive, according to law. No one can claim beliefs or religious teachings to avoid obeying the law or to prevent others from the exercise of their rights.

— PAUL E. SIGMUND —

Paul E. Sigmund is professor of politics and former director of the Program in Latin American Studies at Princeton University. He has published twenty books on religion and politics, most recently Religious Freedom and Evangelization in Latin America, *(Maryknoll, N.Y.: Orbis Books, 1999).*

COUNTRY PROFILES

Population	**36.6 million**
Catholic	87%
Protestant	8%
Muslim	1.5%
Jewish	1%
Other	2.5%
Religious Freedom Rating	3

Background

The Argentine Republic was established after independence from Spain in 1816. Democratic rule was often interrupted by military coups. The end of Juan Peron's authoritarian rule in 1955 led to a series of right-wing military dictatorships and left-wing and nationalist violence. Argentina returned to elected civilian rule in 1983 after seven years of vicious repression of suspected leftist guerrillas and other dissidents.

As amended in 1994, the 1853 constitution provides for a president elected for four years with the option of reelection to one additional term. The legislature consists of a 257-member Chamber of Deputies elected for six years, with half of the seats renewable every three years, and a seventy-two-member Senate nominated by elected provincial legislatures for nine-year terms, with one-third of the seats renewable every three years.

In October 1997, President Carlos Menem's Peronists experienced their first nationwide defeat in a decade. An alliance of the Radical Party and the center-left Front for a Country in Solidarity won nearly 46 percent of the vote. Menem's party won 36 percent. Fears of an impending opposition victory led Menem to direct a campaign against federal prosecutors investigating government corruption. In December 1999, Fernando de la Rua won election and was sworn in as president.

Citizens can change their government through elections. Constitutional guarantees regarding the right to organize political parties, civic organizations, and labor unions are generally respected. Under Menem, legislative authority has been circumvented by the use of more "necessity and urgency" decrees than by all other previous civilian and military regimes combined.

Journalists and human rights groups are generally allowed to operate freely, but both have been subject to anonymous threats and various forms of intimidation, including more than one thousand beatings, kidnappings, and telephone death threats during Menem's rule. Labor is dominated by Peronist unions. Union influence has diminished, however, due to corruption scandals, internal divisions, and restrictions on public-sector strikes. Menem's authoritarian practices and manipulation of the judiciary have undermined the country's separation of powers and the rule of law.

Menem has used the Supreme Court to uphold decrees removing the comptroller general and other officials mandated to probe government wrongdoing. In general, the judicial system is politicized, inefficient, and riddled with the corruption endemic to all branches of government. In 1990, Menem pardoned military officers convicted of human rights violations committed during the country's so-called "dirty war," in which the guerrilla threat was vastly exaggerated in order to justify a 1976 coup. Police misconduct, often apparently promoted by senior government officials, has resulted in a number of allegedly extrajudicial executions of law enforcement officers. The investigation of a 1994 car bombing of a Jewish organization has languished in part due to poor police work at the crime scene but also reportedly in part due to complicity by members of the security forces with the terrorists.

Freedom House's 1998–99 _Freedom in the World_ rates Argentina as a three in civil liberties and in political rights. The political rights rating is a drop from two the previous year due to growing spying on politicians, indifference to corruption, packing of the Senate, and campaigns against federal prosecutors.

Religious Freedom

The vast majority of Argentina's population comes from nineteenth- to mid-twentieth-century immigration from Spain, Italy, and other European countries. Although most of these immigrants were Roman Catholic, many from Spain brought with them a strong anticlerical bias. In the early part of this century, a significant number of Eastern European and German Jews also immigrated to Argentina, and they comprise, with some three hundred thousand people, the largest Jewish community in Latin America. There are also a similar number of Arab Christians and Muslims, many coming from Lebanon and Syria; the current president, Carlos Menem, is an Alawite Syrian who, although publicly he has proclaimed his adherence to Christianity, is believed to practice Islam in private as well. The Protestant minority is heavily centered in the country's Anglo-Argentine population.

Historically, there has been a strong bond between the Catholic Church and the Argentine state, which continues to finance the Church. Other religious organizations say the _patronato regio_ tradition by which the state governs its relationship with them is discriminatory, as taxes paid by members of all faiths are earmarked for just one religion. In 1994, a constitutional amendment removed the requirement that the president and vice president had to be Catholics, despite opposition to the move by some Catholic prelates. Non-

Catholics still have to receive permission from a Catholic priest in order to act as hospital chaplains, and only Catholic chaplains are appointed to the army. The Catholic hierarchy is often described as the most conservative in Latin America, and most supported the military dictatorship.

The constitution provides for freedom of religion. There is practical freedom to worship and to train and appoint clergy. Religious bodies have rights of self-government, of religious education, to carry out charitable activities, to own and acquire property, and to maintain social institutions. Religious instruction may be provided outside of school hours in both public and private schools, though it is mandatory in Buenos Aires public schools. They can produce, print, and distribute literature; receive donations; and have contact with coreligionists domestically and overseas. Individuals can adopt, change, or leave a religion freely, with no change of civil status. A 1988 law forbids discrimination by providing prison terms of up to three years for anyone who arbitrarily obstructs or restrains a person based on several characteristics, including religion. In April 1998, a court sentenced three Buenos Aires youths to three years in prison for assaulting a man in 1995 whom they believed was Jewish.

The ruling Peronist party traces its original ideological roots in part to the social doctrines of the Catholic Church, particularly the encyclical _Rerum Novarum_, but in the 1950s it clashed head-on with the Church on issues of prostitution and the role the Church was playing with the party's working-class base. Today, however, the Peronist government advocates neoliberal economic policies and, for this reason, is frequently the target of criticism from the Catholic hierarchy. The other dominant political grouping, the centrist Radical Civic Union, was historically seen as having a more secular focus. There is a very small Christian Democratic party.

The Secretariat of Worship of the Foreign Affairs Ministry has the authority to permit religious groups to function throughout Argentina by registering them in a national religious register. Conservative elements of the Catholic Church have supported government proposals for limitations on the activities of so-called "sects," although the government's concerns appear to be based primarily on concerns about child welfare and public safety. The Human Rights Ecumenical Movement (MEDH) views proposed legislation on religious regulation as restrictive in that it contains criminal provisions and, MEDH says, runs against the republican principle of separation of powers.

Random acts of anti-Semitic violence continue to be a problem in Argentina, and they are believed to be the work of fringe elements in the military and the police, as well as some ultraright organizations. In recent years there have been a number of acts of vandalism against Jewish graveyards, a number of which the local press has attributed to recently purged members of the Buenos Aires provincial police. In May 1998, a two-year prison term and three two-year suspended sentences were handed down to four men convicted of distributing anti-Semitic literature—a violation of the 1988 law.

Suspected high-level security force complicity in the carrying out and/or cover-up of the 1992 bombing by Islamic extremists of the Israeli Embassy and the 1994 bombing of the city's Jewish community center (AMIA) might have been responsible for lack of progress in bringing those guilty of the terrorist outrages to trial. Upon taking office in 1989, President Carlos Menem restored several well-known thugs, some of whom were associated with anti-Semitic acts, to Argentina's military, police, and intelligence agencies. Menem's praise for former and current members of the military and police associated in the public mind with death squad activity and other violations of human rights have disconcerted those most active in trying to clear up the two attacks—the largest attack against a noncombatant Jewish population since World War II.

Armenia

Population	**3.8 million**
Armenian Apostolic Church	**78.5%**
Muslim	**3.3%**
Protestant	**0.5%**
Atheist/Agnostic	**17.7%**
Religious Freedom Ranking	**4**

Background

The landlocked, predominantly Christian Transcaucus republic of Armenia was ruled at various times by Macedonians, Romans, Persians, Mongols, and others. Prior to their defeat in World War I, Ottoman Turks controlled a western region and, between

1894 and 1915, engaged in a systematic genocide. The Russian region came under communist control and was designated a Soviet republic in 1922 after western Armenia was returned to Turkey. Armenia declared its independence from the Soviet Union in September 1991.

Prior to 1995 parliamentary elections, ARF-Dashnak and eight other parties were banned, thereby ensuring the dominance of Petrosian's ruling ANM coalition. In March 1995, Prime Minister Robert Kocharian, who was appointed by Petrosian in 1997 and formerly served as president of Nagorno-Karabakh, was elected president with the support of the formerly banned Armenian Revolutionary Federation (ARF-Dashnak).

In Nagorno-Karabakh the cease-fire in force since 1994 continued to be largely observed, but no major progress was registered in international peace negotiations. Armenia continued to insist that Nagorno-Karabakh abandon its goal of outright independence from Azerbaijan and that Baku drop its insistence on a conventional autonomous status for the disputed region. On October 27, 1999, extreme nationalists, claiming to be staging a coup, assassinated Prime Minister Vazgen Sarkisian, as well as the speaker, two deputy speakers, the energy minister, and two other members of Parliament.

All print, radio, and television media must register with the Ministry of Justice. Papers routinely permit government censors to review material, and self-censorship is common to avoid suspension. Scores of private newspapers operate independently, however, or in open affiliation with opposition political parties. Libel laws have been used to intimidate the media. More than 120 television and radio stations are registered. Freedom of assembly is generally respected, although permits are needed for demonstrations. The judiciary is not independent, with the president appointing all judges.

The right to private property is enshrined in the constitution. Regulation and an inefficient and sometimes corrupt bureaucracy and court system hinder business operations. Key industries remain in the hands of oligarchs and influential clans who received preferential treatment in the early stages of privatization.

Because of the legalization of the leading opposition party and reasonably free presidential elections, Freedom House's 1998–99 *Freedom in the World* improved Armenia's political rights rating from a five to a four.

Religious Freedom

Armenia was the first state in history to adopt Christianity as its official religion (A.D. 301). The Armenian Apostolic Church, one of the ancient oriental churches and monophysite in theology, has maintained its traditions, liturgy, church structure, and architecture almost intact from the earliest days to the present. Ethnicity and religion are indissolubly linked, with no tradition of non-Armenians converting to the Apostolic Church and the historic fact that all Armenians have been—at least nominally—members of the state church. This history explains present attitudes.

Events in the twentieth century have profoundly affected religious liberty and cemented national religious consciousness. After the systematic genocide in the West at the hands of the Turks between 1894 and 1915, the East fell under Soviet control, and so for the next sixty-nine years Armenia's religious destiny was inextricably linked to Soviet antireligious policies. The sole difference was that, because of the

Armenian diaspora, containing many wealthy families, the republic became a showcase of "successful" Soviet nationality policies. Contributions were even accepted from the outside to maintain a rump of religious and historical institutions. With the collapse of the Soviet Union, the Armenian Apostolic Church became virtually the state religion.

Whereas in Soviet times the number of functioning churches was severely limited (some thirty in the postwar decades) and monastic institutions and seminaries limited to one, in Echmiadzin, the ancient Christian capital, now the Armenian Apostolic Church functions as freely as economic deprivation allows. In April 1995, an enlightened Oxford-educated new Catholicos (Patriarch) was elected, coming from the second diocese of Cilicia, the alma mater of the Armenian diaspora in the Middle East outside Armenia itself. This development seemed promising for religious liberty, not least because Catholicos Karekin I had played a prominent role in the affairs of the World Council of Churches. However, he was dogged by ill health and died in June 1999. In recent years a lay "brotherhood" movement has emerged, which is virtually an evangelical wing of the Apostolic Church and is not rejected by it.

Article 23 of the Constitution states: "Everyone has the right to freedom of thought, conscience and faith," but in practice, the virtual state church severely limits this guarantee. The "Law of the Republic of Armenia on Freedom of Conscience and Religious Organizations," passed in July 1991, completely overturned its Soviet predecessor and amplified the constitutional guarantee in detail. However, to be recognized as a legal entity, a religious community must be registered. An ap-

plication can be refused or rescinded "if it does not comply with existing legislation." There is officially separation of church and state, but it is "subject to protection from the Republic of Armenia within the limits of The Armenian Apostolic Church international legal norms."

Despite constitutional guarantees, religious persecution has become endemic in Armenia. Attacks have affected even registered communities and are, to some degree, inspired by the State. On December 22, 1993, then-President Levon Ter-Petrosyan signed a decree giving greater powers to the State Council on Religious Affairs (itself an echo of Soviet practice in the control of religion) to limit the activities of religious minorities. Further restrictions were overwhelmingly approved by the National Assembly on June 9, 1997; these called for raising the minimum registration requirement from fifty to two hundred members and banned outside funding for foreign-based churches. For churches other than the Armenian Apostolic, prior permission must be sought from the State Council for Religious Affairs for religious activities in public places, foreign travel, or inviting foreign guests. In practice these laws have not yet been implemented. Jehovah's Witnesses continue to be denied registration, and the number of Hare Krishnas has fallen below fifty.

In 1995, there was a propaganda campaign in the press against "sects," and the minister for military affairs, Vazgen Sarkissian, made a television request for the public to help provide information on where the "sects" were meeting. Personnel in military-style clothing attacked people and places where, for example, Jehovah's Witnesses were known to meet. Most of those affected seemed to be males who refused military service; the law does not allow a pacifist alternative. Hare Krishna devotees have asked the American Embassy in Yerevan for political asylum on grounds of religious persecution.

None of those affected has had adequate protection under the law, and police have stood by while mob violence has occurred. On April 14, 1995, police armed with machine guns interrupted a Jehovah's Witness meeting in Yerevan and seized nine young men aged seventeen to nineteen. They were held at a police station for two days and released, only after they showed they were students and therefore temporarily exempt from military service. As of June 30, 1999, six Witnesses were in detention.

Other incidents have affected Armenian Baptists and American-led Protestant missions. On April 26, 1995, in Gyumri in Northwest Armenia, unidentified attackers threw Molotov cocktails through the window of a kindergarten attached to an evangelical church, and an unidentified assailant threw a grenade through the window of the house of the principal of a kindergarten, also used for Pentecostal worship. No one was injured in these attacks.

Five charismatic Christians belonging to a group called "Warriors for Christ" spent six months in prison in 1995 before being released at the end of the year. They had been charged with "hooliganism" (an old Soviet portmanteau word), but not sentenced, following an attack on their meeting by neighbors with cudgels. The perpetrators were never brought to justice, and this religious community has not been permitted to register, despite repeated applications.

In Nagorno Karabakh, Azeri aggression has destroyed Armenian Apostolic churches and caused extensive damage. Instances of violence have become less frequent, and the influence of Catholicos Karekin was unquestionably a factor in an improving situation. The war with Azerbaijan over the disputed Armenian enclave has become a focus for heightened nationalism, and almost all of the Muslim population has left the country. This nationalism grew with the commemoration on April 24, 1995, of the genocide by the Ottoman Turks and (ironically, for such an irenic individual) the election of the new Catholicos in the same month. In the popular mind, minority groups have become virtually synonymous with foreign influence, and it has become almost obligatory for clerics speaking in the media to condemn their activity.

Austria

Population	**8.1 million**	**None**	**9%**
Catholic	**78%**	**Religious Freedom Rating**	**2**
Protestant	**6%**		
Other Christian	**3%**		
Muslim	**2%**		
Jewish	**0.1%**		
Other (Mormon, Jehovah's			
Witness, Baha'i, Buddhist)	**1.9%**		

Background

Until the end of World War I in 1918, Austria was a monarchy whose constitution dated back to 1867. The First Republic of Austria comprising nine federal states (Bundesländer) was created on October 1, 1920, and a new constitution was adopted. This constitution, which is still in force, comprises elements of the Fundamental Federal Law on Common Rights of Citizens and provisions of the Peace Treaty of St. Germain (1919). Occupation by the Western allies and the Soviet Union ended in 1955 under the Austrian State Treaty, which guaranteed Austrian neutrality and restored national sovereignty. In July 1998, Austria assumed the presidency of the European Union (EU), thereby leading a major international institution for the first time since the end of the Hapsburg empire seventy years ago. Austria is divided over neutrality or NATO membership. The nationalist Freedom Party and its anti-Semitic leader, Jorg Haider, continue to gain political influence. The party now commands the support of approximately one-fourth of the electorate. In October 1999 general elections it received 27.3 percent of the vote, compared to 33 percent for the Social Democrats and 26.9 percent for the People's Party.

Austrians can change their government democratically. The country's provinces elect members of the upper house of parliament. Voting is compulsory in some provinces. The judiciary is independent. A 1955 treaty prohibits Nazis from exercising freedom of assembly or association, and Nazi organizations are illegal. In 1992, public denial of the Holocaust and justification or approval of Nazi crimes against humanity were outlawed. Austrian media are free: restrictions on the grounds of public morality or national security are rarely invoked.

Law prohibits women from working at night except as nurses, taxi drivers, and a few other occupations. The ruling SPO party has pledged to begin to address gender biases by ensuring that women occupy 40 percent of all party and government posts by 2003. Under the informal *proporz* system, many state and private sector appointments are made on the basis of affiliation with the two main political parties. Trade unions retain an important independent voice in Austria's political, social, and economic life. Fifty-two percent of workers are organized in fourteen national unions. Although not explicitly guaranteed, the right to strike is universally recognized. Freedom House's 1998–99 *Freedom in the World* rates Austria as a one in political rights and in civil liberties.

Religious Freedom

Article 14 of the Fundamental Law of 1867 states: "Full freedom of belief and conscience is guaranteed to everyone. The enjoyment of civil and political rights is independent of religious adherence; however, civic duties may not be prejudiced by religious adherence. No one can be forced to observe a ritual act or to participate in an ecclesiastical ceremony insofar as he is not subordinate to another who is by law invested with such authority." Article 63 § 2 of the Treaty of St. Germain guarantees the right to free exercise, in public or private, of every kind of belief or religion insofar as it does not conflict with public order morality.

Relations between the state and religion are rooted in a principle of the recognition and nonrecognition of religions. Until 1997, there was a two-tiered system with some churches and religious societies recognized as such by law and others, since 1992, registered according to the Law on Associations. Now a third category has been added: religious denominational communities officially registered but not by a law.

Twelve religions fall into the first category. According to Article 15 of the Fundamental Law, they are corporations of *public* law. This gives exemption from taxes on property and on commercial activities such as sales of publications, rights to collection of church taxes, engagement in religious education in public schools, receipt of subsidies for private schools, air radio and TV broadcasts, and immunity from securing work or residence permits for foreign religious workers.

On December 10, 1997, the Parliament passed a controversial law that changed the recognition procedure for "state recognised religions." This blocked applications by about twenty religious associations (including Jehovah's Witnesses, the Church of the Seventh-Day Adventists, the Federation of Baptist Congregations in Austria, the Free Christian Church in Austria, the Pentecostal Church) and was meant to avoid recognizing "cults," which the Administrative Court in 1997 had said was required under current law. Before then the government had ignored these applications.

Under the new law a religious group can acquire legal status after waiting six months and if it has at least three hundred members. For nonreligious associations the waiting period is shorter and membership requirements minimal. The Federal Minister of Education and Culture can deny legal status in the interest of public security, public order, health, and morality, or where youth will be adversely affected psychologically or when psychological methods are used improperly.

To achieve the higher status of a "state recognised church or religious society" now requires a ten-year wait and proof of twenty years existence in Austria. The number of adherents must be sixteen thousand. Only four of the currently recognized religious societies meet this standard, so there is in effect a double standard for newer religions. The state can also deny legal status to so-called "dangerous cults," such as evangelical and Pentecostal churches, while the twenty-one thousand Jehovah's Witnesses, who have been applying for thirty years, will now have to wait another ten years to apply. Moreover, Andreas Khol, chairman of the People's Party, said in 1997 that Jehovah's Witnesses would be denied recognition because "they reject the state as such," an assertion that they deny. The governing coalition—the Socialist Party and the People's Party—voted for the new legislation while the Green, Liberal, and Freedom parties voted against it.

The following are "Recognised Churches and Religious Societies": Catholic Church (78%); Protestant Church Augsburg and Helvetic (5%); Greek Oriental Church, Old Catholic Church, Methodist Church, Mormons: about three to four thousand; Armenian Apostolic Church, New Apostolic Church, Syrian Orthodox Church, Israelite Religious Society: about seventy-three hundred; Islamic Religious Society: about 160,000; Buddhist Religious Society: about one thousand. The "Registered Religious Denominational Communities" are: Federation of Baptists, Congregations of Austria, Federation of Evangelical Congregations in Austria, Federation of Free Christian and Pentecostal Congregations, Christian Movement for Religious Revival in Austria, Church of the Seventh-Day Adventists, Coptic Orthodox Church in Austria, Jehovah's Witnesses, and Baha'i Religious Communities of Austria. The "Religious and Philosophical Groups

Registered as Associations" are all other religions (Sahaja Yoga, Hindu Mandir Society, Scientology, etc.) that were registered as ordinary associations and not as religious associations, more than one hundred in all.

Individuals have the right to freedom of religion and belief if they respect public order and public morality. Everyone belonging to a registered religious group automatically has civil duties, especially concerning church taxes. No one can be forced to remain a member of a church or a religious society. The minimum age for the free exercise of belief and conscience is different from the age of majority (19 years). At fourteen, every inhabitant can freely choose or leave a religion. At twelve, one cannot be forced by one's parents to leave a religious group and can be exempted from otherwise compulsory public schools' religion classes. A member of a registered group who leaves it and wants this decision to have legal consequences, such as the end of church tax liability, must officially declare the resignation to the administrative authority of the state. The person is then officially considered as "without religious adherence." Entry into another registered group is regarded as an internal affair of the other group.

The rights of the clergy and freedom of worship are fully respected, and religious marriage is possible, even if not preceded by civil marriage, but it has no civil consequences. The right to self-government is given to legally recognized groups (Article 15 of the Fundamental Law). However, when groups apply for a higher form of recognition, the state exercises some preliminary control on church teachings and membership. Recognized groups can levy taxes on their members and call upon the state's assistance in cases of nonpayment.

Freedom of religious education and instruction is recognized and respected by the state. According to Article 174 of the Fundamental Law, only recognized groups can hold religion classes in public schools. They also receive funding for private schools. In public schools, every pupil must attend the religion classes of their registered group, unless a valid notice of nonattendance is given to the director. Parents or guardians can provide this until age fourteen. After this, youth can give such a notice themselves. In public and similar schools a cross must be in all classrooms if the majority of pupils are Christian. All religious groups can carry out charitable activities.

In July 1998, some religious communities were "promoted" from "third-class" to "second-class" religion six months after the new religious legislation. This status allows them to have a bank account or to own property, but it obliges them to wait for ten years (at least if they have enjoyed a juridical personality for a minimum of twenty years) before application for "first-class" recognition is admissible. The application of Sahaja Yoga was turned down.

No religious group except legally recognized ones has the right to levy taxes, hold religion classes in public schools, receive subsidies for private schools, or air radio and TV broadcasts. There have also been difficulties in securing residence permits for Baptist ministers, Quaker missionaries, and others. Private schools not founded by religious groups have no right to financial help from the state. There are some discrepancies between some legally registered groups due to different common-law regulations. The Orthodox Church has no right to state assistance recovering unpaid church taxes.

On August 20, 1998, a law was published creating a "Documentation and

Information Center on Matters Related to Cults" under the authority of the Ministry for Environment, Youth and Family. This Center widely distributes information on alleged harmful groups, even Jehovah's Witnesses although they are registered. In 1993, the European Court made Austria pay the expenses of a woman who had been denied child custody because she was a Jehovah's Witness. Austrian evangelicals have protested their new status, which denies them the rights and advantages granted to others, and called for a revision of the 1997 religious legislation. In 1997, the People's Party executive passed a resolution excluding members of alleged "cults" from their ranks, which was widely criticized as unconstitutional. In April 1999, the Party's convention formally accepted the executive's decision.

Azerbaijan

Population	7.7 million
Shi'a Muslim	65%
Sunni Muslim	30%
Russian Orthodox	2%
Armenian Apostolic	2%
Other (Jewish)	1%
Religious Freedom Rating	5

Background

Persia and the Ottoman Empire competed for Azeri territory in the sixteenth century, with the former gaining control in 1603. The northern sector, ceded to Russia in the early 1800s, briefly joined Armenia and Georgia in the Transcaucasia Federation after the 1917 Bolshevik Revolution. It proclaimed its independence the following year but was subdued by the Red Army in 1920. In 1922, it entered the Soviet Union as part of the Transcaucasian Soviet Federal Republic. It became a separate Soviet Socialist republic in 1936. Azerbaijan declared independence from the Soviet Union after a referendum in 1991.

Haydar Aliyev, a former KGB general and Soviet-era politburo member, was re-elected president on October 11, 1998. The election was boycotted by leading opposition parties. The key political issues in 1998 were the presidential election and indications that some segments of the ruling Yeni Azerbaijan were dissatisfied with official corruption and with the grooming of President Aliyev's son as a successor. The Central Election Commission announced that President Aliyev received 72 percent of the vote, more than the two-thirds necessary to avoid a runoff election. Mamedov finished second with 11 percent. Western observers reported "serious irregularities."

At year's end, international mediation efforts over control of the disputed enclave of Nagorno-Karabakh remained inconclusive. Azerbaijan continued ostensibly to support a phased approach through which Armenia would return occupied Azeri territory, the blockade of Armenia would be lifted, and refugees would be returned prior to a final decision on the enclave's status.

Azerbaijan's citizens cannot change their government democratically.

President Aliyev has imposed a totalitarian regime while building a cult of personality. The 1995 constitution gives the president control over the government, legislature, and judiciary. While a 1992 media law and the 1995 constitution enshrine the principles of press freedom, in reality the print media in Azerbaijan are subject to harassment, and the state-run electronic media are firmly in the hands of the government and President Aliyev. Several articles in the criminal code limit criticism of government officials. Forty-seven radio and television companies are registered with the government, but only eight are operating. Most private newspapers operate with precarious finances and depend on government-controlled printing and distribution facilities.

Freedoms of assembly and association have been curtailed. Scores of demonstrators were arrested during several rallies in September 1998, but most were subsequently released. More than forty-five parties applied for official registration prior to the 1995 parliamentary vote, but only thirty-two were recognized by the Ministry of Justice. Since 1996, several parties and opposition organizations have been banned. The largest labor organization is the government-subsidized, post-Communist Azerbaijan Labor Federation. The largest independent union is the oil workers' union, which represents approximately 80 percent of the industry's workers.

The constitution provides for a judicial system of limited independence. With parliamentary approval, the president appoints Supreme Court and Constitutional Court judges. The judicial system is subject to the influence of executive authorities and is inefficient and corrupt. The constitution enshrines the right to property and freedom of enterprise and business. Privatization has led to a rise in small businesses, mostly in the retail and service sectors, and a significant segment of urban housing has been privatized. Bureaucratic hurdles and rampant corruption at all levels of government and services are common. These factors severely limit equality of opportunity. Most Azeris, particularly refugees from Nagorno-Karabakh, live in privation. Cultural traditions often impede resolution of social problems and perpetuate discrimination and violence against women. Freedom House's 1998–99 *Freedom in the World* rates Azerbaijan a six in political rights and a four in civil liberties.

Religious Freedom

The government is secular, officially recognizing no state religion, and it guarantees religious freedom in the constitution. However, the dominant faiths of Muslim, Russian Orthodox Christianity, and Judaism are considered "traditional" and so receive preferential treatment in comparison to minority faiths. Despite this preferred status, all three "traditional" religions are subordinate to government control and scrutiny. About 90 percent of the population is Muslim, both Sunni and Shi'a, which is primarily an ethnic identity rather than a practicing religious association, while Christianity claims 4 percent (a number halved in recent years due to conflict with Armenia) and Jews 1 percent. The government generally protects the free religious practices of the Jewish communities although anti-Semitic references surface periodically. Most of the population is only nominal in its religious adherence.

The end of Soviet rule produced a renaissance of religious activity. In 1992, a generous law on religion was passed, banning state interference with religious practices. Yet, as nationalistic identity grew, harassment and control of religious activity reemerged in late 1995. Although religious freedom is explicitly recognized in the constitution, legislation substantially infringes upon this guarantee. In particular, foreigners and religious minorities are targeted.

In recent years new laws seriously contravene international human rights standards concerning religious liberty and override constitutional protections. In 1996, the Azeri parliament passed restrictive amendments to the 1992 religion law. Additionally, on January 6, 1997, the president issued a decree titled "On Banning the Activity of Foreigners in the Sphere of Religion." This decree has been used to harass foreign missionary activity, denial of registrations, and promotion of government surveillance of religious organizations, and scurrilous media campaigns.

Restrictive legislation is aimed specifically at religious minorities. Two primary targets are fundamentalist-oriented Muslims and Protestant Christians. Regarding Muslims, the government is wary of losing control of traditional congregations if political Islam gains greater regional influence. This engenders surveillance of apolitical, peaceful Muslim groups. The activities of Muslims are governed through the Spiritual Directorate for Caucuses Muslims. Muslim women won the right to wear scarves in passport photos but only through a lawsuit decided in their favor in June 1999.

Protestant Christians are targeted for three apparent reasons: their minority status, their relatively new status in Azerbaijan, and the religious tensions produced by local civil wars (albeit Muslim *vs.* Orthodox, not Protestant). Generally, Protestants have been apolitical in this suspicious atmosphere, yet

allegations abound that an increase in the Christian population will rent the nation along religious lines, citing the Nagorno-Karabakh ("NK") conflict with Armenia.

Armenians continue to claim the NK region, which lies within the Azeri territory. Although some human rights advocates might differ with this characterization, the NK conflict can be described as a nationalistic dispute between Armenian Orthodox Christians located in a still isolated enclave fighting for independence from Azerbaijan. Apart from major casualties suffered by the Armenian population, the conflict has produced eight hundred thousand internally displaced Azeris, approximately 10 percent of the Azeri population. A substantial amount of humanitarian aid for these refugees, who are primarily ethnic Azeri Muslims, is provided by Christian international aid organizations. Consequent extreme animosity against Armenians has resulted in the closure of all Armenian churches, even though up to thirty thousand Armenians still remain in Azerbaijan.

Other regional disputes are used by the government to justify religious controls on the minority Christian population. These conflicts include neighboring Orthodox Christian Georgia and its strife with the subject Muslim Ossetian people. Also, the Muslim Chechens' fight for independence from Russia is personalized due to Chechen raids against Azeri-Russian oil pipelines.

The primary means of control over religious activity is the registration of organizations. Currently, according to government reports, approximately 190 Muslim groups and 50 other religious organizations are registered. The national government frequently denies or delays registration years. In the last six years, only the Roman Catholic Church has received legal registration status, and this only after intervention by the American Embassy. Numerous groups have been refused registration including the nondenominational Word of Life Church, the Ichthus Baptists, and the Jehovah's Witnesses.

Unregistered groups are considered as illegal gatherings and are subject to a range of harassment including loss of rental halls, fines, slanderous media campaigns, deportation of foreigners, detentions, and even incarceration. Government raids made upon unregistered groups have involved turning off gas and heat to close them physically. Once a group exceeds ten adults, registration is mandated, which involves a litany of national government offices including the Department of Religious Affairs, the Ministry of Justice, and the Council of Ministers. This bureaucratic maze is famously employed to extract "payments" from minority religious organizations before the coveted registration is granted.

At the beginning of 2000, there were contradictory signs concerning registration as two Protestant churches were granted legal status while a Lutheran congregation was raided as "illegal." Though several minority religious groups have been denied registration, the only group to appeal their denial to the courts has been Word of Life, a nondenominational charismatic Christian group located in Baku. (Typically groups are cowed into not appealing.) Word of Life was denied legal status after a three-year struggle culminating in a final adverse court decision in May 1998. Consequently, the church suffered several rounds of harassment as an illegal organization. In July 1998, forty members were arrested for illegally meeting in a private home. In April 1999, security forces interfered with several other Word of Life meetings. In August 1999, another sixty members were taken into police detention for being an unregistered worship gathering.

Denial of registration brings harassment. When the largest Protestant Bible school in Azerbaijan was denied registration, it was forced to move eight times in one year. Many of the larger meeting halls are still government owned, and denial for registration results in this common form of harassment. Jehovah's Witness meetings were interrupted repeatedly in 1998 and 1999, which resulted in fines for approximately forty people in one April 1999 incident. A Jehovah's Witness pastor was imprisoned when he attempted to register his organization, his home was raided, his wife and congregation members were interrogated, and one member was treated for a broken eardrum as a result of interrogation. Police surveillance and restrictions on distributing religious literature are means of control of minority religious groups.

Scurrilous media propaganda is another popular means of harassment of minority religious groups. Media attacks on churches increased significantly since the president's bans on foreign missionary activity in 1996 and 1997, receded in 1998, and then regained momentum in 1999. Antimissionary propaganda in the national press was particularly fierce in 1996 and 1997, which reflects a general governmental bias against Protestant missionary activity. Even though tensions persist against foreigners and missionaries, these groups continue their activities. In August 1999, alleging an "illegal" gathering, the security police interrupted a Sunday service of the one-hundred-year-old German Lutheran Church in Baku, filming the congregation and taking their names.

On September 5, 1999, police raided the duly registered Baku Baptist Church and arrested sixty congregants for conducting an "illegal religious meeting." Eight foreigners were charged and deported for "organizing illegal meetings and speaking against the Muslim faith of the country," and two Azeri pastors were incarcerated for fifteen days.

Bangladesh

Population	125.7 million
Muslim	86.6%
Hindu	12.1%
Buddhist	0.6%
Christian	0.3%
Other (Sikh, Baha'i)	0.4%
Religious Freedom Rating	6

Background

Bangladesh won independence in 1971 after a brief war with occupying West Pakistan. After fifteen years of often turbulent rule by a succession of generals, the country's democratic transition began with the resignation of General H. M. Ershad in 1990 in the wake of pro-democracy demonstrations. Elections in 1991 brought the centrist Bangladesh Nationalist Party (BNP) to power under Khaleda Zia. In June 1996 elections, which were held with 73 percent turnout, the Awami League won 146 of 300 parliamentary seats. (Thirty additional seats are reserved for women.) In August 1997, the BNP quit parliament, returning in March 1998 to protest alleged harassment of its workers and a proposed treaty giving India transit rights through Bangladesh. Despite constant tensions, the Awami League and the BNP differ little on domestic policy. Their disputes mainly reflect intense personal rivalry. In summer 1998, Bangladesh's worst flooding ever caused approximately fifteen hundred deaths, left millions of people homeless, and caused more than $4.3 billion in losses.

Bangladeshis can change their government through elections. The 1996 elections were the freest in Bangladesh's history despite some violence and irregularities. The military's influence in politics continues to diminish. Political institutions are weak. Politics are frequently conducted through strikes and demonstrations that are marred by violence. The judiciary is independent, but corruption and severe backlogs plague lower courts. In practice, poor people have limited recourse through the courts. Torture, rape, and other abuses of suspects and prisoners are routine, widespread, and rarely punished. Both the Zia and Hasina governments have used the 1974 Special Powers Act, which allows authorities to detain suspects without charge for up to 120 days, against political opponents. The print media is diverse, outspoken, and under pressure. At least five journalists were arrested in late 1998. Party activists and Islamic fundamentalists also harass journalists. Broadcast media are state owned, and coverage favors the ruling party.

Rape, dowry-related assaults, acid throwing, and other violent acts against women are apparently increasing, with minimal police intervention. A law requiring rape victims to file police reports and obtain medical certificates within twenty-four hours of the crime in order to press charges prevents most rape cases from reaching the courts. In rural areas religious leaders arbitrarily impose floggings and other punishments on women accused of violating strict moral codes. Women face discrimination in health care, education, and employment. Approximately fifteen thousand women and children are sent each year to Pakistan and other countries for prostitution and other forced labor, and domestic child prostitution remains a problem. Union formation is hampered by a 30 percent employee approval requirement and restrictions on organizing by unregistered unions. Workers suspected of union activities can be legally transferred or fired. Child labor is widespread. Freedom House's 1998–99 *Freedom in the World* rates Bangladesh a two in political rights and a four in civil liberties.

Religious Freedom

Bangladesh was established as a secular state after its independence from Pakistan in 1971, but in 1972, the eighth amendment to the constitution declared Islam as the state religion. Despite a stress on Islamization, the Bangladeshi Constitution formally grants religious freedom. Radical Muslims have expressed dissatisfaction with the "pseudo-Islamization" of the country and want it to be renamed the "Islamic Republic of Bangladesh" with a constitution based on *shari'a* (Islamic law). The Bangladeshi government has so far resisted pressure from these groups and their sympathizers. Most religious leaders have sought amicable relations with other groups.

Since the creation of Bangladesh, people belonging to minority religious groups have suffered various kinds of social discrimination and persecution. These include destruction of property;

kidnap; murder of leadership; rape of young girls; and discrimination in education, employment, and property rights. Most Hindus have lost lands under old Pakistani laws against "enemies," which, in practice, has meant Hindus. Destruction of places of worship stems back to 1971, when a number of Hindu temples, Christian churches, and Buddhist monasteries were destroyed by the Pakistani army returning home following independence. Violent acts of this nature have continued since then, and hundreds of premises belonging to all religious communities have been destroyed. In 1995, a school run by a Catholic social organization, Caritas, was burned down. In the same year a campaign was organized by Muslim fundamentalist groups to deport foreign church workers from the country.

Deliberate attempts by different Islamic groups, such as Jam'at-a Islami, to arouse antiminority, and specifically anti-Christian, sentiment has increased dramatically since the Gulf War. In April 1998, an announcement was made over the loudspeakers of a mosque in Dhaka stating that Christians were demolishing a mosque. This caused anger even among ordinary Muslims, who took to the street and attacked churches and other properties, causing extensive damage to St. Xavier's Girls School, Holy Cross Church, and nearby Baptist and Saint Thomas' Church. Death threats were made against priests and staff workers.

Hindu women complain of being forced to dress like Muslim women, not being allowed to wear bangles or put vermilion on their forehead, which is considered a religious duty by many Hindus. Hindu men are also afraid to wear Dhoti (unstitched cloth that is wrapped around the waist) for fear of attacks by Muslim radicals. As evidence of their persecution, Hindus point to the decline of their population from 28 percent to 12 percent. A notable source of irritation to the community is also the fact that the famous Hindu Temple of the Goddess Kali, which was destroyed by the Pakistani army, has never been reconstructed. Some Hindus and Christians also complain of being forced to convert to Islam under duress.

Persecution of the Buddhist Chakmas is perhaps the most systematic of all the faith communities. The Chakmas are a tribal people who have lived in the Chittigon hills for thousands of years. They are a retiring people who have their own culture and religion (Buddhism) and have always depended on the natural resources of the Eastern hills. However, as a result of scarcity of land, tens of thousands of Muslims began populating the Chittigon hill area in the 70s. Since that time Chakmas have been subject to a systematic policy of rape, torture, and killing, and the destruction of their cultural and religious identity at the hands of Muslims. More than fifty thousand have fled to India. Minority rights groups in Bangladesh describe the persecution of Chakma people as the holocaust in the hills and allege the involvement of military personnel. International concern coupled with condemnation by bodies such as the European Commission has led to some positive initiatives by the Bangladeshi government since 1998.

Discrimination against religious minorities has been legalized in the form of the Vested and Non-resident Ordinance, also known as the Enemy Property Act 1976, in spite of constitutional guarantees of equal treatment. A circular issued in 1979 declared properties belonging to members of the non-Muslim minority as vested properties. Under the terms of the Ordinance, these properties can be confiscated at any time and released only by the ministry responsible. Minority rights groups in Bangladesh claim that 60 percent of the property belonging to members of minority communities has been illegally confiscated by Muslims in positions of authority. Human rights groups all over the world have taken up this issue and campaigned vigorously against this law, but it has been suggested that if the Enemy Property Act were repealed, many Muslims would lose their properties.

Religious minorities also face discrimination in employment, and, despite excellence in many fields, people from minority faiths are poorly represented in government service. Other implicit policies of exclusion are noticeable in the allocation of aid. The minority population, which is particularly concentrated in the Southern districts of Bangladesh (Khulna, Jessore, Satkhira), often find themselves deliberately omitted from development programs. This discrimination extends to Ahmadiyas, whom many Muslims regard as heretical. In January 1995, the Ahmadiya worship center in Kushtia was attacked by a mob and its adherents harassed.

Disturbing acts of violence against minority women continue to the present day. Sanahar, a thirteen-year-old Christian girl, was raped by a Muslim man and became pregnant. She had to face a trial for her "crime" in a village court. It is extremely difficult for a rape victim to receive justice as she has to find four Muslim adult male witnesses to prove her allegations. Human rights activist Issac Baroi has documented other atrocities committed against members of the minority communities, including a four-year-old girl who died after being raped. In her novel *Lajja*, famous writer

Tasleema Nasreen depicts accounts of gang rapes of Hindu girls returning from school. She was accused of blasphemy by Muslim fundamentalists, forcing her into exile in Sweden, despite the fact that the court acquitted her. In September 1998, she returned to Bangladesh and faces two blasphemy suits.

Constitutional guarantees of religious freedom mean that there is no direct legal restriction on freedom of worship in Bangladesh and that religious communities can manage their own affairs and run their own institutions, including schools. They can also have contacts with coreligionists overseas. However, since Bangladesh came into being, there have been hundreds of cases of persecution of minority group members. The Vested and Non-resident Ordinance is evidence of increasing antiminority sentiment in the country.

Population statistics also suggest that the minority population in Bangladesh has decreased from 14.6 percent in 1974 to 13.4 percent in 1990.

Amid calls from NGOs for the implementation of more stringent measures to improve the human rights situation and protect minority rights in Bangladesh, Prime Minister Hasina Wajid has taken some initiatives, including plans to establish a National Human Rights Commission. She has also promised to abolish laws that discriminate against minorities. In the meantime, Christian, Hindu, and Buddhist leaders in Bangladesh continue to report human rights violations against members of religious and ethnic minorities across Bangladesh, and it remains to be seen how effective and far-reaching government reforms will be.

Belarus

Population	**10 million**
Orthodox	**48%**
Roman Catholic	**22%**
Jewish	**1.1%**
Protestant	**1%**
Muslim	**0.2%**
Agnostic/Atheist/Other	**27.7%**
Religious Freedom Rating	**5**

Background

Belarus was part of the tenth-century Kievan realm. After a lengthy period of Lithuanian rule, it merged with Poland in the 1500s. It became part of the Russian Empire after Poland was partitioned in the 1700s and became a constituent republic of the Soviet Union in 1922. With the collapse of the Soviet Union in 1991, nationalist leader Stanislaw Shushkevich became head of state. A pro-Russian parliament ousted Shushkevich in 1994, and Lukashenka, a former state farm director and chairman of the parliament's anticorruption committee, won the newly created post of president. After his election Lukashenka gradually reintroduced censorship and Soviet-era textbooks and national symbols, banned independent trade unions, ignored the Supreme Court when it overturned his decrees, limited the rights of candidates in parliamentary elections, and sought reintegration with Russia. In 1996, Lukashenka extended his term and amended the country's constitution by referendum to enable the president to annul decisions of local councils, set election dates, call parliamentary sessions, and dissolve parliament. Parliament was restructured into a bicameral legislature consisting of a house of representatives with 110 deputies and a senate, with the president appointing one-third of the senators. In July 1999, Semyon Sharetsky, opposition leader and former speaker of the parliament, fled the country. On December 8, 1999, Russia and Belarus signed an agreement to enter into a confederation analogous to the European Union.

The citizens of Belarus cannot change their government democratically; freedom of the press is strictly curtailed; the law bars the importation of newspapers that include reports that may do harm to the political and economic interests of the country; public rallies and demonstrations require government approval; and a 1997 presidential decree curtailed freedom of assembly. Even charitable organizations have faced government pressure: arbitrary and contradictory tax policies have led several international humanitarian groups to cease operations in Belarus. The judicial system is essentially the same three-tiered structure that existed in the Soviet era. Judges continue to be influenced by the political leadership, and the Criminal Code includes many provisions that are susceptible to political abuse, including a host of antistate activities. All citizens must still carry internal passports, which are required for travel, permanent housing, and hotel registration. The right to choose one's place of residence remains restricted in practice. All citizens are required to register their places of residence and may not change them without official permission. Freedom House in the 1998–99 *Freedom in the World* rates Belarus a six in political and civil liberties.

Religious Freedom

Belarus looks both East and West in its religious allegiance. The Orthodox Church predominates and carries with it a strong Russianizing tendency. Its influential head, Metropolitan Filaret of Minsk and Slutsk, refuses to allow any use of Belarusian in the liturgy, which helps Lukashenka's declared intention of eventually reintegrating Belarus with Russia. In the west of Belarus, the ties with Poland are strong, with a large number of ethnic Poles and consequently a strong allegiance to Roman Catholicism (although there are many Catholics of Belarusian nationality also). As the Soviet Union did not permit the training of Catholic priests, except for a small number in Lithuania, the needs in these western dioceses were acute, and Polish priests entered the country in considerable numbers after 1991.

Historically, the nearest Belarus came to having a truly national church was Catholicism of the Eastern Rite (Uniate), but it never became a defining characteristic of the nation, as it did in Western Ukraine. Tsar Nicholas I abolished it in 1839, and it reemerged only after independence in 1991. Since then it has not regained its one-time influence. There is, however, a patron saint—Euphrosyne of Polotsk, a twelfth-century princess and nun—who is universally admired as an educator of the nation.

A law on freedom of conscience and religious organizations, similar to its 1990 Soviet predecessor, was passed on December 17, 1992, and overturned the old Soviet Stalinist decree of 1929, thus guaranteeing a large measure of religious liberty (like its Soviet counterpart in 1990). However, the subsequent 1994 constitutional guarantee of religious liberty is unambiguous. Article 16 reads: "All religions and faiths shall be equal before the law. The establishment of any privileges or restrictions with regard to a particular religion or faith in relation to others shall not be permitted. The activities of denominational organizations, their bodies and representatives, that are directed against the sovereignty of the Republic of Belarus, its constitutional system and civic harmony, or involve a violation of civil rights and liberties, shall be prohibited."

This final statement immediately raises the question of the definition of what is an activity directed against the "sovereignty" of the republic and whose decision this is. In practice, this necessitates the existence of a state body to adjudicate. Not only does the name of the former communist watchdog body, the Council for Religious Affairs, reappear here; it is even directed by Alexei Zhilsky, who was formerly head of the Communist Party of the Minsk region.

On July 3, 1995, President Lukashenka issued a new decree limiting the powers of Catholic priests: "Priests are forbidden to hold mass publicly without permission from the regional authorities." Contravention is liable to a fine between two and ten million Belarusian rubles. If the priest is Polish, he is liable to deportation from Belarus. Despite this, the number of Polish Catholic priests has grown from 75 in 1992 to 180 in 1996, serving an estimated 800,000 Catholics in 318 parishes (8% of the population, of whom some 450,000 are Poles). Deportations have been frequent but not on a massive enough scale to be effective. Nor have they been accompanied by violence. It should be noted that the Constitution (Article 11) guarantees resident foreign nationals equal rights with Belarusian citizens, unless otherwise specified in the constitution, the laws, and international agreements.

The Russian legislation restricting the activities of religious minorities (q.v.) has clearly influenced similar moves in Belarus. Discussions took place in 1997, which were advocating what we may call "legislation for privilege." The Russian influence becomes even more obvious in the light of these close parallels: Judaism and Islam are named alongside Orthodox Christianity and Roman Catholicism as the "traditional" faiths of the country, despite the fact that there are only 1.1 percent of Jews and 0.2 percent of Muslims. Other faiths—including Protestants, Eastern-Rite Catholics, and Old Believers—would receive the right to function under restrictions harking back to the Soviet era, while "destructive" faiths would be banned outright.

Where did these proposals originate? A document circulated that bore no signature, but the word was that the sponsorship came from the Belarusian Orthodox Church. Insofar as it is possible to draw any conclusions from contradictory statistics, it would seem that some one hundred thousand believers fall into various categories of nontraditional religions. Of these, mainstream Protestants would be permitted to function but not to carry out active missionary work. They could teach, instruct, and sell their literature but only on their own premises. They could not hire halls or stadiums for large gatherings, thus ruling out Billy Graham-type campaigns. The activities of some extremist sects contravene the laws of democratic societies, so their banning is not so controversial, except that the main "crime" of some of these is refusal to bear arms. Under such a rubric not only would Jehovah's Witnesses be banned but also Quakers. No specific sects are mentioned, but the tenor of the whole is an unmistakable copy of its Russian counterpart.

In April 1998, this letter moved forward more concretely to take on the form of draft legislation. Its preamble is a simple rewrite of the Russian original, placing Orthodoxy above other faiths and recognizing its "special role in the history of Belarus, in the formation of spiritual, cultural and state traditions of the Belarusian nation." At the same time, the new law "respects Catholicism and other Christian denominations, as well as Judaism, Islam and other religions constituting an inalienable part of the history and culture of the nation of the Republic of Belarus."

The draft goes on to state (Article 6) that "religious organisations are equal before the law . . . no religion may be established as a state religion or obligatory." Religious knowledge may be taught in state schools at all levels and all religious organizations may conduct teaching on their own premises (Article 7). There are considerable restrictions on the registration of minority groups, and they must furnish information to the state about their activities. The Committee for Religious Affairs is given wide powers—not only to maintain a database but also to ensure adherence to the law.

The Belarus Cabinet of Ministers issued a four-page decree on February 23, 1999, further restricting foreign workers. It even, by implication, denies women the limited rights enjoyed by foreign men. It stipulates that foreign clergymen, specifically, may engage in religious work in Belarus only if invited by the headquarters of a religious organization. This latter must apply to the State Committee for Religious and Ethnic Affairs. The individual must be theologically qualified. Opinions may be sought, and the process may last up to a year. If the application is granted, the clergyman is restricted to work in one specific area.

Most of these restrictions are potential rather than actual at the moment. Indeed, Belarus, because of its geographical position, is open to outside influences, particularly from Poland. It seems unlikely that any large-scale threat to the Roman Catholic Church will emerge. It is seen as essential to guarantee the overall friendliness of Poland—on the way to joining Nato and the European Union—and it would not be wise to prejudice this by picking minor disputes over the expulsion of Polish priests. When eleven priests were deported in 1996 for not having the correct registration documents, they were quickly replaced. An Eastern-Rite Catholic priest, Valeri, the abbot of a monastery in Polotsk, was given an expulsion order in 1995, but this was rescinded on appeal. Despite the heavy posturing in favor of Russia, the steady expansion of the number of Catholic priests is indicative of this policy.

The head of the Catholic Church is Cardinal Kazimierz Swiatek, Archbishop of Minsk, age eighty-four in 1999. He was imprisoned for ten years in 1939, after the commuting of a death sentence. In 1991, he became the first Catholic bishop in Belarus for fifty years, and he has been active in restoring parishes and church buildings. He has opened a seminary, which graduates the (still insufficient) number of twenty-five priests per annum.

Catholicism is gaining in influence due to several factors, perhaps most of all the high level of education and experience of the Polish priesthood. Unlike the Orthodox, who still celebrate the liturgy in Church Slavonic, they encourage the vernacular, whether it is locally Polish, Russian, or Belarusian. Religious instruction for children is well organized and effective, with laity sharing in this to make up for there being fewer priests than parishes.

Any violence against believers is isolated and affects minorities only. In March 1998, Bishop Petro Hushcha, leader of the Belarusian Church of the Augsburg Confession (Lutheran—4,000 members), was arrested, beaten, and temporarily detained by the police. Charismatic Protestant churches have had difficulty getting permission to meet.

Metropolitan Filaret is aged but a tough survivor from the Soviet period. It is known from the KGB archives that he collaborated with the state organs, but the extent of this seems to have been minor compared with some other senior clerics. He was once in charge of the Department of External Affairs and therefore has good contacts outside his country. He enjoys complete freedom in his activities and has overseen a remarkable expansion of his church since the Soviet period (a threefold increase in the number of parishes).

Minsk itself is resplendent with newly restored churches. There are now 918 parishes in ten dioceses, which have the same number of bishops. There is a theological academy and a seminary, as well as six convents and two monasteries. There is also open access to the media.

At the same time, Metropolitan Filaret is a great Russianizer. Politically,

he supports President Lukashenka's ambitions of reuniting his country with Russia, and the Orthodox Church insists on promoting its Russian aura. There are a small number of parishes belonging to the Belarusian Autocephalous Orthodox Church, which are coming back into existence following suppression in the Soviet period. However, there are not at present enough of these to cause serious worry to the main body, which fulfills in all but law the function of a state church.

Belarus has never had a strong national identity, having fallen successively under Lithuanian, Polish, and Russian rule. It achieved somewhat unwilling independence in 1991, with the collapse of communism. Its language (Belarusian) is far from universally spoken; even President Alyaksandr Lukashenka lacks this facility. Since independence, Belarus has degenerated into one of the more dictatorial states of the former Soviet Union. Lukashenka, ousting the reformist Stanislav Shushkevich in 1994, has systematically reduced the scope of civil liberties and achieved international notoriety in 1997 by confiscating the land on which several foreign embassies were situated, leading in some instances to a severance of diplomatic relations.

Belgium

Population	**10.2 million**
Catholic	74%
Protestant	1%
Orthodox	0.5%
Islam	3%
Secular Humanism	20%
Other (Jehovah's Witness, Buddhist, Mormon, Baha'i, Scientology, Other)	1.5%
Religious Freedom Rating	3

Background

Modern Belgium dates from 1830, when the territory broke away from the Netherlands and formed a constitutional monarchy. Constitutional amendments have devolved power to regional councils at the expense of the central government in Brussels. In 1996, it was formally transformed into a federation of Flanders, Wallonia, and bilingual Brussels, with the German-speaking area accorded cultural autonomy. The weak central government continues to oversee only foreign policy, defense, justice, monetary policy, taxation, and the management of the budget deficit. Political parties are split along linguistic lines. Numerous small ethnic parties and special interest groups have emerged, leading to a decline of the Social Democrats, Christian Democrats, and Liberals. Belgium continues to be plagued by political scandals, ethnic tensions, and decreased confidence in its government, judiciary, and police forces. This produced a major drop in the ruling parties votes in the July 1999 elections.

Belgians can change their government democratically. Nonvoters are subject to fines. The country's judiciary is independent but has continued to experience criticism due to the country's ongoing political and criminal scandals. While freedoms of speech and the press are guaranteed, Belgian law prohibits some forms of pornography as well as incitements to violence. Libel laws have some minor restraining effects on the press, and restrictions on the right of civil servants to criticize the government may constitute a slight reduction of the right of civil speech. Belgium has enacted measures to promote sexual equality, including the prohibition of sexual harassment. Legislation mandates that in parliamentary elections 33 percent of the candidates be women. Approximately 60 percent of the work force are members of labor unions, which have the right to strike—a right they frequently exercise. Freedom House's 1998–99 *Freedom in the World* rates Belgium a one in political rights and a two in civil liberties.

Religious Freedom

The constitution guarantees the rights and freedoms of ideological and philosophical minorities (Article 11), freedom of worship and its public practice, including the freedom to manifest one's opinions in all matters (Article 19). No one can be compelled to take part in the activities and ceremonies of a religion (Article 20). The state may not intervene in the appointment of religious ministers (Article 21). It guarantees the respect of philosophical, ideological, or religious beliefs of parents and their children at school and provides for religious education in schools (Article 24). It guarantees the payment of the wages and retirement pensions of ministers of recognized religions and their secular equivalents.

The Belgian system of relationships between the state and its religion, including philosophies, is historically rooted in the principle of recognition and nonrecognition of religions. Catholicism (1802), Protestantism (1802), and Judaism (1808) have enjoyed de facto state recognition. Anglicanism was recognized in 1835, Islam in 1974, and Orthodoxy in 1985. Despite its recognition, Islam has failed to form an administrative umbrella organization with which the state could negotiate. Consequently, Islam has not yet been financed. Elections are due to take place, which should lead to a body to represent it. The recognition of Anglicanism and some Protestants seems an arbitrary recognition within larger religious groupings. Other Protestant groups are now applying. Secular humanism (*la laicite*), the symbol of which is the torch, is recognized through the Central Secular Council (Conseil Central Laique), but only a portion of secular humanists, free thinkers, agnostics, and atheists consider themselves part of this organization.

Recognition entails several material benefits. The Ministry of Justice covers the wages, allowances, and bonuses of religious ministers and moral secular advisers. The Ministry of National Defense pays the wages of army chaplains and of Catholic nuns in military hospitals. The Foreign Ministry pays the wages of missionaries, as well as their medical expenses and traveling expenses. The Ministry of Public Works finances the rehabilitation of places of worship. Subsidies are given to various faculties of theology and religious broadcasts, including masses and religious offices. These advantages are denied to nonrecognized religions, which also have no access to radio and TV.

Jehovah's Witnesses have a clear structure and leadership but have been denied recognition. They did not request any financial advantages but only the ability to bring spiritual assistance to their members in hospitals and detention places. Other small religious groups have been denied state recognition with the same negative outcome.

Individuals have the right to freedom of religion and belief if they respect democratic values and public order. However, in Brussels and in a number of municipalities, the distribution of printed material, whatever its content (religious, philosophical, political, cultural, commercial) is forbidden in certain parts of the town, such as in the vicinity of schools, (Christian) churches (but not synagogues, mosques, or any other non-Christian places of worship), military barracks, and so forth. Any distribution of printed material may only be carried out with the written approval of the mayor and payment of a small fee. Some Jehovah's Witnesses have been taken to a police station in Brussels on

this ground, and a school principal lodged a complaint against Gideons' distributing New Testaments outside schools.

Freedom of worship is respected by the state, but only recognized religions (except Islam) get subsidies from the state for worship activities. According to the Constitution (Article 21), religious marriages may not be performed prior to civil marriage. All religious communities, philosophical movements, and other associations are allowed to carry out charitable activities. The independence of the clergy and the right of self-government are recognized and respected by religious bodies, as is freedom of religious education. According to Article 24 No. 1, public schools are neutral, which implies "the respect of the philosophical, ideological or religious beliefs of the parents and the pupils." Schools give a choice between instruction in one recognized religion or a nonreligious ethics course until the age of eighteen. In the French-speaking community, young Jehovah's Witnesses complain that they are compelled to attend classes that conflict with their beliefs. In the Flemish community they are exempted. In Catholic schools only Catholic religious classes are organized. There are also some Jewish schools and some Protestant primary schools that teach only their own religion. All the schools are subsidized by the state.

The report of the parliamentary enquiry commission on cults contained many factual errors and deepened the gap between "good" and "bad" religions. The commission did not verify numerous unfounded accusations, made by former members of minority religions, yet they were published by the parliament. The accused were not even aware of the accusations, nor could they defend themselves. A blacklist of religious movements mentioned during the hearings was also published in the report. In May 1999, the Anthroposophical Society filed a complaint in the Court of Arbitration against the government information center on cults, but in 2000 the Court of Arbitration found the observatory legal. A bank closed the account of the Raelians because they were on the blacklist. The Raelians are bringing a lawsuit against persons they say libeled them before the commission. Adventists, Evangelicals, Pentecostals, and the Baha'i have experienced some difficulties in renting public halls since they were on the blacklist. In September, police raided the homes and facilities of many Scientologists. In November 1999, a court hearing brought by the "Vibrating Heart" group, challenging its placement on the blacklist, was postponed as the government had still not submitted the relevant documents. The Ministry of Justice has refused to meet representatives of a minority religion on the basis that it "only deals with recognized religions." There are reports that children of parents who belong to named "cults" have been harassed at school, and in one divorce case a member of the Sahaja Yoga "cult" was denied custody of her child in favor of a father who was a drug addict and an ex prisoner. Currently, the income taxes of about 130,000–140,000 Belgian citizens who belong to nonrecognized religions are used to finance recognized religions and secular humanism, which are sometimes openly hostile to their own beliefs.

Bhutan

Population	**0.8 million**
Buddhist	**50–70%**
Hindu	**25–45%**
Muslim	**5%**
Christian/Other	**<1%**
Religious Freedom Rating	**6**

Background

Britain began to run this Himalayan land's affairs in 1865 and installed the ruling Wangchuk dynasty in 1907. Britain's role ended with a 1949 treaty that gave India control over Bhutan's foreign affairs. Since then, New Delhi has continued to support the Wangchuk absolute monarchy. In 1972, Jigme Singye Wangchuk, the current monarch, succeeded his father to the throne. The 150-member National Assembly has little independent power. Every three years, village headmen choose one hundred National Assembly members, while the king appoints members to forty seats. Religious groups appoint members to ten seats.

By the mid-1980s, the government, dominated by minority Tibetan-descended Ngalong Drupe ethnic group, viewed the country's Nepali-speakers, known as Southern Bhutanese, as a threat to its absolute power. Between 1990 and 1992, soldiers raped and beat Southern Bhutanese villagers and forcibly expelled tens of thousands. There are currently some 94,500 Bhutanese refugees in Nepal. In 1994, dissidents from the country's third and perhaps largest major ethnic group, the Sarchop community in Eastern Bhutan, launched the Druk National Congress

(DNC) party in exile. By July 1997, authorities had arrested scores of suspected DNC members and sympathizers.

In June 1998, the king dissolved the cabinet, removed himself as its chairman, gave parliament the theoretical power to remove the king, and allowed the legislature to elect most of the cabinet. Analysts said the changes were limited in practice.

The Bhutanese people lack the democratic means to change their government. The king wields absolute power, and policy-making is centered on the king and interrelated Ngalong elites. The National Assembly is often a forum for diatribes against the Southern Bhutanese. Political parties are prohibited in practice. The rule of law is nonexistent. Between 1990 and 1992, the army and police committed grave human rights violations against Southern Bhutanese, including arbitrary arrests, beatings, rape, destruction of homes, and robbery. Few if any of those responsible have been punished. The army continues to harass residents and intimidate police and local officials.

The rudimentary judiciary is not independent. The king appoints and can dismiss judges, most of whom have little legal training. Several detainees and prisoners have reportedly died in custody. According to Amnesty International, since July 1997, authorities have reportedly arrested and held more than 150 suspected DNC sympathizers incommunicado and tortured them. Freedom of speech is restricted, and criticism of the king is not permitted, except indirectly during National Assembly discussions. Satellite dishes are banned. Freedom of assembly is nonexistent, although some business and civic organizations are permitted. The government has banned the Nepali language as a subject of instruction in schools. Southern Bhutanese are required to obtain official "No Objection Certificates" (NOCs) to enter schools, take government jobs, and sell farm products. Many Southern Bhutanese children have no local schools to attend.

Independent trade unions and strikes are not permitted. Villagers are often forced to contribute "voluntary" labor for state projects. Property rights are limited. Freedom House's 1998–99 *Freedom in the World* rates Bhutan a seven in political rights. Its civil liberties rating rose from a seven to a six due to a change in Freedom House methodology to reflect an easing of state intrusions into the personal lives of citizens.

Religious Freedom

Religion continues to play a pervasive role in Bhutanese national life and politics. The shamanistic Bon religion is the oldest in the country and, while it now has few priests, is generally respected by other religious groups. Tibetan influences brought Buddhism to present-day Bhutan in the seventh century. In the seventeenth century, Tibetan-born Shabdrung Nagawang Namgyal unified Bhutan as an independent "theocracy" under the Drukpa Kagyupa school of Mahayana Buddhism. After Britain began shaping Bhutan's affairs in 1865, it gradually pushed the country toward a more secular form of rule. In 1907, the British helped install the ruling Wangchuk dynasty, nominally ending "theocratic" rule.

Nepali-speaking settlers began arriving in southern Bhutan in the mid-nineteenth century. Many were Hindus, although some followed Buddhism. A 1958 Citizenship Act granted most Nepali-speakers citizenship. By the mid-1980s, the government increasingly viewed the Nepali-speaking community as a threat to its absolute power and to its ethnic and Buddhist hegemony. The regime introduced cultural restrictions in 1987 and began applying the discriminatory 1985 Citizenship Act to arbitrarily strip thousands of mostly Hindu Southern Bhutanese of their citizenship.

Southern Bhutanese 1990 pro-democracy demonstrations were generally peaceful, although some leftist groups carried out arson and violence. The army systematically raped and beat Southern Bhutanese villagers, expelled tens of thousands from the country, and arrested thousands more. The government claimed it was expelling recent illegal immigrants, but most of the ninety-four thousand Bhutanese refugees currently in Nepal appear to possess documentation of Bhutanese citizenship. The government has radically reduced its estimates of the numbers of Bhutanese in recent years, largely for political reasons. This is one reason population figures from here are even less reliable than other countries.

In the mid-1990s, dissidents from the country's third major group, the Sarchop community in eastern Bhutan, formed the multiethnic Druk National Congress to press for democratic reforms. Like the dominant Ngalong Drukpas, the Sarchops adhere to the Mahayana school of Buddhism, but their Nyingmpa school is outside the Ngalong's Drukpa Kagyupa sect. Once again the mix of religious differences and calls for democracy led the authorities in 1997 and 1998 to respond by arresting scores of Sarchop sympathizers and closing several Nyingmpa monasteries.

Bhutan has no written constitution or bill of rights, and there are no legal guarantees of freedom of religion. The Drukpa Kagyupa sect of lamaist Buddhism is the state religion, and it is subsidized by the state. By law Hindus,

Muslims, Christians, and other non-Buddhists may not proselytize, and conversions to a nonapproved religion are illegal. Public worship by those other than Buddhists and Hindus has been proscribed, as it has for some forms of Hinduism. Family legal matters are adjudicated according to Buddhist law for Buddhists and Hindu law for Hindus. Non-Buddhists suffer political and social discrimination.

The government considers the symbols and values of the Drukpa Kagyupa sect of Buddhism to be an integral part of Bhutanese national identity. In practice, there is a close relationship between state power and the Buddhist clergy. Buddhist monks are represented in the national assembly, the royal advisory council, and other state institutions. The government subsidizes monasteries and shrines and provides support to several thousand of the kingdom's twelve thousand monks. All state functions begin with Drupe rituals.

The pro-democracy movement in Bhutan has been driven by two of Bhutan's three main ethnic groups—the Nepali-speakers (who in fact consist of several Nepali-speaking ethnic groups that originally came to Bhutan from Nepal) and the ethnic Sarchops from eastern Bhutan. While religious freedom per se is not the focus for the pro-democracy movement, religion is intimately linked to the political situation. The Nepali-speakers are primarily Hindu, although they also include many Buddhists. The Sarchops are Buddhists and are thought to be the most numerous ethnic group, but their Nyingmpa school is outside the Drupe Kagyupa sect of the ruling Ngalong Drukpas. Given the overarching influence of Drukpa Kagyupa lamaism on the state structure and on national life, religion effectively creates a barrier between the ruling

Ngalong Drukpas and the Nepali-speakers, and, to a lesser extent, the Sarchops.

In the 1960s and 1970s, the government generally tried to integrate the Nepali-speakers into the Drukpa lifestyle and culture. But by the late 1980s, government policy had shifted toward a more aggressive assimilation. The sixth Five Year Plan (1987–92) introduced a program of "One Nation, One People" that promoted Driglam Namzha, the national dress and customs of ruling Ngalongs. A 1989 royal decree made Driglam Namzha mandatory for all Bhutanese, although enforcement is sporadic. These cultural codes did not affect religious practice directly, but they have a major indirect effect in a society where Ngalong culture is intimately linked to religion.

Major Hindu festivals are national holidays, and the royal family participates in them. Moreover, Hindus can generally worship freely except during crackdowns in the south. But the overall status of religious freedom is shaped by the close relationship between Drukpa Kagyupa Buddhism and the state, by the government's poor human rights record, and by the absence of a free press and an independent national assembly where grievances over religious rights and other issues can be aired. In effect, Bhutan has freedom of worship. Other religious freedoms may be present but only as sufferance depending on the political situation.

In 1992 and 1993, Christians in the Cirang district were fired from their jobs, beaten by police, and expelled from the country. The September 1997 closure of thirteen monasteries of the Nyingmpa School of Buddhism in the crackdown against Sarchop pro-democracy activists in eastern Bhutan stemmed from the authorities' belief that the learning centers were being used to organize campaigning activities. Among the scores of people detained were dozens of monks and religious teachers. Exile-based dissident groups reported that authorities killed a Sarchop monk during a crackdown in October 1997.

Botswana

Population	**1.5 million**
Christian	59%
Indigenous	40%
Baha'i	0.8%
Muslim	0.2%
Other	0.2%
Religious Freedom Rating	2

Background

Elected governments have ruled Botswana for the more than three decades since it gained independence from Britain in 1966, and it is now Africa's longest continuing multiparty democracy. Economic progress has been built on sound fiscal management and low rates of corruption, but most of the country's people remain poor. In the past two years, the government has increased defense expenditures because of tensions with Namibia.

The legislative elections through which Botswana's 1.5 million citizens choose their government are now considered free and generally fair, despite accusations that the Botswana Democratic Party, which has held power since independence, has regularly manipulated elections. Election conduct has steadily improved. Botswana's human rights record is outstanding in Africa. Several laws regarding sedition and allowing detention without trial remain on the books, but they are rarely invoked. Another law bars "uttering words with intent to bring into ridicule the president of Botswana." The courts are generally considered to be fair and free of direct political interference. Political debate is open and lively, and there is a free and vigorous print media in cities and towns. Government critics, however, receive little access to the government-controlled broadcast media. In May 1998, the government dropped charges of "spreading false rumors likely to cause alarm" against a resident British journalist.

Treatment of Botswana's indigenous Basarwa, known as "Bushmen," has drawn local and international concern. Government-relocation schemes reportedly include forcible evictions of Basarwa from their traditional lands, and they are subject to widespread discrimination and abuse.

Women's rights are not fully respected. Married women may not take a bank loan without their husbands' permission, and women, especially those in rural areas, face traditional discrimination. Domestic violence against women is reportedly rampant. Concentration of economic power has hindered labor organization. While independent unions are permitted, workers' rights to strike and to bargain for wages are restricted. Freedom House's 1998–99 *Freedom in the World* rates Botswana a two in political rights and in civil liberties.

Religious Freedom

Botswana has a long tradition of religious tolerance and accommodation. More than half of the country's population is regarded as Christian although, as in many other countries, elements of traditional beliefs have often been adapted or incorporated into religions introduced later. This is especially true in independent Christian churches not accountable to external bodies. Many traditional spiritual and magical practices also remain current, including divination and healing ceremonies. Others are related to witchcraft and sorcery, and, as in neighboring countries, accusations of harmful sorcery occasionally lead to assaults, burnings, and lynchings.

The Lutheran Church is the strongest single Christian denomination, a result of early missionary activity. Anglican and Methodist churches are strong, and there are also Catholic, Mormon, and Reformed churches. Evangelical groups are increasingly active and operate a Bible school. There is a very small, but economically influential, Muslim population, mostly made up of immigrants of South Asian origin whose forebears arrived in South Africa early in this century, and a relatively large Baha'i community. Indigenous practices vary among ethnic groups, and reported discrimination against Basarwa people mainly arises from ethnic biases and is expressed in economic exploitation. However, the frequent dispossession of their land has desecrated several of their religious sites and so has *de facto* damaged several of their traditional religious practices.

Botswana's constitution clearly guarantees rights of religious freedom. Several provisions of chapter 2, "Protection of Fundamental Rights and Freedoms of the Individual," deal directly or by inference to religious rights. Chapter 2's introductory clause says that all rights are enjoyed regardless of creed and lists freedom of conscience, expression, and assembly, as well as protection of property. These rights are further defined in Sections 12 and 13. Chapter 2, section 11, deals entirely with religious rights. Section 11 (1) states that "no person shall be hindered in the enjoyment of his freedom of conscience," which is defined to include religion and belief. It also states the right to change religion and "alone or in community with others, and both in public and private, to manifest and propagate his religion or belief in worship, teaching, practice and observance." The right to provide religious instruction and maintain religious schools is included in Section 11 (2). Sections 11 (3) and 11 (4), respectively, prohibit imposition of religious instruction without consent and any requirement to take an oath against religious beliefs.

All these rights are subject to qualifications listed in Section 11 (5). This lists a set of conditions that may be allowed in laws if they are "reasonably required" "(a) in the interests of defense, public safety, public order, public morality or public health; or (b) for the purpose of protecting the rights and freedoms of other persons, including the right to observe and practice any religion without the unsolicited intervention of any other religion, and except so far as that provision or, as the case may be the thing done under the authority thereof is shown not to be reasonably justifiable in a democratic society." In practice, the government respects religious freedom, and any limitations conform to international law. There are no reports of misuse of this constitutional authority to restrict or direct religious practice, though the government has made the Bible part of its compulsory curriculum.

All religious organizations are required to register, but this is a relatively simple process. The only group to be denied registration was the Unification Church in 1984. The church's petitions to be registered have been denied, but it is still allowed to operate.

There is freedom to propagate one's faith, freedom of worship, and freedom to train and appoint clergy. Religious bodies have rights of self-government and of religious education, to carry out charitable activities, to own and acquire property, and to maintain social institutions. They can produce, import, and distribute literature and have contact with coreligionists domestically and overseas. Individuals can adopt, change, or leave a religion freely, with no change of civil status.

Brazil

Population	168 million	None	3%
Catholic	68%	**Religious Freedom Rating**	2
Protestant	21%		
Spiritist	4%		
Buddhist	0.7%		
Muslims	0.7%		
Indigenous	0.15%		
Other (Jewish, Orthodox, Jehovah's Witness)	2.4%		

Background

After gaining independence from Portugal in 1822, Brazil retained a monarchical system until a republic was established in 1889. Democratic rule has been interrupted by long periods of authoritarian rule, most recently under military regimes from 1964 to 1985. A new constitution went into effect in 1988 providing for a president elected for four years and a bicameral Congress.

Civilian rule has been marked by corruption scandals, including the impeachment by Congress and resignation of President Fernando Collor de Mello (1989–92). As his anti-inflation plan appeared to work dramatically, the formerly Marxist then market-oriented finance minister Fernando Henrique Cardoso won the presidency in 1994, with 54 percent of the vote. In 1997, he secured congressional approval for a constitutional amendment to drop the one-term limit in the presidency, and he won again in 1998, though at the time his government was implicated in bribery and a phone-tapping scandal. Land issues remain important, with encroachments on Indian land and peasant takeovers of fallow land. Peasant activism has contributed to scores of violent conflicts between peasants and the military, police and private security forces, which act with virtual impunity.

Citizens can change governments through elections. The 1998 elections were considered free and fair, with opposition candidates winning three large governorships. Parliament remains dominated by the executive branch. The constitution guarantees freedom of religion and expression and the right to organize political and civic organizations. Cardoso is credited with initiating a sea change, with improvements in attitudes concerning international criticism on rights issues, and has created a ministerial-rank secretariat charged with defending human rights. He has also proposed making all violations of rights (including by the police) federal crimes, thus moving their investigation from the jurisdiction of state, civil, and military police forces.

A weak judiciary reinforces a profound climate of lawlessness and insecurity. Brazil's Supreme Court is granted substantial autonomy by the constitution, but the judicial system is small and vulnerable to the chronic corruption that undermines the entire political system. There is organized crime and a national breakdown in police discipline. Human rights, particularly of socially marginalized groups, are violated with impunity on a massive scale. Brazil's police are among the world's most violent and corrupt with torture, death squads, and extra judicial killings, especially against the poor. Officers are rarely punished. Since 1994, the federal government has deployed the army in order to quell police strikes and bring order to Rio de Janeiro's four hundred slums. Public distrust of the judiciary has resulted in hundreds of reported lynchings and mob executions. The press is privately owned, and the print media have played a central role in exposing official corruption, although journalists have been attacked, and some murdered.

Brazil has one of the most concentrated land distribution patterns in the world. Land disputes have risen sharply in recent years with innumerable invasions of "unproductive" land by rural activists to draw attention to the plight of an estimated 4.8 million families without land. Violence against women and children is a common problem since protective laws are rarely enforced. In 1991, the Supreme Court ruled that a man could no longer kill his wife and win acquittal on the ground of "legitimate defense of honor," but juries tend to ignore the ruling. Forced prostitution of children and child labor are widespread. One report claims that, on average, three street children are killed every day in Rio, many by police. Violence against Brazil's 250,000 Indians continues. The 1988 constitution guarantees indigenous peoples land rights covering some 11 percent of the country, but these rights are consistently undercut. Industrial labor unions are well organized and politically connected, and many are corrupt. The right to strike is recognized. Freedom House's 1998–99 *Freedom in the World* rates Brazil a three in political rights and a four in civil liberties.

Religious Freedom

Compared to Spanish-speaking countries, Brazil has a history of comparative religious freedom in Latin America. In colonial times one "new Christian" of Jewish descent, Antonio Jose da Silva, was sent back to Portugal and burned for political reasons. Dutch Jews were driven from the Brazilian Northeast in the sixteenth century, but only because all the Dutch of whatever faith were expelled en masse from their settlements there. Catholicism was the state religion until the 1988 constitution ended its status. Minority religions suffered discrimination and repression until after World War II. However, the Brazilian Church was never very powerful by Latin standards. Portuguese rulers had the right to name bishops. There was some suppression of Protestantism, African, and indigenous religions, but generally Brazil has been a more tolerant country than its Spanish-speaking counterparts.

Brazil's history as a colony of Portugal caused other differences from the Spanish colonies. Because enslaved Africans were allowed to remain together as whole tribes, syncretism between Roman Catholic and African beliefs (Umbanda, Candomble, and other forms) has existed for centuries and

continues to flourish. Most Catholics tend to combine their Catholicism with other religious practices, which means that the statistics given above for "spiritism" may be markedly understated: many "Catholics" are also spiritists and vice versa. Numerous small indigenous tribes, with perhaps 250,000 total members, practice their own religions in many parts of the vast Brazilian countryside. Though some religious arrogance towards the tribes still exists among missionaries, for the most part the churches have taken steps to train missionaries to be sensitive to indigenous cultures and beliefs. Tribal wars occasionally seem to lead to interference with religious practice among the indigenous peoples themselves. The government controls access to tribal lands.

In the nineteenth century an offshoot of the French Positivist movement founded by August Comte created positivist "churches," some of which still exist. Freemasonry was pervasive at the highest levels of society. Presbyterians, Methodists, and Baptists from the southern U.S. immigrated to Brazil shortly after the American Civil War. (There is an American cemetery in São Paulo state where the Confederate flag is still flown.) More recently the evangelical explosion that has taken place in Spanish-speaking Latin American countries has had similar success in Brazil, with perhaps as many as thirty-five million Brazilians belonging to one or another type of Protestantism, about 80 percent of them charismatic. The Assemblies of God alone has attracted more than five million members, while several other Protestant groups with North American affiliations probably have slightly under a million members each. The Catholic Church has responded with a lay-led charismatic movement of its own.

Brazil went through military rule during the Cold War from 1965 to 1985. The Brazilian generals harassed and repressed individuals and institutions that promoted liberation theology, a blend of Christianity and social revolution. Several Brazilian theologians and bishops were among the most prestigious leaders of that movement in the world. The generals also sought to curtail the numerous "base communities" and other religious groups that might be viewed as weakening national unity by separatist tendencies or criticism of injustices. These government abuses of religion have ceased almost entirely in the fifteen years since Brazil's return to democracy, though other humans rights violations are rampant. Struggles continue, however, between religious groups, often within the same denomination, who see socialist leaning liberation theology as the religiously dictated path to social justice, and those who think participation in a capitalist economy (a position denigrated as "neoliberalism" by its opponents) will perform the same miracle in Latin America as in parts of Asia.

The 1998 constitution provides that freedom of conscience must not be violated. At a legal level there is full religious freedom. There is freedom to propagate one's faith, freedom to worship, and freedom to train and appoint clergy. Religious bodies have rights of self-government of religious education, to carry out charitable activities, to own and acquire property, and to maintain social institutions. Church-run orphanages, hospitals, and schools have their own media. They can produce, import, and distribute literature, receive donations, and have contact with coreligionists, domestically and overseas. Individuals can adopt, change, or leave a religion freely, with no change of civil status. The principal barrier to religious freedom is the corruption and violence that permeates the society and impedes the practical manifestation of human rights of all kinds. This especially affects indigenous people.

Though tensions between religious groups have not entirely ceased, there is widespread participation in ecumenical councils in Brazil today. Many Protestant groups gather in the ecumenical forum VINDE. One current bone of contention is the Universal Church of the Kingdom of God, an immensely successful movement (about 3 million members) founded in 1977, which preaches a gospel of prosperity. One of the Universal Church's leaders provoked a Catholic reaction when he flagrantly insulted an image of the Virgin Mary on Brazilian television in 1995. Alleged financial irregularities and shady practices have led to government scrutiny of the Universal Church. In 1999, there was also ecclesiastical and media animosity toward the Unification Church ("Moonies") near Jardim on the Paraguayan border.

Although Jews have been present in Brazil longer than in any other nation in the Western hemisphere, and serve at high levels of the government, some anti-Semitism exists. Large German communities in the southern Brazilian states have given rise to some neo-Nazi and separatist movements, and large Arab communities have imported some elements of anti-Zionism. Though worrisome, to date these groups have not been very influential. More harmful to the 100,000 to 150,000 Jews living in Brazil is a long-standing social prejudice against them, which sometimes makes them reluctant even to identify themselves as such. Intermarriage with non-Jews has further weakened religious adherence among Brazilian Jews.

Religion is part of the basic school curriculum, and schools make an effort to coordinate religious education with the wishes of parents and students. Religious groups, especially Protestants, are a strong presence in all the forms of media. The obstacles to freedom of religion that remain largely consist of finding better ways for religious groups to respect one another.

Bulgaria

Population	**8.2 million**
Eastern Orthodox	85%
Sunni Muslim	12%
Shi'a Muslim	1%
Catholics	0.6%
Protestants	0.27%
Armenian Gregorian	0.1%
Jewish	0.03%
Other	1%
Religious Freedom Rating	4

Background

Bulgaria was occupied by Ottoman Turks from 1396 to 1878 and did not achieve complete independence until 1908. The communists seized power in conjunction with the "liberation" of Bulgaria by the Soviet Army and ruled from 1944 until 1989. With the exception of a short-lived democratic government elected in 1991, Bulgaria continued to be governed by former communists until 1997. In April 1997 elections, which were labeled free and fair by international observers, the Union of Democratic Forces and its allies won 52 percent of the vote and 137 of 240 parliamentary seats.

In 1998, the government faced growing pressure to implement reforms and battle endemic corruption. Obstacles to investment continued to be widespread and included violations of intellectual property rights. In May of that year, the World Bank reported that Bulgaria's track record in transition had been "very weak."

Bulgarians can change their government democratically. The 1997 parliamentary elections and 1996 presidential vote were free and fair. In 1997, the UDF-led government pledged to pass a new media law that would minimize partisan interference in the state-owned broadcast media. In June the Constitutional Court ruled that three penal code articles proscribing "libel" and "insult" against state authority were not unconstitutional. Virtually all print media are privately owned. There are more than sixty private radio stations and several privately owned regional television stations. The country's economic crisis has caused hardship for the independent press.

The constitution provides for the right to peaceful assembly. Permits are required for demonstrations and outdoor rallies but are routinely granted. Approximately two hundred political parties and associations are registered. The constitution prohibits the formation of political parties along religious, ethnic, or racial lines. Nevertheless, the overwhelmingly ethnic Turkish Movement for Rights and Freedoms operates freely and is represented in parliament. Bulgaria has two large labor union confederations, the Confederation of Independent Trade

Unions, a successor to the communist-era union, and Podkrepa, an independent federation founded in 1989.

Under the constitution, the judiciary is guaranteed independence and equal status with the legislative and executive branches. Corruption and lack of experienced personnel continue to hamper the system. Police frequently mistreat prisoners and detainees. Free movement within the country and emigration rights are generally respected. Private property is formally protected, and, in general, private property rights are respected in practice and enforced by the judiciary. High rates of corruption, widespread organized crime, and continued government control of significant sectors of the economy impede competition and equality of opportunity. Women are well represented in administrative and managerial positions and in higher education. Freedom House's 1998–99 *Freedom in the World* rates Bulgaria a two in political rights and a three in civil liberties.

Religious Freedom

The Eastern Orthodox Church was a preserver of the Bulgarian identity during the five centuries of Ottoman rule and, as in other Balkan countries, was a core around which the Bulgarian national revival during the eighteenth and nineteenth centuries centered. As a separate institution, it was formed by an Ottoman decree as an ethnically based religious community. After liberation from the Ottomans following the Russian-Turkish War, the church helped form Bulgarian statehood and was instrumental in propaganda for the "national idea" among Bulgarians abroad. It was dominant and privileged compared to other denominations. After World War II, the clergy suffered repression from the communist government, and many were accused of collaborating with the previous regime and punished. The government effectively forced the church into only low profile activities.

The Muslim community has three groups: Turks, the largest minority, are descendants of the Ottomans; Bulgarian-speaking Muslims (also known as Pomaks), who are Slavs converted during Ottoman rule; and the Muslim Roma. Muslims have always been under government control and suffered discrimination, especially during the last years of the communist regime, when the names of 850,000 Muslims were changed by force. Shi'a Muslims, although a relatively large community, have never been recognized separately and officially have always been under the umbrella of the Sunnis.

Catholics and Protestants, although religious minorities, are traditional communities, present in Bulgaria under the Ottomans. Both are composed mainly of ethnic Bulgarians. During the first years of communism, they suffered severe persecution when most of their clergy were executed after show-trials. Before World War II, different religious communities had judicial powers over personal status and in some cases (e.g., the Muslim courts) also on distribution of property after divorce. This was abolished soon after the war.

Currently about 60 percent of Bulgarians declare some type of religious belief, and 10 percent regularly attend worship. The statistics for religious adherents noted above reflect the 1992 census's "historical believing" of people. People of no religion and some Protestants are often included as "Orthodox." Religious attendance is higher among Muslims and Catholics, and it is almost complete amongst Protestants.

The 1991 Constitution of Bulgaria proclaims religious freedom (Art. 13.1 and Art. 37.1), provides for separation of religious institutions from the state (Art. 13.2), and obliges the state to encourage respect between churches and between believers and nonbelievers (Art. 37.1). It also provides for restrictions on this freedom, some of which are vague and others in contradiction to international law. It prohibits the use of religion for political purposes (Art. 13.4) and the formation of political parties along religious lines (Art. 11.4). Most restrictions are the same as in the international law, that is, public order, health and morals, rights and freedoms of others, with the notable exception of "national security" (Art. 37.2). "National security" arguments have been invoked on a number of occasions to restrict religious freedom. The constitution also establishes the Eastern Orthodox Church as the "traditional religion" of Bulgaria. Although this was initially a mere declaration, there have been repeated attempts to make grounds for legislative privileges.

The principal law concerning church and state in Bulgaria is still the 1949 Denominations Act. Article 23 prohibits all religious denominations with centers abroad from establishing missions, religious orders, or charitable organizations in Bulgaria. Article 20 prohibits activities relating to children and young people. Article 10 prohibits foreigners from holding ecclesiastical positions in Bulgarian churches. Article 14 gives the Council of Ministers full power over the existence and programming of religious schools. The act establishes a directorate for religious affairs as a special office of the Council of Ministers. The head of the directorate appoints religious officers abroad (Art. 9); supervises the communications and documents of all churches, including banning them (Art. 15); grants preliminary permission for relations with organizations based abroad (Art. 22); and allows or denies receipt of donations from abroad (Art. 24). Article 12 gives its head the right to dismiss religious officers if they "are breaking the laws, disturbing public order, undermining good morals, or are working against the democratic structures of the state."

During the first years after 1989, those restrictive provisions were not applied. Most of the churches recognized so far were registered during 1990–1992. A number of new churches, mostly Protestant, mushroomed and were incorporated as private associations to avoid administrative control and/or because of dissatisfaction with the old leaders. Confiscated church property gradually began to be restored to traditional communities.

The government first used the restrictive provisions of the Denominations Act in 1992, when for purely political reasons it removed much of the Orthodox and Muslim leadership from office. In decision 5/1992 the Constitutional Court declared seven articles of the Act unconstitutional, including Article 12. However, it left the government the right to recognize or refuse religious leadership. Article 12 has not subsequently been applied, but interference in the internal affairs of groups has nevertheless increased. Each new government has used its power to recognize leaders for its own political ends. The courts do not interfere on the grounds that the law gives the government "free discretion."

Beginning in 1993, a public defamation campaign against "nontraditional" churches began. Most targets were Protestant groups, including churches registered under the Denominations Act and established in Bulgaria for centuries. The trend gradually spread to all media. The word *sect* was used to denote all that is not "traditional," and the groups were accused of all kinds of crimes—kidnapping, instigation to suicide, brainwashing, perverted sex, and drug abuse.

The government amended the Law for Persons and the Family in February 1994. This affected religions registered as not-for-profit organizations rather than as denominations with the Directorate for Religious Affairs. Article 133A required all already registered juridical persons dealing with religious matters to reregister with the courts within a three-month period, requiring the approval of the Council of Ministers. A special transitory provision required that those groups that lost their juridical status must cease their activities.

More than forty groups were refused permission from the government to reregister. Some sued, but most were reluctant. For the most part the courts again applied a principle of "free discretion" and refused to reverse executive decisions. Only the Jehovah's Witnesses appealed to the European Commission of Human Rights and, in 1997, concluded a "friendly settlement" with the government and were recognized as a church.

Deprivation of juridical status led to a series of diverse discriminatory practices. Victims of these practices were members not only of groups that did not receive reregistration but also members of officially recognized churches. Most victims were Protestants, but Hare Krishnas, members of the Unification Church, and nontraditional Muslims were also affected. In several cities municipal councils passed ordinances restricting the activities of religious organizations that had registration with the central government, forcing them to shut their doors.

In 1994, municipal authorities systematically denied access to premises used by religious groups for ceremonies. Peaceful assemblies were disrupted, organizers fined, and religious materials confiscated. Proselytizing groups, such as Jehovah's Witnesses and Mormons, suffered unabated communal violence and police brutality. Employers, especially in public education, checked employees' religious affiliation and fired or otherwise discriminated against a number found to belong to "unwanted" groups. The National Security Service (secret police) created a special task force for surveillance of "suspect" religions.

Although the 1991 constitution required a law to be passed within three years giving a conscientious alternative to compulsory military service, no law was passed for seven years. During this period several Jehovah's Witnesses were prosecuted and two imprisoned for refusing military service. The 1998 law provides for alternative service, which is twice the length of military service. It also specifies an annual quota for conscientious objectors and does not permit them to work in nongovernmental organizations. Conscientious objectors may switch from alternative to regular military service, but not vice versa.

With the noncommunist United Democratic Forces coming to power in 1997, the pressure on religious communities has eased. The 1949 law is, however, still in force, and the several drafts introduced in the Parliament to replace it are not much better. The 1998 draft presented by the Directorate of Religious Affairs would give the Directorate new powers, including refusing the building of new places of worship. Activities of unregulated groups are forbidden, and there could only be one institution per religious base. Debate still continues about draft religion laws. Individual discrimination towards members of religious communities, although not as acute as several years ago, continues to take place.

Burma (Myanmar)

Population	**48.1 million**
Buddhist	**87.5%**
Christian	**6%**
Muslim (mainly Sunni)	**4%**
Animist	**1%**
Hindu	**0.5%**
Other	**1%**
Religious Freedom Rating	**7**

Background

Following Japanese occupation in World War II, Burma achieved independence from Britain in 1948. The army overthrew an elected government in 1962. During the next twenty-six years, General Ne Win's military rule impoverished the country. In 1988, an estimated three thousand people were killed in an army crackdown on massive, peaceful pro-democracy demonstrations. Army leaders created the State Law and Order Restoration Council (SLORC) to rule the country. In 1990, in the first free elections in three decades, the opposition National League for Democracy (NLD) won 392 of the 485 parliamentary seats. The SLORC refused to cede power and jailed hundreds of NLD members. In 1995, the SLORC released Aung San Suu Kyi, the NLD leader and the country's preeminent pro-democracy campaigner, after six years of house arrest.

In November 1997, SLORC reconstituted itself as the nineteen-member State Peace and Development Council (SPDC) and sidelined at least fourteen of the twenty-one SLORC members. By early 1998, the junta had also removed numerous corrupt ministers in an apparent effort to improve its international image. Lieutenant General Khin Nyunt, the intelligence chief and formerly one of the junta's top five members, continues to be the regime's strongman. In April 1998, the regime reportedly detained nearly 250 lawyers, Buddhist monks, and student leaders in an intensified crackdown.

The minorities that comprise more than one-third of Burma's population have been fighting for autonomy since the late 1940s. Since 1989, the SLORC has coopted fifteen ethnic rebel armies with cease-fire deals. Many warlords have become drug traffickers. Recent years have seen intense fighting between the army and the predominantly Christian Karen National Union (KNU), the largest active insurgency.

Burma is effectively a garrison state ruled by one of the most repressive regimes in the world. The junta controls the judiciary, and the rule of law is nonexistent. The SLORC has imprisoned or driven into exile most of its vocal opponents and severely restricted freedoms of speech, press, association, and other fundamental rights. The army is responsible for arbitrary beatings and killings of civilians; the forced, unpaid use of civilians as porters, laborers, and human mine sweepers under brutal conditions, with soldiers sometimes killing weakened porters or executing those who resist; summary executions of civilians as alleged insurgents or insurgent sympathizers; and widespread incidents of rape.

Gross human rights violations during counterinsurgency operations against ethnic rebel groups have driven more than one hundred thousand mainly Karen, Karenni, Shan, and Mon refugees into Thailand. In January 1998, Danish doctors who examined two hundred Burmese refugees in Thailand reported that two-thirds were victims of rape and other abuses.

The junta is equally brutal towards dissidents. In April 1998, opposition leader Aung San Suu Kyi estimated that there are between one thousand and two thousand political prisoners in Burmese jails. One dissident was jailed for three years for illegal possession of foreign currency after a search of his house found his toddler playing with two Singaporean coins. Prison conditions are abysmal: torture of both political prisoners and common criminals is routine. The press is tightly controlled; there are no independent publications or broadcast services. In 1996, the government subjected unauthorized Internet use to lengthy jail terms. Universities are closely monitored and have largely remained closed since late 1996. Criminal gangs have forcibly sent thousands of Burmese women and girls, many from ethnic minority groups, to Thailand for prostitution. Freedom House's 1998–99 *Freedom in the World* rates Burma a seven in political rights and civil liberties.

Religious Freedom

All of the larger world religions can be found in Burma, with Buddhism constituting the majority faith numerically.

Allegiance varies by ethnicity, with the Burmans being majority Buddhist and the minority ethnic groups having significant Christian, Muslim, and animist communities. The Chin are about 70 percent Christian. The Naga and Karenni have significant numbers of Christians. The Wa are mainly animist. The Rohingyas are almost 100 percent Muslim. Many tribal groups are more animist than Buddhist in practice, although official accounts tend to record them as Buddhist. The Karen are believed to be somewhere between 20 and 50 percent Christians. Unofficial figures claim that the Karennis are 90 percent Christian.

While there is some freedom of worship in Burma, anything other than simple worship faces overwhelming problems. The UN Special Rapporteur on Burma, reporting in 1997, stated that "there is essentially no freedom of thought, opinion, expression or association in Myanmar." All gatherings of five or more people are illegal, and families must register all houseguests or face imprisonment or forced portering for the Army. Association with "illegal" (i.e., unregistered) organizations is punishable by multiyear prison sentences with hard labor. The UN Rapporteur noted that such legislation, along with a complex array of security laws, seems to be used arbitrarily. These requirements and restrictions naturally impact upon religious communities in Burma. Gaining permission for Christian and Muslim places of worship is a problem. Planning considerations usually ignore these religious needs, and decisions have even resulted in the destruction of Christian cemeteries and Buddhist graves.

Any association or institution not controlled by the state is perceived as a threat to government loyalty. Indeed, since seizing power in 1988, the SPDC (formerly known as SLORC) have used the promotion of Buddhism as one aspect of their goal to Burmanise the country and thereby to forge "national solidarity." Further proof of this use of Buddhism as a political tool is the fact that the Religious Affairs Ministry is found in the grounds of the World Peace Pagoda (Kaba Aye) in Rangoon, which is the residence of the most senior committee of Buddhist monks.

The Ministry's main functions are the propagation of Buddhism—both nationally, particularly amongst ethnic minorities, and internationally. However, this is not undertaken independently by Buddhist clerics but instead at the direction of the government. Hence, this promotion of Buddhism does not mean that Buddhists enjoy freedom of religion. Buddhist clerics are themselves monitored, and action is taken against those dissenting from the regime. In many areas the network of monasteries provide a link for underground opposition groups, and this, in part, may explain why significant state monitoring of religious activity takes place. Buddhists report that in some areas the local authorities have taken control of religious activities, using them to raise money and promote local unity. In the 1990s, violent crackdowns on monasteries by the regime led to the arrest of thousands of monks. Many remain in detention, and it is believed that eighteen have died. In July 1999, government officials in Mandalay forbade monks to travel without written government permission.

The government monitors most international networks, and religious groups are no exception. While it is not actually forbidden to contact coreligionists, all lines of communication are monitored. Muslims have been permitted to make the Hajj. Foreign religious representatives are usually only allowed tourist visas and are not permitted to preach, evangelize, or remain to carry out religious work. Indeed, under the 1976 constitution, foreigners are denied the right to practice any religion (Article 156a) and are denied the right of association (Article 158), thus making missionary work seemingly impossible. Permission for permanent missionary establishments has not been given since the 1960s, although some Catholic groups do function. A number of seminaries and Bible colleges are allowed to operate.

All teaching in SPDC schools must be in Burmese, and no other languages are taught or tolerated. Therefore, most ethnic non-Burmans are denied formal education in their own language, literature, or culture, in spite of clauses in the Child Law that accord freedom of speech and expression to children. Teachers are subjected to heavy ongoing political indoctrination. The media are heavily censored and controlled. Press Scrutiny Boards monitor every aspect of the written word, including song lyrics, and film and video scripts. Non-Burmese literature is particularly strictly censored. In this context all religious publications are subject to control and censorship. There is a shortage of Bibles and Korans and other religious literature in indigenous languages. This is partly because of strict import restrictions and partly because of translation difficulties in the context of more than one hundred languages.

Ethnic Burmese citizens are clearly favored, both through legislation and government practice, and this policy of Burmanisation has been closely associated with the promotion of Buddhism. Religious persecution is thus a natural extension of these twin policies. Historically many of the ethnic minority groups have been opposed to the regime, and many continue to fight against it, compounding historical tensions.

Discrimination is demonstrated by key aspects of government legislation, including the citizenship law of 1982, under which full citizenship is granted only to those who can trace the families of both parents back to pre-1824 Burma. Identity cards are color coded according to citizenship categories, and most carry information on religion. They have to be shown for the smallest of transactions, such as buying bus tickets, and are also necessary for applications for educational courses and employment, making discrimination on the grounds of ethnicity and religion a real and easy possibility. In 1997, the UN Special Rapporteur noted that, "There are still cases of torture, arbitrary killings, rapes and confiscation of private property. . . . They seem to be taking place most frequently in border areas by military soldiers in the course of military operations, forced relocations and development projects. Many of the victims of such atrocious acts belong to ethnic national populations."

Denied many basic cultural and political rights, the ethnic minorities find themselves suffering the worst human rights abuses by the government. These abuses often have a significant religious dimension, as demonstrated by the plight of Karen and the Rohingyas. Rohingya Muslims in Arakan state are targeted by the regime primarily because they are deemed to be illegal immigrants. As such, the regime has sought to drive them from their land. (More than 250,000 fled in 1989 and a further 25,000 in 1997.) Most have returned but still suffer oppressive conditions. The religious dimension of these attacks shows in the regime's determination to remove everything that goes to make up the Rohingya identity, including mosques. The government's ethnic and religious "cleansing" includes massive murder, rape, and other assault on a scale with few parallels elsewhere in the world. Isolated incidents of religious persecution of Indian Muslims have also taken place, although Chinese Muslims, known as "Panthays" seem to have escaped such discrimination. It is reported, however, that all Muslims are targeted for portering or other forced labor. In March 1997, anti-Muslim riots, reportedly instigated by the regime, resulted in the destruction of dozens of mosques in several cities.

The Karen have also suffered terribly at the hands of the regime, and more than one hundred thousand are now in refugee camps on the Thai-Burma border. At least thirty thousand have died, and some three hundred thousand have been displaced. Acts of religious persecution against the Karen can be traced back for many years. On Christmas Eve 1949, Burmese soldiers massacred more than two hundred Karen men, women, and children by burning them to death in a church. Massacres involving women and children continued throughout the war. In July 1999, twenty Karen, including a baby and two children ages eight and two, were killed by the military, some after rape and torture. In 1998, the UN Special Rapporteur said such acts were not isolated but were government "policy." More recently the SPDC has been involved in forced conversions of Christians, compelling some to become Buddhist nuns or monks. Incidents have also taken place in which individuals who refused to convert to Buddhism were killed. Clerics have been specifically targeted. The UN Special Rapporteur for Myanmar reports that SPDC officials sent a letter to Buddhist leaders in refugee camps on the border stating that while Buddhist families would be able to return to Burma, no Christian would be given safe passage.

Tension between Buddhist and Christian Karens has been deliberately exacerbated by the regime. The Democratic Karen Buddhist Army, now allied to the SPDC, reportedly left the Karen National Union in 1994 as a result of a dispute over the missionary activities of a Buddhist monk, U Thuzana, and complaints of domination by Christian leaders. KNU sympathizers and leaders are specifically targeted by the DKBA, and poor relations between the two may also account for random acts of persecution against Christians by DKBA commanders. These have included posting death threats for attendees on church doors, destruction of church buildings, and acts of violence, including extrajudicial killings. The KNU's human rights record is not unblemished, but no religious motive can be identified.

The military has disrupted church services and destroyed churches among the Naga. In Chin state, which in many northern areas is almost 100 percent Christian, the government has recently prohibited self-supporting schools. Christian children have been taken forcibly and initiated as Buddhist novices. Financial incentives and exemption from porterage or labor duties have been offered for those who convert to Buddhism. Whole villages have been forced to attend sessions on Buddhism which denigrate the Christian faith. In one operation in Chin State, unmarried SPDC soldiers were deliberately chosen and encouraged, through offers of higher rank and privileges, to marry and convert Christian Chin women. Christian sites and graveyards are actively demolished by the SPDC, who replace them with pagodas, often using forced labor from amongst the Chins. Three evangelists were killed by SLORC in 1993, and there are continuing reports of government-instigated violent attacks on clergy.

Little regard is paid to any religious legislation that does exist. Lt. Gen. Khin Nyunt, the first secretary of the SPDC, said in 1992 that under military rule there was essentially "no law at all."

Chile

Population	**15 million**
Catholic	**73%**
Protestant	**20%**
Other (Muslim, Jewish, Baha'i,	
Jehovah's Witness, Indigenous)	**1%**
None	**6%**
Religious Freedom Rating	**3**

Background

The Republic of Chile was founded after independence from Spain in 1818. Democratic rule predominated in this century until the 1973 overthrow of the Marxist Salvador Allende by the military under Augusto Pinochet. The 1980 constitution provided for a plebiscite in which voters could reject another presidential term for Pinochet. In 1988, 55 percent of voters rejected eight more years of military rule, and competitive elections were scheduled for 1989.

Christian Democrat Patricio Aylwin, the candidate of the center-left Concertacion for Democracy, was elected president, and the Concertacion won a majority in the Chamber of

Deputies. With eight senators appointed by the outgoing military government, however, it fell short of a senate majority. A right-wing Senate bloc stymied Aylwin's government in efforts to prevent Pinochet and other military chiefs from remaining until 1997. In 1993 elections, the Concertacion's Eduardo Frei also won handily. Pinochet remained a senator for life. In December 1999, Joaquin Lavin, the conservative candidate, won the presidential election.

In 1998, Pinochet was detained in Britain on a Spanish extradition warrant for the torture and deaths of thousands of opponents following the U.S.-backed coup in 1973. This produced a strong political polarization in Chile and, according to one top general, has left the country in a "critical situation." Subsequently, Pinochet was released by Britain on health grounds and returned to Chile.

Citizens can change their government democratically, but the Pinochet extradition crisis shows that Chile's democracy remains incomplete and requires constitutional reforms to ensure civilian control of the military. Frei has wrested some power from the armed forces, but his failure to eliminate some of the 1980 constitution's most egregious features has heightened the sense of emergency.

The 1990 Truth and Reconciliation Commission to investigate rights violations under military rule implicated the military and secret police leadership in the deaths or forcible disappearance of 2,279 people between 1973 and 1990. In 1978, however, the regime gave amnesty for all political crimes, and the Supreme Court, packed by Pinochet before he left office, has blocked all efforts to lift it. Hundreds of cases involving incidents after 1978 have come to civilian courts but with few convictions. Military courts can bring charges against civilians for sedi-

tion, including any comment that may affect the morale of the armed forces or police. Physical abuse of prisoners, particularly by the Carabinero uniformed police, is common. The 1958 State Security Law punishes those who "defame, libel, or calumniate" the president, government ministers, parliamentarians, senior judges, and the commanders in chief of the armed forces. In January 1998, two journalists were jailed overnight for claiming a former Supreme Court justice was "old, ugly, and had a murky past." Diverse media present all points of view, although self-censorship regarding Chile's recent political history is widespread.

Chile has a strong trade union movement. Government corruption is comparatively minor for the region, although military graft has not been investigated. A 1993 indigenous rights law guarantees that Indian lands cannot be embargoed, sold, expropriated, or taxed, but new government-promoted development projects continue to threaten Mapuche Indian lands in the south. Freedom House's 1998–99 *Freedom in the World* rates Chile a two in civil liberties and a three in political rights, a drop from two in the previous years due to worsening civil-military relations following Pinochet's detention.

Religious Freedom

In Chile there are an estimated five thousand different religious organizations or new movements. Roman Catholicism, brought to Chile in the sixteenth century, is practiced by an overwhelming majority of Chileans (nearly 80 percent). Small groups of Anglicans and Protestants, whose forefathers arrived from Europe in the nineteenth century, have in recent years gained ground—in part because of difficulties between the Catholic Church and a seventeen-year military regime—as have the Church of Latter Day Saints (Mormons), the Jehovah's Witnesses, and the Pentecostal churches. There is a small Jewish community (15,000 people), and a Muslim community mostly drawn from the largest Palestinian community outside the Middle East (300,000). About 6 percent of Chileans say they have no religious preference or are atheists.

Current practice on freedom of conscience and religion reflect two centuries of evolution in the Chilean constitution. Under the 1833 constitution, in force until early in the twentieth century, the state officially recognized and supported the Catholic Church. The prohibitions on the public exercise of other religions, however, were usually observed in the breech, as non-Catholics were allowed private exercise of their religions and the establishment of their own schools and cemeteries. By the turn of the century, legal reforms established civil marriages and cemeteries. The state was officially separated from the Catholic Church and freedom of conscience and religion guaranteed. However, the Catholic Church, along with the Antiochian Orthodox Church, still had privileged status, retaining a formal constitution recognition by the state. The 1980 constitution in Article 19.6 explicitly recognized "freedom of conscience, manifestation of all beliefs and the free exercise of all religions." This is subject to the requirements of "morals, good customs or public order." Religious groups can "build and keep churches" depending on "conditions of hygiene and security" and are generally exempt from taxes. Its framers held that all churches and religious denominations have public legal personality, in keeping with the principle of equality under the law. The constitution provides for equality before the law, but it does not specifically ban discrimination

based on race, sex, religion, or social status. The criminal code (Articles 138 and 139) has penalties for disturbing the religious freedom of another.

In the 1990s, Protestant churches and other religious groups have pushed to end the practice of conferring legal personality on religious institutions through executive decree. They maintain that this practice infringes on the principle of separation of church and state and, by leaving this to state authorities, is reflective of religious tolerance rather than freedom, permission rather than right. In June 1999, Protestant groups organized in the Committee of Evangelical Organizations proposed a bill, The Judicial Constitution of Churches and Religious Confessions, that would eliminate the situation in which the Catholic Church is recognized as a public institution while other confessions are private corporations with fewer rights. The Chilean Bishops Conference (CECH) has opposed the law, arguing that its historical role in the country should be recognized as a distinct status.

By 1993, Congress approved constitutional reforms for the purpose of ensuring respect for Chile's minority indigenous community (approximately 10 percent of Chileans) by protecting or exempting their customs. It established the right of Native Americans to community activities in sacred sites, cemeteries, and ngullatun courts (Mapuche ceremonial sites).

Catholic rites are celebrated in the official ceremonies of the armed forces. Protestants have established military missions but say that they do not have the institutional support enjoyed by their Catholic counterparts, pointing to the absence of Protestant armed forces chaplains and difficulties for pastors in visiting military hospitals. Proposed legal reforms would mandate that military, police, and penal institutions facilitate, as far as practicable, the physical space and means to carry out religious activities for all groups.

Chilean legislation has never required those holding high public office to be Catholic—at variance with historical practice in most other Latin American countries. The ruling Christian Democratic party, while largely composed of Catholics, is not confessionally affiliated. The Catholic Church does, however, continue to have strong influence in the areas of education, in the media, and in legislation. Chile remains one of the few Latin American countries that does not have civil divorce. (The Chamber of Deputies approved a divorce bill in September 1997, despite heavy opposition from the Catholic Church; the bill is still awaiting Senate action.) In Santiago, the capital, two of the six regular television channels are owned by religious organizations; in outlying areas the percentage is higher.

Post-Vatican II relations between the Catholic Church and other faiths have shown dramatic improvement, particularly with Chile's Jewish community. However, increasing adherence to Protestantism has caused negative feelings in a church that has seen a slow ebb of the faithful to other denominations due to evangelism by Protestants, especially Pentecostal groups.

Although it is not mandatory and in fact is legally open to other faiths, in practice a predominately Catholic religious education is given in public schools. This can result in social pressure to adhere to Catholicism, given that the usually few non-Catholic children are placed in an awkward position of accepting Catholic courses or standing apart. Religious bodies have the right to train and appoint clergy, self-government, religious education, carry out charitable activities, own and acquire property, and maintain social institutions. They can produce, import, and distribute literature, receive donations and have contact with coreligionists domestically and overseas.

During the military dictatorship (1973–90), the Catholic Church was the object of several attacks, particularly against members of the clergy who were outspoken in denunciation of official human rights abuses. In the 1990s, the four-hundred-thousand-member Church of the Latter Day Saints has been the object of violence, with scores of churches destroyed or damaged. Many believe that the attacks, which have been followed by lackadaisical police work, are inspired, at least in part, by anti-Americanism. Jehovah's Witnesses also suffer forms of discrimination, especially when their beliefs conflict with the law, such as differing views on the appropriateness of medical treatment, especially blood transfusions. While there is no formal right of conscientious objection, the military formally asks potential draftees about their religion in an apparent attempt to identify and exempt Jehovah's Witnesses from military duties because of their faith. There was one false bomb threat against a Santiago synagogue in late August 1998. People detained by the police for questioning are asked about their religious affiliation. The practice, which has been accepted by the Supreme Court, is employed to identify people summarily detained for street crime.

Population	1,242 million
Asian (including Falun Gong)	16%+
Buddhist	8%+
Christian	6%+
Muslim	3%+
Atheist	10%+
Religious Freedom Rating	6

Background

Chinese Communist Party (CCP) Chairman Mao Zedong proclaimed the People's Republic of China in 1949 following victory over the Nationalist Kuomintang. Mao's death in 1976 largely ended the brutal, mass ideological campaigns that had characterized his rule and resulted in millions of deaths. Deng Xiaoping emerged as paramount leader and, in 1978, began market reforms that included ending collectivized agriculture. The army's bloody crackdown on pro-democracy demonstrators near Tiananmen Square in 1989 signaled the government's wholesale rejection of political reform. Deng selected hard-liner Jiang Zemin, the Shanghai mayor and party boss, to replace the relatively moderate Zhao Ziyang as CCP secretary general.

In 1993, Jiang assumed the presidency. Since then, the CCP has attempted to maintain its monopoly on power by improving living standards through economic reform, while stifling dissent. By 1997, Jiang had consolidated his power to the extent that Deng's death, once seen as a possible prelude to upheaval in this fractious country, passed unremarkably.

As in past years, the annual meeting of the National People's Congress (NPC) in 1998 served mainly to approve the CCP leadership's closed-door decisions. With hard-liner Li Peng having served the two terms as premier permitted under the constitution, the NPC approved conservative technocrat Zhu Rongji,

sixty-nine, as premier. Jiang began a second term as state president. Zhu's reforms included closing thousands of unprofitable state-owned industries, cleaning up the technically insolvent banking system, slashing the number of government agencies from forty to twenty-nine, separating the regulatory role of ministries from their business interests, abolishing state-subsidized housing, and encouraging home ownership. The restructuring was predicated on continued strong economic growth that would create jobs for newly unemployed state workers. By autumn 1998, Zhu was forced to scale back his plans.

Chinese citizens lack the democratic means to change their government. The CCP holds absolute power, has imprisoned nearly all active dissidents, uses the judiciary as a tool of state control, and severely restricts freedoms of speech, press, association, and religion. In practice there is little separation between party and state. The NPC, constitutionally the highest organ of state authority, has little independent power and has never rejected legislation.

Under the 1987 Village Committees Organic Law, approximately 60 percent of the country's 928,000 village bodies are chosen through local elections. Campaigns generally focus on local corruption and economic matters, but only prescreened CCP and some independent candidates can compete. In many villages, independents have won seats. However, throughout the country, balloting is characterized by irregularities and unfair procedures. Moreover, unelected CCP village secretaries and county authorities hold real power.

The CCP controls the judiciary. Corruption is rampant, and local governments intervene in cases. Judges are poorly trained and are generally retired military officers selected on the basis of party loyalty. Suspects are routinely tortured to extract confessions.

Authorities can arbitrarily detain dissidents and ordinary criminals through several extrajudicial administrative procedures, thereby contributing to a vast network of forced labor camps. Activist Harry Wu has identified eleven hundred *laogai*, or "reform through labor," camps holding six to eight million prisoners without trial under brutal conditions. Abuse of prisoners, particularly ordinary workers, is routine and widespread, and authorities often encourage inmates to beat political prisoners. There are persistent reports of authorities selling organs of executed prisoners for transplant purposes.

The government admits that it is holding approximately two thousand people for political crimes, although the actual figure is probably much higher. In 1997, as part of revisions to the criminal code, authorities eliminated the category of "counterrevolutionary" crimes, under which courts have imprisoned thousands of dissidents. The revised code still incorporates key elements of the 1993 State Security Law, which authorizes punishment of groups and individuals for working with foreign organizations or individuals, expands the criminal concept of "state secrets," and creates a separate article aimed at pro-independence and autonomy movements in Xinjiang, Inner Mongolia, and Tibet. (*A separate report on Tibet appears later.*) Unrelenting police harassment prevents many dissidents from holding jobs or otherwise leading normal lives. In April 1997, authorities allowed Wang Dan, one of China's few prominent political prisoners, to go into exile in the United States.

The media never directly criticize the CCP's monopoly on power or top leaders. At least a dozen journalists are in prison, some merely for meeting with Western counterparts. Since 1996, Jiang has tightened control over the media and the arts. The government has introduced regulations to control Internet access. The market-driven press is allowed to report on inefficient government agencies, environmental damages, official corruption, and other issues that dovetail with Beijing's interests. The government has tolerated the existence of several thousand nongovernmental organizations (NGOs) that focus on areas the government does not consider to be politically threatening, including the environment and the rights of women and migrant workers. Authorities use a complex process to weed out any groups that could potentially oppose the government.

Freedom of assembly is limited. In recent years, authorities have tolerated some public protests on labor, housing, and local government issues, while forcibly ending others. China's harsh family planning policy limits urban couples to one child, while in rural areas parents of a girl can petition authorities for permission to have a son. Some local officials zealously enforce the policy through sanctions and even forced abortion and sterilization. Couples adhering to the policy receive preferential education, food, and medical benefits while those failing to comply face a loss of benefits and fines. Dissidents in Xinjiang report that authorities often force Muslim women to have abortions and sterilizations after their first child. Women face social and economic discrimination and sexual harassment in the workplace.

Independent trade unions are illegal. All unions must belong to the CCP-controlled All-China Federation of Trade Unions. Strikes are occasionally permitted in foreign-owned factories to protest dangerous conditions and low wages. In March the U.S.-based National Labor Committee accused American clothing manufacturers of avoiding direct responsibility for labor rights by subcontracting production to non-American-owned factories in China where workers receive low pay, are forced to work overtime, have no contracts, and are subject to arbitrary dismissal. Most prisoners are required to work and receive little if any compensation.

Urban middle-class Chinese enjoy increased freedom to work, travel, enter into relationships, and buy homes as they choose. However, for many urban dwellers the state controls everything from the right to change residence to permission to have a child. Freedom House's 1998–99 *Freedom in the World* rates China a seven in political rights and a six in civil liberties, the latter a rise due to an easing of state intrusion into personal life.

Religious Freedom

To a greater or lesser extent, China has repressed religion throughout the fifty years of Communist Party rule. Its aim has been to make religion serve the interests of the communist state until it disappears from Chinese society. This remains the dominant view. State religious policy, as explained by Chinese President Jiang Zemin in March 1996, is to "actively guide religion so that it can be adapted to socialist society." Ye Xiaowen, the hard liner heading the Religious Affairs Bureau (RAB), in 1996, also urged the "handling" of religious matters according to the dictates of Lenin and declared that "we will gradually weaken the influence of religion."

In the 1950s, Mao Zedong sought to control religion through government-controlled religious groups and the total suppression of uncooperative

religious leaders through brutal labor camp terms, murder, or exile. In the Cultural Revolution of the sixties and seventies, Mao closed all places of worship and tried to extinguish religion altogether. Since Mao's death in 1976, the government has tolerated some religious expression but only within government-registered organizations. The constitution, in Article 36, guarantees freedom of religious belief, but elsewhere it sets forth sweeping exceptions and qualifications to the right and states that it only protects religious activities that are "normal," without defining the term.

The collapse of Soviet Communism and the Tiananmen Square democracy demonstrations in June 1989 profoundly shook the leaders in Beijing. In 1991, the government issued Document 6, which called for a crackdown against unregistered religious groups and reaffirmed its goal of creating a "materialistic," "scientific," and atheistic society. Repression against underground religious groups rose again in 1994 after Beijing issued decrees 144 and 145, mandating the registration of religious groups.

This campaign to "eradicate" unregistered groups intensified during the late 1990s. The new anticult provision of the Criminal Code was being used by late 1999 to impose long prison sentences on leaders of the Falun Gong and Zhong spiritual movements as well as Protestant house church leaders. At the turn of the millennium, unregistered Catholic, Protestant, Tibetan Buddhist, Muslim, and various Asian religious groups, such as Falun Gong, report that many of their followers endure arrests, fines, imprisonment, and severe economic discrimination, and that some of their leaders have even been tortured and killed.

Clerics, pastors, monks, imams, and other religious leaders cannot preach outside of their own area, and they and their venue must be approved by the government. In early 2000, the government "ordained" five Patristic priests as bishops of the Patrisitc Church without Vatican approval, an act that was strongly condemned by the Vatican. Religious services and members are subject to monitoring. Sermons must stick to approved topics under penalty of arrest. Children are barred by law from being educated in religion and from attending public worship services.

Many unregistered places of worship have been shut down or bulldozed in recent years. The *Far Eastern Economic Review* reported that in the first half of 1996, "police have destroyed at least fifteen thousand unregistered temples, churches, and tombs." In 1999, the government demolished more than a dozen Catholic churches in the Fujian area, including some, like St. Joseph's Church, that were of distinguished architecture, and in 1998, a Qing dynasty mosque near Chengdu's Muslim quarter. The popular Catholic shrine to the Blessed Mother Mary in Donglu, Hebei Province, was demolished by military forces in 1996, and the traditional annual pilgrimage—which drew tens of thousands in 1995—banned.

China's stringent birth-control campaign, designed to achieve zero population growth by midcentury, is objectionable on religious grounds to members of Christian and Muslim groups, among others. Women, restricted in the number of children they may bear, must seek state permission before becoming pregnant in a particular year. Compliance is coerced through steep fines; job loss; demolition of housing; denials of birth certificates; educational opportunities for children; and forcible abortion, sterilization, and infanticide. In 1999, Australia was in-

vestigating the case of a woman who, after being deported back to China, was forced to undergo an abortion ten days before the birth was due. In a notorious case in 1989, two Catholic villages were raided and devastated and their residents tortured and jailed for violating population-control policies.

Beijing controls the five "authorized" religions (Protestantism, Catholicism, Buddhism, Islam, and Taoism) by the RAB, which is controlled by the United Front Work Department, which is itself controlled by the Central Committee of the Communist Party. In turn, Party officials by law must be atheists. The RAB registers and controls all religious groups through the Three-Self Patriotic movement and the China Christian Council for Protestants, the Catholic Patriotic Association and Bishops Conference for Catholics, and similar patriotic associations for Buddhists, Muslims, and Taoists.

The heightened crackdown may stem from frustration and political insecurity as authorities observe the astonishing revival of religion throughout China, particularly through unsanctioned groups. Along with the current crackdown, China's government pushes an aggressive public-relations campaign to convince the West that there is no religious persecution in China, that whatever incidents of repression occur are either the unauthorized acts of "overzealous cadres" or else necessary measures against dangerous criminals, cultists, and practitioners of "abnormal" religious activities.

Since the end of the Cultural Revolution, China's Christian churches, registered and underground, Catholic and Protestant, have been experiencing explosive growth. Registered Catholics number five million, and, according to the Vatican, unregistered about seven.

Thirteen million Protestants are registered with the government, while unregistered Protestants may number more than fifty million, in house churches, so named because services are held in houses.

After issuing decrees 144 and 145 in 1994, government authorities attempted to induce registration by providing incentives—such as making Bibles available—and by forcing house churches to close. In July 1995, Ye Xiaowen was appointed to direct the RAB, and the government began its "Strike Hard" campaign against unregistered churches.

In an effort to undermine all influence of the Roman Catholic Church within the Patriotic Catholic Church, the Chinese Communist Party Central Committee reportedly issued a sixteen-page document dated August 16, 1999, calling on authorities to tighten control of the official church and "eliminate the underground Church if [it] does not bend to total government control." The document endorses the use of harsh treatment for those who lead "illegal" activities.

Registration requires that churches desist from preaching to minors and speaking about the Second Coming of Christ, the gifts of the Spirit, the story of Creation in Genesis, certain sections of the Catholic Catechism, and the evils of abortion. For Catholics, registration also means severing ties to the Vatican; submitting to bishops appointed by the communist government, not the Pope; and rejecting the spiritual authority of the Pope. The "Patriotic" Protestant churches have to be organized in the same undifferentiated church body.

China has more Christian prisoners and detainees than any other country in the world. Arrests increase around Christian feast days and before national events. Protestants leaders have been arrested and tortured for holding prayer meetings, preaching, and distributing Bibles without state approval. Roman Catholic priests and bishops are currently imprisoned or under house arrest for celebrating Mass and administering the sacraments without official authorization. Three years of "reeducation" in labor camps is the norm for such prisoners. Like political and other prisoners, Christian prisoners are held in deplorable conditions, with many forced to work as veritable slaves in labor camps.

Protestant Pastor Peter Xu (Yongze), a leader of the large evangelical "New Birth" house-church network, was sentenced in 1997 to a Henan penal colony for being a "heretic," "cultist," and "disturbing public order." Catholic Bishop James Su Zhimin was arrested in Hebei in October 1997, after issuing an appeal to authorities for greater religious freedom for Roman Catholics, and has not been seen since. Protestant Philip Xu, a former resident of California, was sentenced to a labor camp in Jiangsu in 1997, without a trial, for teaching the Bible. Bishop An Shuxin, one of ten Catholic bishops under detention, house arrest, or restriction, is imprisoned for leading the pilgrimage to the Marian shrine in Donglu. Zheng Yunsu, head of the large Jesus Family in Shandong, is serving a twelve-year sentence at the Shengjian Motorcycle Factory Labor Camp for "disturbing the peace," and his sons were sent to labor camp for appealing on his behalf.

Prominent Protestant pastor Zhang Ronglian and five others along with millions of followers were accused by authorities of leading superstitious "cults," a criminal offense that could bring the death sentence. They were among thirty-one Christian leaders arrested in August 1999, twenty-five of whom were released after paying fines of hundreds of dollars. In 1998, Zhang gave an unprecedented petition to two American journalists, appealing for the release of Christian prisoners, an end to attacks on churches, and a dialogue with authorities.

Underground Christians report brutal beatings that have resulted in paralysis, coma, and even death in some cases. By late 1998, the trend seemed to be worsening. According to credible reports, three evangelicals and two Catholic priests have been beaten to death by police since 1996 because of independent religious activities. Xiuju, a thirty-six-year-old Protestant woman, was beaten to death by police during an arrest for underground Christian activities in Henan on May 26, 1996. The Rev. Yan Weiping, a thirty-three-year-old administrator of the Catholic diocese of Yixian, Hebei, was arrested while offering Mass in Beijing in May 1999 and found dead on the street a few hours later. In an alarming development, as reported by the government's Xinhua News Agency on October 14, 1999, the Rev. Liu Jiaguo, a prominent Protestant house-church leader, was executed by firing squad in Xiangtan City, Hunan province, on what Chinese Christians maintain are false charges.

Police beatings during arrest and torture to exact confessions also seem to be rising. Underground Catholic seminarian Wang Qing was arrested in Hebei province in May 1999 and tortured for three days, being suspended by his wrists, beaten, and force-fed with contaminated liquids that caused severe injury and illness. Catholic priest, the Rev. Peter Hu Duo, suffered broken legs in police beatings in Hebei on December 20, 1998, shortly after being released from labor camp. On December 24, 1998, in Liangzhuang village, Xushui County, a masked mob set fire to a prayer meeting place and blindfolded and beat with electric batons and

other devices three Catholic lay leaders, who then required hospitalization. Around the same time, a twelve-year-old girl who told interrogators she became a liturgy lector was beaten so badly she also had to be hospitalized. In November 1998, Cheng Meiying, a Protestant woman from Henan, suffered brain damage in beatings by police. Throughout 1999, the government arrested many more Christians, particularly when it was concerned about Falun Gong (see below).

Bibles and other religious literature can be printed only with government permission and legally obtained through government-approved sources. More than eighteen million Bibles are in print, and the demand for more is large. The government bans the baptism of children, forbids evangelizing them, and bars religious schools for children. Seminaries and schools for theological training exist but are tightly controlled: students must be considered "politically reliable" by Chinese authorities. Some are permitted by the government to study in seminaries abroad. There is an acute shortage of clergy and trained religious leaders.

There are several cases of churches and clergy being barred from registering for unstated, but presumably political, reasons. A 1997 directive from the Communist Party in Tong Xiang states, without explanation, that the Protestant church Wu Tong Ba-zi-qiao will not be allowed to register and "will not be protected by law." In one widely publicized case "Patriotic" Pastor Yang Yudong from Guangwashi Church in Beijing was forcibly dragged from his pulpit on December 4, 1994, by riot police for deviating from the party line.

In many areas the boundaries between registered and underground churches are blurred, as members and even leaders move back and forth.

There are priests and bishops in the Patriotic Catholic Church who are also recognized by the Vatican, and some of the official Protestant churches cooperate with underground Christians. On December 10, 1999, the Pope wrote a reconciliatory letter to the Catholic Patriotic Association calling the "Shepherds and faithful of mainland China who cannot yet set forth in a full and visible way, their communion with this Apostolic See."

Reports of persecution of practitioners of Buddhism and Taoism are more scarce, perhaps because these groups' emphasis on escape from worldly suffering are viewed as less threatening by state authorities. Perhaps many Chinese practice some form of syncratic religion. The government estimates there are slightly more than one hundred million Buddhists, but followers claim much higher numbers because many do not participate in public religious activities. Their public worship has been restricted, their leaders must be government approved, and thousands of unregistered shrines have been demolished or otherwise closed by the state during the 1990s.

Falun Gong, founded in 1992 by Li Hongzhi, now in exile in New York, is similar to the increasing number of groups in China inspired by Buddhism and Taoism and mixed with beliefs and practices from the syncretistic world of Asian religions. It claims more than seventy-five million adherents in China, including many Communist Party members. Falun Gong has the hallmarks of a religious group, with a philosophy of life and death, a moral code, and a central treatise, the Zhuan Falun. Its leadership may deny that Falun Gong is a religion because it is not one of the five state-sanctioned religious groups, and followers would be liable for punishment were they to claim it as such.

In April 1999, more than ten thousand practitioners staged a silent sit-in outside the red-walled Chinese leadership compound in Beijing and requested state approval. The protest shocked China's rulers, and in July they banned the group, destroyed two million of its manuals, and issued an international appeal for Li's arrest, charging him with the deaths of more than seven hundred followers and "disturbing public order." According to Associated Press reports, the Chinese government plans to prosecute ten publishers of books and literature on Falun Gong, as well. In September 1999, China's Health Ministry newspaper published further restrictions, banning from "important public places" the widely practiced slow-motion exercises called qigong; and, in October 1999, the legislature passed a law, directed at Falun Gong, banning "heretical cults." The state arrested and beat thousands more who defied the ban throughout the fall of 1999. Amnesty International estimates that up to thirty-five thousand Falun Gong members were arrested in the latter part of 1999. Several members were given lengthy sentences of up to eighteen years in prison, and seven have died from abuse in custody.

Reliable outside sources estimate that Muslims number forty million, though Chinese government sources report only eighteen million. About eight million Muslims from the Uigur and Kazak ethnic groups are concentrated in Western China in the Xinjiang Uighur Autonomous Region (East Turkestan), which was conquered by the Qing dynasty in the nineteenth century.

In Xinjiang, religion is culturally important and plays the greatest political role. The Chinese government has used vast areas of Xinjiang as a base for conducting nuclear and missile testing, among other things. The Cultural

Revolution caused the same brutal extinction of public worship and non-Maoist culture as elsewhere in China. In addition, Beijing has encouraged the influx of the dominant Han ethnic group into the area. All these factors have led to growing discontent, particularly among the Uighurs.

Both Islam and pan-Islamic links with the rest of Central Asia have been reestablished among the Uighurs in recent years. With the establishment of independent states in Central Asia following the demise of the Soviet Union, the government fears an independence movement in Xinjiang and has responded with severe oppression. This has given further impetus to the formation of clandestine nationalist opposition groups, some of which have resorted to violence and bombing attacks directed against the government.

As with the other religions, the government restricts the building of mosques, the training and appointment of religious leaders, and the content of sermons. Minors are barred from attending mosque services and from receiving religious education, and those who travel abroad for study without state approval are liable to lose their social benefits, like health care and public

education, when they return. These controls were tightened after a series of violent incidents in Xinjiang in 1997.

There are informants and spies who infiltrate mosque congregations as well as the delegations making hajj (pilgrimage) to Mecca. Some Muslims have been arrested and tortured for having challenged the government-appointed mullahs' interpretation of Islamic teaching. Uighurs have attested that government officials make attempts to undermine Muslim piety and traditions by pressuring them to drink alcohol and break fasts during the holy month of Ramadan. Muslims reportedly have been fired from government posts for praying, and many are afraid to be seen praying publicly for fear of losing their jobs.

A harsh crackdown on suspected Uighur "separatists" and "religious extremists" has been underway in Xinjiang since 1996. Authorities repress any activities suspected of supporting the separatist movement, including peaceful religious gatherings. In April 1999, Amnesty International reported that at least 210 people, mostly Uigurs, had been sentenced to death over the previous two years and that reports of police torture to force confessions was commonplace.

China-Tibet

Population	4.6 million*
Tibetan Buddhist	97%
Muslim	1%
Bon	1%
Other	1%
Religious Freedom Rating	7

*This figure from China's 1990 census includes Tibetans living in the Tibet Autonomous Region (TAR) and in areas of Eastern Tibet that, beginning in 1950, were

incorporated into the Chinese provinces of Sichuan, Qinghai, Gansu, and Yunnan. Independent observers estimate that there are at least six million Tibetans under Chinese rule.

Background

Prior to the Chinese invasion in 1949, Tibet had been a sovereign state for the better part of two thousand years, coming under modest foreign influence only during brief periods in the thirteenth and eighteenth centuries. China invaded Tibet with one hundred thousand troops in late 1949 and, in 1951, formally annexed the country. In 1959, popular uprisings against Chinese rule culminated in mass pro-independence uprisings in Lhasa, the capital. Over the next several months, China crushed the uprisings, killing an estimated eighty-seven thousand Tibetans in the Lhasa region alone. The Tibetan spiritual and temporal leader, the fourteenth Dalai Lama, Tenzin Gyatso, fled to Dharamsala, India, with eighty thousand supporters. In 1960, the International Commission of Jurists called the Chinese occupation genocidal and ruled that, prior to the 1949 invasion, Tibet had possessed all the attributes of statehood as defined under international law. In 1965, China created a Tibet Autonomous Region encompassing only half the territory of preinvasion Tibet. The rest of Tibet had, since 1950, been incorporated into four southwestern Chinese provinces.

During 1998, authorities strengthened their already harsh campaign to erode support among Tibetans for the Dalai Lama and his exile government and for independence from China. In November, the Tibet Information Network (TIN) reported that authorities were now searching the homes of Tibetan officials in Lhasa for shrines and religious objects and had renewed a requirement for Tibetan members of the Chinese Communist Party to withdraw their children from exile schools in India.

Tibetans lack the right to self-determination and cannot change their government democratically. In a 1997 report, the International Commission of Jurists called for a United Nations supervised referendum on self-determination. China appoints compliant Tibetan officials to some largely ceremonial posts to provide a veneer of self-rule but in reality controls all major policy decisions and sharply restricts basic rights and liberties. In 1997, TIN reported that only 44 percent of regional or higher-level government department heads are Tibetan, and sixty-two of seventy-two county-level deputy heads are Chinese, who wield actual power behind Tibetan figureheads. Chinese officials also dominate the military and police.

Arrests of political dissidents and torture in prisons have increased since July 1994, when the Chinese government decided to tighten political control over the region. In 1997, the Dharamsala-based Tibetan Center for Human Rights and Democracy said there were 1,216 known Tibetan political prisoners. In 1997, the Boston-based Physicians for Human Rights reported that of 258 Tibetan refugees surveyed in Dharamsala in 1996, 15 percent said they had been tortured in Tibet, including 94 percent of those who had been detained for political activities. Security forces routinely rape imprisoned nuns. Political prisoners are reportedly subjected to forced labor.

Although Beijing's draconian family-planning policy ostensibly does not extend to Tibetans and other minorities, the one-child rule is generally enforced in Tibet. Beijing's Sinification policy includes granting employment, education, healthcare, and housing incentives to lure ethnic Chinese into migrating to Tibet. This has altered the demographic composition of the region. Beijing's attempts to indoctrinate Tibetan primary and middle-school students include daily ceremonies to raise the Chinese flag and sing the Chinese national anthem. Schools and universities are increasingly using Mandarin as well as Tibetan as the language of instruction. Freedom House's 1998–99 *Freedom in the World* rates Tibet a seven in political rights and civil liberties.

Religious Freedom

Prior to the arrival of Buddhism from India in the mid-eighth century, a native animist religion named "Bon" dominated Tibet's spiritual landscape. Elements of this were incorporated into the newly arrived Buddhism. This unique brand of Buddhism was woven through the political, social, and practically all other dimensions of Tibetan life and thrived until the Chinese Communist invasion in 1949. Preinvasion Tibet's central institutions were Buddhist monasteries, wherein hundreds of thousands of monks and nuns studied curriculum designed to produce an enlightened, skillful, and ethical person. This stress on education and its opposition to basic tenets of Maoist Marxism made these institutions primary targets for eradication by the Chinese Communist state.

The position of the Chinese government in relation to Tibetan Buddhism has followed three semi-distinct phases, though each has been based on Mao's famous statement made to the Dalai Lama in 1953 that "religion is poison." The post-invasion Seventeen Point Agreement (drafted by China and accepted under duress by the Tibetan government) included respect for the religious beliefs of Tibetans and the protection of monasteries. However, the Chinese government did not consider these provisions applicable to Tibetan areas outside central Tibet. Consequently, in eastern Tibet in the early 1950s, monastic Buddhism was attacked and Tibetan monks were subjected to "strug-

gle sessions," torture, and imprisonment. In mid-1999, China, with the aid of a World Bank loan, was planning to introduce fifty-eight thousand ethnic Chinese to the Tibetan areas of Qinghai.

The flight of the Dalai Lama in 1959 eliminated the last obstacle to complete Chinese control of Tibet. According to Chinese census figures, the clerical population of central Tibet dropped from an estimated 9.5 percent in 1958 to 1.44 percent by 1960. Monasteries and temples, the repositories of Tibetan wealth and culture, were stripped of articles of value, including religious icons and sacred texts. The Legal Inquiry Committee to the International Commission of Jurists concluded "that acts of genocide had been committed in Tibet in an attempt to destroy the Tibetans as a religious group." During the Cultural Revolution the destruction of almost all of Tibet's remaining monasteries was completed. Virtually all religious practice was banned. Monks and nuns were forced to copulate in public and made to marry. Others were killed or put in labor camps.

In 1979, post-Mao liberalization heralded a second phase. Tibetans were allowed to devote a portion of their regained economic assets to the revival and support of religion. The restoration of monasteries was allowed, as was the ordination of monks and nuns. For example, the Jokhang Temple in the heart of Lhasa was reopened, and the iron fence that prevented Tibetans from prostrating was removed.

In the mid-1980s, in its current phase, China again moved to restrict religious freedom. Democratic Management Committees (DMCs), first initiated in Tibet in 1959 to diminish the role of abbots within monasteries, came under increasing government control. Monks were subjected to indoctrination on patriotism and the Chinese version of Tibetan history. Admission of new monks was restricted. The 1994 Third Work Forum on Tibet identified the influence of the Dalai Lama as the "root of Tibet's instability," and new policies were aimed at undercutting his spiritual and political authority. Residents of monasteries and nunneries have been required to study official tracts, memorize and recite affirmations of Chinese policy, denounce the Dalai Lama, declare support for China-appointed Panchen Lama, accept that Tibet has long been an "inalienable part of the motherland," and promise to oppose any views to the contrary.

On January 8, 1999, a meeting of the propaganda department of the Chinese Communist Party in Lhasa decreed that atheism is necessary to promote economic development in the region and to assist the struggle against the influence of the Dalai Lama. The launch of this "atheism campaign" was announced on the same day China reaffirmed a policy of protecting religious freedom during a meeting between Ye Xiaowen, director of China's State Administration of Religious Affairs, and Robert Seiple, current ambassador at large for International Religious Freedom. Under Chinese law, officials who illegally deprive a citizen of freedom of religion are subjected to up to two years imprisonment. To date no officials have been prosecuted in Tibet under this clause.

The UN High Commissioner for Refugees reports that half of the three thousand escapees from Tibet each year are monks or nuns fleeing harsh restrictions on religious freedom, or who have been forbidden to return to their monasteries, or who have been imprisoned for political activities. In January 1998, the Rakhor Nunnery, the oldest in Tibet, was destroyed after forced "patriotic education," started in July 1997, was deemed unsuccessful. Youning Monastery forcibly had to retire forty-nine monks older than sixty in October 1998. The expulsion of senior monks is extremely rare since their importance to the religious tradition is immense.

Most Tibetan political prisoners are religious workers. Current reports indicate that monks and nuns from 131 religious institutions are behind bars. Nuns make up 80 percent of all female prisoners, and monks represent 65 percent of all male prisoners. Torture is routine: a female prisoner in Drapchi (TAR Prison #1) has a one in twenty chance of not surviving the consequences of imprisonment. Average sentences are increasing in length, and prison officials are lengthening periods of solitary confinement to isolate "unreformed" political prisoners. The mortality rate of female prisoners was pushed up sharply by the deaths of six nuns—Khedron Yonten, Tashi Lhamo, Dekyi Yangzom, Lobsang Wangmo, Choekyi Wangmo, and Ngawang Choekyi—after prisoner demonstrations in Drapchi prison in May 1998.

The most popular acts of political protest are demonstrating, putting up posters, and distributing leaflets. Other common reasons for detention include: shouting or writing slogans, possessing even a small rudimentary image of a Tibetan national flag; possessing photographs, videocassettes, or literature pertaining to the Dalai Lama; or failing to declare support for official positions.

The Chinese government's interference in 1995 in the selection of the Panchen Lama, the second-most prominent figure to the Dalai Lama within Tibetan Buddhism, has been a source of serious discontent amongst Tibetans. After the Dalai Lama, according to religious tradition, announced his recognition of the Panchen Lama's reincarnation, the Chinese government swiftly denounced it. The six-year-old child, Gedhun Choekyi Nyima, along with his family and teachers, was arrested and a campaign was launched to denounce the Dalai Lama for making his announcement without official Chinese government sanction. The Chinese government then officially announced and installed their own candidate as Panchen Lama. Gedhun Choekyi Nyima and his family remain in government custody, and in spite of numerous high-level international appeals, his whereabouts and well-being remain closely guarded state secrets.

Colombia

Population	**38.6 million**
Catholic	**93%**
Protestant	**4%**
Tribal	**0.5%**
Muslim	**0.2%**
Baha'i	**0.1%**
Jewish	**0.1%**
Nonreligious/Other (Mormon,	
Orthodox, Jehovah's Witness)	**2.1%**
Religious Freedom Rating	**4**

Background

After independence from Spain in 1819 and a long federation with what are now Venezuela, Ecuador, and Panama, the Republic of Colombia was established in 1886. Politics have since been dominated by the Liberal and Conservative parties, led largely by the country's traditional elite. Under Liberal president Cesar Gaviria from 1990 to 1994, Colombia approved a new constitution that limits presidents to a single four-year term and provides for an elected bicameral Congress.

Modern Colombia has been marked by the corrupt machine politics of the Liberals and Conservatives, left-wing guerrilla insurgencies, right-wing paramilitary violence, the emergence of vicious drug cartels, and gross human rights violations committed by all sides.

Liberal Ernesto Samper, a former economic development minister, won the presidency with 50.4 percent of the vote in 1994. With strong U.S. encouragement, Samper presided over the dismantling of the Cali drug cartel, but there is evidence that the cartel gave six million dollars to Samper's campaign. In 1996, Samper was charged with fraud and other offenses, but the Liberal-dominated Chamber of Representatives acquitted him. In the 1998 election Andres Pastrana won the presidency in an impressive victory over the Liberal Party.

After three decades of fighting, guerrillas have pushed their insurgency ever closer to the major cities and are now believed to control more than 40 percent of the country. In November, in an effort of peace, Pastrana oversaw the withdrawal by a dispirited military from a demilitarized zone of five southern districts.

Citizens can change their government through elections. The 1991 constitution provides for broad participation including two reserved seats in congress for the small Indian minority. Political violence and a generalized belief that corruption renders elections meaningless have helped to limit voter participation. In 1998, President

Pastrana proposed broad reform to combat corruption. He offered the guerrillas a pardon and guarantees for post-peace participation in legal political activities.

The justice system remains slow and compromised by corruption and extortion and can treat drug traffickers lightly. The country's national police, once very corrupt, have been reorganized and are now respected. Constitutional rights regarding free expression and the freedom to organize political parties, civic groups, and labor unions are severely restricted by political and drug-related violence and by the government's weakness. Political violence in Colombia continues to take more lives than in any other country in the hemisphere. In the past decade an estimated thirty-five thousand have died, and one million have been displaced from their homes. More than 90 percent of violent crimes are never solved. Prison conditions are awful.

Human rights violations have soared to unprecedented highs, with atrocities being committed by all sides in the conflict. Human rights workers in Colombia are frequently murdered. Paramilitary groups have grown exponentially. In May 1998, a military intelligence unit was disbanded after credible reports tied it to support for death squads. In 1998, left-wing guerrillas used as many as four hundred villagers as human shields against aerial bombardment. Perpetrators of political violence operate with a high degree of impunity.

Journalists are frequently the victims of political and revenge violence. There is also "social cleansing," the elimination of drug addicts, street children, and other marginal citizens. Indigenous groups suffer from attacks on their land. Murders of trade union activists continued as Colombia remained the most dangerous country in

the world for organized labor. Freedom House's 1998–99 *Freedom in the World* rates Colombia a four in civil liberties and a three in political rights; the latter upward trend is an improvement from a four the previous year due to the election of an apparently uncorrupted president in free and fair elections.

Religious Freedom

For much of its troubled history, Colombia recognized the Catholic Church as the official national religion and discriminated against other beliefs. Between 1948 and 1960, evangelical Protestants could be subject to the destruction of their church buildings, robbery, rape, and murder. The Church in Colombia remains one of the most conservative in Latin America and claims a high percentage of the people as members, more than 93 percent. However, since the 1991 adoption of a new constitution, a large measure of religious liberty exists in Colombia in both theory and practice. Protestantism has grown more slowly in Colombia than in other Latin countries and currently includes about 4 percent of Colombians.

Official government policies toward all religions are, with few exceptions, evenhanded. With the exceptions noted below, in terms of the law in Colombia, individuals have the right to freedom of religion and belief if they respect public order and morality. There is freedom to propagate one's faith, freedom of worship, and freedom to train and appoint clergy. Religious bodies have rights to self-govern religious education, to carry out charitable activities, to own and acquire property, and to maintain social institutions. They can produce, import, and distribute literature, receive donations, and have contact with coreligionists domestically and overseas. Individuals can adopt, change, or leave a religion freely, with no change of civil status. Hence, there are no specific limits on religious freedom per se.

Religious education is usually handled sensitively by state schools. Official exceptions to religious freedom are generally when religion affects the political structure, especially concerning military service. A Mennonite seminary was ordered to close in 1997, primarily, it appears, because the government wished to discourage the pacifism of the church and avoid giving exemptions from military service for the dozens of men enrolled as students. Jehovah's Witnesses, too, have experienced some conflicts with the government because of their commitment to absolute pacifism. Though military rules officially allow pacifists to perform alternative service, the Jehovah's Witnesses claim that they have been denied the opportunity to do so. In Colombia's complicated political climate, people regard pacifism or neutrality in various quarters as partisan stances.

However, religious freedom is not merely the freedom to carry out certain narrowly prescribed religious activities but is also the freedom to live in the social and political world according to one's beliefs. Hence, religious freedom is necessarily limited when the society, itself, is fragmented, repressive, or in turmoil. In Colombia, though there is no targeting of religion per se, religious freedom is restricted by the corruption, intimidation, and repression that affect all human rights.

Various forms of religious repression exist, however, as the result of Colombia's social and political turmoil. As elsewhere, where Marxist guerrilla groups seeking revolution continue in Latin America, religious workers involved in human rights activities are subject to intimidation both by the government and by guerrillas. In 1996, a Jesuit priest, Sergio Restrepo, was assassinated on the steps of his parish church. In 1997, three workers at the Jesuit Center for Research and Popular Education were murdered. On May 19, 1998, gunmen killed two more workers in a Jesuit-run office. In November in the northeast, a Catholic priest and a human rights worker were killed, and in a separate incident a Catholic missionary was kidnapped. No suspects have been identified in these attacks, but it is highly likely from such evidence as exists that the attackers were government agents or associated paramilitaries.

In 1997, the pastor of the country's largest Protestant church, Cesar Castellano, and his wife were machine-gunned to death by terrorists. In the first half of 1999, there were reports twenty-five Protestant pastors were killed and up to three hundred Protestant churches closed. Church leader Pedro Leon Camacho was murdered by rebels of the "Popular Liberation Army" (EPL) on May 18, 1999. On May 30, the "Army of National Liberation" (ELN) abducted dozens of churchgoers from a mass in Cali. Some abductees were not released until December. ELN rebels kidnapped Roman Catholic Archbishop Jose de Jesus Quintero on August 15, 1999, but he was released thirty-five days later. Other murders and kidnapping of priests occurred in November. So-called Peasant Defense Groups (ACCUs) and Rural Watch Cooperatives (CONVIVIRs), though seemingly popular organizations, are in fact often organized by paramilitaries or large landowners against suspected insurgents.

Given these circumstances, it is not surprising that insurgents demanding they declare their political allegiance for or against the current government have also threatened churches in rural areas of Colombia. In 1998, even attempts by the community of San Jose de Apartado to remain neutral among the various political factions resulted in a FARC reprisal. Foreign missionaries, too, have been targeted for kidnappings, because of both their religious views and their nationalities. The Revolutionary Armed Forces of Colombia (FARC), perhaps the most powerful guerrilla movement, kidnapped three people from the New Tribes Mission in 1994. Their whereabouts are still unknown. In order to deter further acts, U.S. policy does not allow negotiations with kidnappers or ransom payments, though the U.S. government is

working to free the three detainees through third parties. FARC and the ELN, which is led by the Spanish priest Manuel Perez, are thought to be holding about two hundred prisoners total; government forces are probably responsible for a similar number of illegal detainees.

Jews in Colombia (a small community of about 5,000) practice their religion freely and have developed an extensive network of schools and organizations. They participate strongly in the nation's professional, business, and intellectual life. Anti-Semitism is not a serious social problem in Colombia.

Cuba

Population	11.2 million
Catholic	40%
Protestant	10%
Santeria	2–10%
Other (Jewish, Orthodox, Jehovah's Witness)	1%
None	40%
Religious Freedom Rating	6

Background

Cuba achieved independence from Spain in 1898 as a result of the Spanish-American War. The Republic of Cuba was established in 1902 but was under U.S. tutelage under the Platt Amendment until 1934. In 1959, Fidel Castro overthrew the dictatorship of Fulgencio Batista, who had ruled for eighteen of the previous twenty-five years. Since then, Castro has transformed Cuba into a one-party police state. Communist structures were institutionalized by the 1976 constitution. The constitution provides for a National Assembly that, in theory, designates a Council of State that appoints a Council

of Ministers in consultation with its president. In reality Castro, as president of the Council of Ministers, chairman of the Council of State, commander in chief of the Revolutionary Armed Forces (FAR), and first secretary of the Communist Party (PCC), controls every lever of power in Cuba. The PCC is the only authorized political party, and it controls all governmental entities.

Since the collapse of the Soviet Union and its subsidies, Castro has sought Western foreign investment. A U.S. embargo has been in effect since 1960. The government claims that the economy has rebounded in the past three years, but the "special period" austerity programs remain in place. The legalization of the dollar in 1993 has heightened social tensions, with a minority having access to dollars from abroad emerging as a new moneyed class.

Neither the Fifth Congress of the PCC in 1997, at which one-party rule was reaffirmed, nor the one-party national elections held in 1998 provided any surprises. At the congress, Castro named as successor his brother, Vice President Raul Castro.

The number of dissidents confirmed to be imprisoned has dropped from 1,320 in 1996 to 381 in June 1998. Part of the decline was due to the release of 140 of 300 prisoners whose freedom was sought by Pope John Paul II. At year's end, however, four top opposition leaders faced sedition charges after being arrested in July 1997.

Cubans cannot change their government through democratic means. Opposition and dissident groups are forbidden to present their own candidates. All political and civic organization outside the PCC is illegal. Political dissent, spoken or written, is a punishable offense. There are sentences, frequently of years of imprisonment, for seemingly minor infractions, even possession of a fax machine or a photocopier. Although there has been a slight relaxation of strictures on cultural life, the educational and judicial systems, labor unions, professional organizations, and all media remain state controlled. A small, courageous group of human rights activists and dissident journalists and activity by the Catholic Church are the only glimmer of a civil society.

The executive branch controls the judiciary. There is continued evidence of torture and killings in prison and psychiatric institutions, where some dissidents arrested are held. Since 1990, the International Committee of the Red Cross has been denied access to prisoners. Local human rights activists report that more than one hundred prisons and prison camps hold between sixty thousand and one hundred thousand prisoners of all categories. Cuba has one of the highest per capita rates of imprisonment for political offenses of any country in

the world, with vague charges such as "disseminating enemy propaganda" or "dangerousness." Groups that exist apart from the state are labeled "counterrevolutionary criminals" and are subject to systematic repression.

The press in Cuba is the object of a targeted campaign by the government. Independent journalists, particularly those associated with five small news agencies, have fallen victim to endless repression. Foreign news agencies must also hire local reporters only through government offices. On a more positive note, in November the government announced that, after twenty-nine years, the Associated Press would reopen its bureau in Havana. Freedom of movement and the right to choose one's residence, education, or job are severely restricted. Attempting to leave the island without permission is a punishable offense. In the post-Soviet era, the right of Cubans to own private property and operate joint ventures with foreigners and non-Cuban businesses has been recognized. In practice, those who do not belong to the Cuban Communist Party have few rights. Freedom House's 1998–99 *Freedom in the World* rates Cuba a seven in political rights and civil liberties, with a slight upward trend due to increased freedom and the release of some political prisoners.

Religious Freedom

Since the 1959 revolution, the communist government of Cuba under Fidel Castro has engaged in systematic repression of religion. Pre-Columbian empires imposed religious uniformity to bolster political power, as did the Spaniards in many places after their arrival. But no American regime before revolutionary Cuba has so thoroughly opposed religion per se. Recent concessions by the regime, under duress, have not basically altered that pattern.

The current Cuban constitution formally allows freedom of religion and purports to treat all religions equally. However, these strictures are not followed, and its clauses mask widespread official and unofficial discrimination against believers and limitations on religious exercise. For many years, active believers were both openly and subtly threatened about the consequences of continued practice. Some were simply arrested and given long prison sentences as counterrevolutionaries. Others were dismissed from government posts and forced to take menial jobs. Still others were—and still are—denied access to the more prestigious educational institutions that are the gateway to employment in the entirely state-owned economy. The few exceptions prove the rule.

The regime claims that religion was never very strong on the island and that it largely functioned as a prop for exploitative elites. However, nominal Catholics probably still constitute about 40 percent of the population, though only 2 percent attend Mass. Protestantism is growing and may now claim 10 percent of the Cuban population. The government likes to point to Santeria, a combination of African, indigenous, and Catholic practices that poses few challenges to the regime, as the most widespread form of spirituality on the island. However, after decades of control, it is difficult to determine the religious makeup. Castro himself was educated by the Marxists and Jesuits, and he and his brother Raul were saved from execution by the intervention of Bishop Enrique Perez Serrantes, a family friend, when they were tried by the Batista regime for the 1953 attack on the Moncada Barracks.

From before the triumph of the revolution on January 1, 1959 to early in the 1960s, when the move to communism became apparent, many in the churches supported the apparently ideologically uncommitted revolutionaries. Many priests, supported by bishops, served as chaplains to the revolutionaries. But Catholic concern for social justice did not extend to the embrace of Marxism, whose basic atheism conflicted with the Church. In the early days of the revolution, most Christians regarded Castro as an idealist. The divide was Fidel's December 1960 declaration, "To be anti-Communist is tantamount to being anti-revolutionary." Earlier he had explored the possibility of a National Church, independent from Rome, on the Communist Chinese model.

After the failed U.S.-supported Bay of Pigs invasion in April 1961, the regime immediately arrested many Catholic laymen, priests, and all the bishops. The next month, all private religious schools, Catholic and Protestant, were "nationalized." That fall, more than a hundred priests were expelled, public religious observances were banned, and discrimination against believers began in earnest. The 1976 constitution declared Cuba an officially atheist state. Building permits for churches were withheld, repairs were unauthorized, and activities strictly regulated. Even so, churches remained the only partly independent sector: politics, the press, labor, education, and almost the entire economy were in party hands. The government has been careful not to make martyrs; its self-proclaimed goal has been to create apostates.

In the last decade there has been some slight opening to real freedom of practice. This "special period within socialism," that is, the period in which Cuba no longer receives Soviet subsidies, has made slight accommodation with the churches a necessity.

Christmas was permitted as a legal holiday in 1997 in anticipation of Pope John Paul II's visit in January 1998. (In December 1998, the regime announced it would make that arrangement permanent.) Havana's Cardinal Ortega was allowed to broadcast a message about the pope's pilgrimage to the island over Cuban television and radio. Some church figures now have limited access to the media. Open-air masses have been allowed, and a procession took place in downtown Havana at Eastertime 1998.

These accommodations seem to be tactical necessities in difficult times. Caritas, a Catholic relief organization, has been allowed to import medicines and other materials, but the regime has demanded a large percentage of those imports for its own hospitals and services as the price for the private relief efforts. After the 1998 papal visit, Cuba expelled an American missionary who had been promoting human rights in Santa Clara, a warning to native and other foreign priests that strict limits on the church's social role still exist.

The regime attempted to use the papal pilgrimage to Cuba as a chance to gain international sympathy. Upon the pope's arrival, Castro stressed that Cuban Communism and Roman Catholicism shared a common vision of social justice, regarding liberation theology, a blend of Catholicism and elements of Marxist social analysis, as an ally. The pope distanced himself from this, pointing to other elements in Cuban history, culture, and religion. Though he and the Cuban bishops have long condemned the U.S. embargo, they continue to push for basic human rights. The Rapid Response Battalions, used to squash any expression of dissent, were kept out of sight during the pope's visit, and policemen were or-

dered to patrol without weapons. But the government filmed and kept careful records of all public demonstrations.

Prior to the visit, Catholics and Protestants in Cuba, like elsewhere in Latin America, competed. Except for those Protestant groups that collaborated with the regime, Protestants were stifled like the Catholics but lacked the Catholic Church's more substantial presence, and so existed at the margins of society. However, Protestants joined with Catholics in the public celebrations of the pope's visit, building on the fact that most of the current religious leadership of the island, among them Jaime Ortega, cardinal archbishop of Havana, were among many young Catholics and Protestants who in the 1960s were imprisoned together in the "Military Units to Aid Production" (UMAP), in reality concentration camps.

The 1992 constitutional revisions allowed Christians to become members of the Communist Party, with attendant social and economic benefits. The clause declaring Cuba an atheist state was modified so that Cuba is now officially "secularist." But the constitution still stipulates that no rights may be used "contrary to the Cuban people's decision to build socialism and communism."

Religious groups must be registered, and the Ministry of Justice can refuse registration. The construction of new churches is nominally forbidden. There is no right of conscientious objection. The constitution gives guarantees of religious freedom, freedom of conscience, and freedom to change religion, as well as outlawing discrimination on the basis of religion. Nominally, religious groups can own property for what the government regards as their "legitimate" needs. However, all of these freedoms are subject to government override when it wishes. Nevertheless, even this small opening seems to have led to a sharp increase in religious practice. Religious meetings in homes have been tolerated. There have been tens of thousands of baptisms, many of adults. Religious weddings, confirmations, and first communions have also increased sharply. Catholic and Protestant churches are growing.

The government continued to send mixed signals on religious freedom. In late 1998, it approved the admission of nineteen Catholic priests and twenty-one religious workers. Since then it has been more restrictive, and, in early February 1999, it was reported that the government burned thousands of Bibles imported by Protestants from the United States. However, in May and June it allowed a large series of public evangelical Protestant celebrations to take place throughout the country, with national television coverage. On June 20, a Protestant rally in Havana drew one hundred thousand people, including Castro, and was broadcast live on national television. However, a significant number of evangelical denominations refused to take part, saying it was an event to garner support for the regime. Out of 129 denominations in the Cuban Council of Churches, only forty-nine took part. On some previous occasions the regime has given more latitude to Protestants when it wanted to undercut Catholics. The recent Catholic and Protestant public celebrations, and accompanying media coverage, are major departures from Castro's previous practices. Nevertheless, other restrictions remain in place, and, in October, Osmany Dominguez Borjas, president of Cuba's United Pentecostal Church, was arrested for "convoking" an evangelical gathering in the city.

East Timor

Population	**778,000**
Catholic	**80%**
Other (Muslim, Buddhist,	
Protestant)	**20%**
Religious Freedom Rating	**5**

Background

The Portuguese arrived on Timor around 1520, and in the nineteenth and early twentieth centuries took formal control of the island's eastern half. In 1974, Portugal agreed to hold a referendum on self-determination. In November 1975, the leftist Revolutionary Front for an Independent East Timor (Fretilin) declared an independent republic. Indonesia invaded in December and in 1976 formally annexed East Timor as its twenty-seventh province. By 1979, Indonesian soldiers had killed up to two hundred thousand Timorese. Skirmishes between Indonesian forces and the poorly armed resistance continued.

On November 12, 1991, Indonesian soldiers fired on a peaceful pro-independence march to the Santa Cruz Cemetery in the territorial capital of Dili. Between 150 and 270 civilians were killed. In 1992, ten soldiers were court-martialed and given light prison sentences ranging from eight to eighteen months. In November, Indonesian soldiers captured resistance leader Jose "Xanana" Gusmao. In

1993, in a sham trial, a court sentenced Gusmao to life imprisonment, subsequently reduced to twenty years.

The 1996 award of the Nobel Peace Prize to East Timor Roman Catholic Bishop Carlos Felipe Ximenes Belo and Jose Ramos Jorta, the leading East Timorese exile activist, brought renewed international attention to Indonesian abuses in the territory. During and after the May 1997 Indonesian parliamentary election period, attacks by East Timorese National Liberation Army (*Falintil*) guerrillas on military and civilian targets killed at least nine suspected collaborators and other civilians, as well as thirty-three soldiers, police, and guerrillas. The army responded by arbitrarily detaining and often torturing hundreds of civilians, and there were reports of killings and "disappearances." In August 1998, the Indonesian military said it had completed the withdrawal of all combat troops from East Timor, leaving some five thousand "territorial personnel." Yet by September, residents and church groups were reporting a new combat troop buildup.

The United Nations did not recognize Indonesia's 1976 annexation of East Timor. Suharto's ouster (see profile of Indonesia) left most of the existing Indonesian power structure intact, and civil liberties improvements in East Timor up to mid-1999 were modest. The judiciary was not independent, particularly for trials of dissidents. The trial of Jose "Xanana" Gusmao (see above) fell well short of international standards. While the Habibie government released 120 political prisoners throughout the archipelago, it still held several East Timorese political prisoners. Many were held for peaceful activities. Under Suharto, the army and police committed arbitrary arrests,

detention, torture, crackdowns; soldiers arbitrarily detained and often tortured civilians to extract information. Under Habibie, many of these practices apparently continued.

In October 1998, thousands of East Timorese demonstrated in Dili and Bacau demanding a referendum on independence, acts that would have brought a swift crackdown from security forces only a few months earlier. Yet, overall, authorities continued to restrict freedoms of speech, press, assembly, and association. Jakarta-appointed governor Abilio Soares warned civil servants that they risked being fired if they opposed Indonesia's proposals on granting East Timor autonomy but not independence.

In the spring of 1999, Indonesian President B. J. Habibie called for a referendum on East Timorese independence, which was held on August 30. Ninety-nine percent of those eligible to vote did so, and 78 percent of those opted for independence. In the period leading up to the vote, "militias"—armed and supported by the Indonesian military—attacked pro-independence figures. After the vote they unleashed a campaign of terror. The Indonesian military either stood aside or else actively supported militia violence. In the subsequent carnage, many people were killed and two hundred thousand made refugees. About 75 percent of homes were destroyed, as well as other infrastructure. Many of the two hundred thousand who fled to Indonesia-controlled West Timor continued to be attacked by militias, and most still remain in West Timor. After growing international pressure, the Indonesian government acquiesced in accepting a UN peacekeeping force. On September 18, a 7,500-member force, with a core of 4,500 Australian troops, began to arrive, and the Indonesian military withdrew. In

October, the Indonesian Parliament said it would accept East Timor's independence, as did new Indonesian President Abdurrahman Wahid. At the end of 1999, the territory was under United Nations control, and preparations were underway to create a government.

Freedom House's 1998–99 *Freedom in the World* rated East Timor a seven in political rights and a six in civil liberties, the latter an increase from the previous year due to slight easing of freedom of expression due to Suharto's ouster. Subsequently, East Timor has been in political and social turmoil.

Religious Freedom

Prior to the Indonesian invasion, the majority of the seven hundred thousand East Timorese were animist, with minorities of Catholics (30%), Buddhists, and a small number of Muslims. Even though the Portuguese government favored Catholicism as the state religion, there were never any religious conflicts among the four "religious groups." Now Catholics represent about four-fifths of the population.

East Timor has been widely recognized as one of the world's worst places for human rights abuse. However, there was limited evidence of restrictions on or abuses targeted specifically at religion. The Catholic Church has been active, and there was little evidence of specific restrictions on the other four officially recognized religions: Protestantism, Islam, Hinduism, and Buddhism. However, as in other situations, religion is not an isolated category but is intertwined with other political, social, and national aspirations. Hence, one of the leading political spokespersons was Nobel Prize winner Bishop Belo, the head of the Catholic Church. One priest observed: "The Church in East Timor is regarded as the main obstacle to the in-

tegration policy of the Indonesian government. It is the only organization that still survives in occupied East Timor." Consequently, the Indonesian authorities used religion to create division and unrest.

One major incident was riots in Bacau in June 1996, which were believed to have been provoked by an Indonesian Muslim soldier insulting the Roman Catholic religion. The soldier was reportedly seen placing a desecrated picture of the Virgin Mary on the door of a mosque in Baguia, a subdistrict of Bacau. These riots resulted in the arrest of approximately 165 East Timorese, many injuries, and up to three Timorese killed.

There were other reports of the Indonesian army instigating violence by insulting Catholicism. Their purpose, according to the East Timor Human Rights Committee (ETHRC in Australia), was "to ensure that East Timor remains in turmoil, thereby justifying a policy of repression and the continued high military presence." In 1995, an Indonesian prison official, Zakarias Sake, made derogatory remarks about Catholicism, which provoked riots in Maliana, Dili, and Viqueque. Sake and, subsequently, another prison official, Sanusi Abubakar, were both sentenced to four years imprisonment for insulting another religion. ETHRC maintained, "There has been a pattern for many years of deliberate provocation of so-called 'religious conflicts' in East Timor, which appear to be aimed at presenting unrest in East Timor as primarily a matter of conflict between Christians and Muslims." There were instances of apparently Muslim attacks on the church, but pro-government forces likely also instigated these incidents.

Where religious figures, notably Bishop Belo, have been persecuted, it has been due to the political stance they have taken. Another notable religious figure was Bishop Martinho de Costa Lopes, bishop of Dili from 1977 to 1983. He was an outspoken advocate for human rights and a fierce critic of the Indonesian authorities. In particular, he criticized the forced conscription of fifty thousand men and boys and later denounced the Indonesian army for war crimes. In 1983, he was forced to retire after General Murdani and the Indonesian government persuaded the Papal Pro-Nuncio in Jakarta to advise the pope to request his retirement. The bishop moved to Lisbon and died in 1991.

Bishop Belo has been the head of the East Timor Catholic Church since 1983 and a bishop since 1988. In 1989, he wrote to the pope, the UN secretary-general, and the president of Portugal calling for a referendum on East Timor and for international help for the East Timorese. Two years later he gave sanctuary in his own home to youths escaping from the Santa Cruz massacre. He was reportedly under constant surveillance, and attempts were allegedly made to assassinate him, notably by the Indonesian Special Forces on December 24, 1996.

The Indonesians tried to collaborate with the church in order to influence the Timorese people and gain their trust when, in October 1996, in a rare visit, President Suharto came to the capital, Dili, to inaugurate a giant statue of Christ as a gesture of religious tolerance.

The Indonesian policy of "forced integration" involved the imposition of Bahasa Indonesia as the official language, the banning of Portuguese in schools (including seminaries and church schools), and reeducation in the official Indonesian state ideology of Pancasila (the five principles of one God,

humanitarianism, nationalism, democracy, and social justice). Furthermore, according to the constitution, all citizens were required to register as adhering to one of the official religions: Islam, Protestantism, Catholicism, Hinduism, and Buddhism. One reason the number of animists decreased was that it was literally illegal to be one. The Indonesian policy of immigration to East Timor from the more crowded areas of the Indonesian archipelago also had the effect of introducing a large Islamic element, and, as these newcomers were often given favorable treatment, this created further religious tension.

These conflicts were due to the nature of the Indonesian occupation of East Timor, the resistance movement, and the high-profile role the church played in the resistance movement. The East Timor conflict has been territorial but necessarily has religious consequences. By and large, religious freedom in East Timor was restricted for political and nationalistic reasons. Much of the repression would have happened even if the Timorese were of a different religion, but, since there is a religious difference with the majority of Indonesians, political repression necessarily involved religious repression.

In the slaughter carried out by Indonesian militias following the August 30 vote for independence, there were signs of specifically anti-Christian violence. Bishop Belo, who had downplayed any religious element in the occupation, now spoke of "a planned strategy against the Catholic Church," and of "religious persecution." He was forced to flee the territory on September 7. His home was burned, and priests and nuns were apparently singled out for attack.

After the arrival of UN peacekeeping troops, the bishop returned, and the

Catholic Church and other religious bodies are cooperating with one another and with the administration in the reconstruction of the territory. There are currently no legal or political restrictions on religious freedom within the territory itself. However, since the infrastructure of civil society has been destroyed and perhaps a quarter of the population are still refugees in Indonesia, the practical impediments to religious freedom are still massive.

Egypt

Population	**66 million**
Muslim	**87.5%**
Christian	**12%**
Other	**0.5%**
Religious Freedom Rating	**5**

Background

Egypt gained formal independence from Great Britain in 1922, though the latter only surrendered the Suez Canal Zone in 1956. Colonel Gamel Abdel Nasser became head of state in 1954, after leading a coup that overthrew the monarchy, and ruled until his death in 1970. A constitution adopted in 1971 under Nasser's successor, Anwar al-Sadat, grants full executive powers to the president, who is nominated by the 545-member People's Assembly and elected to a six-year term in a national referendum. Islamic militants assassinated Sadat in 1981 for making peace with Israel. Under his successor, Hosni Mubarak, the ruling National Democratic Party (NDP) continues to dominate a tightly controlled political system. In 1999, Mubarak won a third presidential term with 94 percent approval in a national referendum. Opposition groups boycotted the ballot.

Years of repression by authorities appear to have neutralized the threat of Islamic terrorism. The leaders of the major militant groups, along with thousands of their followers, remain in jail or in exile. More than seventy political prisoners have been executed since 1992 under special military courts set up to handle terrorist offenses. Popular support for militant Islamists has dwindled as their campaign has focused more on violence than on alternative policy. In March 1999, *al-Gama'at al-Islamiya* (the Islamic group) declared a unilateral cease-fire inside and outside Egypt.

Yet threat of unrest remains. While the economy is currently growing at a rate of 5 percent a year, some 10 to 30 percent of the workforce is unemployed or underemployed. There is widespread frustration with a government that is perceived to be corrupt and unresponsive. The Egyptian government has quickened the pace of economic reform prompted by a sharp decline in tourism after the 1998 massacre of tourists in Luxor, declining oil prices, and the Asian financial crisis. It has relaxed its opposition to privatization of public utilities.

Egyptians cannot change their government democratically. Widespread fraud and irregularity characterized parliamentary elections held in 1995. Political violence led to the deaths of 51 people and wounded over 850 more. Elections took place in June 1998 for half of the 264-member Shura Council; the president appoints the other half. The upper house of parliament has no legislative authority; its role is restricted to issuing opinions and reports on topics of its choosing. The landslide victory of the ruling NDP (97 percent of the seats) came as a surprise to no one; opposition leaders called the elections "fraudulent and corrupt." Requests to form political parties are routinely denied by the state-controlled Political Parties Committee (PPC), usually because their platforms are unoriginal.

The militant Islamist battle against the government, now contained mainly in the Assiut and al-Minya provinces, has resulted in more than twelve hundred deaths since 1992. Security forces have been accused of extrajudicial killings of militants during antiterrorist operations. The Emergency Law has been in effect since Sadat's assassination in 1981 and is up for renewal every three years. Its provisions allow for detention of suspects without charge for up to ninety days. By some estimates, twenty-five thousand activists have been jailed or detained since 1992. International human rights groups regularly condemn arbitrary arrest, abuse, and torture of detainees by police, security personnel, and prison guards. It is not uncommon for security forces to arrest friends or family members of suspects.

The Egyptian judiciary enjoys limited independence. The president appoints both the general prosecutor and the head of the Court of Cassation, Egypt's highest court. Under Law 25/1996, the president may refer civilian cases to military courts. There is no appellate process for verdicts by military courts. While convicted members of the terrorist Islamic Group are frequently executed, Muslim brothers have never been sentenced to death, reportedly because of wide popular support.

The Press Law, the Publications Law, the Penal Code, and libel laws all restrict press freedom. Critics of the pres-

ident, members of the government, and foreign heads of state may incur heavy fines or imprisonment for violations. Newspapers published outside Egypt can be distributed only with government permission. The Ministry of Information owns and operates all domestic television production.

The Interior Minister may withhold approval for public demonstrations under the Emergency Law. The Ministry of Social Affairs has broad powers to merge and dissolve nongovernmental organizations. Human rights organizations such as the Egyptian Organization for Human Rights (EOHR) and the Arab Program for Human Rights Activists (APHRA) are frequently subject to harassment by the government. In the spring of 1999, the government introduced legislation to control human rights and other nongovernmental organizations. It would give the government power to control their boards and to dissolve them.

Women face discrimination in many legal and social matters. The 1976 law on labor unions sets numerous restrictions on the formation and operation of unions and the conduct of elections. Article 124 of the Penal Code criminalizes labor strikes. Child labor is a serious problem. Freedom House's 1998–99 *Freedom in the World* rates Egypt a six in political rights and in civil liberties.

Religious Freedom

The majority of Egypt's sixty-six million people are Sunni Muslims. There are about five thousand Shi'ite Muslims, small numbers of other Islamic groups, Baha'i, and a Jewish community now numbering only several hundred. Apart from Muslims, Egypt's largest religious group is Christians, usually referred to as "Copts." Egypt's Christians number between six and ten million, the largest Christian community in the Middle East, of whom over 90 percent are Coptic Orthodox, but also including Greek Orthodox, Catholics, Protestants, and others.

Article 2 of the constitution states that "Islam is the religion of the state. Islamic Jurisprudence [*sharia* law] is the principle source of legislation." Until the nineteenth century, *sharia* was the law of Egypt. Since then more secular rulers have introduced alternative civil laws, partly to facilitate economic relations with the Western world. In 1955, Gamal Abdel-Nasser abolished *sharia* courts except in the area of family law. The 1971 constitution described *sharia* as "*a* principle source of legislation" (emphasis added). However, in 1980, President Anwar Sadat introduced an amendment making *sharia* law "*the* principal source" of Egyptian law (emphasis added). Although the main body of Egyptian law remains civil, the influence of *sharia* law is increasing.

Sharia decrees are not given the full weight of Egyptian law or applied directly. Rather, they are used increasingly as an interpretive mechanism for state law, which then gradually takes on its color. In this process the opinions of Islamic teachers are becoming increasingly influential. One illustration is the case of Dr. Nasr Hamed Abu Zeid, a relatively liberal Muslim and a professor of Islamic studies at Cairo University. A colleague thought Abu Zeid's views were a departure from Islam and that he was, thus, an apostate. While Egypt has no law against apostasy, his accusers used two features of *sharia* in Egypt. One was a ninth-century principle of *sharia* called *hisbah*. Under this principle, any Muslim may pursue a case before the court if he thinks Islam has been harmed, whether or not he is himself personally involved. The other was that family law still came under the ju-

risdiction of *sharia*. Hence, in 1993 they tried to make a case that, as an apostate, he could no longer be married to his Muslim wife and must divorce her. The appeals court declared him an apostate and ordered him to divorce his wife. In August 1996, the Court of Cassation, Egypt's Supreme Court, upheld the Court of Appeals. According to many observers, this would have been impossible thirty years ago.

Extralegal attacks against moderate Muslim intellectuals have escalated in recent years. In 1992, Dr. Farag Fouda was murdered by Islamic extremists after being accused of "apostasy"; in 1994, Naguib Mahfouz, the Arab world's only recipient of the Nobel prize for literature, was stabbed by Islamic extremists; and several other writers have been threatened with death.

In the 1920s, Islamic movements emerged and claimed that departure from a pure Islam was responsible for many of Egypt's social and economic problems. The most important was the *Al-Ikhwan Al Muslimeen*, or the Muslim Brotherhood. The group splintered when some elements called for the use of violence in order to achieve a fundamentalist Islamic state. During the 1970s several of these violent splinter groups, such as *Al-Takfir wa al-Higra*, were formed. In the 1980s and 1990s, other violent groups emerged, such as *Al-Jihad al-Islami* (Islamic Holy War or *Jihad*) and *Al Gama'at al-Islamiya*. Especially since 1992 they have attacked security forces, tourists, and Copts. By mid-1999 it appeared that terrorism was on the wane. However, two Muslim Brothers were convicted for the murder of a Coptic priest on September 2, 1999, and were given the relatively light sentence of seven years. Two other priests were also injured in attacks in late 1999. From 1994 onwards, even peaceful members of the Brotherhood have been arrested because of a ban on religion-based parties. The Brotherhood has not been allowed to rein in elections though some of its members run as independents.

As part of its efforts to combat terrorism and extremism, the government is extending its legal control to all mosques, which by law must be licensed. The government appoints and pays the salaries of the imams officiating in mosques (though not for Christian clergy) and proposes themes for, and monitors, sermons. The Egyptian penal code forbids "any clergy, who delivered in a place of worship, or in a religious gathering, while performing his duty, an insult or criticism of an act by the administration." Of the country's approximately seventy thousand mosques, nearly half remain unlicensed and operate outside the control of government authorities. The government has announced its intention to bring all unauthorized mosques under its control by 2000. The imams of all newly appropriated mosques are required to attend state-run religious indoctrination courses. Female students who wear the traditional *munaqabat,* a veil covering the entire body, have been ordered to adopt standard school dress or be dismissed. Egyptian security officials have been brutal in their suppression of Islamicism and have often detained people only on suspicion.

The Copts, while generally able to practice their religion, are threatened in varying degrees by terrorism from extreme Islamic groups, by the abusive practices of local police and security forces, and by discriminatory and restrictive Egyptian government policies.

The arrest and torture of up to twelve hundred Copts followed the murder of two Copts in El-Kosheh in August 1998, allegedly by five Muslims. Several observers believe that the arrests were intended to portray the murders as within a religion and so preempt any sectarian violence that might otherwise result. The government continued to deny that this has happened and has arrested clergy, including Coptic Bishop Wissa, and human rights groups that have reported it. Following an international outcry, Mubarak remarked that "El-Khosheh has become more famous than the pyramids," and following his visit to the United States in July 1999, an inquiry into the incident was reopened. In October there were reports that this inquiry too had been closed.

Copts are severely underrepresented in government, diplomatic, and academic positions. None have been elected to the legislature, though six have been appointed to the People's Assembly by President Mubarak. The government has given media access to Islamic preachers who have engaged in hate speech against Copts, while denying Copts the chance to reply. This has contributed to an environment that can encourage terrorist violence. In 1999, discriminatory programming diminished.

The government also enforces restrictions on building or repairing churches, restrictions that do not apply to mosques. The requirements for building and repairing churches or church-owned buildings are cumbersome and frequently arbitrary. These now culminate in the requirement that the state president must personally approve all building applications, and the provincial governors must approve all applications for repairs. In recent years the pace of approval for construction and repair has improved, but many churches have still been unable to secure permission. At the end of 1999, President Mubarak dropped the requirement for permission for repairs *within* churches.

Egypt has several educational systems. One is the state-funded *Al-Azhar* school system, which is oriented toward inculcating Islam in its pupils. Apart from this is the regular state school system. Christians and Muslims have their own separate and required religious instruction classes. However, in history, language, and literature classes, Coptic elements are almost entirely absent. In 1999, the government formed a committee of academics to revise the curriculum, and exams have been rescheduled so as to conflict with Christmas.

Vulnerable young Christian women and girls are targeted by some extremist Muslim groups and are pressured to convert to Islam, sometimes with the cooperation of local police. Pastors who have worked with such girls have been threatened and assaulted by extremists. In other incidents, Muslim militants killed ten young Copts in a prayer meeting in a church in Abu-Qurqas. In April 1998, two Coptic farmers were shot dead in Ibshadat. On August 13, 1998, three Copts were killed as they were sitting outside their house in Minya.

On January 2 and 3, 2000, the worst anti-Coptic violence in decades took place in El-Kosheh, a town still simmering from police violence in 1998. In several days of riots, more than one hundred homes and workplaces were destroyed and twenty-two Christians and one Muslim killed. President Mubarak has blamed "foreign elements" for the violence, while more than one hundred people have been charged.

Since 1992, some Islamic terrorist groups have maintained that non-Muslims (Christians and Jews) should be given *dhimmi*, or separate and subordinate status under *sharia* law, and must pay a special tribute to secure their protection. Those who refuse may have their homes or businesses attacked and themselves or their families beaten, maimed, or killed. Some observers claim that thousands of Copts have paid *jizya* in recent years and that dozens of Christians have been killed for failing to pay.

Converts from Islam to Christianity have been imprisoned and tortured by the police. In recent years the security forces have tended not to attack publicly known converts directly but to inform their families, in which cases the families may attack them, often with impunity. While neither the constitution nor the civil and penal codes prohibit proselytizing, some Christians have been arrested on charges of violating article 98(f) of the penal code, which prohibits citizens from ridiculing or insulting "heavenly religions" or inciting sectarian strife.

On July 26, 1999, Mohammed Ibrahim Mahfouz, an alleged cult leader, was sentenced, along with thirteen of his followers, to jail terms of up to five years. Other nonconforming Muslim groups have faced heresy trials before state security courts.

There have been no anti-Semitic acts in recent years directed at the tiny Jewish community. However, anti-Semitism in the Egyptian press is found in both the official government and unofficial press.

Baha'is have resided in Egypt since 1868. Persecution of the Baha'i community began in 1925, when the Supreme Religious Court of Cairo annulled the marriage of a Baha'i and a Muslim woman and declared the Baha'i faith to be a dangerous heresy. Since that time, Baha'is have endured harassment, public slander, loss of property and jobs, and periodic arrest. In 1969, President Nasser dissolved all Baha'i assemblies. All Baha'i properties and assets were confiscated, and Baha'i activities previously conducted by these assemblies were banned. It was officially announced that the restrictive measures were directed only at the Baha'i administrative institutions and their activities and that individuals remained free to believe and practice the Baha'i faith. In practice, however, Baha'is have been imprisoned and harassed on several occasions over the past thirty years. They continue to hold gatherings on a very limited scale and are able to observe Baha'i holy days in small groups. Nasser's ban on Baha'i institutions has never been rescinded.

El Salvador

Population	**5.9 million**
Catholic	**75%**
Protestant	**20%**
Baha'i	**0.5%**
Other (Jewish, Mormon,	
Jehovah's Witness)	**2.5%**
None	**2%**
Religious Freedom Rating	**3**

Background

El Salvador's independence from Guatemala was declared in 1841, and the Republic of El Salvador was established in 1859. A century of civil strife and military rule followed. Elected civilian rule was established in 1984. The 1983 constitution provides for a president elected for a five-year term and a unicameral National Assembly elected for three years. A decade of civil war, with more than seventy thousand dead, ended with peace accords signed in 1992 by the Farabundo Marti National Liberation Front (FMLN) and the conservative government of President Alfredo Cristiani.

The FMLN participated in the 1994 elections. In the March 16, 1997, elections, the conservatives won twenty-eight seats, the FMLN twenty-seven, with other parties splitting the difference. In 1998, the FMLN's electoral chances in the 1999 elections appeared to be dim, as the party split into hard-line Marxist and reformist camps. Although Social Democratic leader Facundo Guardado, a former guerrilla leader and leading reformist, was the party's presidential nominee, many worried whether the party was still committed to social revolution. In the March 1999 presidential election, Francisco Flores of the Alianza Republicana Nacionalista was victorious with more than 51 percent of the vote.

Citizens can change their government democratically. Political parties have agreed to a set of electoral reforms needed to improve the process. Political rights improved significantly in 1997, as evidenced by the fact that the left-wing FMLN nearly equaled the vote of the ruling ARENA in contests generally considered free and fair. ARENA accepted their losses without threatening extralegal action; the once-feared army remained neutral. Random killings, kidnappings, and other crimes—particularly in rural areas—have reinforced the country's reputation as one of the most violent countries in Latin America.

The constitution guarantees free expression and the right to organize political parties, civic groups, and labor unions. Although the 1992 peace accord has led to a significant reduction in human rights violations, political expression and civil liberties are still circumscribed by sporadic political violence, repressive police measures, a mounting crime wave, and right-wing death squads. The judicial system remains ineffectual and corrupt, and a climate of impunity is pervasive. El Salvador is one of the few Latin American countries to restrict military involvement in internal security. The National Civilian Police (PNC), which incorporated some former FMLN guerrillas, has yet to prove capable of the task of curbing the country's rampant crime while protecting human rights. Police accountability is a problem. Prisons are overcrowded, and conditions are wretched.

The media are privately owned. Election campaigns feature televised interviews and debates from across the political spectrum. Left-wing journalists and publications are occasionally targets of intimidation. Labor, peasant, and university organizations are well organized. The archaic labor code was reformed in 1994, but the new code lacks the approval of most unions because it significantly limits the rights to organize in certain areas. Unions that strike are subject to intimidation and violent police crackdowns. Freedom House's 1998–99 *Freedom in the World* rates El Salvador two in political rights and a three in civil liberties.

Religious Freedom

During the protracted guerrilla warfare of the late 1970s and 1980s, religious figures in El Salvador were subjected to various forms of repression and intimidation. To speak in favor of peace or social reform—even without trying to take sides—was hazardous. Salvadoran military units and "death squads" responded to terrorist violence by striking not only at secular communities perceived as supporters of the insurgents but at religious figures working for social justice as well.

In 1980, Oscar Romero, archbishop of San Salvador and a long-standing religious conservative, was shot and killed while celebrating Mass at the capital's cathedral. Romero had begun to speak out eloquently for an end to human rights violations. Assassins operating with the support of the Salvadoran military carried out the act. At his funeral, thirty-nine people died when a bomb exploded and gunfire was exchanged. That same year, four American churchwomen working in El Salvador were brutally raped, tortured, and murdered. (In 1998, the four former Salvadoran national guardsmen who had been convicted of the crime confessed that they had been told that the order had come "from higher levels, and nothing is going to happen to us.") At the other end of the decade, in 1989, army units killed six Jesuits and a housekeeper at the University of Central America in San Salvador. The Romero assassination and the massacre of the Jesuits frame an entire decade of violence against religious figures.

Since the end of large-scale civil strife, however, conditions in El Salvador have improved tremendously for religious freedom. While struggles still occur over issues of human rights and social justice, nothing even remotely comparable to the regular atrocities of the past against the religious occurs in El Salvador today. A new law was adopted in 1996, which went into effect the following year, requiring all nongovernmental organizations and non-Catholic religious bodies to register with the government. While this still gives the Catholic Church a privileged status in law compared to other groups, the interior minister said it would not affect other churches. At passage, it was also promised that the law was intended for purposes of public order, not for purposes of control or repression. So far, that promise seems to have been kept. In 1998, there were no complaints about government violation of freedom of belief as prescribed under the Salvadoran constitution.

Individuals have the right to freedom of religion and belief if they respect public order and morality. There is freedom to propagate one's faith, freedom of worship, and freedom to train and appoint clergy. Religious bodies have rights of self-government of religious education, to carry out charitable activities, to own and acquire property, and to maintain social institutions. They can produce, import, and distribute literature; have access to the media; receive donations; and have contact with coreligionists, domestically and overseas. Individuals can adopt, change, or leave a religion freely, with no change of civil status. The principal limit on religious freedom is the violence and corruption that circumscribes all civil liberties in El Salvador.

One of the few recent conflicts over religious practice arose when about one hundred Japanese members of the Unification Church, headed by the Reverend Sun Myung Moon, were deported because they were proselytizing. Salvadoran law requires all missionaries to seek immigrant status before working actively in the country. The missionaries had been admitted with tourist visas and had been allowed to return as tourists.

Though, as elsewhere, the figures are uncertain, El Salvador has been experiencing a growth in evangelical churches. Official figures claim that Roman Catholics make up almost 90 percent of the population; the reality is probably 10 percent lower. The Assemblies of God are the largest Protestant body. Though there are some tensions among denominations, these have not resulted in serious infringement upon one another's activities. A small Jewish community of about ten families participates fully in the economy.

Estonia

Population	1.47 million
Protestant (mainly Lutheran)	38.4%
Orthodox	20.3%
Roman Catholic	1%
Muslim	1%
Jewish	0.3%
Nonreligious/Other	39%
Religious Freedom Rating	1

Background

Dominated by Sweden in the sixteenth and seventeenth centuries and annexed by Russia in 1704, Estonia became independent in 1918. Soviet troops occupied the country during World War II, following a secret protocol in the 1939 Hitler-Stalin pact, which forcibly incorporated Estonia, Latvia, and Lithuania into the Soviet Union. Under Soviet rule, approximately one-tenth of the population was deported, executed, or forced to flee to the West. Subsequent Russian immigration decreased the population, with ethnic Estonians comprising 88 percent of the population before World War II and just over 61 percent in 1989. Estonia regained its independence with the disintegration of the Soviet Union in 1991 and has since made rapid economic progress.

In early 1998, the ruling Coalition Party/Rural Union (KMU) minority government was unable to increase its support in parliament. Finding it increasingly difficult to carry out his political programs, including reforms for European Union membership, Prime Minister Siiman called for early elections through a no-confidence vote in his government. The ruling coalition ultimately rejected the proposal; elections were held in March 1999. The turnout, though, was considered to be an all-time low.

In December 1998, parliament adopted controversial legislation requiring all elected officials and candidates for public office to demonstrate sufficient proficiency in Estonian to participate in debates and understand legal acts. Max van der Stoel, the Organization for Security and Cooperation in Europe's (OSCE) High Commissioner for National Minorities, criticized the new legislation as unfairly limiting the voters' choice of candidates and inhibiting the integration of Russian-speakers into Estonian society. The language requirements entered into force in May 1999 after the March elections.

Estonians can change their government democratically, but the country's citizenship law has disenfranchised many Russian-speakers who arrived in Estonia during the Soviet era. According to international observers, both the 1995 national and 1996 local elections were conducted freely and fairly. Political parties are allowed to organize freely, although only citizens may be members. The government respects freedom of speech and the press, and the media routinely conduct critical investigative reports. There are several major independent television and radio stations and dozens of privately owned national and regional newspapers. The constitution guarantees freedom of as-

sembly, and there were no reports in 1998 of government interference in political rallies or other mass gatherings. Workers have the right to organize freely and to strike, and unions are independent of the state as well as of political parties. The judiciary is independent.

Of Estonia's population of just under 1.5 million, more than 1 million are Estonian citizens, of which 105,000 have been naturalized since 1992. Almost 330,000 are stateless but hold Estonian residence permits, and more than 100,000 are citizens of other countries, mostly of Russia. On December 8, 1998, parliament amended the Citizenship Law, easing citizenship for the children of stateless persons. Freedom House's 1998–99 *Freedom in the World* rates Estonia a one in political rights and a two in civil liberties.

Religious Freedom

Estonia's political independence in 1991 has allowed it to reverse totally the persecution and control of the Lutheran Church in the Soviet period, and it is now a model of religious liberty. Articles 40–42 of the Constitution read in part: "Everyone shall have freedom of conscience, religion and thought. Everyone may freely belong to a church or a religious association. There shall be no state church. Everyone shall have the freedom to practise his or her religion, unless it endangers public order, health or morals. No state or local government authority or their officials may collect or store information on the persuasions of any Estonian citizen against his or her free will." A law of 1993 requires registration (minimum of twelve members to qualify), but de facto there are no restrictions on unregistered groups. Registration is necessary if a religious community seeks the return of property seized by the Soviet authorities after 1945. All sorts of small groups exist and organize themselves without interference.

Problems for the main churches, especially the majority Lutherans, arise not from restrictions but from the legacy of communism. As part of their attempt to subjugate the population, the Soviet authorities engaged in brutal deportations to Siberia, which included not only the political and cultural elite but also virtually the whole leadership of the churches. Up to the emergence of Gorbachev, this act of terror ensured that the leadership of the Lutheran Church remained complaisant, which had a debilitating effect on church membership, especially as religious education for children remained illegal in any form.

However, religious stirrings reoccurred, and the churches remained alive. For example, in 1970, at the age of forty-two, a lawyer called Harri Motsnik gave up his career to become a Lutheran pastor, and sermons became manifestos of religious (and even national) liberation. The KGB harassed him, and before long his health gave way. The church did not play the decisive role in the overthrow of communism that it did in Lithuania, but its moral influence was far from negligible.

With the easing of restrictions, the Lutheran Church has resumed control of its own affairs, appointed its own leadership, and begun rebuilding its institutions, inhibited only by the serious lack of trained personnel, especially clergy. Finnish Lutherans, living nearby, contributed extensively to the financial restoration of church buildings and to the reestablishment of Christian educational institutions. The mutually comprehensible languages of Finland and Estonia also contributed to this. The Lutheran Church became very active internationally. Archbishop Kuno Pajula invited representatives of the World

Council of Churches to come to Tallinn, the capital, in January 1989, and this was followed in the next month by the setting up of an Estonian Council of Churches, the first such ecumenical body on Soviet soil. In mid-August the first major Christian youth festival ever to be held in the USSR took place.

The Methodist Church, while very small, has benefited from being able fully to renew its international contacts and send its best students abroad for training. The Roman Catholic Church received a visit from Pope John Paul II in September 1993, and President Lennart Meri welcomed him in a speech of remarkable warmth for a head of state of a non-Catholic country.

The freedom of religion that Estonia enjoys also entails the freedom of churches to engage in extensive polemic. Relations between churches have remained positive, but the Orthodox Church has been driven by an internal dispute. In the Soviet period the Orthodox Church was an instrument of Russification—almost Sovietization. Linguistically and culturally, Russian dominance was complete, despite the original tradition that the Orthodox liturgy would use the language of the people. This was clearly epitomized by the present Patriarch of Moscow, Alexi II. He was the dominant religious figure in Estonia during the last thirty years of the communist era. He became bishop of Tallinn at the age of thirty-two in 1961. With the surname Ridiger, his father was German aristocracy, but his mother was pure Russian. The Soviets thought he would help render the Russian overlordship in Estonia acceptable to the people. He did, however, protect his own churches; the persecution of the Khrushchev period (1959–64) devastated Estonia less than other parts of the Soviet Union. He became metropolitan of St. Petersburg, while retaining his old diocese in plurality, and became a leading international ecumenical figure (which the Soviets encouraged in order to spread political influence).

With independence in 1991, a split was inevitable between the Russian Orthodox Church and Estonian Orthodoxy, which had grown during the brief independence of the interwar years. This "autocephalous" (independent) Estonian Apostolic Orthodox Church was summarily abolished by the Soviets in 1945. It continued its existence in exile and then conflicts emerged in the mid-1990s. These problems often divided individual parishes. Not all Russians wanted to come under the Moscow Patriarchate; not all Estonians wanted their leaders to join the Ecumenical

Patriarchate of Constantinople. The debate, though sharp, was pursued without violence. The two patriarchates engaged in bitter polemics, even briefly breaking fellowship with each other, but the internal split was formalized in 1997 and is now irreversible. In May 1998, Finnish Orthodox Archbishop Ioann of Karelia consecrated the sixty-five-year-old Russian, Simon Krushkov, as the first bishop of the autonomous Estonian Orthodox Church.

Estonia broke the shackles of communism with remarkable rapidity and currently demonstrates a model of religious liberty. Church leaders have not exhibited the paranoia about the activities of foreign evangelists that has been evident in other newly independent countries.

Finland

Population	**5.2 million**
Lutheran	86%
Orthodox	1%
None	12%
Other (Evangelical,	
Jehovah's Witness, Mormon)	1%
Religious Freedom Rating	1

Background

Finland declared independence in 1917, following eight centuries of foreign domination. Under its current constitution, from 1991, the directly elected president holds considerable power since the proportional representation system hinders any party from gaining a parliamentary majority. The president can initiate and veto legislation and dissolve parliament at any time. He also appoints the prime minister. The president currently holds

primary responsibility for national security and foreign affairs, while the prime minister's mandate covers all other areas.

Under current prime minister Paavo Lipponen, Finland's coalition government has sought closer integration into the European Union. Lipponen's Social Democratic Party (SDP) heads a "rainbow" coalition with the country's Conservative, Green, Swedish minority, and ex-Communist parties.

Finns can change their government by democratic means. Legislation passed in 1992 provides all Finnish citizens with the right to their own culture and equal protection under the law, but Gypsies, who have lived in Finland for nearly five hundred years and who outnumber the indigenous Saamis (or Lapps), often report being treated as outsiders by the largely homogeneous population. Discrimination on the basis of race, religion, sex, language, or social status is illegal.

The media are varied and not subject to control or censorship. Finnish workers have the right to organize, bargain, and strike, and an overwhelming majority belong to trade unions. Only sixty thousand people in the country are foreign residents. While a strict refugee quota of five hundred persons per year maintains the homogeneity of the population, those refugees who are admitted receive generous benefits. To prevent ethnic "ghettoes," some refugees are placed in small villages, and the government educates children about their new neighbors. Freedom House's 1998–99 *Freedom in the World* rates Finland a one in both political rights and civil liberties.

Religious Freedom

The Finnish people have lived on their present territory for thousands of years. After Swedish King Eric introduced Christianity to the region in 1154, the Finns began a seven hundred-year political affiliation with Sweden. Since the Protestant Reformation, the country, like Sweden, has been overwhelmingly Lutheran. The small Russian minority, which predominately adheres to the Orthodox Christian faith, and the indigenous Lapps (Saami) are notable exceptions. Today, although most citizens pay state church taxes as part of their income taxes, many are only nominal adherents. About 10 percent attend church monthly and 2 percent weekly. In recent decades small numbers of Finns have become Jehovah's Witnesses, Mormons, and evangelical Protestants.

Finland provides for freedom of religion in both law and practice. Citizens and other residents enjoy the right to freedom of conscience. They may worship, observe religious holidays, and publish and broadcast religious information freely. Under legislation passed in 1992, all citizens have the right to their own ethno-religious or other cultural practices and beliefs and to equal protection under the law. By law, the media cannot identify people by race, which is often linked to religion. The only significant barrier to freedom of religion in Finland is pressure to conform in this extraordinarily homogeneous society. This, however, is a largely nonquantifiable social impediment rather than a legal restriction.

Nontraditional religious groups may practice their faiths, provided that they are registered by the government as religious communities. Mormons, evangelical Protestants, and other groups have been registered, thereby enabling them to receive tax-free donations. Although they have applied for status as a religious community, Scientologists have been registered only as an association, the first time a group has been denied status.

The Lutheran and Orthodox churches are established by the state through special taxes on citizens' incomes. These funds are used to cover the building and other operating expenses of these two churches. Adherents who do not wish to pay these taxes may be exempted through notifying the tax office. Citizens are free to worship both publicly and privately, including on nonofficial premises. They may build and maintain official premises without wrongful impediment. They may organize processions and pilgrimages, provided they register for appropriate permits, which are issued on a nondiscriminatory basis. They may choose their priests and other leaders and personnel without government interference or discrimination.

Religious leaders may perform the rites and customs of their faiths with the texts and music and in the language of their own choosing. They may also preach according to the doctrines of their faiths without threat or interference by the state. Religious leaders of all faiths enjoy access to prisons, hospitals, military installations, and other relevant bodies in order to minister to the congregants.

Communities of believers may implement and operate their own educational, institutional, and hierarchical structures. The state religions are incorporated in the public school curriculum, but those who are not members of state churches may substitute general classes on religion and philosophy. They may also designate and otherwise assign their officials and train them freely in their own institutes and other bodies. They may import and otherwise acquire and circulate holy books and other religious publications. They are also free to print and circulate their own publications from within Finland. They also enjoy access to public communication. They are free to establish and maintain relations with individuals and communities of their choosing, both within Finland and internationally. They may also receive voluntary individual and institutional financial contributions both domestically and internationally.

Citizens have access to higher education, employment, the judiciary, military service, and public office without regard to their religious faith. They also enjoy freedom of expression, movement, emigration, association, assembly, marriage, and access to information without regard to religion.

France

Population	**59.1 million**
Roman Catholic	**80%**
Islam	**7%**
Protestant	**1.22%**
Jewish	**1.18%**
Buddhist	**1%**
Orthodox	**0.2%**
Eastern Catholic	**0.2%**
Jehovah's Witness	**0.2%**
Other/None	**9%**
Religious Freedom Rating	**3**

Background

After World War II France established a parliamentary Fourth Republic. This was governed by coalitions and ultimately failed due to the Algerian war.

The Fifth Republic began in 1958 under Prime Minister (and later President) Charles de Gaulle. Election of the president by popular suffrage began in 1965. In 1992, French citizens narrowly approved European political and economic union under the Maastricht Treaty.

In 1998, his second year in office, Socialist Prime Minister Lionel Jospin presided over a slight rebound in the French economy with a government of "cohabitation" with conservative president Jacques Chirac. Although the Socialists won an absolute majority in the National Assembly, Jospin named some communist ministers. The communists pressured Jospin to increase taxes and social reforms, halt privatization, and stay out of the European Monetary Union and the European Union's Amsterdam Treaty. In recent years the National Front, a far-right party led by the racist Jean-Marie Le Pen, has exerted strong influence in regional politics. In 1998, however, it suffered a number of setbacks.

French citizens can change their government democratically by directly electing the president and National Assembly. The constitution grants the president significant emergency powers, including rule by decree under certain circumstances. The president may call referenda and dissolve parliament but may not veto its acts or routinely issue decrees.

Decentralization gives mayors significant powers. The judiciary is independent. France has drawn criticism for its treatment of immigrants and asylum-seekers. Border guards have used excessive force to discourage crossings. The status of foreigners in France is confused by contradictory immigration laws. The National Front and others have gained popularity by blaming immigrants for high unemployment. Soon after taking office, Prime Minister Jospin eased the country's residency rules by giving illegal immigrants a one-year period to apply for legal residency. In August 1998, the government further eased residency requirements.

The press in France is free, although the government's financial support of journalism and the registration of journalists have raised concerns. Publication of opinion polls results is prohibited in the week preceding any election. Labor rights are respected in practice, and strikes are widely used to protest government economic policy. Incendiary racist remarks by National Front leader Le Pen led to the introduction of legislation to punish the publication of xenophobic and racist ideas. Freedom House's 1998–99 *Freedom in the World* rates France as one in political rights and a two in civil liberties.

Religious Freedom

From the sixteenth-century religious wars to the Revocation of the Edict of Nantes in 1685, a recurrent political-religious conflict opposed the Catholic majority and the Protestant minority. In the eighteenth century, opposition to Catholicism came from the Enlightenment and led to the landmark 1789 Revolution. Monarchy by divine right was replaced by constitutional monarchy and the Rights of Man were officially proclaimed. Protestants recovered the rights lost by the Revocation of the Edict of Nantes. In 1790, Jews received citizenship. With these events ended the privileged position of the Catholic Church which, as a state church, had previously enjoyed financial, social, and political advantages. In 1801–02, Napoleon recognised four religions: Catholic, Reformed, Lutheran, and Judaism.

At the turn of the twentieth century, the French government's secularization process stirred up conflict with the Catholic Church. This came to a climax in 1903–04, when religious orders were expelled from their premises by the army and the Vatican broke off diplomatic relations until 1921. A law on the separation of state and religions was introduced in 1905, which put an end to the recognition and financing of religions by the state (except in Alsace-Moselle, which was then under German rule; French Guyana also remains outside the 1905 law and is ruled by an 1830 royal order providing for a privileged Roman Catholic Church). The state was now neutral concerning religion.

Since the beginning of the twentieth

century, the status of religions has been ruled by these laws. Religious associations can be registered as "worshiping associations" according to the 1905 law if their activities are limited to worship and they do not disturb public order. This status, granted by the Ministry of the Interior, gives financial advantages such as exemption from transfer taxes on "hand donations." "Worshiping associations" can also be registered under a 1901 law on nonprofit associations, but they do not enjoy any material advantages.

The Catholic Church forbade its parishes and institutions to be registered under the 1905 law because the hierarchical structures of the Church were incompatible with the legal structure of "worshiping associations." But in 1907, a special law let them register under the 1901 law. In 1923–24, a compromise between the 1905 law and papal claims led to the creation of "diocesan associations": these respect both civil law and Catholicism since bishops were automatically their presidents.

France does not recognize any religion, except in the three departments of Alsace-Moselle (Bas-Rhin, Haut-Rhin, and Moselle). The current 1958 constitution states in Article II: "France shall be an indivisible, secular democratic and social Republic. It shall ensure the equality of all citizens before the law, without distinction of origin, race or religion. It shall respect all beliefs." The Declaration of the Rights of Man, now appended to the constitution, states in Article X: "No one ought to be disturbed on account of his opinions, even religious, provided their manifestation does not derange the public order established by law."

France currently is perturbed by the emergence of so-called "new religious movements." In 1996, the National Assembly published the "Guyard Report" listing 172 supposedly harmful or dangerous cults, and compared them to "private militias" and "combat groups," which can be legally banned. Subsequently, an Observatory on Sects was established, which at the end of June 1998 published its first yearly report, claiming that about fifty organizations were "indoctrinating children" in 1998, as against twenty-eight in 1996. It recommended increased legal standing for anticult groups, controls on professional training to prevent cult members "infiltrating" the professions, creating special magistrates for targeted religions, and reinforcing existing laws prohibiting private militias and extending them to "sects." It concluded that "cults" represent a real threat for the state. Subsequently, the prime minister and the president jointly issued a 1998 decree creating a task force against cults that has broad investigatory powers. Laws also grant anticult groups extensive powers to initiate legal actions against minority religions. In December 1999, the Senate approved a proposed law permitting the dissolution of groups that "threaten public order" or "constitute a major danger to individuals."

Individuals have the right to freedom of religion and belief if they respect democratic values and public order. Only about 14 percent of the Catholic population attend church regularly. Freedom of worship is guaranteed for larger groups, but minority religions complain about sudden unexpected difficulties in renting premises. The rights and the independence of the clergy are respected as is the right to self-government by religious bodies. However, the Muslim community has not yet constituted an uncontested umbrella organization that the state could recognize as representing all groups.

Freedom for religious education is recognized and respected. Chaplaincies can be created in public schools but are not financed by public authorities. No religious classes are held in public schools except for the recognized religions in Alsace-Moselle. Private schools can be denominational: 95 percent are Catholic and can have access to state financing. Wearing religious symbols in public schools is not forbidden unless it is regarded as provocation, proselytism, or propaganda. All religious communities, philosophical movements, and other associations are allowed to carry out charitable activities.

Despite the separation between state and religions, religions have unequal rights. A two-tiered system exists between religious associations registered under the 1901 law or under the 1905 law. The status of the 1905 law requires restriction to exclusively worshiping activities and not disturbing public order. Groups with this status can receive donations and gain tax exemptions on donations and places of worship. Activities of a general nature carried out in a denominational framework (Catholic hospitals, homes for elderly people, etc.) can be financed by the state. Some Muslim cultural centers have been financed by municipalities, but most have not. Departments or municipalities can also finance chaplaincies.

New religious movements do not enjoy the privileged status of the 1905 law, even if they fulfill its conditions. Chaplains of recognized religions and moral advisers of secular humanism officially have access to prisons, and so forth; other religions do not. The Muslim community complains that it cannot have chaplaincies in public schools, the army, hospitals, and prisons, and that the state has not financed their schools. Catholic cathedrals belong to the state, and churches built before 1905 belong to local governments, and they are lent to the Catholic Church for worship. Consequently, public authorities must pay for maintenance and repairs. New religious movements and Islam must finance their own places of worship. In Alsace-Moselle, most inequality stems from its system of recognized and nonrecognized religions. The Catholic Church, Reformed Church, Lutheran Church, and Judaism enjoy a state label of quality and receive material advantages while nonrecognized religions do not.

The "Guyard report" has increased intolerance. Many media have been libeling minority religions, and these religions have been marginalized and stigmatized. Access to public halls has been denied or made more difficult. Children and adults have been stigmatized as members of cults. The French tax administration enforced a 60 percent transfer tax on "manual donations" made by more than two hundred thousand Jehovah's Witnesses in the last four years. The amount of taxes owed is about fifty million dollars, and any donation made to cover it will itself be taxed again on a 60 percent basis. A court has ordered seizure of their assets. The tax administration said they were not a worshiping association but a sect and cannot benefit from requested tax exemption. The small Evangelical Church of Besançon is also hit by this fiscal measure. It remains to be seen if tax collectors will "limit" their actions to the 172 "cults" listed in the French parliamentary report or if they will extend it to Catholic, Protestant, Jewish, and Muslim associations, about 90 percent of which are not official worshiping associations either.

In 1995, the Church of Scientology of Paris was liquidated by a Trade Court after the French Ministry of Finance refused to authorize the importation of funds that would have enabled the church to pay its tax assessment of forty-eight million French francs. The Church of Scientology had tried for many years to agree with the Ministry of Finance to resolve the contested amounts—a common practice in France—but the authorities chose to try to destroy it financially. In July 1997, the Minister of the Interior publicly voiced disagreement with the Lyon Appeal's Court decision that Scientology could claim to be a religion.

Jehovah's Witnesses have lost teaching jobs even though they were not guilty of any professional misconduct. In divorce cases some judges tend to grant child custody to parents who are not members of cults, violating the 1998 decision of the European Court in the case of *Hoffmann v. Austria*. The Mandorum group claim that the funeral of its spiritual leader was disrupted and its statue of the Cosmo-Planetery Messiah was demolished by the government, an act upheld by a Court of Appeals on June 15, 1999.

Georgia

Population	**5.38 million**
Georgian (and Russian) Orthodox	**57%**
Muslim	**21.2%**
Armenian Apostolic	**5%**
Catholic (Greek-Catholic)	**0.8%**
Protestant (mainly Baptist)	**0.5%**
Jewish	**0.5%**
Atheist/Agnostic	**15%**
Religious Freedom Rating	**4**

Background

Absorbed by Russia in the early nineteenth century, Georgia proclaimed independence in 1918, gaining Soviet recognition two years later. In 1921, the Red Army overran it. In 1922, it entered the USSR as a component of the Transcaucasian Federated Soviet Republic, becoming a separate union republic in 1936. Georgia did quite well economically, partially due to the fact that Stalin and hated Soviet Police Chief Beria were born there. Georgia declared independence from a crumbling Soviet Union after a referendum in April 1991.

Nationalist leader and former dissident Zviad Gamsakhurdia was elected president, but his authoritarian and erratic behavior led to his violent ousting by opposition units.

In early 1992, Eduard Shevardnadze, the former Soviet Foreign Minister was asked by a temporary State Council to head a new government, and he was subsequently elected speaker of the parliament, making him acting head of state. In 1993, Georgia experienced the violent secession of the long-simmering Abkhazia region and armed insurrection by Gamsakhurdia loyalists. Although Shevardnadze blamed the Russians for arming and encouraging Abkhazian separatists, he legalized the presence of nineteen thousand Russian troops in five Georgian bases in exchange for Russian support against Gamsakhurdia, who was defeated and reportedly committed suicide. In early 1994, Georgians and Abkhazians signed an agreement in Moscow that called for a cease-fire, the stationing of Confederation of Independent States (CIS) troops under Russian command along the Abkhazian border, and the return of refugees under United Nations supervision. On February 9, 1998, a presidential motorcade was attacked by a group of assassins. President Shevardnadze was not hurt, but two bodyguards and one assassin were killed.

Throughout 1998, numerous clashes along the Georgian-Abkhaz border involved Georgian paramilitary groups, Abkhazians, and Russian peacekeepers. On October 19, several hundred soldiers in western Georgia, led by Akakiy Eliava, a former Gamsakhurdia commander, revolted and moved on the city of Kutaisi. The insurgency was put down in one day, and thirty-one rebels were arrested. Many in Georgia blamed Russian intrigue. Relations with Russia remained strained. In the general election of November 1999, the governing party, which supports Shevardnadze, held off a challenge from a pro-Russia party.

Georgians can change their government democratically. The November 1995 elections were judged generally free and fair by international observers. Article 24 of the constitution allows for free expression and open dissemination of information. Under a 1991 press law, journalists are obliged to "respect the dignity and honor" of the president and not impugn the honor and dignity of citizens or undermine the regime. Publications can face legal action for "malevolently using freedom of the press, [and] spreading facts not corresponding to reality." Freedom of assembly is guaranteed under the constitution and under law and is generally respected. More than one hundred nongovernmental organizations are registered, some of which enjoy tax exemptions. These are trade unions, and workers are allowed to strike. The

judiciary is not fully independent. Corruption is endemic and reaches all levels of government. Freedom House's 1998–99 *Freedom in the World* rates Georgia as three in political rights and four in civil liberties.

Religious Freedom

History says that the Georgian Orthodox Church was founded in 330, but tradition has it that St. Andrew the Apostle preached in the coastal area of Abkhazia in the middle of the first century. Under Stalin's Soviet law of 1929, most churches and all religious educational institutions were closed, and the Orthodox Church lost its independence to Moscow while retaining a titular head as patriarch. The end of World War II saw some improvement, but it was only after 1991 that Georgia gained anything recognizable as religious liberty. However, in the late Soviet period, most of Georgia's venerable Jewish community received permission to emigrate to Israel.

Despite his extremist political position, the first president of independent Georgia, Gamsakhurdia, guaranteed equal rights for all national and religious minorities. In an interview with Austrian television in June 1991, he said: "No one will discriminate against them or oppress them, and all their cultural rights are guaranteed. . . . They can use their own language, their own schools. Religion, culture—all this is retained. There is no danger for them in Georgia, nor will there be." A new law in 1991 reflected this (Article 19): "Every individual has the right to freedom of speech, thought, conscience, religion and belief. The persecution of an individual for his thoughts, beliefs or religion is prohibited, as is compulsion to express opinions about them. These rights may not be restricted unless the exercise of these rights infringes upon the rights of other individuals."

It seems, however, that this liberal statute will not long be allowed to remain in force, despite the apparent liberalism of Gamsakhurdia's successor, Shevardnadze. By the end of 1998, all the other countries of the former Soviet Union, except the Baltic States, had brought in or were considering new restrictive laws based on the Russian model. The debate was continuing in Georgia. The Ministry of Justice presented a restrictive draft bill to parliament in February 1997, but it failed to gain agreement and was returned for revision. In the new version, not yet ratified, there is recognition for five "traditional religions": the Georgian Orthodox Church (as the state religion), the Armenian Apostolic Church, the Catholic Church, Islam, and Judaism. An alternative draft, which has little chance of success even though it emanates from Tbilisi State University, cites the Georgian Orthodox Church as the sole traditional religion.

The Protestant Church receives no mention, even though Baptists have been "traditional" in Georgia since the 1860s. Though a tiny minority, Baptists are strong and have achieved unity of national identity since breaking away after independence from the Moscow-dominated All Union Council of Evangelical Christians and Baptists, under the strong leadership of Bishop Malkhaz Songulashvili. His personal relations with the Orthodox have been excellent, at least until an element of greater nationalism began to creep into Orthodox circles in the late 1990s. There are no reported instances of physical violence against the "mainstream" religious minorities in general, and they enjoy a good measure of religious liberty.

However, along with the intention of introducing a new law, there is a hardening of attitudes toward other groups. Individual priests have agitated, especially against the Jehovah's Witnesses. In October 1999, in Tbilisi, a priest who broke away from the patriarchate, Fr. Basil Nikolaishvili, led his flock of twelve hundred members in seizing and burning a huge bonfire of Witness literature, and he called on the public and the authorities to join him. In September 1999, the patriarchate itself called for the Witnesses to be banned. In the region of Abkhasia the Witnesses have been under particular pressure.

While most Georgians are now strongly committed to the Orthodox Church (and many did not abandon it, despite the restrictions of the Soviet period), the religious picture is complex, owing to the ethnic complexity of the whole Caucasus region. Some Abkhazians are Muslim, but they form only about 20 percent of their "own" separatist region. Islam is also strongly present among other minorities, such as the Azeris and Ossetians. Despite the civil war—or even partly because of it—Muslims are able to enjoy virtually complete religious liberty.

The Georgian Orthodox Church has moved quickly to recoup the losses it suffered in the communist period. There are now some five hundred parishes, as well as twenty-seven monasteries, but there are reports of some disputes over property. The Armenian Church claims that some of its property is in the hands of the Georgians. Also, government agencies still occupy some church property, especially former possessions of the Armenians, Catholics, and one synagogue in Tbilisi.

There are schisms in the Orthodox Church. Earlier disputes have focused on the extent of the collaboration of the hierarchy with the Soviet system and full archival and documentary evidence on this has not become available. More recently the question is involvement in the ecumenical movement, specifically the World Council of Churches, of which the Georgian Orthodox Church was a member, apparently an enthusiastic one. However, in an unsuccessful effort to avoid schism, the Georgian Orthodox Church withdrew from the WCC in May 1997. Five monasteries had rebelled against the patriarch, accusing him of "ecumenical heresy" for his travels abroad and reception of fraternal church delegations. The Holy Synod stripped the monks of their rank, but this led to an outcry by Archimandrite Ioann Sheklashvili, who had campaigned against the (Soviet-encouraged) ecumenical links since 1984. The patriarch has refused to cut links with the Ecumenical Patriarchate of Constantinople, as well as with other ecumenically engaged Orthodox churches.

In November 1999, the pope visited Georgia, urging reconciliation between the two churches, divided since the schism of 1054. However, Patriarch Ilia II welcomed him only as a head of state (the Vatican), spoke of deepening "friendly relations" between "our countries," and did not pray with him. The Georgian church also instructed its members not to attend the Papal Mass.

These accusations and counteraccusations may be a sign of religious freedom, but overall the climate is deteriorating, as in most other countries of the CIS. While the country remains so sharply politically divided, there can be no long-term guarantee of religious liberty.

Germany

Population	82 million
Evangelical (Lutheran)	33.8%
Catholic	33.6%
Orthodox	1%
Other Christian	1%
Muslim	3.4%
Other (Jewish, Baha'i, Hindu, Buddhist)	0.2%
None	27%
Religious Freedom Rating	3

Background

After World War II, Germany was divided into Soviet, U.S., British, and French occupation zones. Four years later the Allies helped to establish a democratic Federal Republic of Germany, while the Soviets oversaw the formation of the communist German Democratic Republic (GDR). The division of Berlin was reinforced by the 1961 construction of the Berlin Wall. After the collapse of Erich Honecker's hard-line GDR regime in 1989 and the destruction of the wall in 1990, citizens voted in the country's first free parliamentary election, in which parties supporting rapid reunification triumphed.

In October 1998, Gerhard Schroeder of the Social Democratic Party (SPD) replaced Helmut Kohl, Europe's longest serving leader, as chancellor of Germany. The SPD, which received approximately 40 percent of the vote, formed a coalition with the Green Party.

German citizens can change their government democratically. The federal system provides for a considerable amount of self-government among the sixteen Lander (states). Individuals are free to form political parties and to receive federal funding as long as the parties are democratic in nature. The country's judiciary is independent. The Basic Law (Constitution) provides for unrestricted citizenship and legal residence immediately upon application for ethnic Germans entering the country. Individuals not of German ethnicity must meet certain requirements, including legal residence for ten years (five if married to a German) and renunciation of all other citizenship. Germany has no antidiscrimination law to protect immigrants.

The German press and broadcast media are free and independent, offering pluralistic viewpoints. Nazi propaganda and statements endorsing Nazism are illegal. Nazi-related, antiforeigner, anti-immigrant, and racist incidents have all increased in recent years, and xenophobic political policies and pronouncements continue to find support among some voters. In June 1998, the government drew criticism from human-rights groups for tightening the country's liberal asylum law.

Labor, business, and farming groups are free, highly organized, and influential. In recent years, however, trade union federation membership has dropped sharply due to the collapse of industry in the East and layoffs in the West. Freedom House's 1998–99 *Freedom in the World* rates Germany as a one in political rights and a two in civil liberties.

Religious Freedom

Germany generally has freedom of religion, worship, and religious auton-

omy. However, there is continual hostility to new immigrant groups and non-traditional religions (including charismatic Christian churches), often called "cults." Both trends are manifestations of opposition to "foreigners."

Article 4 (1) of the 1949 constitution guarantees freedom of religion, freedom of belief and conscience, and freedom to express religious or philosophical convictions. Article 4 (2) guarantees "the undisturbed practice of religion." The right to freedom of religion has been held to require the principle of the "philosophical-religious neutrality" of the state. Under Article 140, civil and political rights may not be determined on the basis of religion, and access to the civil service may not depend on religion. It also stipulates that no one can be obliged to declare their religious beliefs or to participate in religious practices and that each religious community is free to organize and arrange its own affairs independently. Religious communities are entitled to legal personality if they can show by their constitution and number of adherents that they are likely to be permanent. These provisions apply equally to "philosophical" communities.

Religious education in state schools is a constitutional requirement for most Lander, and this education must be provided "in accordance with the principles of the religious communities." Article 7 (4) and (5) give a right to establish private schools, and these are state subsidized. Islam is taught in schools in some federal states. The use of Christian symbols in state education has been challenged, especially in Bavaria.

The two main churches— Evangelical (Lutheran) and Catholic— remain pre-eminent in German society and are involved in education, social work, and Third World development aid. About 5 percent of Lutherans and 18 percent of Catholics attend church weekly. After the state, they employ more people than any other organization. However, church attendance is less than 10 percent. A church tax is collected by the state on behalf of the two main churches and other religions recognized as institutions of public law. The tax is mostly raised as an additional surcharge of 8 or 9 percent on income tax. The money is collected by the state and transferred to the churches or religious communities. The money is collected from baptized members, though they are allowed to opt out. Most religious bodies are tax-exempt.

There is no state church, but, as in several other European countries, there are different degrees of legal status for religions. Religious bodies are either recognized as public entities by the Lander in an inconsistent fashion or else, as nonrecognized bodies, must function as civil entities, like clubs or associations. This creates both discrimination between religious groups and gives power to the state authorities whether to recognize a religion. The primary impact of this discrimination comes in tax concessions by the authorities. The state is also involved in determining whether the content of a religion is conducive to the "public good." Further, this treatment does not seem to depend on whether the religious body is well established. The Muslim communities still remain to be recognized as a religious public entity (although the government is considering Muslim military chaplains) and the Jehovah's Witnesses have had a long struggle to be so. The Berlin State government has refused them public law status. Since there is no legally designated Muslim representative body, Islamic groups can-

not officially shape the teaching about Islam in schools.

The hostility of the German state to new religions has been manifested in a wide and arbitrary use of the term *cult*, a term that has a dangerous meaning in Germany. Throughout the 1990s the Church of Scientology has been regarded as a dangerous cult, and the state has taken excessive measures to prevent the effective functioning of this group. Members of the Church of Scientology are denied employment opportunities in the public sector and face frequent discrimination in the private sector, including most political parties. Since June 1997, it has been under surveillance by the security services, an action highly unusual in modern European societies. The purpose to which such information is to be put remains to be seen. This move was severely criticized by many governments, including the United States. In June 1999, the State Social Appeals Court of Rhineland-Palatinate ruled illegal a 1994 directive from the German Ministry of Labor that denied Scientologists the right to own or operate employment agencies.

Another example has been the treatment of the Christliche Gemeinde Church in Cologne. This is a Christian charismatic group based in the United States that has become established in Germany. After being continually recognized as a religious public entity from 1983 to 1996, their status was removed following a crude campaign in the local media. The removal was at the instigation of the tax authorities, one of the grounds being that they believed in the complete truth of the Bible and the authorities thought that this was contrary to the public good. Once the church was deemed not to be conducive to the public good, its tax status was removed and the church was required to pay taxes on all "collections" and "gifts," and those who had given to it were also required to pay taxes. The tax demand was backdated to 1990 and placed severe stress on the ability of the church to survive. The Federal Constitutional Supreme Court rejected their appeal within two months, a time scale that appears indicative of a hostility to the emergence of charismatic churches originating from the United States. This case is likely to go before the European Court of Human Rights. In June 1998, a commission established in 1996 to investigate "sects" and "psycho-groups" reported and said such groups did not pose a threat to society: it did, however, suggest strengthening consumers law regarding "psychological claims" and called on the government to publicize the dangers of such groups, especially Scientology.

The requirement of vigilance in the area of anti-Semitism in Germany is important for historical reasons. Jews are a recognized religious public entity, and the Jewish community has full religious rights. It is a crime to deny the holocaust. The growth in neo-Nazi groups has been a matter of concern because of hostility to Jews and immigrants. Though anti-Semitic acts have decreased, they still occur, including a December 1998 bomb that destroyed the gravestone of the Jewish community of Berlin.

In 1998, in Frankfurt and Stuttgart, Turkish Muslims were refused permission to establish mosques, and in Stuttgart a school district did not hire a Muslim women because she would wear a head scarf while teaching.

Greece

Population	10.5 million
Orthodox	87%
Old Calendar Orthodox	8%
Catholic	2%
Muslim	1.2%
Jehovah's Witness	0.5%
Protestant	0.3%
Other (Baha'i, Jewish, Buddhist, Hare Krishna, Protestant)	1%
Religious Freedom Rating	4

Background

Greece was under Ottoman rule for about four hundred years. In 1821, the Metropolitan Bishop of Patras, Father Germanos, launched the rebellion movement against the Ottomans from the Greek Orthodox monastery of Agia Lavra. In 1830, Greece was recognized as an independent state but was placed under the protection of France, Great Britain, and Russia. From 1833 to 1862, Othon I of Bavaria, an autocratic monarch imposed by the great powers, governed the country. After a putsch in 1843, Othon I had to accept a new and very conservative constitution. Occupation by the Axis powers in 1941 was followed by civil war between non-communist and communist forces until 1949. Following a 1967 military coup, a failed countercoup by naval officers in 1973 led to the formal deposition of the monarch and the proclamation of a republic. The current constitution, adopted in 1975, provides for a parliamentary system with a largely ceremonial presidency.

Greeks can change their government democratically. Change of voting address is not permitted, hence nearly 650,000 people must travel to prior residences as voting is compulsory. The judiciary is independent. The media have substantial freedom, but the public prosecutor may charge publishers and seize publications deemed offensive to the president or to religious beliefs. The law bans "unwarranted" publicity for terrorists.

Western Thrace's Turkish Muslim minority, whose religious rights are guaranteed under the 1923 Treaty of Lausanne, objects to being classified as "Turkish" rather than "Muslim" and to the government's power to choose its mufti, or Muslim community leader. The country's ethnic Slavic minority, not recognized by the state, makes similar objections. Gypsies, who may number three hundred thousand, encounter discrimination in education and social benefits. In June the parliament abolished a discriminatory law that had stripped nonethnic Greeks of citizenship if they left the country for an extended period and that primarily affected 120,000 Muslims in border areas.

Greeks enjoy freedom of association, and, except for security personnel, can join unions and strike. In 1997, the government passed a new law allowing conscientious objectors to perform alternative, civilian service, but it requires objectors to serve twice as long as military conscripts. Freedom House's 1998–99 *Freedom in the World* rates Greece as a one in political rights and a three in civil liberties.

Religious Freedom

The Preamble to the 1975/1986 Constitution opens, "In the name of the Holy and Consubstantial and Indivisible Trinity." Article 3 § 1: says, "The prevailing religion in Greece is that of the Eastern Orthodox Church of Christ. The Orthodox Church of Greece, acknowledging our Lord Jesus Christ as its head, is inseparably united in doctrine with the Great Church of Christ in Constantinople and with every other Church of Christ of the same doctrine, observing unwaveringly, as they do, the holy apostolic and synodal canons and sacred traditions. It is autocephalous and is administered by the Holy Synod of serving Bishops and the Permanent Holy Synod." Article 3 § 3 reads, "The text of the Holy Scripture shall be maintained unaltered. Official translation without prior sanction by the Autocephalous Church of Greece is prohibited."

Article 5 § 2 provides for full protection of the laws "irrespective of nationality, race or language and of religious or political beliefs." Article 13 § 1 holds that freedom of religious conscience is inviolable. Enjoyment of individual and civil rights does not depend on the individual's religious beliefs. Article 13 § 2 holds that all known religions shall be free and their rites of worship shall be performed unhindered. Proselytism is prohibited. Article 13 § 3 holds that the ministers of all known religions shall be subject to the same supervision by the state and to the same obligations toward it as those of the prevailing religion. Article 13 § 4 holds that no person shall be exempt from discharging his obligations to the state or may refuse to comply with the laws by reason of his religious convictions. Article 14 § 1: "Every person may express and propagate his thoughts orally, in writing and through the press in compliance with the laws of the state."

The Greek Orthodox Church was rewarded by the prohibition of any form of proselytism [enshrined in the first Hellenic Constitution (1844)] for the decisive role it had played in the national independence movement. Under the Metaxas dictatorship (1936–41), non-Orthodox were made subject to law that required a state permit for setting up non-Orthodox places of worship, could expel foreigners engaged in proselytizing, restricted entry of foreign non-Orthodox clergy, and imposed discriminatory regulations on the publishing and distributing of non-Orthodox religious literature. Although these laws were enacted in 1938 and 1939, when the Greek Parliament was suspended, they are still fully implemented. The provisions about proselytism were revised but never disappeared and in 1975 were extended beyond the Orthodox Church, to any "known religion."

The identification of Hellenism with Orthodoxy has partly degenerated into hypernationalism. This explains the concept of "known religion," the only status that merits constitutional provisions guaranteeing religious freedom. Among the "known religions," Greek Orthodoxy is paramount. The state pays clergy salaries and finances church construction and upkeep. The lesser status of "corporations under public law" is given to Islam and Judaism. Other "known religions" such as Old Calendar Orthodox, Catholics, Jehovah's Witnesses, and Seventh-Day Adventists are "corporations under private law," while Protestants, Buddhists, Mormons, Baha'i, and others can be "religious corporations under private law."

Greek citizens have the right to choose or change a religion or belief of their choice, but, despite objections by the European Parliament, the law requires that religious adherence be shown on identity cards. (The Justice Ministry announced in 2000 that this provision would be dropped.) The Orthodox Church has opposed the European Union's Schengen Agreements on free passage of people because religious adherence would not be mentioned on identification documents. In Thessaloniki and in some villages, municipalities refuse to record conversion of former Orthodox believers to Jehovah's Witnesses. The Orthodox Church backs this by segregation and denial of burials in the local cemetery. In some villages the local authorities have not allowed the burial of Jehovah's Witnesses. Orthodox clerics treat these converts as apostates and heretics. In 1997–98, the Greek branch of the WatchTower recorded more than a hundred cases of assault by Orthodox priests and fanatics and harassment by police officers. Since the enactment of the anti-proselytism laws, about twenty thousand Jehovah's Witnesses have been arrested. From 1983 to 1988, more than two thousand known cases of prosecution and four hundred convictions on grounds of proselytism were recorded.

In 1993, the European Court in Strasbourg condemned the Greek State in the case of *Kokkinakis v. Greece* but did not condemn Metaxas' laws against proselytism per se, and they are still in force. Kokkinakis, an eighty-three-year old Jehovah's Witness, had been sentenced to a prison term because he had been preaching from door to door. The sentence was converted to a fine.

In 1998, the European Court condemned Greece again in a proselytism case involving Pentecostals. Courts are generally heeding the European Court's decision, but a Hare Krishna was sentenced to two years for proselytism in 1997. The right to manifest one's beliefs in public is also restricted for minority religions. The government closed a Protestant television station in 1994 and radio station in December 1999. In 1997, Dimitris Iliadis was arrested again for holding public evangelism meetings in

Thessaloniki. Before the conscientious objection law of 1997, about four hundred objectors, almost all Jehovah's Witnesses, were in prison. In December 1999, the European Court of Human Rights was due to hear *Thlimmenos v. Greece*, in which Mr. Thlimmenos says he was denied a position as a chartered accountant because he had previously been convicted for refusing to perform military service. School authorities punish Jehovah's Witness pupils for refusing to salute the flag. In July 1999, in Halkidiki, a mob, urged on by the mayor and local bishop, obstructed the construction of a Jehovah's Witness lecture hall.

The Orthodox Church fully enjoys freedom of worship, but under the "Law of Necessity, 1672/1939," the Ministry of Education and Religions can ask for the advice of the Orthodox Church on any application for another religion to operate a place of worship. Although this advice is theoretically not binding, it fully influences the minister's decision. In most cases the Orthodox Church gives a negative answer. This has victimized Muslims, Protestants, and Jehovah's Witnesses. In November 1999 an evangelical minister in Thessolonika was taken to court for operating a "house of prayer" without permission from the local Orthodox bishop. In the town of Kimeria (region of Xanthi, Western Thrace), seventeen Muslims were arrested for adding a minaret to their mosque and were sentenced to four months in prison in January 1997. In June 1997, an appeals court reduced the sentence to two months with a three-year suspension period. Despite the European Court's challenging these restrictions, they continue to be applied.

Religious ministers of "known" religions can perform the rites and customs established by their religious community, but, according to the constitution, only the version of Holy Scripture published or approved by the Orthodox Church can be used. However, this provision is not implemented. The Macedonian language is forbidden in any place of worship, and some Orthodox priests have been prosecuted on that ground.

Interference by the Greek government in the internal affairs of Islam is a source of permanent tension. The government refuses to recognize muftis chosen by the Muslim community and has appointed other muftis, which are widely rejected by the Muslim community. Relations between the appointed muftis and a significant portion of the Muslim minority are very limited. A mufti may be relieved of his functions by presidential decree. In 1991, two muftis, elected by the community, were rejected by the government and convicted of usurping titles and signing illegal documents. In December 1999 the European Court of Human Rights judged that the conviction of one of these muftis, Ibraim Serif, had violated his religious freedom and ordered the Greek government to pay a fine.

Freedom of religious instruction at home is respected. Greek Catholics complain that they lack the right to create further private schools. In the public schools, only the Orthodox religion is taught. Since 1995, exemption from religion classes has become legally possible. In 1997–98, there were twenty cases of discrimination and religious intolerance against Jehovah's Witnesses in schools. Four students were suspended for one day from school because they refused to participate in nationalistic school parades.

The Catholic Church has had difficulty receiving recognition of legal personality, and, although the Council of State recognized Jehovah's Witnesses as a "known religion," the military consistently refused to exempt their clerics from mandatory military service. In May 1997, the European Court of Human Rights found this practice violated the European Convention on Human Rights. Subsequently, the Ministry of Defense requested all recruiting offices to conform to the Strasbourg decisions. Residence permits for foreign Catholic nuns and monks have been denied or not renewed. Greek Catholics and Protestants complain that they cannot have a career in the police or army. Until recently, non-Orthodox

teachers have been fired from public and even private schools, but this practice has dramatically diminished in recent years. Access to jobs in public services has been denied to Jehovah's Witnesses because they have been imprisoned as conscientious objectors. In several divorce cases lower courts have denied child custody to parents who were Jehovah's Witnesses because they refused blood transfusions. The right to create religious charities is obstructed for all minority religions.

Guatemala

Population	**12.3 million**
Catholic	**60%**
Protestant	**35%**
Animist	**2%**
Other	**1.5%**
None	**1.5%**
Religious Freedom Rating	**3**

Background

The Republic of Guatemala was established in 1839, eighteen years after gaining independence from Spain. The nation has endured a history of dictatorship, *coups d' etat*, and guerrilla insurgency, with only intermittent democratic rule. Amended in 1994, the 1985 constitution provides for a four-year presidential term and prohibits reelection. An eighty-member unicameral Congress is elected for four years.

After UN-mediated talks were launched between the government and the Guatemalan National Revolutionary Union (URNG) left-wing guerrillas, the latter called a unilateral truce for the 1995 election and backed the left-wing New Guatemala Democratic Front (FDNG). In 1996, Guatemala City

mayor Alvaro Arzu Irigoyen of the National Advancement Party (PAN) won the presidential election with 36.6 percent of the vote. Soon after taking office, Arzu reshuffled the military, forcing the early retirement of generals linked to drug trafficking, car-theft rings, and human rights abuses. After a brief suspension of peace talks in October 1996 because of a rebel kidnapping, subsequent agreement on the return of rebel forces to civilian life and a permanent cease-fire led to the December 1996 peace accords. In 1997, Arzu's government won plaudits for important advances in implementing the peace process. In April 1998, Guatemala was shaken by the murder of Auxiliary Bishop Juan Gerardi, a case that has become a test of the government's willingness to control the armed forces and to hold accountable those who abuse human rights. In 1999, the Guatemalan Republican Front (FRG), founded by Rios Montt (see below), easily won both the presidential and the parliamentary elections.

Citizens can change their governments through elections, but recent voter turnouts suggest that people are increasingly disillusioned with the process. The constitution guarantees religious freedom and the right to organize political parties, civic organizations, and labor unions. However, political and civic expression is severely restricted by a climate of violence, lawlessness, and military repression. The rule of law is undermined by the systemic corruption that afflicts all public institutions, particularly the legislature and the courts.

Despite penal code reforms in 1994, the judicial system remains a black hole for most legal or human rights complaints. Drug trafficking is a serious problem. In general, the justice system suffers from chronic problems of corruption, intimidation, insufficient personnel, lack of training opportunities, and a lack of transparency and accountability. Native Americans are largely excluded from the national justice system. Guatemala remains one of the most violent countries in Latin America and ranks fourth in the number of kidnappings in the region. In a positive development, the first convictions on war crimes charges were handed down in November 1998 when three pro-government paramilitary force members were sentenced to death for their role in a 1982 massacre of Indian peasants.

The press and most of the broadcast media are privately owned, with several independent newspapers and dozens of radio stations, most of which are commercial. Five of six television stations are commercially operated. However, journalists remain at great risk. The Runejel Junam Council of Ethnic Communities (CERJ) represents the interests of the country's Indians, a major-ity of the population, who have faced severe repression and violence by the army and allied paramilitary organizations as well as being manipulated by the URNG guerrillas. Workers are frequently denied the right to organize and are subjected to mass firings and blacklisting, particularly in export-processing zones where a majority of workers are women. Existing unions are targets of systematic intimidation. Guatemala is among the most dangerous countries in the world for trade unionists. Freedom House's 1998–99 *Freedom in the World* rates Guatemala a three in political rights and a four in civil liberties.

Religious Freedom

Until 1873, it was illegal to be an adherent of anything other than the Catholicism that had displaced traditional Mayan beliefs. In 1873, a freedom of conscience act was passed that allowed room for the growth of Protestantism. Since then, Guatemala has officially separated church and state.

Many of the victims of human rights abuses during the civil conflict were indigenous peoples of the various Mayan groups in the country, who constitute about half the population. As elsewhere in Latin America where Spanish settlers intermingle with large indigenous groups, religion in indigenous areas was and remains a syncretism between Catholic and traditional Mayan beliefs. Rural indigenous people were economically marginalized to a great extent during Guatemala's history by the concentration of land ownership within a small percentage of the population. When liberation theology began to emerge in the 1970s throughout Latin America, some of the Guatemalan proponents of that movement organized indigenous communities to challenge perceived injustices.

Massive human rights abuses were visited upon individuals and groups who saw in their religious commitment obligations to reform governmental practice and promote social justice. Government forces, death squads, and "civilian patrols" violently repressed anyone seen as an "enemy of the people" during the civil war. Guerrilla forces, too, if in lesser numbers, attacked indigenous communities they perceived as loyal to the government. Many indigenous people crossed the border into southern Mexico; others were displaced to different areas within Guatemala.

Though the worst of these attacks have largely ended since the signing of the peace accord, the basic tension over gross economic inequality remains. Religious people of both Catholic and Protestant churches continue to call for land reform and economic justice. Rampant criminality and rampant security atrocities to suppress it, including the killing of street children, have already become another focus of human rights contention in religious sectors.

In terms of the law in Guatemala, individuals have the right to freedom of religion and belief if they respect public order and morality. There is freedom to propagate one's faith, freedom of worship, and freedom to train and appoint clergy. Religious bodies have rights of self-government, of religious education, to carry out charitable activities, to own and acquire property, and to maintain social institutions. They can produce, import, and distribute literature; receive donations; and have contact with coreligionists, domestically and overseas. Individuals can adopt, change, or leave a religion freely, with no change of civil status. Hence there is no specific limitation on religious freedom per se. However, since religious freedom is not merely the freedom to carry out certain narrowly prescribed religious activities but is also the freedom to live in the social and political world according to one's beliefs, then it is necessarily limited when a society is repressive. In Guatemala, though there is no targeting of religion per se, religious freedom is restricted by the corruption, intimidation, and repression, which affect all human rights.

Guatemala's long history of widespread and flagrant abuse of human rights continues, sometimes in old ways, sometimes in new ones, which involve religious issues. The most graphic confirmation occurred on April 26, 1998. Just two days after issuing "Guatemala: Never Again!" a fourteen-hundred-page report that blamed the Guatemalan army or government paramilitaries for more than 80 percent of the dead and for 401 out of 422 documented massacres, Juan Jose Gerardi, a seventy-five-year-old Catholic bishop and founder of the Guatemala City archdiocesan human rights office, was brutally murdered. The official government investigation has tried to place the blame on a priest who lived in the same house, alleging that the violence was the result of a homosexual relationship gone bad. But there is no evidence confirming this charge. Such evidence as there is, phone records and vehicles reported to have been outside the residence that night, points to figures named in the human rights report. In June 1999, a former judge filed a complaint accusing Guatemala's incoming defense minister, General Marco Tulio Espinoza Contreras, and two other senior military officials of the murder.

Guatemala has created a Truth Commission to try to sort out responsibility for human rights violations committed in the past. The Guatemalan Catholic bishops have founded the Project to Recover Historic Memory and assembled a forensic team to exhume and examine bodies of massacre victims. As these investigations continue, other members of religious groups involved in pursuing justice and reconciliation are likely to be the targets of death threats and intimidation and perhaps will suffer further outrages.

Guatemala has the distinction of being the most Protestant Latin American nation and may even have a majority Protestant population in the next century. The reasons for this development are several. Like other Latin peoples, Guatemalans have been attracted to evangelical and Pentecostal Protestant churches because of their good effects on people's lives, families, and fortunes. But in Guatemala an additional factor has been operating. Because of long-standing Catholic involvement in Guatemala society—for most of its history as a prop for the elites, in recent decades more often as a critic of injustice—identifying oneself as a Catholic may suggest some political orientation. The Jesuit order in particular has in recent decades been identified with reform and even revolutionary currents in Guatemala. Jesuits have therefore been generally targeted by repressive elements. Some Protestants are closely identified with the ruling elites, and several Protestants, including General Efrain Rios Montt, have been elected president during the 1980s and 1990s. But for many ordinary Guatemalans, identifying oneself as a Protestant can also be a statement of political neutrality and of a desire to work quietly within the status quo. In addition, in some areas the armed forces allowed only Protestant missionaries, who for the most part had North American views of the superiority of capitalism to liberation theology. Protestant missionaries who preached social revolution, however, have also found themselves targets of repression.

Catholicism was the official religion of Guatemala and the only legal Christian denomination until late in the nineteenth century. When freedom of conscience was proclaimed, German and American Protestants invested in Guatemala and made vigorous missionary efforts. In strictly legal terms, limitations on religious liberty have been minimal since that time in Guatemala except when political factionalism has made religious groups the targets of one political group or another. For example, Guatemala's small Jewish community (about 1,000) enjoys freedom of worship and has created a network of freely operating social and religious organizations. Anti-Semitism has been minimal, and Jews play important roles in the professions, business, and the life of the nation. Though numbers of Jews took up temporary residence in other countries during the worst periods of the civil war, most have now returned. The peace accord has led to a sharp reduction in the kinds of politically driven attacks on religious groups that were characteristic of the past. But until Guatemala achieves profound social reform, human rights violations against religious reformers are likely to continue.

Hungary

Population	**10.1 million**
Roman Catholic	**61.7%**
Protestant	**24.4%**
Nonreligious/Other	**12.5%**
Jewish	**0.8%**
Orthodox	**0.3%**
Marginal	**0.2%**
Muslim	**0.1%**
Religious Freedom Rating	**3**

Background

With the collapse of the Austro-Hungarian Empire after World War I, Hungary lost two-thirds of its territory under the 1920 Trianon Treaty, leaving 3.5 million Hungarians as minorities in neighboring Romania, Slovakia, Serbia, Croatia, and Ukraine. After World War II, Soviet forces helped install a communist regime. In 1956, Soviet tanks quashed an armed uprising by Hungarians. The ouster of Janos Kadar in 1988 led the way to political reform and the eventual introduction of a multiparty system in 1989.

The run-up to the 1998 parliamentary elections saw decreasing popularity for the coalition headed by Gyula Horn. In 1994, the Socialists had defeated the conservative-populist MDF with promises to ease the transition to a market economy. But in 1995, it adopted an unpopular reform package that saw radical spending cuts, a devaluation of the forint, and stepped-up privatization. In 1996, the government was rocked by a privatization scandal, the so called "Tocsik affair," which centered on a record-consulting fee paid to an independent expert.

Despite macroeconomic gains attributed to its austerity program, which have given Hungary the fastest growing economy in East-Central Europe, Hungarians have been disillusioned with corruption, crime, and an unequal distribution of wealth. In its foreign policy it has supported membership in NATO and the EU.

In the May 1998 parliamentary elections, Fidesz captured 148 seats (up from 20 in 1994); the Socialists won 134 (down from 209); the Smallholders, 48 (up from 26); and the Democratic Forum, 17 (down from 37). The extreme-right Justice and Life Party, led by anti-Semitic demagogue Ivan Csurka, won 14 seats. The Christian Democrats, who won 22 seats in 1994, did not win a seat.

Hungarians can change their government democratically under a multiparty system enshrined in an amended communist-era constitution. The 1998 elections were free and fair. A 1995 media law was meant to end years of political wrangling over control of the electronic media. It provided for the privatization of TV-2 and Radio Danubis and the operation of public service television and radio as joint-stock companies run by public foundations. There are three national public television channels, around twenty-six private commercial television stations, more than two hundred regional cable outlets, and more than thirty radio stations. A wide variety of independent newspapers and publications offers diverse opinions.

Freedoms of assembly and association are respected. Some two hundred political parties, movements, and associations have been registered since 1989, though the number of viable parties is about twenty. The two largest trade unions are the Democratic Confederation of Free Trade Unions (LIGA) and the Hungarian Workers Council. The National Federation of Hungarian Trade Unions (MSzOSz) is a successor to the communist-era union.

The judiciary is independent, and the Constitutional Court has ruled against the government on several occasions, notably nullifying aspects of the 1995 austerity economic program and the 1997 referendum issues. In 1997, a four-tier model that includes regional courts replaced the country's three-tier judicial system. Criteria for would-be judges were made more rigorous, calling for four rather than two years of preparatory practice as a lawyer. Court procedures are often slow.

Hungary's half-million Roma (Gypsies) continue to suffer discrimination in employment, housing, and education. Major ethnic groups such as Roma, Bulgarians, Germans, Slovaks, Poles, Armenians, Greeks, and Serbs have special units of self-government that receive funds from the central budget proportional to the size of their respective minorities.

There is freedom of movement, and the state does not control choice of residence or employment. Property rights are formally guaranteed by the constitution and are upheld de facto by contract and property laws. Foreigners are not allowed to acquire land. Many Hungarians, particularly outside the large cities, are employed in the so-called "black economy," which accounts for about 30 percent of the GDP.

Women are represented in government, business, and education, and several organizations represent women's issues. Freedom House's 1998–99 *Freedom in the World* rates Hungary a one in political rights and a two in civil liberties.

Religious Freedom

By 1600, Hungary's religious affiliation was 90 percent Protestant; however, in the seventeenth century Counter-Reformation period, many reverted to Catholicism. During the subsequent growth of the Austro-Hungarian Empire, Catholicism was the only public religion permitted until 1781, when Austro-Hungarian Emperor Josef II declared the Edict of Toleration. According to this declaration, Catholicism remained the state church; however Hungary's Protestant population regained fundamental rights to public worship and religious association. Currently, Hungarians cannot be asked their religion, which makes data collection difficult.

From 1948 to 1988, the communists controlled the churches and other religious groups by means of discrimination, intimidation, and infiltration. During the liberation period, in 1990, the famous Hungarian Religion Law Number 4 (Law on the Freedom of Religion and Conscience) was promulgated and recognized for its liberal approach to religious activity. Among international organizations and human rights advocates, it was seen as a model for European states. Under this law the registration of religious communities took place in a Hungarian court. The court did not examine the doctrines of the group but simply required that the founders present a written declaration that the intended activities of the group would not be illegal under civil law. In addition, with a one-hundred-member minimum stipulation for registered organizations, underground churches from the communist era could surface and obtain legal status. These groups usually wished to remain separate from established organizations of like doctrine, which had collaborated with the pre-1989 communist state officials. Despite these liberalizations, the last is marked by a series of attempts to pass stricter religious regulations that would reinforce traditional churches but worsen religious liberty for all others.

In 1989–90, the Hungarian Constitution was changed radically in order to comply with the major international and European human rights standards. In 1990, Hungary joined the Council of Europe and ratified the European Convention on Human Rights. The constitution guarantees fundamental human rights, including freedom of religion or belief. Furthermore, Article 8 (Fundamental Rights), paragraph 4 highlights a test that religious freedom can only be restricted in the case of a compelling state interest. However, under Article 60, "belief" is further protected and may *not* be suspended or restricted even under this compelling state interest test. According to Article 8, paragraph 4, "During a state of national crisis, state of emergency, or state of danger, the exercise of fundamental rights may be suspended or restricted, with the exception of the fundamental rights specified in Articles 54–56, paragraphs (2)–(4) of Article 57, Article 60, Articles 66–69, and Article 70/E." According to Article 60 [Belief], "(1) In the Republic of Hungary everyone has the right to freedom of thought, freedom of conscience and freedom of religion. (2) This right shall include the free choice or acceptance of a religion or belief, and the freedom to publicly or privately express or decline to express, exercise and teach such religions and beliefs by way of religious actions, rites or in any other way, either individually or in a group. (3) The church and the State shall operate in separation in the Republic of Hungary. (4) A majority of two-thirds of the votes of the Members of Parliament present is required to pass the law on the freedom of belief and religion." The legal guarantees of the Hungarian Constitution are enforced through the Constitutional Court.

However, in 1992, government officials introduced a serious threat to the 1990 Religion Law. The government's motive was to withhold financial support from four allegedly "destructive" religious minorities: the Unification Church, the Church of Scientology, Krishna Consciousness, and the Jehovah's Witnesses. The legislature wanted to amend Law Number 4 so that the state could increase the number of members required for registration from one hundred to ten thousand. This proposal was intended to defend the financial interests of the traditional churches. Although the measure was not debated, the four "destructive" religious minorities in question were denied state financial support.

In 1993, a new proposal to change the religious freedom law contained four proposed alterations. First, the state would determine whether the religious community potentially was harming "generally recognized moral principles." Second, in order to do this, special state authorities would check each religious community's creed. Third, legal registration would require ten thousand members or one hundred years historical presence in Hungary. Fourth, this quota membership stipulation would amend the law *retroactively,* which would mean that 80–90 percent of the previously legally registered religious communities would lose their acquired rights and legal status. Although heated legislative debate ensued, a tight General Assembly schedule meant that the amendments did not come out of committee to the General Assembly for discussion. In 1993, fifty-four religious communities had registered with the state; however, only thirty-two groups received state support.

According to the U.S. Department of State, as of 1997, there were seventy-nine officially recognized churches in Hungary; however, only fifty-nine of the officially recognized churches received government subsidies that year.

State financial assistance amounted to $5.4 million. A 1996 law permitted Hungarian citizens to donate 1 percent of their income tax to the church or nonprofit agency of their choice, but, in 1997, only 1 percent of the donated total went to churches, while the majority was donated to schools and animal welfare groups. This reflects the fact that, while nominal adherence is as shown in the statistics above, about 40 percent of Hungarians do not describe themselves as Christian.

The Hungarian government signed a 1997 treaty with the Vatican to return church property confiscated by the communist regime. Additionally, the treaty provided for a minimum state subsidy of $7.8 million to the Catholic Church. Reparations to the Jewish community included life pensions to 17,800 Holocaust survivors born after May 9, 1945, and 2,040 additional persons are to receive pensions when they reach sixty years of age. In reference to confiscated Jewish properties, a 1998 agreement made a compensatory payment of $2.7 million and returned nine properties. Additionally, several synagogues have been built since World War II.

Before the 1998 election, opponents of the 1990 Religion Law rallied their political constituents in support of the traditional and dominant churches. Hence, in effect, Hungary's current intolerance of cults is secular not religious. In addition to the alterations proposed in 1993, opponents suggested that the state should take into account the special social significance of a religious community so that legislation should express the degree to which a certain religious community has contributed to Hungary's historical and cultural heritage. Upon election, opponents of the 1990 law officially introduced such a proposal so that the classification of religious communities would be based on value judgments made by the state. This principle violates constitutional Article 60, paragraph 3: "The church and the State shall operate in separation in the Republic of Hungary." According to this paragraph, "A majority of two-thirds of the votes of the Members of Parliament present is required to pass the law on the freedom of belief and religion." Although a change of the law would require a two-thirds vote of agreement of the General Assembly, Zsolt Semjen, deputy secretary of state of the Ministry of National Cultural Heritage, declared that "whether they will have a two-third majority or not, the law will get through."

On April 27, 1999, a conference on "Religion—Society—Legislation" was organized by the Committee on Human Rights, Minorities and Religion of the General Assembly of the Republic of Hungary. In his introductory remarks, Joseph Hamori, the Hungarian Minister of National Cultural Heritage, informed the audience of the immutable intention of the government to differentiate between traditional churches and other religious communities. The proposed amendments to Law Number 4, of 1990, would mark a severe deterioration of the freedom of conscience and religion in Hungary.

Population	**986 million**
Hindu	78%
Muslim (mostly Sunni)	12%
Christian	3%
Indigenous	2.5%
Sikh	2%
Buddhist	0.9%
Jain	0.5%
Parsi	0.3%
Baha'i	0.2%
Jewish	0.1%
Nonreligious	0.5%
Religious Freedom Rating	5

Background

India achieved independence from Britain in 1947 with the partition of the subcontinent into a predominantly Hindu India and a Muslim Pakistan. Until recently, the centrist, secular Congress Party has ruled continuously except for periods in opposition in 1977–80 and 1989–91. In the late 1980s, a non-Congress administration introduced government job quotas for "backward" castes, triggering violent protests. In the aftermath, lower caste-based parties increasingly championed caste causes, and angry upper-caste voters increasingly supported the Hindu Nationalist Indian People's Party, the BJP. During the campaign for the 1991 elections, a suspected Sri Lankan Tamil separatist assassinated former premier Rajiv Gandhi, heir to the political dynasty of Congress standard bearers Nehru and Indira Gandhi.

In the mid-1990s, Congress lost eleven state elections due to a string of corruption scandals, a backlash against economic reforms by poor and lower-caste voters, and Muslim anger over the government's failure to prevent communal violence. Regional parties in southern India, lower caste-based parties, and the BJP in the northern Hindi-speaking belt made large gains. In 1998, the BJP campaigned as the only party that could deliver strong, stable government and fight corruption. The party also promised to introduce protectionist economic policies; eliminate the separate *shari'a* (Islamic law) code for marriage, divorce, and inheritance, followed by the country's 120 million Muslims; build a Hindu temple at the site of the Babri mosque; and consider "inducting" nuclear weapons into the country's arsenal. It won a plurality of seats and formed a government with twelve smaller parties.

The BJP gave up most of its religious agenda in order to attract secular parties into its coalition. In May 1998, India carried out a series of underground nuclear tests, which the government said were in response to a growing Chinese military threat. Many urban Hindus initially supported the tests as an assertion of the country's geopolitical aspirations. Many observers believe Home Minister Lal Krishna Advani, the hard-line BJP leader, is the real power behind the Vajpayee government. More broadly, observers suggest that the government is ultimately controlled by the National Volunteer Service (RSS), a far-right Hindu group modeled after 1930s European fascist parties. Vajpayee and other BJP leaders are RSS members, and the RSS reportedly vetted key cabinet appointments. In April 1999, the BJP government collapsed but, in fall elections, along with its partners, was returned to power with 284 of the 543 seats in the lower house of Parliament. The opposition Congress Party, led by Sonia Gandhi, Rajiv's widow, won 130 seats.

Indian citizens can change their government democratically; however, widespread official corruption and the criminalization of politics perpetuate poverty, disease, and illiteracy and contribute to civil liberties violations. The 1996 and 1998 elections were the fairest in India's history. Since the 1970s the criminalization of politics has accelerated. In February the *New York Times* cited studies showing that more than a third of state legislators in Uttar Pradesh, India's most populous state, have criminal records. The situation is worst in the impoverished northern state of Bihar. Many legislators reportedly lead criminal gangs and buy their way into politics.

The constitution allows the central government to dissolve state governments following a breakdown in normal administration. Successive governments have misused this power. Overall, economic reforms are steadily devolving power to the states. The judiciary is independent and in recent years has been active in response to public interest litigation over official corruption, environmental issues, and other matters. However, the judicial system has a backlog of more than thirty million cases, is widely considered to be subject to corruption and manipulation at the lower levels, and is largely inaccessible to the poor.

Police, army, and paramilitary forces are responsible for rape, torture, arbitrary detentions, "disappearances," and staged "encounter killings." They occasionally destroy homes, particularly in Kashmir, Punjab, and the northeastern states. The 1983 Armed Forces (Punjab and Chandigarh) Special Powers Act grants security forces wide latitude to use lethal force in Punjab, where a brutal army crackdown in the early 1990s largely ended a Sikh insurgency that began in the early 1980s. The broadly drawn 1980 National Security Act allows police to detain suspects for up to one year (two years in Punjab) without charges. Police torture of suspects and abuse of ordinary prisoners, particularly low-caste members, is routine, and rape of female convicts remains a problem.

The seven states of the northeast continue to be swept by antigovernment militancy and intertribal, internecine conflict among its two hundred ethnic groups. In recent decades hundreds of thousands of migrants from other parts of India and Bangladesh have generated local unrest over land tenure and underdevelopment. More than forty mainly indigenous-based rebel armies are seeking either greater autonomy or independence. The 1958 Armed Forces (Special Powers) Act grants security forces broad powers to use lethal force and detention in Assam and four nearby states and provides near immunity from prosecution for security forces acting under it. Maoist Naxalite guerrillas control large areas and kill dozens of police, politicians, landlords, and villagers each year in Andhra Pradesh, Madhya Pradesh, Bihar, and Orissa. Guerrillas run parallel courts in parts of Bihar.

The private press is vigorous. The Official Secrets Act empowers authorities to censor security-related articles, and authorities occasionally use it to limit criticism of the government. Journalists are occasionally harassed and attacked by government officials, party activists, militant Hindu groups, and others. Radio is both public and private, although the state-owned All India Radio is dominant, and its news coverage favors the government. The government maintains a monopoly on domestic television broadcasting. Section 144 of the Criminal Procedure Code empowers state authorities to declare a state of emergency, restrict free assembly, and impose curfews. Authorities occasionally use Section 144 to prevent demonstrations. Police occasionally react to demonstrations that turn violent by opening fire on protesters. Nongovernmental human rights organizations generally operate freely but face harassment in rural areas from landlords and other powerful interests.

Each year dowry disputes cause several thousand women to be burned to death, driven to suicide, or otherwise killed, and cause countless others to be harassed, beaten, or deserted by husbands. Although dowry is illegal, convictions in dowry deaths are rare. Rape and other violence against women are prevalent, and authorities take little action. Muslim daughters generally receive half the inheritance a son receives. Tribal land systems, particularly in Bihar, deny tribal women the right to own land. The constitution bars discrimination based on caste, but in practice members of so-called scheduled castes and scheduled tribes, as well as religious and ethnic minorities, routinely face discrimination. Scores of people are killed each year in caste-related violence.

Numerous religious traditions that place children in positions of servitude contribute to child sexual exploitation in rural India. Major cities have tens of thousands of street children, many of whom work as porters, vendors, and in other informal sector jobs. UNICEF estimates that up to sixty million children are forced to work in industry and agriculture. Several million are bonded laborers. Trade unions are powerful and independent, and workers exercise their rights to bargain collectively and strike. Freedom House's 1998–99 *Freedom in the World* votes India a two in political rights and a three in civil liberties, the latter an increase from four in the previous year.

Religious Freedom

Apart from the ancient set of religions collectively known as Hinduism, several other world religions have also exerted considerable influence on India. Islam's influence began with the Arab contacts of the ninth century, followed by a succession of Muslim conquests, which have left their mark on Indian society. Christianity first came to India in the first century A.D. but long remained confined to the coastal area of Kerala. With the arrival of the Portuguese in the fifteenth century and the British in the eighteenth century, Christianity's influence increased.

The constitution describes India as "a sovereign socialist secular democratic republic." It also contains detailed provisions for religious rights for all citizens. The constitution also empowers the courts to declare invalid any law passed by the parliament or a state government that contravenes the constitution. Article 25 guarantees freedom of conscience, free profession and practice of religion, as well as the right to propagate religion. Article 28 states that no religious instruction shall be provided in any wholly state-funded establishment, and parental consent in other institutions is required. This constitutional provision is currently under threat as a result of demands by Hindu nationalists for all schools in the country to conform to the concept of India as a Hindu nation. Article 30 guarantees religious minorities the right to establish and administer educational institutions. While minority institutions have enjoyed a certain degree of autonomy in the past, in recent years they have been increasingly subjected to restrictions and scrutiny, and there have been cases in which the courts have unjustly intervened in their internal affairs. Article 51 of the constitution also imposes a positive duty on citizens to promote harmony and the spirit of common brotherhood among all people of India transcending religious boundaries, but failure to abide by these provisions cannot be challenged in the courts.

Provision is made in the area of personal law for Hindu, Muslim, and Parsi communities. These personal law provisions are intended to safeguard religious liberty by providing for accepted religious differences. While, in 1965, the Indian government removed some of the anomalies of Hindu personal law, Muslim personal law remains strictly governed by the principles of *shari'a*. Among other disputes that have risen surrounding the issue of religious freedom for Muslims, an Allahbad High Court ruling in 1994 is significant: It states that unilateral divorce (*Talaq*) initiated by a Muslim husband is unconstitutional. This followed a ruling by the All-India Muslim Personal Law Board, which had upheld this provision as "a legitimate Islamic provision" for Muslim men. There is no separate personal law for Christians or the microscopic Jewish community. Under the 1869 Indian Divorce Act, Christian women are not usually entitled to seek divorce from their husbands even if they are mistreated. However, a court in Kerala state did allow a Christian woman to divorce her husband on the grounds of cruelty and desertion. Changes to the law have been proposed, but many Christians fear that these could become means of legal control.

Because of legal confusion over the status of religious personal law, matters affecting the religious freedom of minority groups are likely to remain unresolved until amendments are passed that clearly outline the rights and responsibilities obtained under different personal laws. In general India, with its constitutional guarantees for religious freedom and its ambiguous provisions to protect sensitive religious feelings, can be called a moderate secular state and not a radically or avowedly secular one. As Dr. Radhakrishnan, the former

president of India, noted, "Secularism is not a positive religion, or the state would assume divine prerogative. We hold that no religion should be given preferential treatment."

In reality, however, the religious freedom of Sikhs, Buddhists, and Jains, who are distinct religious communities, is not guaranteed under the constitution. Although, like other minorities, Sikhs, Buddhists, and Jains enjoy absolute freedom of worship and the freedom to establish and govern their own institutions, the government's refusal to recognize these three traditions as separate from Hinduism has been the subject of controversy. While Buddhist and Jain leaders have made fewer efforts to achieve separate constitutional recognition as religious entities distinct from Hinduism, Sikhs have strongly protested, and it is widely believed that this helped give rise to the Sikh Separatist movement in Punjab State in the 1980s. This has caused considerable bloodshed, including the assassination of then prime minister Mrs. Gandhi in 1983 by two of her own Sikh security guards.

Similar controversy concerning the religious identity of the indigenous (*Adivasi*) people has arisen because of the Indian government's consistent refusal at the United Nations to recognize that the religion of its indigenous people is distinct from Hinduism. This has led to the formation of the Indian Council of Indigenous and Tribal People in 1987. Members of officially scheduled tribes are about 8 percent of the population.

In the last few years, India has witnessed a rise in Hindu nationalism and of militant groups such as the RSS (Rashtriya Swayameseva), Wishua Hunadu Parishad (VHP), Shiv Sena, Bajrang Dal, and the BJP (Bharatiya Janata Party). The rise of *Hindutva* has led to the coming to power of the BJP, the political wing of Hindu nationalism. This ideology encompasses the vision of India as a Hindu state in which minorities must assimilate to the majority culture and language, revere the Hindu religion, and glorify the Hindu "race" and culture. Meanwhile the Indian Supreme Court has held that there is no real legal content to the term "Hindu." In the run up to fall 1999 national elections, the BJP has criticized Sonia Gandhi's foreign roots, and some of its supporters have complained that she is a "Christian" tool.

The presence of a substantial Muslim minority in India has always been perceived by radical Hindus as a threat to national unity because of the alleged potential loyalty of Muslims to Pakistan, which was formed as a separate land for Muslims in 1947. Although, since partition, Muslims have enjoyed freedom of worship, they often complain of discrimination in employment, education, and business. India has a long history of Hindu-Muslim riots, and thousands of people have lost their lives and property. Rising Hindu militancy and anti-Muslim sentiment resulted in the destruction of the sixteenth-century Babri mosque in Ayodha in 1992 by a Hindu mob, with the open support of the BJP state government. This destruction was followed by well-organized communal violence across the country, in which thousands of people were either killed or disappeared. This raised questions as to whether India will be able to remain a secular country or become a Hindu nation, particularly when the election slogan of some radical Hindu nationalists was "Muslims have only two abodes—Pakistan or the graveyard."

In recent years the smaller Christian minority has also become a scapegoat for many of the ills prevailing in Indian society. While Christians are generally regarded as peace loving, they are still perceived by Hindu nationalists to be loyal to a "foreign religion." Systematic antiminority propaganda, fueled by the hate speech of right-wing Hindu nationalists, has unleashed a recent campaign of terror against Christians, especially in Gujarat. Incidents of persecution of Christians include destruction of churches, burning of Bibles in schools, torture in police custody, mob violence to disrupt church services and Christian meetings, rape, and brutal murder. In early 1997, Father Thomas, a Jesuit priest from Belgium and a Christian human rights activist, was brutally killed by militants disguised as police officers. Father Christudas was severely beaten and then paraded naked through the streets by Hindu fundamentalists, in full view of the police.

Since late 1998, the number of attacks has increased. In 1999, nationalists burned to death, along with his two sons, an Australian who worked with lepers. On June 22, India's Central Bureau of Investigation filed charges against eighteen men for this murder. The United Christian Forum for Christian Human Rights has released a document under the title *Open White Paper* detailing 113 reported incidents of attacks, including the rape of four nuns and the murders of twelve Christians by Hindu militants in the last two years. In March 1999, attacks on Christians in the state of Orissa left twelve hundred homeless. In September a Roman Catholic was killed by a mob in Orissa, and a nun was kidnapped in the eastern state of Bihar, while on October 2, a priest was killed in Orissa by Hindu fundamentalists. In November a Christian gathering in Delhi was attacked, and at least twelve people were injured. Muslim and

Christian leaders have jointly protested anti-Christian violence. Attacks have increased in the new year.

Since Indian independence, conversion to Christianity and Islam has been a cause of tension. Despite demands for legislation by radical Hindu nationalists for a ban on conversion to religions of "foreign origins," the constitutional right to choose and propagate a religion has been safeguarded. However, the courts have eroded this right. In 1977, the Supreme Court ruled that the constitutional right to *propagate religion* did not include the right to convert any person to one's *own religion*. While attempts to introduce a bill in the national parliament have failed, in the last five years some state governments have passed acts that outlaw conversion to Islam and Christianity from low-caste Hindu and tribal backgrounds, but they do not prohibit conversion to Hinduism.

Part of the ancient economic and religious system of Hinduism, known as the caste system, has been a dominant force of the socioeconomic life of India for more than two thousand years. A Hindu majority means that the caste system still plays an important part in Indian life, dividing the society according to a strict hierarchy. A majority of converts from Hinduism are outcasts who embrace Islam or Christianity as a way to escape the traditional religious sanctions imposed on them under the Hindu caste system. In November 1999, two hundred *dalit* families near New Delhi threatened to convert to Christianity unless the government reserved more slots for *dalits* in medical and engineering colleges. However, while conversion to Islam or Christianity is perceived by some as an emancipation from the bondage of Hinduism, many converts from a low-caste Hindu background, especially

women, still suffer a certain degree of discrimination from their "high-caste" Christian and Muslim coreligionists.

Hindu rules ban *dalits* (formerly called "untouchables," and about 16 percent of the population) from entering the temples. Although, since independence, legal forms of affirmative action have been introduced, it is an open secret that the great majority of low-caste Hindus in India still continue to be treated as *dalit*. In many parts of the country, it is socially unacceptable to allow low-caste Hindus to visit a Hindu temple or participate in a Hindu religious festival. In 1994, the national parliament was informed that between 1991 and 1993, more than sixty-two thousand cases of atrocities were registered against *dalit* and indigenous people. This, together with legal limitations on their right to convert, adds up to serious violations of religious liberty and creates a system akin to religious apartheid. If *dalits* convert to Christianity or Islam, they lose their eligibility for affirmative action programs, though not if they convert to Buddhism, Jainism, or Sikhism, as these faiths are legally regarded as subsets of Hinduism.

Along with constitutional guarantees of religious freedom and respect for the religious feelings of all, there are restrictions in the penal code intended to protect religion. These include injuring or defiling places of worship with intent to insult the religion of any class, disturbance of religious assemblies, and utterances intended to wound the religious feelings of others. These laws are being increasingly violated, often with the connivance of the authorities. The authorities have consistently failed to take action in the face of mob attacks on religious properties belonging to the minority groups. Despite a Supreme Court ruling in 1995 outlawing hate speech, many Hindu leaders and politicians continue to use antiminority propaganda (particularly against Muslims and Christians) for political gain with virtual impunity. Government figures have denounced those who report on religious violence. Undoubtedly, the ineffectiveness of the judicial system is compounded by the certain degree of independence exercised by some state governments ruled by Hindu groups. For example, in 1998, the Shiv Sena government of Maharashtra decided to disband the National Commission for Minorities, which had been set up to investigate cases of violence against minorities.

While the vernacular press has always been biased against the minorities, the English press has historically had the reputation of being fairly balanced towards all religious communities. With the rise of Hindu nationalism, this has changed, and some leading Hindu intellectuals and journalists, such as Arun Shoorie, have shown increasing sympathy for the cause of fundamentalist Hindu nationalism. While constitutional and legal provisions to safeguard religious freedom remain, the rise of Hindu nationalism and Hindu militancy, along with measures to increase public order, have seriously threatened those tenets.

Indonesia

Population	**211.8 million**
Muslim	83%
Protestant	9%
Catholic	4%
Hindu	2%
Buddhist	1%
Other	1%
Religious Freedom Rating	5

Background

By 1700, the Dutch had colonized most of present-day Indonesia, although Holland did not fully control the entire archipelago until the early twentieth century. Following the Japanese occupation in World War II, in 1945 President Sukarno proclaimed Indonesia's independence. Faced with the task of building a nation out of an archipelago of some 13,600 islands and 300 ethnic groups, Sukarno and other independence leaders sought a compromise between proponents of an Islamic state and their secular Muslim opponents with its Pancasila ideology.

Indonesia effectively became a religious nation without a state religion.

Following an alleged left-wing coup attempt in 1965, the Army Strategic Reserve, led by then General Suharto, led a slaughter of an estimated five hundred thousand suspected Indonesia Communist Party members. In 1968, two years after assuming key political and military powers, Suharto formally became president. Under Suharto's highly centralized regime, economic development lifted millions of Indonesians out of poverty, but the president's family and cronies held privileged business positions, corruption drained economic resources, and authorities heavily restricted political and social freedoms. In 1997, the regional economic crisis led to fears that the private sector would default on some eighty billion dollars in foreign debt. As the rupiah (the currency) plunged, food prices soared. Throughout the archipelago, rioting targeted ethnic Chinese merchants and

Christian churches. The ethnic Chinese comprise only 3.5 percent of the population but control an estimated 70 percent of the country's private wealth and are often scapegoated during times of economic hardship.

The economic crisis led to unprecedented antigovernment demonstrations in early 1998. The army's deadly shooting of six student demonstrators in May, followed by three days of massive riots in Jakarta, forced Suharto to resign on May 21 after thirty-two years of often brutal authoritarian rule. Vice President B. J. Habibie took office as president. As students continued to demonstrate for free elections and an end to the military's formal role in politics, in November parliament agreed to early legislative elections, which were held on June 7, 1999.

Indonesians are enjoying unprecedented, though still limited, freedoms. While the rupiah has stabilized, the banking system is barely functioning, and the economic crisis has caused millions of Indonesians to fall below the poverty level. After three decades during which Suharto forcibly depoliticized society, opposition figures had few grassroots connections on which to draw. Not surprisingly, many of the new political parties formed around existing Muslim organizations. Some fear that this could introduce religion into politics for the first time in decades. Megawati Sukarnoputri competed as the Indonesian Democratic Party's (PDI) candidate on a secular, nationalist platform, and, when the delayed vote counts were released in July 1999, the PDI had won 33.7 percent of the vote, while Golkar received 22 percent. A period of coalition building began. Islamicist parties gathered few votes. Before and during the October meeting of the People's Consultative Assembly, which chose the president, there was much "horse trading" between the par-

ties. Moderate Muslim leader Abdurrahman Wahid emerged as president, and Megawati became vice president. While many of the tight restrictions on political activity that characterized the Suharto era have been lifted, the president was still indirectly elected.

Under the doctrine of *dwifungsi* (dual function), the armed forces are responsible for territorial defense and for maintaining internal cohesion. The military currently holds 15 percent of seats in national, provincial, and district legislatures. Moreover, the overarching consensus-oriented Pancasila philosophy is still considered to be the guiding state ideology.

The most severe rights violations occur in Aceh, East Timor, and Irian Java. In the resource-rich Aceh province on the northern tip of Sumatra, the military's counterinsurgency operation against Aceh Merdeka (Free Aceh) separatists peaked between 1989–92, although there have been continuing reports of killings, incommunicado detentions, and other abuses. Some observers accuse the military of instigating unrest as a pretext for maintaining troops in Aceh. In December 1999, the new government announced that it would not prosecute generals for atrocities committed by their troops.

The judiciary is not independent, and it is rife with corruption. The executive branch appoints and can dismiss or reassign judges at will. Police frequently torture suspects and prisoners. Numerous human rights groups have accused soldiers of instigating and participating in anti-Chinese attacks. In the ensuing months activists investigating the attacks received death threats.

The Agency for Coordination of Assistance for the Consolidation of National Security (BAKORSTANAS) has wide latitude in curbing alleged security threats. The Habibie government has maintained the 1963 Anti-Subversion Law, which allows authorities to detain suspects for up to one year without charge. The Suharto government had jailed hundreds of people, many of them political dissidents, under sedition or hate-sowing statues. In the months after taking office, Habibie released political prisoners, but several dozen are still held. While it is too early to detect any real improvement, the new governments have taken the positive measure of acknowledging that abuses have occurred. Authorities frequently denied the permits required for public assemblies and demonstrations, and police often forcibly broke up peaceful, unsanctioned demonstrations. During Suharto's rule, the approximately 286 private newspapers and magazines operated under frequent threats from authorities to kill sensitive stories. In recent years, authorities had arrested several journalists associated with the Alliance of Independent Journalists or with underground political publications. The Alliance and other press groups now operate legally. Authorities frequently imprisoned nongovernmental organization (NGO) activists, restricted them from public speaking, and raided their offices. NGOs now operate more freely. In addition to being targeted for violent attacks in recent years, ethnic Chinese face severe cultural, educational, and business restrictions. The Habibie government ended the de facto monopoly of the government-controlled All Indonesian Workers Union.

In the spring of 1999, Habibie announced that there would be a referendum concerning independence in East Timor, and it was held on August 30. In the run up to the referendum, militias, supported by the Indonesian military, intimidated and attacked pro-independence leaders. Nevertheless, the Timorese voted 78.5 percent for independence. The militias unleashed a wave of violence, killing hundreds and destroying homes and infrastructure. Hundreds of thousands were left homeless, and many fled the territory. In mid-September, United Nations-authorized troops, predominately Australian, arrived to impose order and peace. They found the territory devastated. (See section on East Timor.)

In addition to the wholesale graft and influence-peddling carried out by the Suharto family, corruption is pervasive at all levels of government. Freedom House's 1998–99 *Freedom in the World* rates Indonesia a six in political rights and a four in civil liberties. Both are improvements over the previous year due to Indonesia's ongoing democratization. Subsequent events in 1999 show further major improvements.

Religious Freedom

Religious practice in Indonesia is a complicated mix of major world faiths and traditional rituals and beliefs. Two powerful, religious-based kingdoms emerged in the region by the end of the seventh century. The Buddhist Srivijaya Empire ruled South Sumatra and much of the Malay Peninsula, while the Hindu Mataram Kingdom controlled Java. The last Hindu kingdom, the Java-based Majapahit, controlled Java, Bali, and the island of Madura until the fifteenth century. By then, Islam, initially introduced by Arab traders, had spread from ports to the inland areas. The Majapahits retreated to Bali, which today is Indonesia's only Hindu-majority area.

The Dutch permitted, and at times encouraged, missionaries to go into isolated interior and mountain regions, and to the small eastern islands, to convert local people to Protestantism. One of their aims was to create Christian enclaves to prevent Islam from becoming a unifying force in the colony. Meanwhile, the Portuguese brought Catholicism to the island of Flores, which they eventually sold to the Dutch, and to the island of Timor, the eastern half of which Lisbon ruled until 1975.

Following Indonesia's independence, in a compromise with various Muslim groups, Sukarno established a type of state ideology cum civil religion—Pancasila. The preamble to the constitution includes the Pancasila philosophy, which states: "The State shall be based upon the following philosophical principles: Belief in a monotheistic God, just and civilized humanity, the unity of Indonesia, democracy guided by the wisdom of deliberations of representatives, and social justice for all the Indonesian people." Article 29 of the constitution states: "1. The State shall be based upon the belief in the One and Only God. 2. The State guarantees all persons the freedom of worship, each according to his or her own religion or belief."

Indonesia is the world's largest Muslim country, and its religious communities have traditionally coexisted peacefully. Especially in Java, Islam is often combined with traditional beliefs. Indonesian law formally recognizes five faiths: Islam, Buddhism, Hinduism, Catholicism, and Protestantism. In practice, the government also permits the practice of Aliran Kepercayaan mysticism, and other religions can rightfully exist even though they are not officially recognized (though their adherents must, for legal purposes, identify themselves with the recognized five). However, authorities have banned some groups, such as the Baha'i and Jehovah's Witnesses, and have placed restrictions on others, especially any Islamic group it regards as heterodox. The government

has also banned atheism on the grounds that it violates the first principle of Pancasila. Conversions between faiths are legal and do occur. Proselytizing is legal, although the government discourages it in some areas where another religion has a large majority. Separate Islamic courts hear Muslim marriage and family disputes. Such matters are adjudicated in civil courts for non-Muslims.

News media are forbidden to carry anything that insults a religion. Individuals have freedom of worship within the limits of Pancasila. Religious groups can train and appoint clergy; carry out educational programs, including having schools and universities; carry out charitable activities; own and acquire property; produce, import, and distribute literature; receive donations; and have contact with coreligionists domestically and overseas. In most cases, religious bodies can manage their internal affairs, but the Suharto government did interfere with the selection of bishops in one Batak denomination in northern Sumatra, and the government requires all religious bodies to incorporate Pancasila as the first article of their creed.

The status of religious freedom in Indonesia must be assessed in the context of the overall human rights situation. In practice religious freedom is generally restricted by extralegal rather than legal means. Sukarno and Suharto were suspicious of politicized Islam and permitted only moderate Muslim parties. Even these parties had little power in Indonesia's tightly controlled political system. Moreover, Suharto systematically depoliticized society and prevented mosques and Muslim religious groups from speaking freely on political issues or openly becoming involved in elections. In general, the lack of a free press and tight limits on the political system prevented any meaningful discussion of economic, social, religious, or ethnic issues. The largest of the new political parties have grown out of Muslim organizations, which has disturbed some more secular politicians. The two largest Muslim organizations are the traditional, rural-based Nahdlatul Ulama, and its rival, Muhammadiyah—the former headed by Abdurrahman Wahid and the latter by Amien Rais. In the 1999 legislative elections, it became clear that radical Islamic parties had little public support. Wahid, however, became president of Indonesia and Rais became speaker of the assembly.

A complex interplay between official policy and social tensions has led to an increasing number of attacks on the ethnic Chinese minority and Christian churches and, to a lesser extent, Buddhist temples. In the unrest following the alleged left-wing coup attempt in 1965, an anticommunist purge killed an untold number of ethnic Chinese on suspicion of being linked to Beijing, or simply to settle old scores. Many Chinese converted to Christianity in the 1960s to show that they were not communists. As president, Suharto granted several ethnic Chinese tycoons trading monopolies in key sectors of the economy, knowing that they would be easy to control since the tiny ethnic Chinese community would never be able to challenge him politically.

Today, many Muslim Indonesians resent the ethnic Chinese community for their wealth, business skills, alleged insider connections, and religion. Ethnic Chinese number just 3.5 percent of the population but hold an estimated 70 percent of Indonesia's private wealth. Yet most ethnic Chinese play a modest economic role as shopkeepers and merchants, and many are poor by any standard. Moreover, ethnic Chinese are pro-

hibited from entering the civil service or military, leaving them little choice but to continue as merchants.

As such, attacks against ethnic Chinese often are motivated by both ethnicity and religion. Even before Indonesia's economic crisis began in 1997, observers had reported an increasing number of attacks on Christian churches. In early 1998, the Indonesia Christian Communication Forum, a nongovernmental organization based in Surabaya, reported that 438 churches had been destroyed since Indonesia declared independence in 1945. Of those, 131 were attacked between 1995 and 1997. In 1998 and 1999, the rate of attacks increased. Some mosques have also been destroyed in West Timor and Irian Jaya.

As the economic crisis sent food prices soaring, Muslims attacked ethnic Chinese shops and churches in Java, Sulawesi, Sumatra, and other areas. By early 1998, the organized nature of some riots led to suspicions that the government had orchestrated the unrest to shift the blame for the crisis onto the ethnic Chinese. At a minimum, security forces often failed to provide adequate protection to ethnic Chinese merchants and to churches, apparently content to let the rural poor blow off steam.

Probably fewer than half of Indonesia's six million ethnic Chinese are Christian, and several attacks on churches have targeted non-Chinese ethnic groups. On November 22, 1998, Muslim mobs burned or damaged thirteen churches in Jakarta. As is often the case in Indonesia, the attacks began after rumors spread that ethnic Ambonese, many of whom are Christians, had burned down a mosque. In Ambon itself, communal fights between Christians and Muslims in early 1999 caused hundreds of deaths.

Fighting flared again in July and November 1999, with hundreds more killed. At the end of 1999, about eighty thousand, a quarter of the population, had fled, and some one hundred thousand were homeless. In the new year, fighting had spread to neighboring islands where it has taken the form not of intercommunal rioting but focused attacks on Christians by radical Muslim elements opposed to Wahid's moderate government. Several thousand "jihad warriors" have been organizing in militia camps in Java.

In a bizarre development, in the fall of 1998, unknown assailants killed more than 140 people in Java, many of them Koranic teachers, and accused others of being sorcerers or black magicians. Villagers occasionally kill alleged sorcerers and black magicians in Java. However, the organized nature of the attacks and the targeting of Koranic teachers led some observers to speculate that authorities had sponsored the violence to divide Islamic groups. Others believe that more militant Islamic groups have targeted the much more tolerant members of Nahdatul Ulama, Indonesia's largest Muslim organization.

A small minority of Indonesians is referred to as "people who do not yet have a religion." These people, in fact, practice uncodified tribal religions. While there is no outward pressure on them to convert, scholars have noted that the very phrase, "do not yet have a religion," implies that they will eventually adopt one of the recognized religions. This is reinforced by the fact that

Islamic religious education is a part of the public school curriculum. The educational system and official policy also promote the concept of *agama*, or freedom to practice a recognized religion, as synonymous with progress, modernity, and loyalty to the state. As such, those who practice tribal religions face social pressures to convert.

East Timor (see separate section) is a former Portuguese colony that Indonesia invaded in 1975. The United Nations has never recognized Indonesia's 1976 annexation. According to the United States Department of State, Carlos Filipe Ximenes Belo (the East Timor Roman Catholic bishop), and other leaders of the majority Catholic population, the government has attempted to alter the territory's religious composition by promoting migration of Muslim Indonesians from other islands. Militia attacks on the Timorese, both before and, especially, after the August 1999 referendum, seemed to target churches and church workers until the United Nations took over the territory. In other areas—especially Irian Jaya, Kalimantan, and the sparsely populated eastern islands—the transmigration programs have raised ethnic and religious tension. Often these tribal areas are largely Christian, and migrants, usually from crowded Java, are usually Muslim. Christians complain that they are being swamped and the country's Java-based power structure favors the Muslims. There are still separatist movements in these areas, especially Irian Java.

Population	66.2 million
Shi'a	87%
Sunni	12%
Baha'i	0.5%
Christian	0.4%
Jewish	0.03%
Parsi (Zoroastrian)	0.04%
Other	0.03%
Religious Freedom Rating	7

Background

Shi'a Islam and the Iranian state have been intertwined since the sixteenth century. In 1979, the pro-Western rule of the Pahlavi monarchy came to an end, following widespread dissatisfaction with the policies of the shah. Shiite religious leaders, under the leadership of the exiled spiritual head of Shi'as, Imam Ayatollah Khomeini, managed to mobilize mass support, claiming Shi'a Islam to be the only valid Islamic system. He evoked the themes of passionate struggle and martyrdom, which are fundamental to Shi'a thought. The Islamic revolution produced a regime controlled by Islamic jurists and clerics committed to the spirit and ethics of Islam as the basis of all political, social, and economic activities.

The constitutional arrangements brought about after the Islamic revolution were designed to ensure that the relative religious tolerance of the monarchy was replaced by an entrenched Shi'a Islam, with the comprehensive principles of state regulated by senior clerics and the *ulama* (religious scholars). These arrangements embody an acknowledgment of the superior, public authority of jurists and scholars under the spiritual leadership of the ayatollah/imam, which is a traditional feature of Shiite Islam. The system has been established and kept in place partly by repressive measures and partly by the exploitation of religious senti-

ment, backed by a pervasive anti-Western nationalism.

Following Khomeini's death in June 1989, Ayatollah Ali Khamenei assumed the role of supreme religious leader and chief of state. Popular disaffection has grown in recent years because of the rising cost of living, a huge foreign debt, and 25 percent inflation. Since the revolution, per-capita income has decreased while prices of basic items such as food and fuel have soared. Furthermore, two-thirds of Iranians are under age twenty-five and do not identify closely with the ideals of the revolution.

In March 1997, Mohammed Khatami's liberal reputation won him the support of intellectuals, women, youths, and business groups who seek greater social openness as well as an end to state interference in the economy. Ninety percent of the electorate turned out to vote, and 70 percent voted for Khatami. However, because of the constraints of a highly restrictive political system, Khatami holds little real power. He is accountable to the conservative-dominated *majlis* and bound by the absolute authority of the supreme leader. He cannot realistically challenge the religious basis of the government and therefore cannot legislate political pluralism. In response to his efforts, his supporters have been harassed, jailed, and in some cases murdered by hardline elements. Nevertheless, women have been increasingly taking liberties in their dress and are allowed increasingly to attend sporting events, and even to participate in recreational activities alongside men. And Iranians have turned out on a number of occasions to protest vociferously against the arrests of dissident clerics and politicians.

Iranians cannot change their government democratically. As all legislative and presidential candidates must support the ruling Council of Guardians, meaningful opposition is effectively barred. Political parties are strongly discouraged, and the few that exist are not allowed to participate in elections. Violations of free expression and low-level harassment of Khatami's campaign marred the March 1997 presidential election. The state continues to maintain control through terror: arbitrary detention, torture, disappearance, summary trial, and execution are commonplace. A penal code adapted in 1996 is based on *shari'a* (Islamic) law and provides for the death penalty for a range of social and political misconduct. The intelligence and interior ministries operate vast informant networks. Security forces enter homes and offices, open mail, and monitor telephone conversations without court authorization. Hard-line factions have used extrajudicial killings to silence political criticism.

The judiciary is not independent. Judges, like all officials, must meet strict political and religious qualifications. Bribery is common. Revolutionary courts try political and religious cases but are often arbitrarily assigned cases that normally fall under civil court jurisdiction. Charges are often vague. Press freedom improved slightly through 1998, though tolerance remains arbitrary and crackdowns occurred. At least eleven journalists were arrested and charged with offenses like "publishing insults and lies" and "propagating anti-Islamic attitudes." Besides official repression, hard-line vigilantism emerged as a new threat to the press. The broadcast media remain closely controlled by conservatives. The print media are enjoying considerable new freedom, and it has been reported that some one thousand new newspapers and journals have been licensed since Khatami became president. Women face discrimination in le-

gal, educational, and employment matters. Women may be fined, imprisoned, or lashed for violating Islamic dress codes, though enforcement of these provisions has slackened somewhat recently. Unlike women in Saudi Arabia and the Gulf states, Iranian women may vote, stand for public office, and drive. However, a woman must have permission from a male relative to obtain a passport. There are no independent labor unions. The government-controlled Worker's House is the only legal federation. Collective bargaining is nonexistent. Freedom House's 1998–99 *Freedom in the World* rates Iran a six in political rights and in civil liberties. The rating for political rights was an increase from a seven the previous year due to the development of a de facto political opposition.

Religious Freedom

The Iranian Islamic regime is based on the concept of a single society based on Shi'a Islam. The notion of religious (or political) pluralism is unacceptable, and where international documents require it, senior Iranian leaders denounce it as a Western aberration even though Iran is a member of the UN and signatory to some of its conventions. The election of President Mohammed Khatami in May 1997 has not led to any perceptible softening in policy towards religious minorities. The degree of political freedom, especially freedom of expression, that is tolerated under Khatami can best be described as "freedom under the shadow of fear." Religious minorities continue to live in this shadow.

State institutions that embody the establishment of Shi'a Islam include: (1) The Wali Faqih (religious leader), initially the late Ayatollah Ali Khomeini, who was declared to be the present representative of Imam Mehdi, the "hidden Twelfth Imam" of traditional Shi'a belief. He sets the moral guidelines for state policy and decisions and controls the security forces and judiciary. (2) The Majlis-E-Khobregan (Council of Experts), comprising eighty-three clerics who choose the successor to the ayatollah if he dies in office. (3) The Shura-E-Nigahban (Council of Guardians), made up of six clerical jurists chosen by the ayatollah and six other Muslim jurists, who ensure legislation is compatible with Islamic precepts. This council must approve all presidential and parliamentary candidates. (4) The Shura-Ye Tashkhis-E Maslahat-E Nezam (Committee to Determine the Expediency of the Islamic Order), comprising senior state leaders who arbitrate on legal and theological disputes occurring within the legislative process. The Ministry of Culture and Islamic Guidance is responsible for the policing and monitoring of all religious minorities in the country. The Islamic credentials of all candidates for election to the Majlis or parliament are closely scrutinized.

According to the constitution, Iran treats non-Shi'a Islam with "complete respect" and gives formal recognition to Zoroastrianism (the ancient religion of Persia), Judaism, and Christianity (faiths whose followers are called "People of the Book" in the *Qur'an* and who, in traditional Islamic practice, are the *dhimmi* or "protected people"). However, Article 19 of the constitution accords equal rights to Iranians irrespective of ethnicity, color, or language but notably excludes diversity of faith. Non-Muslims must state their religion on census forms. Adherents of Zoroastrianism, Judaism, and Orthodox Christianity (but not Protestants or Roman Catholics) have separate, minority representation in the Majlis and are nominally free to practice their ritu-

als and educate their children accordingly, but they may not enter government service or hold commissions in the armed services. University applicants are screened for Islamic orthodoxy and must pass a test in Islamic theology, a condition that obviously restricts applications from the religious minorities.

Conversion from Islam to another faith is a capital crime. Constitutional guarantees of freedom to non-Muslim faiths are crippled by additional words and phrases in the relevant articles that make the guarantees subject to the priority of Islam. Thus, Article 26 allows for the formation of religious societies provided they do not violate "the criteria of Islam or the basis of the Islamic republic." Article 20 guarantees sexual equality "in conformity with Islamic criteria." Article 24 denies freedom of the press to writing "detrimental to the fundamental principles of Islam." Such phrases provide an effective legal basis for varying degrees of oppression and administrative action against non-Muslims, nullifying other constitutional guarantees of equal rights for all. The Baha'i faith, not mentioned in the constitution, derives no benefit even from the limited guarantees given to others. Because of the pressures on non-Shi'a and the need to declare religion on census forms, the numbers in religious minorities are almost certainly understated.

Religious differences do not coincide with ethnic groups, but there are parallels. Shi'a Islam is the dominant faith of the Persian and Azerbaijani majority, while Sunni Islam is largely confined to distinct ethnic groups such as Kurds, Baluchis, Turkmen, Arabs, and Turks. Christians are in several groupings: Chaldean, Latin, and Armenian Catholics, totaling 13,000; Armenian,

Assyrian, and Greek Orthodox, together totaling 122,000 (Armenian 112,000 of these); and Protestants, numbering 8,500. The authorities claim that the *Parsi* (Zoroastrians) community now numbers 90,000, but this figure is considered doubtful by many.

Up to six million people profess to be Sunni Muslim, the form of Islam practiced by the majority of Muslims outside Iran. This is a problem for the regime that presents Shi'a Islam as the system for state governance and the basis for all human relationships. The Sunni community was officially wooed during the conflict with (largely Sunni) Iraq, but Shi'a zealots who have practiced widespread discrimination against Sunni communities have not been rebuked, nor has anti-Sunni violence been punished. However, the Iranian government is careful not to resort to the repressive tactics used against other minorities, which would harm Iran's relations with other Islamic countries. Tension between Sunnis and Shi'as has led to major demonstrations in majority Sunni towns. No Sunni Muslim country or religious leaders have condemned the persecution of Sunni Muslims in Iran.

Under the monarchy, members of the small Zoroastrian community were regarded as "true, ancient Iranians," and the community received official approval as a symbol of pre-Islamic history and culture. Some individuals held high public position; many traveled to reside in Tehran from areas where they were previously in the majority, such as Yazd, Central Iran, and Kerman in the Southeast. Since the Islamic revolution, this situation has been reversed. Individuals have returned to the countryside or gone abroad, and those remaining experience reduced legal rights

and discrimination in education and employment.

The Iranian government, being strongly anti-Israel, is widely suspected of giving support to Palestinian terrorist activity. Jews are suspected of disloyalty and are forbidden to visit Israel on penalty of imprisonment. Jewish families cannot travel abroad together. The sole Jewish member of the national parliament is required to denounce Israel regularly. The government discriminates against the microscopic Jewish community in awarding commercial contracts and in education and employment. Jewish schooling is forbidden, as is the study of Hebrew. Since 1979, the regime has executed at least thirteen Jews, either for religious reasons or allegations of spying for Israel. In February and March 1999, thirteen Jews were arrested in the southern town of Shiraz, home to many of Iran's estimated twenty-seven thousand Jews, and accused of espionage for Israel and the United States. Several reports say they have been tortured. They allegedly had contacts with family members in Israel, had (illegally) imported prayer books from there, and three had reportedly visited Israel. Their trial has been scheduled for the spring of 2000.

In 1994, the then Iranian president, Hasemi-Rafsanjani, said that only Islam had validity, that all nations should accept it, and that Islam was certain to triumph over its oppressors, including Christianity. This statement was consonant with the government's efforts, since 1990, to intimidate, and where possible eliminate, Christian activity in Iran. Congregations of the ancient churches, who worship in older languages not otherwise understood, have agreed not to allow participation by Muslims or Muslim converts, and so they are permitted to function. However, members still experience all the disadvantages that accrue to other non-Muslims.

Major police action has been directed against modern, evangelical forms of Christianity, which is thought to be responsible for the conversion of Muslims. Several Protestant Christian leaders, including those who converted from Islam, have been sentenced to death or assassinated in the last decade. They include Hussein Soodman (1994), Mehdi Debaj (1994), and Mohammed Yussefi, a Western-educated pastor whose body was found hanging from a tree in 1996.

The National Bible Society was closed in 1990; there is a ban on the printing of all Christian literature and constant surveillance of churches and interrogation of those who attend them. The official closure of churches has led to several going underground. Since 1993, churches and their pastors have been required to declare publicly (and falsely) that they have full constitutional rights and that they will not attempt to convert Muslims. Some people suspected of involvement in evangelical activity are alleged to have disappeared for prolonged periods of time and been tortured. The ban on all activity outside church walls and the systematic monitoring of evangelical activity has led to death threats against Iranian Christian converts residing abroad.

Orthodox Islam regards Baha'i, which preaches universal truth and peace and brotherhood, as a heresy. Baha'i teaching is perceived as anti-Islamic and pro-Western. As the Baha'i faith is not mentioned in the constitution, its adherents are regarded as "unprotected infidels" and have no legal right to seek defense against attacks. In 1983, a decree was issued forbidding Baha'is to meet or be formally organized as a community. In 1991, the state authorities produced a secret document planning the eradication of the Baha'i community. Iran's Baha'is have been called the worst persecuted religious community in the world. It is believed that since the Iranian revolution, hundreds of Baha'is have been either executed or assassinated and/or killed by violent mobs.

Repressive anti-Baha'i measures in Iran include the closure of Baha'i holy places and institutions, the seizure of cemeteries, the confiscation of private and business premises, and the loss of employment, along with pension rights and other benefits. The torture and execution of at least two hundred Baha'i, including three in 1998, has been widely documented along with the disappearance and arrest of numerous others. In late 1998, seven Baha'i were on death row, out of an estimated fifty detainees nationwide. In 1998, the community's Open University, formed in 1987 as a response to the refusal of public university places to Baha'i young people, was closed. Thirty-six students in fourteen different cities were also arrested. Severe persecution has forced many Baha'is to emigrate, convert to Islam, or go underground.

Ireland

Population	3.7 million
Catholic	92%
Anglican	3.7%
Other Protestant	1%
Muslim	0.2%
Jewish	0.1%
Other	2%
None	1.0%
Religious Freedom Rating	1

Background

Ireland's twenty-six counties held Dominion status within the British commonwealth from 1921 until 1948, when Ireland became a fully independent state. The six counties of Northern Ireland remained part of the United Kingdom at the insistence of their Protestant majority. Despite Articles 2 and 3 of the Irish constitution, which claim Irish sovereignty over the entire island, the republic has played only a consultative role in Northern affairs, as defined by the 1985 Anglo-Irish accord. As part of the 1998 peace agreement, the Irish voted in May to amend the articles so that a united Ireland may not be established without the consent of a majority of people in both jurisdictions.

Recently economic policy is largely determined by the Maastricht Treaty provisions for European Monetary Union (EMU), and Ireland joined the single currency in January 1999. The current wave of economic prosperity is expected to last well into the next decade. In a referendum on May 22, 1998, 62 percent of Irish voters approved the Amsterdam treaty on closer ties with the European Union.

Current prime minister Bertie Ahern of the Fianna Fail party has had his popularity boosted by his success in helping to bring about a peace settlement in Northern Ireland. The 1998 "Good Friday Agreement" recognized the "principle of consent" in the status of Northern Ireland, created a 108-member assembly to be elected by proportional representation, established a north-south ministerial council to consult on matters of mutual concern to Ireland and Northern Ireland, and established a British-Irish council of British, Irish, Northern Irish, Scottish, and Welsh representatives to discuss particular policy issues. In a May referendum, 94 percent of the southern Irish voted in favor of the agreement.

Irish citizens can change their government democratically. Northern Irish are considered citizens and may run for office in the republic. Currently, only diplomatic families and security forces living abroad may vote by absentee ballot. Civil liberties activists have denounced Ireland's refusal to incorporate the European Convention on Human Rights into domestic law. A fifty-six-year-old state of emergency was lifted in 1995, though the government stopped short of revoking all special powers associated with the emergency law. These include special search, arrest, and detention powers by the police, and the juryless Special Criminal Court (SCC) for suspected terrorists.

The Irish government announced "draconian" measures to combat terrorism after a bombing in Omagh, Northern Ireland, by a radical Republican group in August 1998, that killed twenty-eight people. These measures include curtailing the right to silence so that a court may infer guilt from the silence of a suspected terrorist or member of an outlawed organization and extending the maximum period of detention without trial from forty-eight to seventy-two hours under the Offenses Against the State Act.

The Irish media are free, though they may not publish or broadcast anything likely to undermine state authority or promote violence. In addition to international cable broadcasts, international newspapers, particularly from Britain, are gaining a growing share of the Irish market. The Supreme Court in March lifted an injunction against Radio Telefis Eireann (RTE), whose journalists were investigating an alleged tax-evasion scheme by the National Irish Bank (NIB). A Freedom of Information Act came into effect in April 1998. It allows citizens access to personal information as well as official records held by government departments or other public bodies. Exempted records will include cabinet meetings, law enforcement and public safety, security, defense, international relations, and commercially sensitive information.

Gender discrimination in the workplace is unlawful, though inequality of treatment regarding pay and promotion generally favors men in both public and private sectors. A government task force on violence against women reported in 1997 that domestic violence is a widespread problem. Labor unions are free to organize and to bargain collectively. About 55 percent of workers in the public and private sectors are union members. Police and military personnel are prohibited from striking. Freedom Houses' 1998–99 *Freedom in the World* rates Ireland a one in political rights and civil liberties.

Religious Freedom

The Constitution of the Irish Free State came into force in 1922 when the country became independent. It was replaced by the constitution of Ireland in 1937. The preamble of the current constitution opens as follows: "In the Name of the Most Holy Trinity, from whom is all authority and to whom, as our final end, all actions both of men and States must be referred." Article 44

of the constitution is headed "Religion" and provides as follows: "1. The State acknowledges that the homage of public worship is due to Almighty God. It shall hold His name in reverence, and shall respect and honor religion. 2.1: Freedom of conscience and the free profession and practice of religion are, subject to public order and morality, guaranteed to every citizen. 2.2: The State guarantees not to endow any religion. 2.3: The State shall not impose any disabilities or make any discrimination on the ground of religious profession, belief or status. 2.4: Legislation providing State aid for schools shall not discriminate between schools under the management of different religious denominations, nor be such as to affect prejudicially the right of any child to attend a school receiving public money without attending religious instruction at that school. 2.5: Every religious denomination shall have the right to manage its own affairs, own, acquire and administer property, movable and immovable, and maintain institutions for religious and charitable purposes. 2.6: The property of every religious denomination or of any educational institution shall not be diverted save for necessary works of public utility and on payment of compensation."

Until their repeal by the Fifth Amendment of Constitution Act 1972, Article 44.1.2 and 3 provided as follows: "2: The State recognizes the special position of the Holy Catholic Apostolic and Roman Catholic Church as the guardian of the Faith professed by the great majority of the citizens. 3: The State also recognizes the Church of Ireland, the Presbyterian Church in Ireland, the Methodist Church in Ireland, the Religious Society of Friends in Ireland, as well as the Jewish Congregations and the other religious denominations existing in Ireland at the date of the coming into operation of this Constitution." In *Quinn's Supermarket Ltd. v. Att. Gen. (1972) I.R.*, the Supreme Court held that these provisions merely reflected social reality and had no legal significance, that they did not confer any privilege or impose any disability or diminution of status upon any religious denomination and did not permit the state to do so.

Ireland has signed and ratified the International Covenant on Civil and Political Rights and the European Convention on Human Rights and accepted the right of individual petition as regards the latter. But these instruments were not integrated into domestic law because Article 29.6 of the constitution provides: "No international agreement shall be part of the domestic law of the State save as may be determined by the Parliament."

In December 1994, the government set up a Constitution Review Group, which in 1996 published a seven-hundred-page report containing many detailed recommendations, including adapting the preamble to the diversity of belief in present-day Ireland. Twenty pages were also devoted to the various paragraphs of Article 44. Article 44.1 was considered obscure in its language and imprecise in its legal significance. A majority advocated deletion of the whole section while others proposed to reformulate it as follows: "The State guarantees to respect religion."

A revision of Article 44.2.1, closer to the provisions of the European Convention on Human Rights, was also proposed as follows: "Freedom of conscience and the free profession and practice of religion are guaranteed to every person. These rights shall include the freedom, either alone or in community with others, and in public or in private, to manifest his or her religion or belief, in worship, teaching, practice and observance. The exercise of these rights and freedoms may be subject only to limitations as may be imposed by law and are necessary in a democratic society in the interests of the public, for the protection of public order, health and morals, or for the protection of the rights and freedoms of others." The Review Group did not consider it necessary to prohibit the establishment of religion because of the guarantee contained in Article 44.2.3.

The Review Group also considered the final sentence of Article 40.6.1.i: "The publication or utterance of blasphemous . . . matter is an offense which shall be punishable in accordance with law." It endorsed the 1991 Law Reform Commission recommendation to delete this provision. One of the reasons was that there has been no prosecution for blasphemy in the history of the state and the protection of religious beliefs and sensibilities can be best achieved through other channels.

Ireland was part of the United Kingdom until 1922 and was ruled from London. Until 1870, the small Church of Ireland was the established church, to the great displeasure of the Catholic majority of the population. Four Church of Ireland bishops sat in the House of Lords. An end was put to this discriminatory situation with the 1869 Irish Church Act. Since 1870, all churches have been enjoying the same legal status, that of voluntary associations founded upon contract. From a legal point of view, all religions have since then been on the same footing. Although, since 1922, the island has been divided between two political entities, it continues to be subject to a single ecclesiastical hierarchy in the Roman Catholic Church of Ireland, the Presbyterian Church in Ireland, and the Methodist Church in Ireland. No concordat has ever been negotiated between the Irish State and the Vatican.

Ireland has always been a predominately Roman Catholic country, and religious adherence has been a pervasive force in modern Irish society. Currently about sixty percent of Irish Catholics are active church members. Civil law has reflected Catholic moral views about divorce (prohibited by the 1937 Constitution), homosexuality, contraception, and abortion (a criminal offense, at least since 1861). In the last twenty-five years, however, the consensus that underpinned these societal pillars has broken down. The ban on contraceptives was ruled unconstitutional by the Supreme Court in 1973. In 1979, an end was put to the 1935 law banning the sale or import of contraceptives. Homosexuality was legalized in the 1990s. Legislation was introduced in June 1993 decriminalizing sexual activity between consenting adults over the age of seventeen. In November 1995, a very slim majority (50.28% to 49.72%) in a referendum approved a constitutional amendment allowing for the introduction of divorce. The Family Law (Divorce) Act of 1996 came into force only at the end of February 1997.

Individuals have the right to freedom of religion and belief if they respect public order and morality. There is a new freedom to preach and even to proselytize that was unthinkable some decades ago when there was deep suspicion and even hostility to non-Catholic religious groups propagating their faith and making new members. Consequently, the presence of evangelical churches and groups, new religious movements, and Eastern religions has developed and is more visible. Similarly, humanists and secularists have been able to organize and to lobby freely.

The rights and the independence of the clergy are fully respected by the state. Religious bodies have the right to self-government. The right to religious education is also recognized and respected by the state. Article 42 of the Constitution provides in Articles 1 and 4: "1. The State acknowledges that the primary and natural education of the child is the Family and guarantees to respect the inalienable right and duty of parents to provide, according to their means, for the religious and moral, intellectual, physical and social education of their children. 4. The State shall provide for free primary education and shall endeavor to supplement and give reasonable aid to private and corporate educational initiative, and, when the public good requires it, provide other educational facilities or institutions with due regard, however, for the rights of parents, especially in the matter of religious and moral formation."

Most Irish schools are organized on a denominational basis and, though the state provides substantial funding for facilities, salaries, and so forth, it does not own the premises. The state has been scrupulous in upholding the right of the Protestant and Jewish communities to their own schools financially. However, the state may not and does not discriminate between the schools under the management of different religious denominations. The government cannot pass any legislation either that would affect prejudicially the right of any child to attend a school receiving public money without attending religious instruction at that school.

All religious communities are allowed to carry out charitable activities. They have the right to manage their own affairs, own and acquire property, and maintain institutions for religious and charitable purposes. In conformity with the constitutional principle that "the State guarantees not to endow any religion," churches are not financed by the state. The Protestant religious minorities in Ireland in the past seventy years have occupied a relatively privileged economic and class position; successive governments have been careful to guarantee their control over their own schools and hospitals.

The 1997 Bill on Employment Equality was designed to prohibit discrimination in employment, training, and so forth. While it outlawed discrimination on religious grounds, it featured certain important exemptions: Section 37 (1) provided: "A religious, educational or medical institution which is under the direction or control of a body established for religious purposes or whose objectives include the provision of services in an environment which promotes certain religious values shall not be taken to discriminate a person

for the purposes of this Part of Part II if: a) it gives more favorable treatment, on the religious ground, to an employee or a prospective employee over that person where it is reasonable to do so in order to maintain the religious ethos of the institution; or b) it takes action which is reasonably necessary to prevent an employee or prospective employee from undermining the religious ethos of the institution."

Little discrimination against individuals has been reported. Allegations of discrimination have come from parents who wish their children baptized to ensure their enrollment in local schools, and there has been pressure on parents not to exempt their children from religious instruction classes owing to the lack of teachers to supervise them. Another complaint is that only practicing Catholics are employed as teachers in the great majority of the state's schools because teacher training is in the hands of the Catholic Church.

Israel
(Excluding Occupied Territories)

Population	6.1 million
Jewish (mostly secular)	80.2%
Muslim (largely Sunni)	14.6%
Christian	2.1%
Druze	1.6%
Other	1.5%
Religious Freedom Rating	3

Background

Israel was formed in 1948 from less than one-fifth of the original British Palestine Mandate. Its neighbors, rejecting a United Nations partition plan that would have also created a Palestinian

state, attacked immediately following independence in the first of several Arab-Israeli conflicts. Israel has functioned as a parliamentary democracy since independence. Since 1977, the conservative Likud and the center-left Labor party have shared or alternated power.

Following June 1992 Knesset elections, Yitzhak Rabin's Labor-led coalition government secured an agreement with the Palestinian Liberation Organization (PLO) in 1993. The Declaration of Principles provides for a phased Israeli withdrawal from the Israeli-occupied West Bank and Gaza strip and for limited Palestinian autonomy in those areas. Negotiations on the status of Jerusalem, Jewish settlements, refugees, and Israel's borders were to follow the final Israeli redeployment. On November 4, 1995, a right-wing, religious Jewish extremist, opposed to the peace process on the grounds that it would lead to a Palestinian state in the West Bank, assassinated Rabin in Tel Aviv. Foreign Minister Shimon Peres became acting prime minister and served until the 1996 elections, when Benjamin Netanyahu, leader of the right-wing Likud Party, came to power.

On October 23, 1998, after nearly a year of intense pressure from the U.S., Prime Minister Benjamin Netanyahu signed an interim peace accord with Palestinian leader Yasser Arafat following nine days of talks at the Wye River Plantation, Maryland. The agreement called for Israeli withdrawal from 13.1 percent of the West Bank in exchange for security guarantees from the Palestinians, including a provision for CIA monitoring of Palestinian action to combat terrorism. The Knesset ratified the agreement in November 1998, though a majority of the governing coalition voted against it.

Internal infighting, largely over the continued stagnation of the Middle East peace process, kept Benjamin Netanyahu's fragile governing coalition in crisis throughout 1998. In May 1999 elections he was replaced by Ehud Barak, head of the Labor Party, who was able to form a government with some 75 out of 120 Knesset seats, including most of the religious parties.

The 1967 war formed a watershed in Israel's history. It occupied the Sinai Peninsula (since returned to Egypt), the Golan Heights, and the West Bank. East Jerusalem and the Golan Heights were officially annexed to Israel, while the rest were put under separate military administration. This made the Israelis occupiers of a large segment of land of the Palestinians who were not allowed citizenship rights. The occupation of the West Bank revived latent messianic feelings among some Israeli Jews, particularly among religious Zionists. They started a settlement movement in the occupied territories. Since the 1970s, the Jewish religious parties have gradually widened their ranks, winning approximately 20 percent of the Knesset seats in the 1999 elections. Forming the pivot in the balance between the right and the left blocks in the Knesset, the religious parties have had a growing influence over Israeli government. Controversy regarding war and the occupation of the Palestinian territories has widened the gap between some secular and religious Jews in Israel and sharpened the issues of the Israeli identity.

Israeli citizens can change their government democratically. Although Israel has no formal constitution, a series of Basic Laws has the force of constitutional principles. The judiciary is independent, and procedural safeguards are generally respected. Security trials, however, may be closed to the public on limited grounds.

Freedoms of assembly and association are respected. Newspaper and magazine articles on security matters are subject to a military censor, though the scope of permissible reporting is expanding. In January 1998, an ultranationalist Jewish woman was sentenced to two years in jail for publicly displaying posters depicting the Islamic prophet Mohammed as a pig.

Some nine hundred thousand Israeli Arab citizens receive inferior education, housing, and social services relative to the Jewish population. Of the non-Jewish groups in Israel, only the Druze and the Circassians are conscripted to the Israel Defense Forces. Christian and Muslim Israeli Arabs are not subject to the military draft, though they may serve voluntarily. Those who do not join the army do not enjoy the financial benefits available to Israelis who have served, including scholarships and housing loans.

Workers may join unions of their choice and enjoy the right to strike and to bargain collectively. Three-quarters of the workforce either belong to unions affiliated with Histadrut (General Federation of Labor) or are covered under its social programs and collective bargaining agreements. Freedom House's 1998–99 *Freedom in the World* rates Israel as a one in political rights and a three in civil liberties.

Religious Freedom

Based on Israel's raison d'être as the refuge and center of the Jewish people, the Law of Return was passed in 1950 to allow citizenship to any Jew who immigrates from the Diaspora to Israel. A Jew is defined as a person whose mother or grandmother was born Jewish. Most Israeli Jews define themselves as Jews in national terms, with varying attitudes toward the Jewish religion and its role in the state. Israel desires to become a Western secular democratic state while maintaining Orthodoxy as a kind of official religion.

Freedom of worship exists for all citizens, though with some problems. A weekly day of rest for all is guaranteed by law. Jews must take their day of rest on Saturday. Places of work and entertainment, as well as public transportation, must be closed in Jewish neighborhoods on Saturdays and Jewish holidays. Jewish dietary laws are im-

posed on Jewish public life. These prohibitions are imposed on Jews and Jewish neighborhoods only. Since the 1980s, some businesses have opened on Saturdays in Jewish neighborhoods without a license, and controversy between secular and religious Jews has deepened. Muslims and Christians can choose their weekly day of rest and celebrate holidays in their neighborhoods according to their religious choice. However, none of their holidays is official, and many Muslim and Christian government employees must accommodate themselves to Jewish holidays.

Religious instruction is free to members of all religions and takes place mainly in private Jewish, Christian, and Muslim schools. The Jewish and Arab public school systems do not include religious instruction or prayers in their syllabi except for a particular separate religious Jewish public school system.

Israel has allowed free access to Muslim and Christian holy places since 1948. Difficulties have been caused since the early 1990s due to the Palestinian Intifada (uprising) and Israeli restriction of free access from the West Bank and Gaza Strip to Jerusalem. The Muslim pilgrimage to Mecca has been normalized since the beginning of the peace process with Jordan, which provides a route for the pilgrims. Since Jewish Orthodoxy only is the official religion in Israel, other Jewish religious movements, namely Reform (Israel Movement for Progressive Judaism) and Conservative (Masorti Movement) are not allowed to organize prayers at the Wailing Wall according to their traditions, which does not separate men and women. Their attempts to pray at the Wall have met hostile reaction from some ultraorthodox Jews.

Israel has communal autonomy based on the Ottoman *millet* system, which was continued under the British mandate. It recognizes Jewish Orthodox, Sunni Muslim, Druze, and the major Christian communities, each of which has its own court system and authority over personal status. Jewish Reform and Conservative congregations have no recognized religious communities.

Communal autonomy includes maintaining educational, religious, and socio-cultural institutions, and the management of properties and endowments (*awqaf*). Religious communal law courts have had exclusive jurisdiction in matters of personal status such as marriage, divorce, and child custody. Marriage, divorce, and burials raise major issues since Israeli Jews are obliged to follow Orthodox rules that many do not accept.

Converted members of the unrecognized Reform and Conservative movements, a growing segment of new immigrants, are not recognized by the Orthodox rabbinate as Jews. Reform and Conservative rabbis in Israel have no authority in any matter of personal status. The Ministry of the Interior does not register weddings performed by them as legal marriages. Nonorthodox Jewish groups have resorted to legal action, with some success in Israeli courts, to win funds or better treatment from various authorities, local and national. Growing pressures from Jewish secular circles led in the early 1990s to the establishment of special civil family courts to deal with Jewish family conflicts. The authority for final divorce still rests with the rabbinical courts. Following a Supreme Court decision, the Ministry of the Interior must register couples who were married abroad. Civil cemeteries have gradually been opened since the early 1990s for secular people and persons who do not belong to any official religion.

The lack of civil marriage and divorce also infringes on Muslims and Christians. Interfaith marriages cannot be performed unless one of the spouses converts to the other's religious community. Similarly, Catholics, who cannot divorce under church law, have no option of civil divorce and would need to convert to a church or religion that allows divorce.

As the state religion in the Ottoman Empire, Islam had less communal autonomy, including management of religious endowments. This tradition was largely continued by the British and then by Israel. Hence, the government controls Muslim religious properties and endowments (*waqfs*) and allocates their income to the various Muslim institutions. Continuing the *millet* system, the Christian communities have full autonomy in maintaining their endowments and institutions.

More than 90 percent of the Ministry of Religious Affairs funds are allocated to Orthodox Jewish institutions. Very small amounts are allocated to nonorthodox Jewish organizations, and only 2 percent is allocated to Christian and Muslim groups. In 1998, the state comptroller criticized this distribution of funds.

Freedom of organization on a religious basis is open to members of all religions, as is migration within the state and emigration. Immigration is open to all Jews and their family members under the Law of Return. Such a right of immigration is not given to Palestinian Arabs, Muslims, and Christians alike. Many immigrants, especially from the early 1990s mass immigration of 750,000 people from the ex-Soviet Union, have no basic knowledge of the Jewish religion. A growing number declare themselves as having no religion or as Christians. However, they wish to be assimilated into the Hebrew speaking milieu rather than the Arab Christian one. In many cases social pressure is applied on them to convert to Judaism as a token of joining the Jewish people. But the only way to convert is through the Orthodox, which imposes strict observance of Jewish religious rituals and way of life. Similarly, secular Jews who adopt children from abroad must maintain a Jewish religious way of life to have their adopted children registered as Jews.

Conversion is legal and is common among Christians, Muslims, and Jews, usually to facilitate marriage. In many cases this is due to the lack of civil marriage in Israel. Conversion out of conviction or for spiritual reasons is legal but brings strong social opposition. In the last decade Christian evangelistic work by evangelicals and fundamentalists, often based in the United States, has expanded.

Approximately eighty "Messianic" organizations are active, mainly among new immigrants and mixed families. The major active evangelical groups are the King of Kings, the Church of the Nazarene, and the Baptist church. Some groups such as "Messianic Jews" and Jehovah's Witnesses still consider themselves as Jews but are not accepted as such by most of the Israeli public and by the Israeli government, who regard them as Christians. Evangelical groups in Israel number approximately six thousand people, most of whom organized in the United Christian Council in Israel (ICCI).

Evangelistic groups are often accused by the established churches as well as by Muslims and Jews of bribing people in need in order to convert them, and Christian missionaries are often called "bread Christians." The British Mandate in Palestine had enacted legislation to ensure that converts did not change their religion for eco-nomic reasons. In late 1977, an amendment of paragraph 174b of the Penal Law made it an offense punishable by five years' imprisonment to give a practical benefit as an inducement to change religion. Due to international concern led by church leaders, this law has never been enforced.

A further proposed law was put before the Knesset in 1996, as a private member's bill, by Nissim Zvili, a Labor Party member of parliament (MP), and Yishaya Gafni, an ultraorthodox MP. The bill would make it an offense, punishable by a year's imprisonment, to possess, print, reproduce, disseminate, or import tracts or books in which there is an inducement to religious conversion. Another similar bill was put before the Knesset by Raphael Pinhasi, an ultraorthodox MP, in 1998, and was initially approved by the Netanyahu Cabinet and transmitted to the Judiciary Committee for discussion. After protests in Israel and by the international community, this legislation was frozen in the Knesset. Currently no such restrictive proposals exist.

Hostile attitudes towards Christian evangelistic activity grew in the lead-in to the 1999 elections, with attacks on people suspected of distributing evangelistic leaflets, burning Bible stores, and harassing conferences and meeting places. This also affected Christian institutions that had nothing to do with evangelistic activity. During 1998–99, vandalism took place on Christian churches such as the Scottish hospice and church in Jerusalem. The rabbinate of Bath Yam, a small town near Jaffa, attempted to prevent the celebration of Christmas by the local Greek Orthodox. An appeal to the Supreme Court by the Association for Civil Rights in Israel prevented this prohibition.

Attacks on local Christians have

also been provoked by Muslim fundamentalist circles and have accelerated since the early 1990s. In 1998 and 1999, there has been conflict in Nazareth between the municipality, identified with Christians and moderate Muslims, and a group of Muslim fundamentalists over a tract of land close to the Church of the Annunciation. Some Muslim fundamentalists maintain that the land is actually a Muslim endowment (*waqf*), a claim that has been rejected by Israeli courts, and demand that a huge mosque be erected, one that would actually hide the church. Violence in the spring of 1999 brought the pope's intervention. The Israeli authorities have given permission for a smaller mosque to be built on part of the site, and this has led to protests from nearly all Christian groups, including two-day church closings in December.

Japan

Population	**126.7 million**
Buddhist	**49%**
Shinto	**45%**
Christian	**1%**
Other	**5%**

(Note that in Japan many people adhere to more than one religion: the total number of adherents is about twice the population.)

Religious Freedom Rating   **2**

Background

Following its defeat in World War II, Japan adopted an American-drafted constitution in 1947 that vested legislative authority in the two-house Diet (parliament) and ended the emperor's divine status. The Liberal Democratic Party (LDP) won successive elections, presiding over what became the world's second largest economy, and maintained close security ties to the United States. The LDP's factionalism and corruption led to a loss of power for the first time in the 1993 elections, but it returned to power in 1994 in a coalition government.

Japan's national malaise continued in 1998 as an economy that had been troubled since the early 1990s tumbled into its worst recession since World War II. The two main institutions that oversaw the country's strong postwar growth—the ruling Liberal Democratic Party and the Finance Ministry—were looking increasingly paralyzed. In July the LDP's Keizo Obuchi became premier after voters signaled a desire for leadership and economic reform by punishing the party in upper-house elections.

Japanese citizens can change their government democratically. The lower house is chosen by proportional representation while the upper house has 152 single-seat districts and 100 seats chosen by proportional representation. There have been several corruption scandals in recent years. In the spring of 1998, the government cut the size of the prosecution team investigating corruption and transferred its head to a remote district.

Ethnic Koreans, many of whom trace their ancestry in Japan for two or three generations, face discrimination in housing, education, and employment opportunities; they are not automatically deemed Japanese citizens at birth, must submit to official background checks, and must adopt Japanese names to become naturalized. Both the Burakumin, descendants of feudal-era outcasts, and the indigenous Ainu minority also face unofficial discrimination and social ostracism.

The judiciary is independent. Rights to counsel can be restricted, and there are reports of police abuse of accusees. Human rights groups criticize the penal system's extreme emphasis on regimentation and dehumanizing punishments. Immigration officers are accused of regularly beating detained illegal aliens.

Civic institutions are strong, and freedoms of expression, assembly, and association are generally respected in practice. Journalists often practice self-censorship with sensitive stories. The Education Ministry routinely censors passages in history textbooks describing Japan's World War I atrocities. Women face significant employment discrimination and are frequently tracked into clerical careers. In April 1998, police cracked down on gangsters who traffic Filipino and Thai women to Japan with the promise of regular jobs and then force them to work as prostitutes. Trade unions are independent and active.

Freedom House's 1998–99 *Freedom in the World* rates Japan a one in political rights and a two in civil liberties.

Religious Freedom

Japan's oldest written religious belief system is what is called Early Shinto. Buddhism came from Korea in the sixth century A.D., and Chinese influences later brought Confucianism and Taoism. Confucianism shapes the country's ethics to the present day. Christianity arrived in the sixteenth century but was virtually wiped out in later persecutions. While Christianity has never been influential in Japan in terms of numbers of adherents, its ideas have influenced education, social legislation, and labor organizing. Religion in Japan has often been more a matter of participation in certain religious rituals than adhering to specific beliefs: even so, only about 7 percent of the population regularly take part in religious rituals. Many Japanese follow two or more religions.

Religion has provided a particularly important sense of continuity in Japan over the last 145 years, a period of immense upheavals and change that began with United States naval power opening the country to the outside world in 1853. Thereafter, Japan began modernizing its administrative structure and transforming a feudal society into an industrial power. In 1890, Japan's Meiji rulers chose Shinto as the state religion and restricted religious freedom. The Meiji drew upon Shinto myths to assert the superiority of the Japanese race, Japan's position as a chosen country, and the emperor's divine status. In practice, state Shinto emphasized extreme nationalism and loyalty to the emperor. These beliefs contributed to Japan's conquests in Korea, Manchuria, China, and Southeast Asia, leading to its devastating defeat in World War II.

The United States-imposed 1946 constitution vested legislative authority in parliament, ended the emperor's divine status, and brought religious freedom. The end of religious orthodoxy and the psychologically destabilizing effect of Japan's military defeat contributed to the growth of what are called the "new religions." Many are messianic and draw upon aspects of Buddhism, Shinto, Confucianism, and sometimes Christianity.

Soka Gakkai is the largest of these new religions. Originally developed as a lay organization affiliated with the Nichiren Shoshu Buddhist sect, a dispute led to its independence in the early 1990s. Soka Gakkai was also initially behind the development of the Komeito, or "Clean Government" party, in the 1950s. Komeito advocates reuniting religion and state but under Buddhism rather than Shinto.

Article 20 of the 1946 constitution guarantees religious freedom. Article 89 establishes the separation of church and state. With the exceptions noted below, individuals usually have the right to freedom of religion and belief if they respect public order and morality. There is freedom to propagate one's faith, freedom of worship, and freedom to train and appoint clergy. Religious bodies have rights of self-government, of religious education, to carry out charitable activities, to own and acquire property, and to maintain social institutions. They can produce, import, and distribute literature; receive donations; and have contact with coreligionists domestically and overseas. Individuals can adopt, change, or leave a religion freely with no change of civil status.

Religions do not have to be licensed. The 1951 Religious Corporation Act allowed religious organizations to register as corporations and receive tax exemptions. The Act also permitted courts to disband a religious corporation if it is found to have substantially engaged in secular activities or if it poses a threat to the public. Nearly all groups register in order to receive the tax exemptions.

One area of concern is that in reaction to the 1995 terrorist attacks on the Tokyo subway system by the Aum Shinrikyo religious cult, in 1996 parliament amended the Religious Corporation law to strengthen government oversight of religious corporations and to require greater disclosure of financial assets. The Education Ministry can request detailed financial reports from religious corporations and review membership and activities. In late 1999, after prosecutors had sought the death penalty for two senior members of the Aum Shinrikyo group for their part in nerve gas attacks, the government introduced a bill giving security forces broad powers to monitor and curtail the activities of organizations that have committed "indiscriminate mass murder." In December 1999, after allegations of fraud, police raided seventy-four offices of the "Ho-no-Hana Sampogyo" group. Some religious leaders have expressed concern over this increase in state authority over organized religion and see parallels to the current European fervor over "sects." When newspapers attack a new religion, the public response can be quite hysterical. As part of a "cult" and "sect" scare, press reports indicate that some Japanese families hire "deprogrammers" to kidnap converts to new religions and reintegrate them into mainstream society. Authorities do little to investigate or end these kidnappings.

Another area of concern is that Shintoism is regaining a privileged position. However, a 1997 Supreme Court ruling may curb the state funds used to support Shinto purification ceremonies, as well as certain Buddhist and Shinto temples and shrines considered to be national historic or cultural sites. The Court held that a prefecture government may not contribute money to only one religious organization if the donations support and promote a specific religious group.

Small, far-right nationalist groups continue to call for the reestablishment of state Shinto and the restoration of the emperor's divine status. Most Japanese reject these ideas in their most extreme form, yet there is some support for establishing Shinto as Japan's civil religion. Many mainstream conservative politicians have suggested measures consistent with restoring Shinto's preeminent status, including revising the 1946 "peace" constitution to permit Japanese armed forces to participate in peacekeeping missions abroad and re-nationalizing Tokyo's Yasukuni Shrine. This 1869 Shinto holy site memorializes Japanese who died fighting for their country (including some war criminals) and is an important symbol of Shinto nationalism. Several leading politicians have made controversial formal visits to the shrine.

Kazakhstan

Population	**15.4 million**
Muslim (largely Sunni)	**47%**
Russian Orthodox	**25%**
Lutheran	**2%**
Catholic	**2%**
Jewish	**<1%**
Other	**23%**
Religious Freedom Rating	**4**

Background

This sparsely populated, multiethnic land was controlled by Russia from 1730 to 1840. After a brief period of independence in 1917, it became an autonomous Soviet republic in 1929 and a union republic in 1936. Kazakhstan formally declared independence from a crumbling Soviet Union in December 1991. President Nazarbayev, former first-secretary of the Kazakhstan Communist Party, was directly elected in 1991. In March 1995, Nazarbayev dissolved parliament and ruled by decree. He ordered a referendum extending his rule to the year 2000, and a reported 95 percent supported the measure. A new constitution codified periods of presidential rule by decree.

Kazakhs are an ethnic minority in their own country as a result of Stalinist purges, as well as enforced Slavic immigration during the Soviet era. They now constitute only about 45 percent of the population, while Slavs, both Russian and Ukrainians, constitute 35 percent. The north is mostly Slavic, while ethnic Kazakhs dominate the south. Other ethnic groups include Tatars, Uzbeks, Turks, and Chechens.

In July 1998, the government implemented a package of austerity measures aimed at staving off an economic crisis. Key parts of the economy and government positions continued to be dominated by clans loyal to President Nazarbayev and members of his family. His daughter, Dariga, controls the national television network, while her husband, Rakhat Aliyev, is head of the tax police. Another son-in-law, Timur Kulidayev, is the financial director and vice president of Kazakhoil.

Citizens can participate in multiparty elections, but, under the constitution, power is centered in the hands of President Nazarbayev, whose regime has cracked down on the opposition and the media. Parliament is largely powerless. There are several independent newspapers, including those that reflect oppositionist views. The most popular, *Karavan*, reports on corruption and is critical of the government.

Newspaper distribution is controlled by the state. There are now only four nominally nonstate television channels and three independent radio stations in Almaty. Authorities use libel laws to discourage free speech.

Freedom of assembly is restricted. Police broke up several unsanctioned rallies by workers, pensioners, and the political opposition and detained demonstrators who were protesting deteriorating social and economic conditions. Opposition parties have complained of harassment, surveillance, denial of access to the state-run media, and arbitrary banning from registering candidates. The largest trade union remains the successor to the Soviet-era General Council of Trade Unions, in practice a government organ. The Independent Trade Union Center, with twelve unions, includes the important coal miners' union in Karaganda. A new labor law places restrictions on the right to strike. Workers who join independent unions are subject to threats and harassment by enterprise management and have no legal recourse.

The judiciary is not free of government interference and remains under the control of the president and the executive branch. Judges are subject to bribery and political bias. Rights to an attorney and open trial have been denied political detainees. Corruption is evident at every level of the judicial system.

Russians, Germans, and other non-Kazakhs have charged discrimination in favor of ethnic Kazakhs in state-run businesses, government, housing, and education. Ethnic Germans and Russians have left in droves. Uighurs, who have ethnic ties to their restive kin in China's Xinjiang province, have been banned from demonstrating and holding political meetings. In practice, citizens are still required to register in order to prove legal residence and to obtain city services.

Basic rights of property and entrepreneurship are codified, but bureaucratic hurdles and the control of large segments of the economy by clan elites and government officials who are loyal to President Nazarbayev impede equal opportunity and fair competition. Freedom House's 1998–99 *Freedom in the World* survey rates Kazakhstan a six in political rights and a five in civil liberties.

Religious Freedom

Approximately 80 percent of ethnic Kazakhs identified themselves as Muslims, mainly Sunni, which for many is mainly a cultural affiliation. Fewer Slavs, approximately 60 percent, are religiously identified with the dominant Orthodox church, also generally a nominal religious affiliation. In this multicultural society, national traditions of tolerance and ethnic inclusiveness are valued. As a result, relations between the government and religious groups are relatively open in comparison to other Central Asian nations. Nontraditional religious groups are particular beneficiaries of this comparatively free atmosphere. However, the government does target groups considered "fundamentalist" or "sects." The government also unofficially distinguishes between "traditional" and "nontraditional" religions, suggesting a de facto inequality. In particular, the KNB (successor of the KGB) has publicly stated its dedication to ferreting out Islamic and Christian "religious extremism."

Compared to other Central Asian countries, Islamic fundamentalism as a political movement is not deeply rooted, although it is gaining influence, particularly in the south. This has produced apprehension of influences from Pakistan, Chechnya, Tajikistan,

Uzbekistan, and Afghanistan. There are, however, no violent acts attributed to extremist movements. The KNB is beginning to tighten controls and, for example, in September 1998, detained six Pakistanis who were distributing religious literature and cassettes.

The constitution guarantees religious liberty and a "secular" state with no religion officially preferred, although in practice the two dominant religions are Sunni Muslim and Eastern Orthodox. The 1992 law on Freedom of Conscience and Religious Associations is relatively generous legislation passed immediately following the collapse of the Soviet Union. This law remains in place. New legislation that sharply increased government control over religious associations and practices was defeated in March 1999. This was accomplished though the combined protests of indigenous human rights groups, religious organizations, and American pressure promoting international standards for religious liberty.

The Kazakh government has been commended internationally, including by the Organization for Security and Cooperation in Europe (OSCE), for resisting regional trends to adopt more burdensome laws regarding religious activity. However, the new proposals target minority or "nontraditional" religious groups. One provision requires groups to have existed for more than ten years before eligibility. Groups would be required to produce superfluous and burdensome documentation. Overall, its ambiguous language would have reduced religious freedom.

Usually, religious organizations can officially assemble without registration. In practice, this freedom can be constrained by local officials who might require registration arbitrarily in contravention of national law. Registration

gives the right to conduct corporate activities such as renting, employment, and banking. Even though registration is relatively quick in comparison to other Central Asian countries, groups are subject to delays, such as Jehovah's Witnesses, Korean Protestants, and Muslim and Russian Orthodox who function outside of the official hierarchy.

Government officials can use checks on legal "registration" as a pretext for invading group meetings of minority religious organizations. From March 9 to 14, 1994, six Jehovah's Witness groups were raided by Kazakh officials, ostensibly checking registration, even though all were registered. Procuracy officials have required members to write statements regarding their views on medical treatment and military service, which historically have been contentious issues for the government. Until the mid-1990s, Jehovah's Witness men were incarcerated for refusing military service on religious grounds. Since an agreement in 1997, no Jehovah's Witness have been jailed for draft evasion.

Problems are greater in the rural regions, especially the south. Harassment includes privacy invasions, such as phone tapping and other forms of surveillance. Other scattered incidents occur, such as in Dzamboul, where religious books were burned and Christians were beaten and interrogated by security forces (but no charges were sustained). Approximately twenty to thirty missionary organizations function in Kazakhstan without major impediments, although they experience occasional victimization such as periodic loss of halls in state-owned facilities. Missionaries are required to be registered by the government, although many function freely without this certification. Protestant missionaries report harassment by local officials, particularly relating to allegations of "proselytizing," as well as a close scrutiny of their charitable endeavors, such as schools and hospitals. Sporadic incidents of violence occur, such as a bomb thrown into the Almaty Seventh-Day Adventist Church on November 17, 1997, while empty. The next day the government-owned Palace of Culture canceled the church's contract to hold gospel programs.

Despite some harassment of peaceful religious minorities at the local level, Kazakhstan continues to be a relative haven of refuge for those escaping religious hostility common in neighboring countries such as Uzbekistan. With encouragement, Kazakhstan could bring elevated standards of religious freedom uncommon to most other Central Asian nations.

Korea, North

Population	**22.2 million**
Atheist	**68%**
Ch'ondogyo	**15%**
Other Traditional	**14%**
Buddhist	**2%**
Christian	**1%**
Religious Freedom Rating	**7**

Background

The Democratic People's Republic of Korea (DPRK) was established on September 9, 1948, following the end of World War II and the division of the Korean peninsula. With assistance from Moscow, Kim Il-sung, a former Soviet army officer, became head of the North Korean government. In June 1950, Kim, with Soviet military support, invaded South Korea in an attempt to reunify the peninsula under communist rule. The three-year Korean War ended in a truce after intervention by U.S. and Chinese troops, which left the two Koreas bitterly divided.

Throughout the cold war, Kim solidified his power base in the north through an extensive personality cult and the development of *Juche* (self-reliance), a homegrown ideology said to be an application of Marxism-Leninism

specific to North Korea. In practice, it became an ideological justification for communist leadership under Kim's rule. By the 1990s, the North Korean economy was achieving negative growth rates every year. The disintegration of the Soviet Union in 1991 meant the loss of Pyongyang's cold-war patrons in Moscow and increasing isolation for North Korea. As a result, North Korea has suffered widespread famine and has been forced periodically into negotiations over its nuclear weapons programs in return for food aid to support its malnourished population.

Kim Il-sung died suddenly of a heart attack in 1994, paving the way for his son and appointed successor, Kim Jong-il, to assume power, marking the first-ever communist dynastic succession. Midyear 1998 was marked by elections for representatives of the Supreme People's Assembly (SPA). The balloting was a mere formality.

On September 9, 1998, North Korea celebrated its fiftieth anniversary against a backdrop of economic collapse, mass starvation, and increasing international concern over its suspected nuclear weapons program. The country's deterioration, together with the election of a more conciliatory government in South Korea, led to speculation that the year would yield new openness from the reclusive government in Pyongyang. However, as 1999 drew to a close, North Korea remained one of the world's most closed and secretive societies and showed little sign of change.

The governments of North and South Korea resumed efforts in 1998 to end their long-standing hostilities, though little substantive progress was noted. Direct talks were scheduled for the summer of 2000. These talks are part of a continuing series of negotiations aimed at bringing a formal end to the Korean War, which was ended by a truce but without a formal treaty, leaving the two Koreas technically in a state of war. The border between the two Koreas is the world's most heavily armed, with some two million troops deployed on both sides.

North Korea is arguably the most tightly controlled country in the world. Its citizens cannot change their government democratically. Elections are held regularly, but all candidates are state-sponsored and belong to either the ruling Workers' Party or smaller, state-organized parties. Opposition parties are illegal, and there appears to be little organized dissent due to the regime's repression, widespread internal surveillance, and isolationist policies. Even the most basic elements of a civil society do not exist in North Korea. The rule of law is nonexistent.

Authorities implement arbitrary checks of residences, use electronic surveillance, and maintain a network of informants to monitor the population. At school, children are encouraged to report on their parents. The government as-

signs a security rating to each individual that, to a somewhat lesser extent than in the past, still determines access to education, employment, and health services. North Koreans face a steady onslaught of propaganda from radios and televisions pretuned to government stations.

Prison conditions are characterized by severe mistreatment of prisoners and, by several accounts, frequent summary executions. The regime operates "reeducation through labor" camps that reportedly hold tens of thousands of political prisoners and their families.

Travel within the country generally requires a permit, which is normally granted only for state business, weddings, or funerals, although some reports suggest that internal travel restrictions have been eased slightly. Travel into the capital is heavily restricted. Chinese sources say North Korean agents operating across the border in fact return many North Korean escapees. Those who have tried to flee are often summarily executed. Only a handful of foreign journalists are accredited in North Korea, and entry for foreign visitors is highly restricted.

The government-controlled General Federation of Trade Unions is the sole legal trade union federation, and its affiliates are used to monitor workers. The regime does not permit strikes, collective bargaining, or any other core labor activity. Private property ownership is banned. Freedom House's 1998–99 *Freedom in the World* rates North Korea a seven in political rights and civil liberties.

Religious Freedom

Documenting human rights abuses in North Korea is extraordinarily difficult because it is one of the most closed places in the world. The few Westerners permitted into the country are largely confined to the Pyongyang area, where they are carefully supervised. The government's extremely tight security makes defections of North Korean citizens rare. As a result, little is known about the full extent of religious persecution and the extent of underground activity. The statistics used above reflect this uncertainty. What can be said unequivocally is that, as the U.S. State Department asserted, "genuine religious freedom does not exist."

When Kim Il-sung took power, he began a systematic campaign of indoctrination in his own Stalinist ideology, in which religion had no place. Today, virtually all outward vestiges of religion have been wiped out, and North Korea is regarded as the most hard-line atheistic nation in the world. The government relies on relentless propaganda and a comprehensive surveillance system to control virtually every act, belief, and desire of its citizens. North Koreans are prohibited from making even the slightest deviation from the Communist Party's rigid ideology.

Kim considered religion to be "superstition" and "a hindrance to the socialist revolution." By the early 1960s, his secret police had begun an intense effort against religious believers. All temples, shrines, churches, and other religious sites were closed, and all religious literature and Bibles were destroyed. Religious leaders were either executed or sent to concentration camps.

In place of Buddhism, Christianity and other religions, Kim imposed an alternative religion, a personality cult built around himself and his son. From early childhood, North Koreans were taught to look on the "Great Leader" Kim Il-sung, and now Kim Jong-il, as infallible, godlike beings and the progenitors of the Korean race. The practice continues to the present, long after Kim Il-sung's death.

The government allows and controls three religious organizations: the Buddhist Federation, the Korean Christian Federation, and the Korean Catholic Association. The Buddhist Federation says that there are about four hundred thousand Buddhists, the Protestant Federation claims to have ten thousand members, and the Catholic Association claims about three thousand members. Ch'ondogyo, a traditional Korean religion taken over by the government through the Ch'ondogyo Youth Party, is said to have three million adherents. Another three million are said to practice other forms of traditional worship. Nearly 70 percent of the population is said by the government to be atheist.

Visitors report that some Buddhist temples are operating, and Buddhist practices are probably carried out in homes across North Korea. Although fifty years ago the North Korean capital city of Pyongyang was nicknamed "Asia's Jerusalem" because of the strong influence of Christianity and some two thousand churches dotted the northern countryside, since 1988, in the capital, only three Christian church buildings—two Protestant, and one Catholic—have been erected by the government. They seem to be used solely to impress Western observers. No Catholic priests live in the country, so the sacraments cannot be administered even in the showplace church. Foreign journalists who have attended services in the three churches reported that neither the congregants nor the national leader of the Protestant Federation could name the first three books of the Bible. Others who went unannounced to the churches on Easter Sunday found them locked and empty. Some foreign observers have even questioned whether Christianity still exists behind North Korea's tightly guarded frontiers, though recent reports indicate that there may be many thousands of North Korean Christians who continue to meet secretly in homes. They have almost no access to Bibles, religious literature, or teaching materials.

Christianity is perceived by authorities to be a dangerous threat, with the potential of undermining the Kim dynasty. Underground Christians have told foreign groups that if they are caught in possession of the Scriptures they fear being executed on the spot. Defectors report that Christians are given the heaviest work, the least amount of food, and the worst conditions in prison. Those caught praying in prison are beaten and tortured. A recent defector reports that she saw some Christians working in a foundry put to death with hot irons. Defectors also report that children and grandchildren of Christians also face life imprisonment for the religious beliefs and activities of their forebears. There were reports at the end of 1999 and the beginning of 2000 that up to twenty-three converts to Christianity (some returning from China) had been executed by firing squad.

Korea, South

Population	**46.9 million**
Christian	**48%**
Buddhist	**40%**
Confucian	**3%**
Shamanism, Chodogyo, Other	**9%**
Religious Freedom Rating	**2**

Background

At the end of a century that brought colonization and civil war to the Korean Peninsula, South Korea has emerged as a solid democracy and the world's eleventh largest economy. Following the Japanese occupation from 1905 to '45, the Republic of Korea was established in 1948 with the division of the Korean Peninsula. In the next four decades, authoritarian rulers suppressed civil liberties while undertaking a state-directed industrialization drive. The country's democratic transition began in 1987, when student protests forced military rulers to hold South Korea's first direct presidential election. The 1988 constitution limits the president to a single five-year term and ended his power to dissolve the 299-seat National Assembly. Kim Young Sam merged his party with the ruling party to form the governing Democratic Liberal Party (DLP) in 1990 and won the 1992 presidential election, the first civilian president since 1961. Kim curbed the security services, shook up the military hierarchy, and launched an anticorruption campaign. But his popularity waned as reforms slowed. In an unprecedented development, in 1996 a court sentenced former presidents Chun and Roh to death and twenty-two years' imprisonment, respectively, on charges of corruption and treason. Kim Young Sam reduced both sentences and, later, president-elect Kim Dae Jung pardoned both men.

The 1997 Asian economic crisis produced bankruptcies, a banking crisis, and a plummeting currency. With Kim constitutionally barred from a second term, the 1997 presidential election was an open race. Kim Dae Jung allied with conservative United Liberal Democrats (ULD) leader Kim Jong Pil and pledged to transform the polity into a parliamentary system. He won the December 18 election with 40.4 percent of the vote. He undertook economic reforms, and South Korea's crisis appeared to bottom out. In December 1998, the five largest conglomerates announced that they would sell more than half of their subsidiaries, but many observers greeted the news with skepticism.

South Koreans can change their government democratically, and the judiciary is independent. In a sign of increased anticorruption measures, in 1997 a court sentenced then-president Kim Young Sam's youngest son to a three-year prison term for bribery and tax evasion. Corruption has decreased in recent years but is still pervasive. Despite its democratic status, South Korea still holds hundreds of political prisoners. Most are either labor activists or supporters of North Korea. Authorities apply the broadly drawn National Security Law (NSL), under which hundreds of people are arrested each year for allegedly pro-North Korean statements, for unauthorized ownership of North Korean publications or contact with North Koreans, and for other nonviolent activities. In March 1998, Kim freed seventy-four political prisoners. Political prisoners and ordinary detainees are often beaten and generally do not have access to an attorney during interrogation.

In recent years, courts have jailed several journalists under criminal defamation laws for articles critical of officials or corporations. Authorities reportedly pressure editors to kill critical articles, and the largely private media practice some self-censorship. In October 1999, the government lifted its ban on watching television from North Korea via satellite. Civic institutions are strong, and local human rights groups operate openly. Student protests have become a ritual occurrence and frequently turn violent. Women face social and professional discrimination, and domestic violence is reportedly fairly widespread. Union militancy and forceful responses by authorities frequently characterize labor relations. New 1998 labor laws ended the tradition of lifetime employment but also allowed unions to engage in political activity, and granted state-employed teachers the right to organize. Foreign workers are frequently forced to work longer hours and for less pay and are occasionally abused. Freedom House's 1998–99 *Freedom in the World* rates South Korea a two in political rights and in civil liberties.

Religious Freedom

Religion has historically formed the social fabric of Korean life. Buddhism was introduced in the fourth century. Chinese influence later brought Confucianism to the peninsula. The hierarchical, stratified Confucian belief system continues to influence Korean life to the present day. Catholic missionaries entered the country from 1835 on, but Catholicism was savagely repressed in 1846.

In 1885, missionaries began to introduce Protestantism, especially Presbyterianism, to Korea. In subsequent years Protestant missionaries helped revive and propagate Hangul, a fifteenth-century Korean alphabet, by translating the Bible into Korean using Hangul rather than the more widely used Chinese characters. This helped Koreans become literate in their own language and brought greater awareness of Korean cultural and national identity.

Christians were prominent in Korean nationalism and in opposition to Japanese occupation. Since colonialism in Korea was Japanese, not Western, Christianity has not been associated with Western imperialism. Overall, Christianity's contribution to education, women's rights, and class structure is considered to be one of the most significant developments in Korean history. Christians have also played leading roles in Korea's human rights movement. President Kim Dae Jung, whom past military governments tried to murder, is a Roman Catholic.

The 1987 constitution guarantees religious freedom. Article 19 states, "All citizens enjoy freedom of conscience." Article 20 states, "1.) All citizens enjoy the freedom of religion. 2.) No state religion may be recognized, and church and state are to be separated." In practice, religious freedom is respected. Political power is centralized in a strong executive, and this combined with the fact that the population is almost entirely homogenous, contributes to a uniform situation throughout the country regarding religious freedom and other human rights. There are no legal restrictions on religious freedom, and authorities do not place extralegal restrictions on religious practice.

Unless there is believed to be a threat to national security (a term traditionally defined expansively in South Korea), individuals have the practical right to freedom of religion and belief if they respect public order and morality. There is freedom to propagate one's faith, freedom of worship, and freedom to train and appoint clergy. Religious bodies have rights of self-government, of religious education, to carry out charitable activities, to own and acquire property, and to maintain social institutions. They can produce, import, and distribute literature; receive donations; and have contact with coreligionists, domestically and overseas. Individuals can adopt, change, or leave a religion freely, with no change of civil status.

Citing the need for national security, South Korea does not allow conscientious objection to military service or any alternative civilian service. At any given time, about one thousand men, the majority of them Jehovah's Witnesses, are in jail for an average of two and a half years for refusing military service.

In recent years conflict has continued within the one-thousand-year-old Chogye Order, which is South Korea's largest Buddhist group, with an estimated eight million followers. Leadership disputes within the Order have descended into violent clashes several times in the past three decades. In 1993, the government came under criticism for sending riot police into a temple to end an episode of violence. The latest violence began in November 1998, when dissident monks drove out mainstream monks from the Chogye Temple in Seoul, the Order's headquarters. The dissidents seized the temple after Song Wol-ju announced his candidacy for a third four-year term as chief monk. Song claimed that this would not violate an internal 1994 rule limiting the chief monk to two terms, since he was unable to finish his first term in the early 1980s after fleeing the country in a dispute with the then-military government. In the ensuing weeks, mainstream and dissident monks clashed violently several times, and dissident monks refused to obey a December 11 provisional court ruling to leave the temple. On December 23, riot police evicted the dissidents from the temple. The conflict within the Order's leadership appears to have had minimal impact upon its followers.

Since the restoration of democratic rule in the late 1980s, labor leaders have frequently used the Myondong Catholic Cathedral in Seoul as a haven to avoid arrest on charges of organizing strikes considered illegal by the government. Catholic priests and laypeople, often centered in Myondong, have also been active in protests against government repression, and some have been arrested. Some of them and some liberal Protestants have developed a leftist "minjung" theology, but the vast majority of South Korea's Christians are conservative Presbyterians. Authorities have generally exercised restraint and avoided entering the cathedral because of its religious significance.

Kyrgyz Republic

Population	**4.7 million**
Muslim	**75%**
Russian Orthodox	**20%**
Other (Jewish, Buddhist, Catholic, Protestant)	**5%**
Religious Freedom Rating	**4**

Background

The Kyrgyz Republic declared independence from the Soviet Union in 1991. In what was called the "Silk Revolution," President Askar Akayev, a respected physicist, introduced multiparty democracy and market reforms. But resistance from a Communist-dominated parliament elected in 1990 led Akayev to dissolve the legislature in 1994 and call a national referendum for changes to the constitution. Nearly 75 percent of voters approved a proposal for a new parliament.

The April 1998 government reshuffle came amid growing economic difficulties. The country was mired with a one billion dollar foreign debt, a substantial budget deficit, plunging exports, and little foreign investment. In 1998, President Akayev successfully advocated constitutional amendments that would enlarge parliament, provide for private ownership of land, and limit parliamentary immunity to activities connected with parliamentary duties. The revisions were adopted by public referendum in October.

Citizens can elect their government under a multiparty system. The 1996 constitution codifies strong presidential rule and a weak parliament. Parliamentary and presidential elections in 1995 included such violations as ballot stuffing, inflation of voter turnout, media restrictions, and intimidation. The judiciary is not independent and remains influenced by the executive branch. The procurator, not the judge, is in charge of criminal proceedings, and courts of elders still operate in remote regions. A new system of court administration has improved judicial professionalism.

The new criminal code and press law adopted in 1997 placed restrictions on the publication of state secrets; materials that advocate war, violence, or intolerance of ethnic groups; and libeling public officials. No private local radio or television stations exist. There are several independent papers, among them *Res Publica*, *Asaba*, *Delo No*, and *Vecherniy Bishkek*.

Freedoms of assembly and movement are respected inconsistently. In September 1998, local authorities in southern Kyrgyzstan banned an opposition rally. Major political parties include the Communists on the left, the nationalist Asaba, the Social Democrats, the Republican Party, the Agrarians, and Erkin (Freedom). The largest political movement is the progovernment Democratic Movement of Kyrgyzstan. Most parties are small and weak, with vague platforms and little financial support.

A 1992 law permits the formation of independent unions; most workers belong to the Federation of Independent Trade Unions of Kyrgyzstan (FITUK), the successor to the Soviet-era labor federation. More than 450 nongovernmental organizations (NGOs) are registered, ranging from business groups to sports and charitable associations.

Although the constitution guarantees minority rights, there has been an exodus of educated and skilled Russians and Germans. The Uighur organization Ittipak (Unity) has faced sporadic suspension for "separatist activities." Southern politicians continue to complain about underrepresentation in parliament. Under a Soviet-era law, citizens need official government permission (a *propiska*) to work and settle in a particular area of the country.

The 1990 property law allows foreign and Kyrgyz citizens to own homes, vehicles, means of production, enterprises, and buildings. A 1998 constitutional amendment permitted the private ownership of land. The legal and regulatory environment for business operations is widely regarded as superior to those in neighboring countries. Nevertheless, personal connections, corruption, and insider privatization have put limits on competition and equal opportunity. Women are well represented in the workforce, business, higher education, and NGOs. Domestic violence against women has reportedly increased since 1991. Freedom House's 1998–99 *Freedom in the World* rates Kyrgyzstan a five in political rights and civil liberties, both a decrease from the previous year due to increased authoritarianism.

Religious Freedom

The constitution, through Article 16, provides for religious freedom and the separation of the state from religion. Equal treatment of religions is in principal promoted, with no selection of a preferred or "traditional" religion, unlike several other former Soviet countries. Religious teaching is forbidden in the public schools. Religion is often a facet of national identity, with ethnic Kyrgyz professing Islam, while ethnic Russians are typically Orthodox. Islam is the largest faith, claiming approximately 80 percent of the population (although a large percentage are nominally affiliated) while 17 percent are Russian Orthodox. The remaining population includes a growing Protestant movement, as well as Catholics, Jews, Baha'i, and Buddhists. For different reasons the government has demonstrated a suspicion of radical Islam and non-Orthodox Christian organizations such as Protestants.

The single largest restriction upon religious liberty is the registration process, which remains a prerequisite for legal group assembly. Since 1996, following a presidential decree, all religious organizations must be registered with the State Commission on Religious Affairs (SCRA), as well as the Ministry of Justice. Religious groups that fail to register and continue to assemble are considered illegal gatherings and subject to harassment. Nonregistered groups are prohibited from several activities, including owning property, renting halls, making contracts, and banking. Currently, more than 300 organizations have been registered, including 210 Christian groups, as well as Muslim, Jewish, Baha'i, and Buddhist organizations.

Since 1998, a new, more restrictive religion law has been considered. This reflects a regional trend that the Kyrgyz Republic had resisted to date. The proposed Kyrgyz legislation bans unregistered groups from, among other things, importing literature and other religious material, publicly preaching, or otherwise sharing beliefs. Reportedly, the draft text is ambiguous, inviting the intimidation of nontraditional and unregistered religious groups.

In January 1997, the Inter-Departmental Council for Religious Affairs was implemented through governmental decree, ostensibly to foster interdenominational tolerance. Yet the Council has also been assigned the task of "countering religious extremism" as well as appointing "religious affairs officials to local administrations," inviting undue interference in religious expression. This impetus to control is bolstered by the two main religions, Islam and Orthodox Christianity, which periodically unite to promote their dominance by encouraging closer monitoring of minority religious groups. For example, they encourage the submission of all Muslims to the officially recognized Muslim Spiritual Board, and all Christians to the Russian Orthodox Church, regardless of Christian denomination.

Protestant Christian groups experience discrimination and harassment. Problems typically include registration delays or denials and consequent civil liberty infringements relating to free speech, association, and assembly. This has occurred with Seventh-Day Adventists, some Baptist groups, and the Church of Jesus Christ of Latter-Day Saints. A recent incident occurred in May 1999, when government officials broke up a Baptist evangelistic meeting in the town of Kyzyl Kiya in the Osh region. Ten participants were fined, detained, and expelled from the country. Missionaries are also harassed, with marked tensions particularly in the countryside.

The government closely monitors Islamic groups that it believes might stir up ethnic tensions or political opposition, in an effort to stem the tide of religiously inspired political extremism that has threatened the region. Since late 1997, the government has undertaken a campaign against Muslim fundamentalist groups, derogatorily referred to as "Wahhabis," with the Ministry of National Security assigned to hinder their activity. The Islamic Center was forced to close after their leader was accused of being a "Wahhabi" by the Muslim Spiritual Board, which is a government-controlled Muslim organization. Ethnic Uighurs were arrested in 1998 for possessing "Wahhabi" tapes and, in 1997, alleged movement leaders were expelled from the country. Lately, fears regarding the influence of political Islam have increased dramatically following bombings in Uzbekistan in February 1999. This has resulted in crackdowns and consequent migration to Kyrgystan. In August 1999, seven hundred armed Islamic insurgents engaged in guerrilla warfare, seizing hostages and engaging Kyrgyz security forces.

In recent years there has been much discussion in the national press about issues of religious control. Themes include allegations that extremist religious organizations are increasing and observations regarding the marked number of converts to "nontraditional" religions (including Protestantism). This in turn has elicited calls by politicians, intellectuals, and mainstream religious figures for greater restrictions on "nontraditional" faiths.

Despite some restrictions on religious liberty, the Kyrgyz Republic continues to provide relatively greater freedom in comparison to neighboring Central Asian countries. Yet, increasingly, restrictions of religious freedoms have occurred against perceived fundamentalist Islamic groups, motivated by fear of political extremism. A growing intolerance for "nontraditional" religion is an unfortunate trend given the relative present freedoms.

Latvia

Population	**2.48 million**
Protestant (mainly Lutheran)	**20%**
Roman Catholic	**20%**
Orthodox	**15%**
Jewish	**0.9%**
Muslim	**0.4%**
Atheist/Agnostics/Other	**43.7%**
Religious Freedom Rating	**3**

Background

After centuries of domination by Germany, Poland, Sweden, and Russia, Latvia gained independence in 1918. The country was forcibly incorporated into the Soviet Union during World War II under the provisions of a secret protocol of the 1939 Hitler-Stalin pact. More than fifty years of Soviet occupation saw a massive influx of Russians and the deportation, execution, and emigration of tens of thousands of ethnic Latvians. The proportion of Latvians decreased from 77 percent in 1940 to 52 percent in 1991, the year the country regained its independence in the wake of the USSR's disintegration. In July 1993, the 1922 Constitution was fully restored.

President Guntis Ulmanis was elected to a second term on June 18, 1996. The year 1997 was marked by continual government instability. In the October 1998 national legislative elections, six parties secured enough votes to enter parliament. With only forty-six of one hundred seats in parliament, the current coalition government's future stability and effectiveness remains a question.

Russia's economic crisis had a considerable impact on Latvia in late 1998, with Russian-oriented trade and banking sectors most strongly affected. In November 1998, Latvia was stung by its exclusion from fast-track membership talks to the European Union, although it may be invited to pre-accession discussions sometime in 1999.

Latvians can change their government democratically; however, the citizenship laws disenfranchise the almost one-third of the country's population that immigrated to Latvia during the Soviet period and who must apply for citizenship. International observers determined that the most recent legislative elections in 1998 were free and fair. More than forty political parties are officially registered, although communist, Nazi, and other organizations whose activities would contravene the constitution are banned.

The government respects freedom of the press, and both Latvian and Russian-language newspapers publish a wide range of political viewpoints, while there is a large number of private television and radio stations. Freedom of assembly and association are protected by law, but two events in the spring of 1998 soured already tense relations between Latvia and Russia. On March 3, 1998, police used rubber truncheons to disperse an illegal demonstration of mostly Russian pensioners. Two weeks later Russia and the international community denounced a commemorative march by the controversial Latvian Legion, formed by German occupation forces during World War II.

Workers have the right to form trade unions, strike, and engage in collective bargaining. The judicial system is weak and inefficient, and corruption is reportedly widespread. Most judges are not adequately trained, and many judges' posts remain vacant. In 1998, the country's Law on Citizenship was amended to ease and accelerate the naturalization process. On October 15, parliament amended the constitution with a new chapter outlining twenty-seven generally recognized human rights, which until then had been protected by provisions contained in an interim Constitutional Law. Despite objections from Latvia's ethnic Russian population, parliament passed a constitutional amendment declaring Latvian as the official state language. Freedom House's 1998–99 *Freedom in the World* rates Latvia a one in political rights and a two in civil liberties. The country was held to have improved over the previous year due to changes in the citizenship law.

Religious Freedom

Religion in Latvia has suffered the same vicissitudes as the country as a whole. Christian since the sixteenth century, Latvia turned into a mainly Protestant country following the Reformation, while the eastern province of Latgalia shared the Catholicism of neighboring Lithuania. During the time of the Old Believer's schism in Russia, members of this persecuted minority found refuge in the dense forests of the periphery, where some eke out an existence until today. The Russian population forms a significant bloc of the Orthodox faith.

As with the other two Baltic States, Soviet policy was to sovietize Latvia in the shortest possible time after World War II, with the church leadership of all denominations suffering heavy casualties. Following the thaw of 1956, there was some improvement, with most of those leaders who had survived being able to return to such churches as had remained open. Hopes for greater openness were soon dashed by Nikita Khrushchev's new antireligious policy of 1959–64. Baptist evangelists, especially the Russian Iosif Bondarenko, actively opposed this policy; while being heavily persecuted, they secured a greater freedom.

The Lutheran Church seemed intimidated into silence, yet it, too, received an influx of young enthusiasts in the 1980s. In 1985, a bright theological student at the one seminary, Maris Ludviks, fell foul of the authorities, and the Council for Religious Affairs refused to sanction his ordination. He was then ordained in Lithuania by Bishop Kalvanas, who was prepared to take such a major risk. The advent of Gorbachev came just in time to prevent the imprisonment of all involved.

In the late 1980s, the Rev. Modris Plate, a lecturer at Riga theological seminary, set up a movement called "Rebirth and Renewal," which had a massive effect on the Lutheran Church and public opinion in general. Fifteen pastors signed a petition calling on the faithful to fight for the right to an alternative to military service, to teach religion to children, and for believers to do pastoral work in hospitals and old people's homes. When Archbishop Mesters read this petition, he was terrified and banished Pastor Plate from the seminary, along with the rector for having allowed such a person to lecture. At this point international opinion intervened to support the persecuted group. The eventual outcome was soon to be the reconsecration of Riga cathedral, after decades of secularzation as a concert hall, the institution of religious broadcasts on TV and radio and, most importantly, the voting out of Archbishop Mesters and the election of a new Consistory (synod) in April 1989.

The Rebirth and Renewal movement was closely allied with the political Popular Front, now fighting directly for liberation from the Soviet yoke. Karlis Gailitis, elected in September 1989 as archbishop in place of Mesters, was an overt nationalist but died in a car crash in 1992. However, the freedoms won by these events, unique in Soviet church history, became a permanent gain, and the Lutheran Church had played a strong role in the struggle to liberate the country.

The successor of Archbishop Gailitis was Janis Vanags, who had lost his job as a teacher because of his religious convictions. Aged only thirty-five at his election, he proved surprisingly conservative, opposing the ordination of women, while the Lutheran Church as a whole encourages this. He has also campaigned for state financial support for Christian schools. As a result, the Latvian Lutheran Church has not ratified the Porvoo Agreement, providing for mutual recognition of ordained ministry between Lutherans and Anglicans.

Gorbachev's new law of September 1990 guaranteed religious liberty in theory as well as in practice, which, by that time, existed. This was followed,

after independence, by Latvia's own law. Article 35 of the Constitution reads: "1) The State is separate from the church. 2) The State guarantees the freedom of religious persuasion. People or their associations have the right to practice religious rituals and ceremonies. No one may be forced to participate in religious rituals and ceremonies, or to learn religious doctrine. Religious or ideological motives do not free anyone from their responsibilities to the State and the necessity of observing the law."

However, a somewhat restrictive and controversial law, "On Religious Organizations," was passed in 1995. In a pre-echo of the Russian 1997 law, "new" religious groups must apply for reregistration every year for the next ten years so that "their loyalty to the State and its laws may be proved" (Article 8.4). In 1997, the debate over what are "traditional religions" continued. A draft law of that year names Baptist, Lutheran, Orthodox, Roman Catholic, and Jewish. If the law passed, they would be guaranteed the right to "gather together for social, educational and cultural initiatives and to promote an ecumenical spirit; freedom to visit people in hospitals, orphanages and other state and private institutions; control over the process of returning property to the church and exemption of clergy from military service."

There are no penalties for nonregistration, but with this status there is no access to certain rights. From 1996, the minimum number of members required for registration was reduced from twenty-five to ten. Reports in 1997 claimed that twenty-two individual congregations had been denied registration, including eleven of the Latvian Free Orthodox Church, one of the New Apostolic Church, a Christian Science congregation in Riga, and the Jehovah's Witnesses. In 1998, the Ministry of Justice granted registration to the Jehovah's Witnesses, reversing a decision of two years earlier. Four Pentecostal congregations were stripped of registration in 1996 because they did not submit their reregistration documents on time. Even a group such as the Seventh-Day Adventists, which has existed in Latvia for more than a hundred years, is disadvantaged because its members, traditionally pacifist, are not granted an alternative to military service. Even a technical shortcoming in the filling out of forms may be a ground for refusing legal status, which in its turn denies a congregation the right to sell its publications or raise funds.

The grounds for refusing registration to the Free Orthodox Church are that they do not recognize the Moscow Patriarchate and therefore are superfluous in a country where there is already one major Orthodox Church—a secular judgment that is an intrusion into internal church affairs. Indeed, it is a state judicial body, which unilaterally makes the decisions on which congregations should be registered. Though legally privileged, the Russian Orthodox Church is disadvantaged economically, as the majority of Russians are second-class citizens who do not share in the modest economic growth that Latvia is experiencing. As Latvia is a country that has achieved a high standard of law and order, discrimination against unregistered congregations and individuals belonging to them is legal rather than physical, and there are no reports of attacks against individuals or property. The main religious groups may, on request, provide religious education for students in state (public) schools, according to a new law of 1997.

Lebanon

Population	**4.3 million**
Muslims (Shi'a, Sunni)	**55%**
Christian (Maronite, Orthodox, Melchite, Protestant, Chaldean, Assyrian, Syriac)	**41%**
Druze	**3%**
Others (Jewish, Baha'i, Alawi, Jehovah's Witness)	**1%**

(Accurate demographic figures for Lebanon's religious communities are notoriously hard to attain. These percentages reflect the averages of a number of currently circulating claims.)

Religious Freedom Rating	**4**

Background

Lebanon gained full sovereignty from France in 1946. An unwritten National Pact in 1943 gave Christians a mandatory six-to-five ratio of parliamentary seats over Muslims. After three decades during which non-Christians tried to end this system, a civil war erupted between Muslim, Christian, and Druze militias in 1975, claiming more than 150,000 lives before it ended in 1990. Complicating the situation was the presence of the Palestine Liberation Organization (PLO), which, after having been expelled from Jordan in 1971, used Lebanon as a base for attacks against Israel and constituted an occupying force. Syria sent troops into Lebanon to support the government in 1976. The Syrians, who consider Lebanon part of Greater Syria, continue to occupy the country today with some forty thousand troops, meaning that the Lebanese government is not sovereign in its own country. Syria dominates the country politically and militarily, while Israel's South Lebanon Army (SLA; scheduled to withdraw in 2000) controls a 440-square-mile security zone in the south. The Shi'ite pro-Iranian Hezbollah militia is still active in many southern towns, and Palestinian groups operate autonomously in refugee camps throughout the country.

The balance of power enshrined in the 1989 Taif Accord resulted in overlapping authority among the speaker, prime minister, and president. Religious tensions and conflicting priorities among the three have often led to political infighting and stalled political and economic progress. Syria, meanwhile, has worked to manipulate these tensions. Recently there has been a decreasing emphasis on religious proportions in senior government positions.

Shortcomings in the electoral system limit the right of Lebanese citizens to change their government. Parliamentary elections held in 1996 were neither prepared nor carried out impartially. According to the constitution, a president is to be elected by parliament every six years. In truth, Syria's choice of president is simply ratified by parliament. The U.S. State Department considered municipal elections held in May and June 1998 reasonably free and fair.

The judiciary is also influenced by Syrian political pressure. International standards of criminal procedure are not observed in the military branch of the courts. The average case is tried in minutes. Extragovernmental groups, like the SLA, Palestinian factions, and Hezbollah, administer justice in areas under their control, generally without due process safeguards. Arbitrary arrest and detention are commonplace. Security forces detained dozens and searched homes without warrants after a car bombing in Dora in mid-June 1998. Security forces use torture to extract confessions. Prison conditions do not meet international standards.

The government continues its crackdown on independent broadcasting, which flourished during the civil war. In January a government decree banned two of the country's four satellite television stations from broadcasting news or political programming. The appropriation of frequencies is a slow and highly politicized process. Print media are independent of government, though their content often reflects the opinions of the various local and foreign groups that finance them. Insulting the dignity of the head of state or foreign leaders is prohibited. All foreign print media are subject to government approval. In December 1998, the new government lifted a five-year-old ban on public demonstrations. Public assemblies require government approval.

Citizens may travel abroad freely, though internal travel is restricted in certain areas under Israeli or Hezbollah control. The government does not extend legal rights to some 180,000 stateless persons who live mainly in disputed border areas. Some 350,000 to 500,000 Palestinian refugees live without adequate electricity and water and face restrictions on travel, work, building, and purchasing property. Women often suffer legal and social discrimination under Islamic family law. All workers except those in government may establish unions, strike, and bargain collectively. Employers routinely abuse foreign domestic workers. Freedom House's 1998–99 *Freedom in the World* rates Lebanon a six in political rights and a five in civil liberties.

Religious Freedom

Lebanon has perhaps the Middle East's most diverse religious population. Its Maronites trace their history back to the fifth century A.D. when they moved from what is today northern Syria. In 1180, they entered into communion with the Roman Catholic Church. It is also home to the vast majority of the Druze, an offshoot of Islam that arose in Fatimid, Egypt, and relocated to the Levant, and is considered heretical by mainstream Islam. Lebanon also contains a rapidly growing community of Shi'a Muslims, a Sunni Muslim community mainly in the coastal urban areas, a Greek Orthodox Christian Church, and a Greek Catholic (Melchite) Church that shares in the Antiochian Byzantine tradition, an Armenian community tracing its expansion to the Turkish persecutions of the early twentieth century, a small Alawi community in northern Lebanon, and a Jewish community that has dwindled to number about eighty individuals.

Christian and Muslim communities in Lebanon have benefited from the country's freedom and diversity that have set them apart from much of the Middle East. Despite this, Lebanon's history has been punctuated by recurring instances of religious strife between Christians, Muslims, and Druze brought on in most cases by externals, for example, the Crusades, Ottoman hegemony, European colonialism, and, more recently, Palestinian radicalism, Iranian-inspired militancy, Saudi-funded Islamization, and Israeli and Syrian occupation.

The Lebanese political system is confessionally grounded, meaning that high-level government posts are apportioned along religious lines. The president of the republic should be a Maronite Christian, the speaker of parliament a Shi'a Muslim, and the prime minister a Sunni Muslim. Even mid-level posts in the government bureaucracy and the army follow this scheme. Parliamentary representation also reflects confessional or sectarian propor-

tions. Although the amended constitution of 1998 seeks to move away from this, it still remains.

The Lebanese Constitution guarantees freedom of religion, and it is the only Arab country whose constitution does not declare Islam to be the religion of the state: Lebanon has no state religion. Eighteen religious groups are officially recognized under Lebanese law, and the religious freedom guaranteed in the constitution applies only to them. These are: Shi'a, Sunni, Druze, Alawis, Ismailis, Jews, Maronites, Greek Orthodox, Greek Catholic, Roman Catholics (Latin), Protestants, Syriac Orthodox, Syriac Catholics, Armenian Orthodox, Armenian Catholics, Assyrians, Chaldeans, and Copts. Most of these groups fall under the two broad headings of Christianity and Islam.

Those outside the eighteen, including atheists, Jehovah's Witnesses, Buddhists, and Hindus, are automatically at a very broad legal disadvantage. The reason is that all matters pertaining to personal circumstances or status such as birth, registration, marriage, death, and inheritance are covered by specific laws for each one of the officially recognized groups. The option of civil marriage, for example, is not available in Lebanon because it is not legally sanctioned. Those couples seeking to marry in this fashion must go to Cyprus. This ceremony will be recognized in Lebanon, but it cannot be performed there. In March 1998, President Elias Hrawi introduced a bill to permit civil marriages, but it did not make it past the cabinet. In Muslim communities the marriage partner of any Muslim man or woman, if not already a Muslim, must automatically convert to Islam at the time of the matrimonial union or the marriage is unacceptable. Exceptions happen to this too, but they are usually frowned upon.

During the war years (1975–90)

Lebanon experienced the systematic destruction of places of worship, both churches and mosques. The war also resulted in the massive uprooting of whole communities and the internal displacement of populations. This too happened along sectarian lines. Entire villages of Christians in the Shouf Mountains, Bekaa Valley, and Akkar region in northern Lebanon near the Syrian border were emptied of their inhabitants (i.e. religiously cleansed), and in most cases the villages themselves were looted, burned, and destroyed. As a result, Christians are now compressed into about 20 percent of the territory of Lebanon. While there were massacres of Muslims, notably by Lebanese Christians at the time of the Israeli attack on Beirut, most massacre victims throughout the years of Lebanon's war were Christian, and many claim that during the war they were specifically targeted *as* Christians and that they are currently underrepresented in political arrangements. They also believe that the erosion of the country's freedoms under Syrian occupation has not only affected them but their Muslim countrymen as well.

In 1994, the Syrian-controlled authorities in Lebanon issued a Naturalization Decree that added some three hundred thousand individuals to the country's population, largely Syrian Muslims. This controversial measure upset Lebanon's already strained demographic balance. Christians fear that tampering with demographics in favor of Muslims coupled with a prolonged and open-ended Syrian occupation will reduce them to second-class status. Another fear is that the nearly three hundred thousand largely Muslim Palestinians will remain in Lebanon after the resolution of the Arab-Israeli conflict and the signing of the final peace treaties.

There is freedom to build or renovate places of worship and to proselytize. Since the cessation of hostilities in 1990, a building boom has taken place throughout the country, restoring churches and mosques. Two television stations, Tele-Lumiere for the Christians and Al-Manar for Hezbollah, are allowed to operate freely and broadcast their respective religious messages. Similarly, there are radio stations dedicated exclusively to religious preaching. Religious books, pamphlets, and other publications are freely and openly produced and disseminated.

Despite all this, an increase in Islamic fundamentalism presents a real danger to the future of religious freedom. There is an undeclared competition for Islamization between Iran-backed militant Shi'as and Saudi-financed Sunnis. This Islamization plays itself out in unbridled real-estate purchases, particularly in traditional Christian areas; a concerted drive to Arabize school curricula; asymmetrical appointments to low and mid-level government posts; and an inordinate increase in the number of conscripted Muslims in the army. In late 1999, there were several bombings of churches in Tripoli. In November a well-known folksinger, Marcel Khalife, was put on trial for blasphemy after singing a verse from the Koran. All these gradual pressures plus the deteriorating economic situation, brought on principally by the continuing Syrian occupation, have led to a steady exodus of Christians from the country, swelling the ranks of those who already emigrated during the war. There is also considerable concern among Christians in the south who have cooperated with the Israelis about their fate when Israel withdraws its troops from its occupation zone in 2000.

Present trends seem likely to decrease religious freedom. But currently, despite the upheavals and setbacks that Lebanon has suffered since the outbreak of war in 1975, freedom of religion is greater than in the surrounding Arab countries. Its religious freedom rating of four reflects the fact that much of the country is under the control of non-governmental groups. Within government-controlled areas there is much greater freedom.

Lithuania

Population	**3.7 million**
Roman Catholic	**80%**
Russian Orthodox	**5%**
Lutheran	**1.1%**
Jewish	**0.3%**
Muslim	**0.2%**
Agnostic/Atheist/Other	**13.1%**
Religious Freedom Rating	**2**

Background

One of the leading states of Europe during the Middle Ages, Lithuania merged with Poland in the sixteenth century and was subsequently absorbed by Russia in the eighteenth century. After becoming independent at the end of World War I, Lithuania was annexed by the Soviet Union in 1940 under a secret protocol of the 1939 Hitler-Stalin pact. The country regained its independence with the collapse of the USSR in 1991, having been the first in 1989 to publicly proclaim secession.

In the 1992 parliamentary elections, the Lithuanian Democratic Labor Party (LDDP), the renamed ex-Communist Party, won 79 of 141 seats. In 1996, with two LDDP-led governments tainted by financial scandal, the LDDP was routed in parliamentary elections. Gediminas Vagnorius of the Homeland Union-Conservative Party (HU/LC) was named prime minister. In a second round of presidential balloting held on January 4, 1998, Lithuanian-American Valdas Adamkus narrowly defeated former prosecutor general Arturas Paulauskas. Incumbent prime minister Gediminas Vagnorius was chosen in March to serve a second term.

On May 23, the Lithuanian daily *Lietuvos Rytas* published an article alleging that Vytautas Landsbergis, leader of the Sajudis independence movement, and former Interior Minister Vidmantas Ziemelis had ordered secret surveillance of high-ranking officials and political rivals. However, a parliamentary commission found no proof of wrongdoing. After provoking criticism from the Israeli government, the U.S. State Department, and Jewish organizations, the trial of accused war criminal Aleksandras Lileikis was postponed again in late 1998 due to the ninety-one-year-old defendant's poor health. The trial would mark the first proceeding against an alleged Nazi war criminal in Lithuania. The European Union failed to invite Lithuania to start formal membership negotiations.

Lithuanians can change their government democratically. The 1992 constitution established a 141-member parliament (*Seimas*), in which 71 seats are directly elected and 70 seats are chosen by proportional representation, all for four-year terms. The president is directly elected for a five-year term. The 1996 legislative elections and the 1997–98 presidential vote were declared free and fair by international observers.

The government generally respects freedom of speech and the press. Freedom of assembly and association are also respected, although the Communist Party of Lithuania continues to be banned. Workers have the right to form and join trade unions, to strike, and to engage in collective bargaining, though this is weakened in practice. There have been credible reports of police brutality, and prisons remain overcrowded and poorly maintained. The rights of the country's ethnic minorities are protected. In 1992, Lithuania extended citizenship to all those born within its borders, and more than 90 percent of nonethnic Lithuanians, mostly Russians and Poles, became citizens. Freedom House's 1998-99 *Freedom in the World* rates Lithuania a one in political rights and a two in civil liberties.

Religious Freedom

Lithuania was the first country of Europe officially to adopt the Christian faith (1387), and it held tenaciously to its Roman Catholic faith under the communist system. When, in the later Middle Ages, the Polish-Lithuanian Empire stretched from the Baltic to the Black Sea, the identity of religion and nationalism shaped the country's culture and tradition and was a determining factor in its political destiny, since the church formed the core of opposition to communism and led to the declaration of independence in 1991. This ended a period of almost two hundred years in which Lithuania had been subjugated by Russia and the Soviet Union, except for short independence (1918–40) and German occupation (1941–44). This latter virtually annihilated the richly endowed Jewish community in Vilnius, from which it can never recover. The only other significant religious community is the Lutheran Church, especially in the Klaipeda coastal region, though some 140,000 out of 170,000 fled in the face of communist "liberation" in 1944.

The twentieth-century experience of being thrice oppressed after two decades of independence had a profound effect not only on national identity but also on allegiance to the Roman Catholic Church. Most traumatic of all for the general population at large (as opposed to the Jewish community) was the deportation of some two hundred thousand citizens after the second Soviet occupation of 1944. These included six out of seven bishops and virtually all other senior clergy, as well as prominent laypeople in all walks of life. Church property was nationalized, but even with this massive assault, the number of churches functioning (some 60%) remained the highest per head in the whole Soviet Union. Subsequently, the pattern of religious persecution closely followed that of the Soviet Union in general: some releases from the Gulag during the "thaw" (1956–59), further repression under Nikita Khrushchev (1959–64), the period of *zastoi* (stasis) under Brezhnev, followed by the mold-breaking experience of *perestroika* under Mikhail Gorbachev.

The darkest days were lightened by the solidarity of Lithuanian Christians and the determined leadership of those priests still at liberty. This culminated in 1975 in the first issue of a remarkable clandestine journal, *The Chronicle of the Lithuanian Catholic Church*, which survived, despite assiduous attempts by the KGB to destroy it. The issues were regular, voluminous, and as time has shown, completely accurate, despite the harrowing conditions under which it was compiled. It remains to this day a manifesto of religious liberty and national independence. It was obvious that communist policy of repressing church and nation had failed.

During Gorbachev's *perestroika* in 1988-99, there was an alliance between the Catholic Church and the political independence movement (*Sajudis*). The leader of the latter, Vytautas Landsbergis, was a Lutheran but firmly proclaimed religious liberty for all. The return of Bishop Julijonas Steponavicius to his diocese after twenty-nine years of house arrest and his subsequent repossession of Vilnius Cathedral after more than forty years moved the heart of the nation.

Stalin's Law on Religious Associations of 1929 was extended to Lithuania after the Soviet conquest and remained formally in operation until Gorbachev's replacement guaranteed full religious liberty in 1990. A new constitution for the newly independent country was passed in October 1992. Article 26 reads in part: "Freedom of thought, conscience and religion shall not be restricted. Everybody in the Lithuanian Republic has the right to choose freely any religion or faith, to confess it on one's own, with others publicly or privately, to perform rites, to practice faith and teach it. No one can compel another person nor be compelled to choose, confess, or not confess any kind of religion or faith." Subsequently, in 1995, a law on Religious Communities and Associations was passed, giving them full property rights. Nine are declared "traditional" and therefore qualify for governmental assistance: Roman Catholics, Byzantine-Rite Catholics, Lutherans, the Reformed Church, Orthodox, Old Believers, Jews, Sunni Muslims, and Karaites (an ancient Lithuanian group). In practice, the Roman Catholic Church enjoys most religious freedom

because of its economic advantages compared with the minority groups. It enjoys the full range of freedoms found in traditional Catholic societies of Western Europe: theological seminaries, monastic orders, army chaplains, the right to teach religion in schools, radio and TV studios, and the regular airing of programs and a full range of publications.

Two areas of tension remain. The teaching profession was officially atheist in the communist period, and some residual hostility to the church is expressed in classes. There is also dispute about the return of some church property, particularly land subsequently put to other uses. The church is content to let some architectural monuments remain in the hands of the state, which can provide better protection. There was acrid discussion of the property issue in 1994–95, since in 1992, the "neo-communists" had won the parliamentary elections.

The Lutheran minority, while not influential, enjoys the freedom it needs for its thirty thousand members. It has a role in Lithuania's history since the first texts in the language emanated from the Protestant Reformation. The Soviets tried to abolish the church completely, but it showed remarkable persistence and eventually won the right to send a few theological students to the Lutheran seminary in Riga. The collapse of communism saw the opening of a seminary in Klaipeda, which now has some thirty students.

The present government makes a strong moral gesture towards the surviving Jewish community by maintaining the rich Jewish museum in Vilnius, with a pledge to provide a new building for the collection.

Macedonia

Population	**2 million**
Macedonian Orthodox	**67%**
Muslim	**23%**
Catholic	**3%**
Protestant	**2%**
Other	**5%**
Religious Freedom Rating	**4**

Background

Macedonia, an ethnically diverse mix of peoples, declared independence from Yugoslavia in 1991, though Greece only recognized it under the name of the Former Yugoslav Republic of Macedonia (FYROM). Kino Gligorov, a former communist leader and head of the SDSM (the former Communists), was appointed interim president in 1992 and directly elected in 1994. The country's first parliamentary elections since independence from Yugoslavia, held in October 1994, were marked by fraud and irregularities.

Prior to parliamentary elections, early 1998 saw a series of maneuvers and shifts in alliances. The two leading Albanian parties formed an electoral alliance, and the Liberal and Democratic parties merged. The Crvenkovski government was hurt by charges of corruption and the collapse of the TAT-saving institution in 1997 that affected thousands of investors. A center-right coalition led by the Internal Macedonian Revolutionary Organization-Democratic Party for Macedonian Unity (VMRO-DPMNE), which had boycotted elections four years earlier, won the parliamentary elections in October 1998. VMRO-DPMNE leader Ljubco Georgievski was named prime minister in late November and formed a government that included members from ethnic Albanian parties. Bribery was rife in public administration, the customs department, and among civil servants at all levels. Macedonia held presidential elections beginning in November 1999. After repeated irregu-

larities led to repeated votes, the winner was the moderate Boris Trajkovski.

A key issue in the 1998 campaign was the parlous state of an economy crippled by the 1994–95 trade embargo by Greece as well as the United Nations' ban on trade with the states of former Yugoslavia, lifted after the 1995 Dayton Accords on Bosnia. In March, with the eruption of fighting in Kosovo, the 750-strong United Nations Preventive Deployment Force (UNPREDEP), which was due to withdraw in August, announced plans to stay. In the spring of 1999, several hundred thousand ethnic Albanian refugees from Kosovo fled to Macedonia to escape Slobodan Milosevic's ethnic cleansing campaign. This caused tensions in a country where many were already suspicious of the Albanian ministry, and the Macedonian government was accused of hindering the entrance of refugees.

Macedonians can change their government democratically. The 1998 parliamentary elections were free and fair. The constitution enshrines free speech and access to information and prohibits censorship. Slander and libel laws have led to self-censorship. In October 1998, Georgievski said he was suing the paper *Vecer* for slander for an article that said his party and Albanian parties had agreed to the division of Macedonia. Most major media are government controlled or receive some subsidizes. Critics have argued that the issuance of broadcast licenses has been politicized. There are no significant restrictions on freedom of assembly.

Macedonia has a multiparty system, and some fifty parties are registered. No parties are explicitly illegal or outlawed. The Union of Independent and Autonomous Trade Unions confederation was formed in 1992. The Council of Trade Unions of Macedonia is the successor to the communist labor federation. Some three thousand nongovernmental organizations (NGOs) are registered. The president of the Republican Judicial Council acknowledged in 1997 that political parties, particularly the ruling coalition, play a critical role in the election of judges and that "efforts should be made to eliminate the political influence in the selection of judges." The judiciary is not free of political or governmental interference.

National minorities, particularly Albanians, have complained about abuses at the hands of police and discrimination. Other minority groups include Turks, Serbs, Vlachs, and Roma (Gypsies). Freedom of movement is unimpaired by government regulation. The constitution and laws enshrine property rights. An unreliable legal framework exacerbates bureaucratic delays, which are common in registering a business. Smuggling, drug dealing, and a large gray economy remain serious problems. Freedom House's 1998–99 *Freedom in the World* ranks Macedonia a three in political rights and civil liberties, with an improvement in political rights due to free and fair elections and the inclusion of Albanian parties in the government.

Religious Freedom

Religious tensions in Macedonia reflect its complex religious history, and religion and ethnicity are closely related. Christianity was formally introduced to Macedonia in the fourth century. From the sixth to the ninth centuries, the Slavs invaded, and most of the Balkan Slavs were Christianized. At the same time the priest Bogomil established Bogomilism, considered by many to be a religious heresy, and led his followers in the 869 rebellion in which Macedonia declared independence from the Bulgarian Empire. When, in 1204, the Crusaders attacked Constantinople, they broke off

parts of Macedonia from the Byzantine Empire and disrupted Catholic-Orthodox relations. The introduction of Islam to Macedonia came at the end of the fourteenth century when the Ottoman Turks began their five-century rule over the region. As the Turks migrated to Macedonia, the Muslim population increased while the Christian population shrank, though the two mixed without much discord.

A major rift in the Orthodox Church occurred in 1767 when, for political reasons, the Patriarch of Constantinople abolished the existing Macedonian archbishopric. Constantinople placed Greeks rather than Slavs in the clergy, escalating ethnic tensions between the people. The 1878 Berlin Treaty, ending the Russian-Turkish war, forced Turkey to divide Macedonia into sanjaks, or districts, governed by an equal number of Muslims and Christians. Tensions between the Christians and Muslims escalated during this period, with Christian uprisings and Turkish repression and massacres in 1902. In the First Balkan War in 1912, an Anti Ottoman League was formed to help free "brother Christians" from the Turks. With a large part of Macedonia under Serb rule in Yugoslavia, the Serbian Orthodox Church (SOC) reassimilated with the Macedonian Orthodox Church (MOC) in 1920.

Under Tito the MOC was reestablished, but even today it is not recognized by the other Orthodox churches. Although political relations with other Balkan states have stabilized, in 1995, the SOC declared the MOC schismatic, and there has been considerable conflict in Serbia and Macedonia regarding these opposing denominations over property ownership and church rights. In response, the MOC has developed friendly relations with the Catholic Church and has expanded its social services. The MOC is also the only religious group mentioned in the constitution, and Protestant and Muslim groups say it is favored by the government, a charge that it denies.

In the 1990s, there was a freedom to worship not known under communism and a general congeniality among religious groups, though most religious groups suffer from funding problems. Meetings held without registration or in areas other than the appointed worship place are subject to fines, but this is not uniformly enforced. Access to the media has been generally seen as fair, though registered communities appear to have easier availability to electronic media. Religious education is only permitted in registered places of worship. Muslims find restrictions on religious education particularly troubling. Generally, the main source of injustice reported by religious groups is not from the government but from family and friends of people who have left the MOC. Ethnic Serbs report that they cannot worship freely in the SOC.

In 1997, Parliament passed the Law on Religious Communities and Religious Groups that divided religious organizations into "religious communities," including the Macedonian Orthodox Church and Islam, and "religious groups," which included new or nontraditional groups. The law granted preferential status to these "religious communities." Although the law allowed citizens to establish religious groups, it required registration, including listing the names and addresses of fifty members. Groups not registered are illegal and subject to fines. Access to Macedonia by foreign missionaries and preachers is restricted. Other regulations address proselytism, collection of money, and activities outside of the designated place of worship. Penalties for

violations ranged from thirty thousand to one hundred thousand dinars. Although nineteen religious organizations have been able to register, some harassment and other difficulties were reported by Protestant groups.

The law is not primarily aimed at smaller religious groups but to protect the MOC from the SOC. SOC clergy have been prevented from entering the country and many foreign missionaries have experienced problems. Approximately fifteen foreigners have been deported from Macedonia in the past five years specifically for religious reasons. In 1995, Swedish missionaries' passports were stamped "persona non grata" when they left the country. Foreign workers have been interrogated, sometimes for several days, and only two foreigners are known to have been granted religious-worker visas. Macedonian pastors have been denied health cards and entrance into the social security system. Pressure is often worse outside of Skopje.

On December 24, 1998, the Constitutional Court of Macedonia declared Articles 3, 10, 11, 13, 14, and 22 of the 1997 Law of Religious Communities and Religious Groups unconstitutional. The court challenge was initiated by four Evangelical churches of Macedonia. The challenge was supported by the Macedonian Helsinki Committee for Human Rights, which is planning further legal action. Article 3 prohibited religious activity by nonregistered groups. The court found that this impermissibly violated an individual's religious liberty. Articles 10 and 11 required a fifty-member minimum for registration and filing of detailed information. The court felt that this restricted freedom of religion and association since it was not required of other civic groups. Articles 13 and 14 required an official register of legal religious groups. Article 22 required government permission for the construction or acquisition of religious buildings. The court said that these articles interfered with separation of church and state and restricted religious freedom.

The Macedonian Helsinki Committee plans a challenge to Article 8, which permits only one religious denomination for any particular faith, and Article 19, which requires the permission of the Office for Affairs of Religious Communities and Religious Groups for religious events in public places. The 1997 law is similar to legislation under communism, and there is concern how the recent change in government and new adjustments to the law will affect religious freedom. The election in late 1999 of a Methodist pastor, Boris Trajkovski, as president may signal increased openness.

Malaysia

Population	22.7 million
Muslim	58%
Buddhist/Taoist/Chinese	23%
Christian	8%
Hindu	6%
Sikh/Animist/Other	5%
Religious Freedom Rating	4

Background

The British colonial rulers established their first foothold in Penang in 1786 and gradually brought Indian and Chinese conscripts and indentured laborers to the Malay Peninsula to work on tin and rubber plantations. Malaysia was established in 1963 through the merger of then-independent, ex-British Malaya with the then-British colonies of Sarawak, Sabah, and Singapore. (Singapore withdrew in 1965.) The fourteen-party ruling National Front coalition has captured at least a two-thirds majority in the lower house in nine straight general elections since 1957. Mounting Malay frustration over the economic success of the ethnic Chinese minority exploded into anti-Chinese rioting in 1969. In 1971, the government responded with still-existing quotas for Malays in education, the civil service, and business affairs.

The National Front is dominated by the conservative Malay-based United Malays National Organization (UMNO). The current premier, Mahathir Mohamad, took office in 1981. The government has gained considerable legitimacy by presiding over a rapidly expanding economy. However, authorities exercise significant control over the media and use numerous security laws to restrict freedoms of expression and association and to chill political activity.

By 1997, the effects of a decade of excessive corporate borrowing, financial distortions caused by crony capitalism, a high-current account deficit, and the government's spending on prestige infrastructure projects combined with a regional economic slowdown to send the value of the *ringgit*, the currency, tumbling. In September 1998, Mahathir sacked Anwar Ibrahim—his deputy premier, heir apparent, and sometime rival—after Anwar had openly challenged Mahathir's loose fiscal and monetary policies. Authorities subsequently arrested Anwar on charges of sodomy and corruption, and the man once widely expected to be Malaysia's next premier was convicted of corruption in early 1999. His sodomy trial follows. Police used tear gas and water cannon to break up pro-Anwar demonstrations in Kuala Lumpur and several towns. However, in November 1999 elections, Mahathir was reelected with more than two-thirds of the seats. The main opposition grouping increased its seats, but its composition changed markedly. Islamist parties increased their vote. PAS, an Islamic opposition party, held on as the government in Kelantan and took over the government in the neighboring state of Trengganu.

Malaysians have a limited ability to change their government through elections. The government exercises significant control over the media, uses numerous security laws to restrict freedoms of expression and association, and reportedly punishes opposition-held states by economic reprisals. Nevertheless, PAS has controlled Kelantan state since 1990. The Mahathir government has made legitimate efforts to curb corruption and money politics.

The judiciary is subject to government influence in sensitive political and commercial cases. Mahathir, as home affairs minister, controls all important judicial appointments. _Shari'a_ (Islamic law) courts have authority over family and property matters in the Muslim community. Successive governments have used a series of security laws to detain alleged communists, religious extremists, Vietnamese boat people, and opposition figures. The number of people presently detained is not known. The 1960 Internal Security Act and the 1969 Emergency Ordinance permit detention of suspects for up to two years. The 1970 Sedition Act Amendments prohibit discussion of the privileges

granted to Malays and often sensitive issues. A 1987 amendment to the 1984 Printing Presses and Publications Act (PPPA) bars the publication of "malicious" news and expands the government's power to control publications.

Journalists practice considerable self-censorship. Individuals and companies close to the ruling National Front own all the broadcast media and the major newspapers, and the opposition receives little coverage. In September 1998, courts charged four people with spreading rumors over the Internet of rioting in Kuala Lumpur, Malaysia's first such cases. The 1967 Police Act requires permits for all public assemblies. Since 1969, political rallies have been banned, although indoor "discussion sessions" are permitted. Under the 1966 Societies Act, any association (including political parties) of more than six members must register with the government. Nongovernmental organizations (NGOs) operate openly but face some harassment.

Conditions in detention centers for political asylum seekers and alleged illegal immigrants are grim. In 1998, authorities responded to Malaysia's worsening economic crisis by rounding up and deporting thousands of alleged illegal immigrants to Indonesia. There are considerable restrictions on trade union association and the right to strike. Freedom House's 1998–99 _Freedom in the World_ rates Malaysia a five in political rights and civil liberties. The rating for political rights was a drop from a previous year due to the jailing of the two opposition figures and increased restrictions on freedom of expression.

Religious Freedom

Religion in Malaysia is divided largely along ethnic lines. Historically, several Southeast Asian empires exerted control over all or parts of the Malay

Peninsula, including the Hindu Majapahit Empire in the thirteenth and fourteenth centuries. Islam came to the Malay Peninsula in the fifteenth century, and today it is considered by the government as an essential element of the ethnic Malay identity. The Tamils and other southern Indians brought Hinduism to the region, while the Chinese introduced Buddhism and Taoism. Missionaries also spread Christianity to Sarawak and Sabah on Borneo, which were ruled by the "White Rajahs" of the Brooke family and the British North Borneo Company, respectively, until the Japanese occupation during World War II.

Non-Muslim minorities have expressed concern over their political marginalization and the potential for an erosion of existing religious rights in this relatively secular Muslim country. The increasing power of more militantly Islamic groups in the 1999 elections has raised concerns among religious minorities. Within Islam itself, there are tensions between the progressive political elite, which has ruled Malaysia since independence, and Islamic fundamentalists, who want to strengthen the *shari'a* (Islamic law) courts that cover Muslim property and family matters.

Article 2 of the constitution guarantees religious freedom. The Shafi school of jurisprudence within Sunni Islam is the state religion, and all ethnic Malay Muslims are legally regarded as Muslims. The government sponsors Islamic religion and cultural activity, and Islam has a privileged position in state schools. Non-Malays are free to convert to Islam and to other religions, while conversion from Islam is very strongly discouraged. In 1998, there were proposals inside and outside the government to punish "apostates," but the government has said there would be no punishment as long as people did not defame Islam after their conversion. Non-Sunni forms of Islam are also restricted. The states on the island of Borneo have a high population of Christians (30%) and animists (7%). Most states, especially on the mainland, have laws that either prevent the proselytization of Muslims or strongly discourage it.

Shari'a Islamic law courts have authority over family and property matters in the Muslim community. The 1984 Islamic Family Law Act covers marriage, divorce, and property matters and was intended to provide fair treatment for Muslim women. Parliament revised the law in 1989 to provide better protection for the property rights of married Muslim women and to strengthen their divorce rights. As prime minister, Mahathir Mohamad has advocated a progressive practice of Islam and has criticized religious scholars and the *shari'a* courts for discriminating against women. Mahathir and other religious reformers have also sought to unify the state Islamic laws under a federal system, although state religious leaders have strongly resisted this. The government is also proposing to make the payment of tithes mandatory for all Muslims.

Malaysia is a federation of thirteen states and the Federal Territory of Kuala Lumpur. Nine of the peninsular states have sultans (hereditary rulers). Every five years the sultans choose one of their members to become the Yang di-Pertuan Agong, or "King" of Malaysia. The nine states with sultans control their own Islamic affairs, with the sultan at the apex of the Islamic religious establishment in each state. The sultans are empowered to appoint members of state religious councils, the Islamic judiciary, mosque functionaries, and the registrars of Muslim marriages and divorce. The sultans also direct the *shari'a* courts on legal procedures.

In Penang, Melaka, Sabah, Sarawak, and the Federal Territory, the Islamic religious leadership is assumed by the Yang di-Pertuan Agong. The federal parliament has no legal jurisdiction over the application of *shari'a* in the individual states, only in the Federal Territory. Ethnic Malays face increasing pressure to adhere to the growing number of religious decrees from Muslim authorities. Each state has a department of Islamic affairs, and officers are generally authorized to arrest and prosecute Muslims for not attending Friday prayers, selling alcohol, eating and selling food during Ramadan, building mosques and teaching Islam without state approval, wife abuse, and various sexual offenses. The police and other government institutions often help enforce these strictures.

In 1989, Pahang State authorized mandatory caning of apostates, and large fines, imprisonment, and caning for Muslims involved in propagating other religions. In 1987, the states of Selangor and Pahang introduced legislation requiring Muslim women to wear conservative clothes in public. In 1997, religious authorities in Selangor arrested three Malay women for taking part in a beauty contest, and a *shari'a* court fined them for indecent dressing. Kelantan State is headed by an Islamic fundamentalist party and is the only opposition-controlled state. The state government has imposed restrictions on all female workers, including non-Muslims, that it says are based on Islamic values. Women in Kelantan cannot work at night and must wear conservative dress in the workplace.

Islamic religious authorities have no control or influence over non-Muslims. Non-Muslims are bound only by the civil legal system, which is based on English common law. The constitution's Article 3 (1) says that while "Islam is the religion of the Federation . . . other religions may be practiced in peace and harmony in any part of the Federation." Moreover, the federal government has made an effort to promote respect for the country's religious diversity. For example, Muslim, Buddhist, Hindu, Christian, and traditional holidays are all celebrated either as national holidays or as public holidays in certain states. For non-Muslims there is generally freedom of worship and freedom to train and appoint clergy. They have rights of self-government, of religious education, to carry out charitable activities, to own and acquire property, and to maintain social institutions. Nevertheless, because of its official status and close proximity to state power, Islam has an overarching influence in society.

State governments are often slow in approving building permits for non-Muslim places of worship or land for cemeteries and sometimes deny permits arbitrarily. The government discourages and, in effect, forbids the circulation of a popular Malay-language translation of the Bible within peninsular Malaysia and the distribution of Christian tapes and printed materials in the Bahasa Malaysia languages: it has claimed that some words, like *Allah*, are Islamic and should not be used for the Christian God.

Fundamentalist Muslim leaders are often critical of the government's economic development program, arguing that it will inundate the country with Western ideas and undermine traditional Islamic values. The government has responded by portraying itself as a defender of Islamic values, expanding the Islamic bureaucracy, and helping state authorities to enforce Islamic laws. These efforts are in turn viewed by non-Muslims as evidence of the increasing political power of the Muslim community.

The government has taken a similar

approach to what it considers to be perhaps an even greater threat than fundamentalist Islam: the rise of charismatic or "deviant" Islamic groups. Rather than suppressing these groups, authorities have generally tried to co-opt their leaders. For example, former deputy premier Anwar Ibrahim had been the leader of a charismatic youth movement until 1982, when he crossed over to the government. However, authorities have used authoritarian measures against less tractable groups. In 1994, the National Fatwa Council, a religious body that is empowered to rule on the legitimacy of Islamic groups, declared the messianic al-Arqam group to be illegal and ordered it to disband. The government then ordered it to do so. Previously the government had kidnapped al-Arqam's leader out of Thailand. In 1996, authorities used the Internal Security Act to arrest eighteen al-Arqam leaders. All were released by early 1997. Authorities also restrict the practice of Shi'ite Islam. In 1997, authorities arrested ten people under the Internal Security Act for spreading Shi'ite teachings.

Mounting Malay frustration over the economic success of the Chinese minority exploded into anti-Chinese rioting in 1969. As noted above, the government responded with still-existing quotas and preferences for Malays in education, housing, the civil service, and business affairs. However, since a Malay is defined as a Muslim, these preferences are also religiously discriminatory. If a Malay adopts another religion, he or she will lose access to these benefits. In 1983, Chinese and Indian leaders formed the Malaysian Consultative Council of Buddhism, Christianity, Hinduism, and Sikhism in an effort to open a dialogue with Muslim leaders. In the early 1990s, the government formed the Institute for Islamic Understanding to promote religious tolerance and advance non-Muslim understanding of Islamic beliefs and practices. However, these efforts have been largely symbolic. The official emphasis on promoting harmony among Malaysia's groups, and restrictions on free expression, has meant that in practice there is little true discussion of interreligious issues.

In recent years, overt conflict between religious groups has been rare. However, observers say the regional economic crisis has contributed to interreligious tensions. In March 1998, Muslims in Penang attacked a Hindu temple after its bell ringing allegedly disturbed their prayers nearby, leading to riots between Hindus and Muslims.

Mauritania

Population	**2.6 million**
Muslim (predominantly Sunni)	**99%+**
Christian (predominantly foreigners)	**0.2%**
Religious Freedom Rating	**6**

Background

Mauritania, located in northwestern Africa, is almost entirely a Muslim country. The Berber nomads entered the area and controlled the indigenous population in the first century A.D. The Arabs defeated the Berbers in the sixteenth century and brought Islamic culture with them, and this remains the dominant part of Mauritanian culture. The French colonized the area in the early twentieth century and were the first to abolish slavery. Mauritania declared its independence in 1961 and joined the United Nations in 1978. The Mauritanian people were severely affected by a drought in the late 1960s and 1970s; however, the economy survived, largely because of vast iron and copper deposits that were discovered and exploited.

After a 1978 military coup, Mohammed Ould Haidalla (a former prime minister) became president in 1980 and subjected Mauritania to a strict interpretation of Islamic law. In 1984, Haidalla was ousted by his chief of staff, Maaouya. By 1989, tensions with Mauritania's neighbor, Senegal, had increased so much that 100,000 Mauritanians were forced out of Senegal and 125,000 Senegalese were forced to leave Mauritania. The problems with Senegal brought international attention and increased international and domestic pressure on President Maaouya. In 1991, he made a number of democratic reforms that included a new constitution and the legalization of opposition parties.

Maaouya's Social Democratic Republican Party has ruled the country as a de facto one-party state since the 1996 legislative and 1997 presidential elections. Mauritanians have never been permitted to choose their representatives or change their government in open, competitive elections. Neither the 1997 presidential election nor the 1996 parliamentary vote was free or fair. The absence of an independent election commission, state control of broadcasts, harassment of independent print media, and the incumbent's use of state resources to promote his own candidacy devalued Ould Taya's presidential victory.

The government heavily influences Mauritania's judicial system. Many decisions are shaped by *shari'a* law, especially in family and civil matters. In February 1998, several human rights activists were convicted of operating or associating with "non-authorized" organizations. Several people identified as prisoners of conscience by Amnesty International remain incarcerated. More than twenty political parties and numerous nongovernmental organizations operate, but government registration requirements may now be used to block human rights and antislavery groups. A handful of black African activist groups and Islamist parties are banned. Widespread discrimination against blacks continues. As many as one hundred thousand blacks still live in conditions of servitude tantamount to slavery.

Prepublication censorship, arrests of journalists, and seizures and bans of newspapers devalue constitutional guarantees of free expression. The state owns the only two daily newspapers and monopolizes nearly all broadcast media. State media forbid dissemination of allegations of continued slavery and criticism of Islam. Punishable offenses include "insulting the president" and "promoting national disharmony." Under *shari'a* law, a woman's testimony is only given half the weight of a man's. Legal protections regarding property and equality of pay are usually respected only in urban areas among the educated elite. Female genital mutilation is widely practiced.

Approximately one-fourth of Mauritania's workers serve in the small formal economic sector. The government-allied Union of Mauritanian Workers remains the dominant labor organization. The government has forcibly ended strikes and detained or banned union activists from the capital.

Mauritania is one of the world's poorest countries and faces a virtually un-payable foreign debt. Freedom House's 1998–99 *Freedom in the World* rates Mauritania a six in political rights and a five in civil liberties, the latter a rise from six the previous year due to greater freedom of association.

Religious Freedom

Officially, the Constitution of Mauritania grants "freedom of opinion and thought" (Article 10.1). However, it also declares that "Islam shall be the religion of the people of the state" (Article 5). Though the constitution ostensibly protects minority religions, its laws prohibit Mauritanians from participating in them. A High Council of Islam, consisting of six imams, advises on the conformity of legislation to Islamic principles.

According to the Mauritania Penal Code, Section IV, Article 306:

Any Muslim guilty by word or deed of the crime of apostasy, visibly and obviously will be invited to repent within three days.

If he does not repent during this time, he is condemned to death as an apostate, and the Treasury Department will confiscate his property. If he repents before the sentence is carried out, the Public Prosecution Service will refer the matter to the Supreme Court with the view to restoring his rights, without affecting any penalty provided for in Paragraph one of the present Article.

Any person guilty of the crime of apostasy, will, unless he has first repented, be sentenced to death. . . .

Any adult Muslim who, while acknowledging that prayer is an obligation, refuses to pray, will be invited to do so before the expiration of the time set for the carrying out of the obligatory prayer in question. If he continues to refuse until the end of the set time, he will be sentenced to death.

If he does not acknowledge the obligation of prayer, he will be sentenced to death for apostasy and the Treasury Department will confiscate his property. He will not be allowed the usual religious rites.

In these sections, apostasy includes changing religion from Islam or seeking to abandon Islam entirely. In addition, the government views "proselytizing" as undermining the state and has prohibited non-Muslim groups from "proselytizing."

The constitution also declares that Mauritania is an "Islamic, African, and Arab republic" and requires the president to be a Muslim. An overwhelming majority of the Mauritanian population is Sunni Muslim. Other religious groups among non-Mauritanians are tolerated. Proselytizing is illegal and considered a threat to the state.

While the practice of other religions by non-Mauritanians is usually tolerated, Mauritanians cannot freely practice another religion. To do so, they would be assumed to have converted from Islam, and this is strictly forbidden. Mauritanians are not allowed even to attend non-Muslim religious ceremonies or own sacred books of other religious groups. The archbishop of the Catholic Church, which is the only recognized religious group outside of Islam, has been warned that any Mauritanian who converts to Catholicism will be beheaded, although in practice the government has not carried out such threats. There have been some reports of persecution of non-Mauritanian Christians. In 1995, two priests were attacked by an extremist Muslim at their church in Nouakchott.

Because of these pressures, the official statistic that Mauritanians are 100 percent Muslim may hide any diversity of religion that may exist in the country. Because converting from Islam is prohibited, the presence of other religions is likely to be deeply hidden.

A group of Shi'ite Muslims from Lebanon living in Western Mauritania worships freely. The only non-Muslim religion present in the territory seems to be Christianity. Several Christian churches are located in Nouakchott, Atar, Zouerate, Nouadhibou, and Rosso. The members of these churches are not prohibited from practicing their faith. However, Mauritanians are forbidden to join them. Most of the members are expatriates or from an ethnic group other than Mauritanian. Despite the religious restrictions placed on Mauritanians, the government does seem to respect and protect the religious liberty of non-Mauritanians. The U.S. State Department reports that the Mauritanian government immediately carried out an investigation into death threats received by a Christian nongovernmental organization, however no arrests were made.

Mexico

Population	**99.7 million**
Catholic	**89%**
Protestant	**6%**
None	**3.5%**
Other (Orthodox, Muslim, Jewish, Baha'i)	**1.5%**
Religious Freedom Rating	**4**

Background

Mexico achieved independence from Spain in 1810 and established itself as a republic in 1822. Seven years after the Revolution of 1910, a new constitution was promulgated under which the United Mexican States became a federal republic consisting of thirty-one states and a Federal District (Mexico City). Each state has elected governors and legislatures. The president is elected to a six-year term. A bicameral congress consists of a 128-member Senate elected for six years with at least one minority senator from each state, and a five-hundred-member Chamber of Deputies elected for three years.

Since its founding in 1929, the Institutional Revolutionary Party (PRI) has historically dominated the country by means of its corporatist, authoritarian structure, which is maintained through co-optation, patronage, corruption, and repression. Salinas de Gortari won the 1988 presidential elections through massive and systematic fraud. Until the outbreak of the Marxist-led Zapatista rebellion in the southern state of Chiapas on New Year's Day 1994, it was assumed that Salinas' hand-picked successor, Luis Donaldo Colosio, would win in the 1994 presidential election. The Zapatistas' demands for democracy and clean elections resonated throughout Mexico, and Colosio was assassinated on March 23, 1994. As the PRI stand-in, Salinas substituted Zedillo, a forty-two-year-old U.S.-trained economist with little political experience. Weeks after Zedillo took office on December 1, 1994, the Mexican *peso* collapsed, and the economy fell into a deep, yearlong recession. Mexico became the leading supplier of illegal drugs to the U.S.

In 1996, opposition parties of the left and right won important municipal elections in three states. Post-electoral conflicts took place in several regions. In the southern states of Guerrero, Oaxaca, Tabasco, and Chiapas—where many of Mexico's indigenous people live—political violence continued to be a fact of life. The climate in which Mexicans went to the polls several times in 1997 and 1998 was substantially improved from past elections. These elections were the fairest in the country's history.

Supreme Court judges are appointed by the executive and rubber stamped by the Senate. The judicial system is weak, politicized, and riddled with the corruption infecting all official bodies. Constitutional guarantees regarding political and civic organizations are generally respected in the urban north and central parts of the country. However, political and civic expression is restricted throughout rural Mexico and in poor urban areas. Civic society has grown in recent years: human rights, pro-democracy, women's, and environmental groups are active. However, government critics remain subject to forms of sophisticated intimidation. An official human rights commission was created in 1990. However, it is barred from examining political and labor-rights violations, and cannot enforce its recommendations. For more than four years, the human rights situation has seriously deteriorated, with hundreds of arbitrary detentions, widespread torture, scores of extrajudicial executions, and a number of forced disappearances.

During the outbreak of the still-simmering Chiapas rebellion, the military was responsible for widespread human rights violations. The growing role of the military in internal security—ostensibly to combat domestic terrorism, drug trafficking, and street crime—has contributed to grave human rights problems, particularly in rural areas. Published reports offered continuing evidence of close links between drug traffickers and the armed forces, contradicting official versions that have sought to portray the military as less prone to corruption and drug cartel influence than civilian law enforcement.

The media, while mostly private and nominally independent, depend on the government for advertising revenue. A handful of daily newspapers and weeklies are the exceptions. The ruling party dominates television. Violent attacks against journalists are common. Officially recognized labor unions operate as political instruments of PRI. The government does not recognize independent unions, denying them collective-bargaining rights and the right to strike. Independent unions and peasant organizations are subject to intimidation, blacklisting, and violent crackdowns. Violence against women is rampant, and the government consistently fails to enforce child-labor laws. Freedom House's 1998–99 *Freedom in the World* rates Mexico a three in political rights and a four in civil liberties.

Religious Freedom

Mexico has had a long history of church-state confusion, conflict, and tension. Some of the early Spanish missionaries supported, while others resisted, the exploitative ways of the conquistadors. Later, the Catholic Church was identified with the old ruling class. Finally, there was the expropriation, limitation, and marginalization of the church after the 1917 revolution. In nearly all these cases, relations between Mexico's church and state have undercut religious freedom.

The PRI from its inception took a strong anticlerical line. In the last decade, particularly since the new constitution of 1992, Mexico has drawn closer to a system that basically respects religious rights. But many issues, both theoretical and practical, await resolution. Mexican society still bears many of the marks of the period between 1917 and 1992 when religious practice was strictly regulated. In 1917, the revolutionary government adopted the world's first socialist constitution, with many features detrimental to religion. Under that regime, churches and other religious groups did not have judicial status, were not allowed to engage in public worship outside church buildings, to own real estate, or to receive official recognition for education in religious institutions. Religious orders were technically illegal, and foreign missionaries were not officially permitted. When the pope visited Mexico in 1979, he theoretically violated the constitution by appearing in public in clerical garb. In practice, given Mexico's population of religious believers, ingenious private arrangements often mitigated the absolute character of these regulations.

Only in the 1990s have these highly restrictive laws been changed, and vague language still leaves a great deal of power over religion in state hands. According to the revisions of the 1992 constitution, churches are still expected to celebrate their liturgies only in their own buildings: only in the case of extraordinary events might they be allowed to occur in public spaces, subject to official permission (Article 24). Religious bodies now may receive juridical status (Article 130) and may own property for what is "indispensable" (Article 27) to their religious aims and within other legal limits. Who determines what is "essential" to religious practice is not entirely clear. Private education may be recognized by the state but must conform to the ends proposed for public education (Article 3), again as determined by state officials.

These revisions have improved conditions for the free exercise of religion but reflect a view that these are concessions by the Mexican state to its believing citizens. Among other large-scale restrictions, religious bodies still cannot own or operate radio or television stations. Clergy cannot criticize laws or authorities. Historic anticlericalism seems to continue in prohibitions against ministers of any religion running for political office. Religious groups cannot support parties or candidates. Political parties and groups of whatever kind are forbidden to adopt names for themselves containing "any word of indication of whatever type that relates them with any religious confession" (Article 130). A European-style Christian Democrat party would be ruled out by its very name. There is no formal right to conscientious objection, though sometimes it is recognized.

In addition to historic conflicts between the Catholic Church and the secular Mexican state, new difficulties over religious liberty have emerged. The explosive growth of various evangelical and pentecostal Protestant groups (along with the presence of mainstream Protestants and Mormons) in several areas has created tensions both between

Catholics and Protestants and between state governments and the new Christian groups. The Mexican constitution guarantees freedom of religious belief within the legal restrictions described above, and the Catholic Church professed to want religious liberty for all before the constitutional reform. But these principles are often ignored by both church and state due to existing political alliances. Some members of the hierarchy viewed Protestant growth as the illegitimate fruit of North American interference and sought to get as favorable position for the church as possible against these perceived incursions. Anti-Protestantism is sometimes linked with anti-Americanism in those social sectors that see Mexico's identity as necessarily demanding sharp difference from the United States. In some media portraits, evangelicals are characterized as North American spies and a threat to Mexican culture. However, the Vatican's insistence that the new constitution protect religious liberty across the board has prevailed with the Mexican Catholic hierarchy. (About 30 percent of nominal Catholics actively attend church services.)

Nonetheless, some Protestants continue to be mistreated by local authorities. In some of the southern states, such as Chiapas and Oaxaca, evangelical Protestants have been penalized with jail sentences or fines for refusal to participate in traditional public festivals or communal philanthropic activities that run against their beliefs. Their children have been refused admission to or expelled from public schools. Protestant churches have been burned. In some cases leaders have been murdered, and there are instances of rape. San Juan Chamula in Chiapas has witnessed the eviction of between twenty-five thousand and thirty thousand people since

1974, the vast majority Protestants, but a small number of Catholics as well. Evictions were continuing through spring 1999 in Ejido Saltillo, El Retiro, El Vergel, El Paraiso, and Siberia in Chiapas. On June 15, 1999, thirteen Protestants trying to build a new church in Mitziton, in Chiapas, were arrested by local authorities.

The current turmoil in Chiapas is the result of complicated political, economic, and social factors, but it appears that many of these evictions had religious motivations as well and certainly have exacerbated the other problems. About 80 percent of those expelled from their home are Presbyterians. In the local context this means that they reject the dominate syncretism of local indigenous groups, themselves long neglected by Mexico City, which combines Catholicism with native beliefs. Those same indigenous Catholics also are uncomfortable with Marxist social theory when it comes in the form of Catholic liberation theology or the revolutionary violence of the Zapatistas. The Zapatista National Liberation Army has threatened at least one evangelical pastor in 1998, believed to be supporting government-backed militia groups. Indigenous village chiefs frequently expel or contribute to the deaths of converts.

San Juan Yahe in Oaxaca has expelled people for beliefs that contradict "the customs and traditions of the people." In several cases, these conflicts reflect not only Catholic-Protestant tensions but tensions between the new Protestant groups and indigenous peoples, who, with the collaboration of authorities, have burned homes and fields, and beaten and sometimes killed individuals. Indigenous Caciques often profit from the liquor consumed at traditional festivals and view the Protestant opposition to drinking as a threat not only to cultural unity but to their economic interests. The Caciques have been aligned with the ruling PRI and, despite the national government's long-standing limitation on Catholicism, these political alignments, perhaps sometimes going near to the top of the governmental pyramid, result in national military assistance to indigenous/Catholic elements.

By some estimates, 40 percent of the Indians in some southern states are now evangelicals or pentecostals, and their mistreatment has made them a potent force for opposition parties to the PRI. According to some reports, Catholic catechists in Chiapas—apparently operating under liberation theology principles—have ordered churchgoers to support the Zapatistas under pain of being barred from the sacraments. Those indigenous persons who have not wished to support the revolutionary group have left the Catholic Church and added further to the ranks of those seeking independence from both the traditional bosses and the revolutionary army.

The Catholic Church in Mexico has been criticized for contributing to this infringement of the religious rights of Protestants by the influence it exerts through state and local officials. In some states and municipalities, the traditional power of local bosses is closely tied with certain sectors of the church. But these social habits seem more accidental than programmatic features of Mexican church-state relations. In practice, both religious and secular leaders in various parts of Mexico are seeking to preserve the status quo in direct violation of the official national policies of both the Catholic hierarchy and the Mexican government.

There is a small (50,000) Jewish community in Mexico that basically lives freely with only minor and occasional outbursts of anti-Semitism. Most Jewish young people attend Jewish schools, and Mexican Jews have created vigorous and successful national and international organizations. Though excluded for many years from politics and public service (as were many other classes of Mexicans outside the PRI orbit), Jews in Mexico today have assumed several important posts in the federal structure.

Moldova

Population	**4.3 million**
Russian/Romanian Orthodox	66%
Catholic (Greek and Roman)	2.5%
Protestant (mainly Baptist)	1.7%
Jewish	1.5%
Muslim	0.2%
Agnostic/Atheist/Other	28.1%
Religious Freedom Rating	4

Background

Moldova, 90 percent Romanian-speaking, was annexed by Moscow as a result of the Molotov-Ribbentrop Pact of 1939. After War World II, it was sovietized and forced to use Cyrillic script. This former Soviet republic, bordering Ukraine and Romania, declared independence from the Soviet Union in 1991, when Mircea Snegur, who ran unopposed with the backing of the nationalist Moldovan Popular Front (MPF), was elected president. In 1990, Slavs in the Transdniester region proclaimed the Dniester Moldovan Republic (DMR).

The 150,000-member Gagauz, a Turkic, Christian people, did the same. The fighting in the Transdniester, where local Slavs were supported by elements of Russia's Fourteenth Army, ended with a cease-fire in mid-1992. In 1994 parliamentary elections, the PDAM—a coalition of former communists and moderate supporters of Moldovan statehood, won 56 of 104 seats. In the March 1998 parliamentary elections, the communists, who were banned from running in the 1994 vote, won 40 out of 101 seats and 30 percent of the vote. But a center-right coalition led by Prime Minister Ion Ciubuc formed a new government in April, leaving communists out of the cabinet. On September 9 1998, the country was rocked by the collapse of the lei. The International Monetary Fund took steps to shore up the currency but pressed Moldova to cut its large budget deficit. Talks continue on the withdrawal of Russian troops from the Transdniester region.

Moldovans can change their government democratically under a multiparty system enshrined in the 1994 constitution. International monitoring groups characterized the November 1996 presidential elections and the 1998 parliamentary elections as "free and fair." The constitution and law provide for freedom of speech and press. However, defamation of the "state and people" is proscribed. There are some restrictions on freedom of assembly. Under law, rallies that slander the state or subvert the constitution are banned. Some fifty political parties and groupings span the political spectrum.

In June, teachers went on a hunger strike in Ungheni to protest salary arrears. In October, employees of state radio threatened to strike over unpaid wages. The judiciary is still not fully independent, with the prosecutor's office having undue influence, which undermines the presumption of innocence. Moldova has ratified the Council of Europe's Convention on the Protection of Ethnic Minorities, but discrimination against Romanian-Moldovan speakers continued in the Transdniester. Freedom of movement is not restricted, though Transdniester authorities have searched incoming and outbound vehicles. The government may also deny emigration to anyone with access to "state secrets." Corruption in government, the civil service, and organized crime hinders fair competition and equal opportunity. Political union with Romania remains a sensitive issue. Freedom House's 1998–99 *Freedom in the World* rates Moldova a two in political rights and a four in civil liberties and notes an improvement in political right due to freer elections.

Religious Freedom

The majority Romanian language group and their allegiance to the Orthodox Church dominate religion in Moldova, but the church is seriously divided within itself. When the territory of present-day Moldova was incorporated into the Soviet Union as a result of World War II, the Soviet authorities, as in other instances, forced the Moscow Patriarchate to back the Kremlin and ensure that the Orthodox Church transferred its allegiance from the Romanian Orthodox church, with its patriarchate in Bucharest. The only, and limited, training available for future priests was in the Russian language and outside the country.

Moldova inherited the Stalinist restrictive religious legislation of 1929, which was replaced by Mikhail Gorbachev's law of September 1990 guaranteeing full religious liberty. The new state soon passed its own law guaranteeing religious freedom in April 1992.

This Law on Cults prohibits the state from intervening in church affairs. It permits religious groups to organize themselves as they wish, providing they do not violate general legislation, and forbids any religion from being recognized as a state church. In November 1998, a new law was passed, permitting proselytism, in conformity with the European Convention on Human Rights, and overturning a prohibition contained in the 1992 law. A draft amendment, somewhat unclearly, forbids "abusive proselytising."

The government has interfered in a basic conflict within the Orthodox Church. In 1992, the Orthodox Church in Bessarabia, the "southern tier" of Moldova, asserted its right in a newly independent state to realign its allegiance. It argued that since most of Moldova's territory formerly belonged to Romania, the church should now come under the Romanian patriarchate in Bucharest instead of Moscow. This Bessarabian Metropolia, as it called itself, under Bishop Petru Paduraru claims the allegiance of some 10 percent of the population of the country. However, the State Service for Denominations, under its head Gheorghe Armasu, a secular bureaucrat, refused to give it independent registration, saying that there should not be two Orthodox churches in the country. He ruled that the church property of the forty or so secessionist parishes should be returned to the main church, under Archbishop Vladimir of Chisinau and Moldova, whose allegiance was to the Moscow patriarchate.

In August 1992, men, reported to be clergy representing the "anti-Romanian" majority, broke into Petru's residence and seized documents and cash. The police investigation never identified the culprits. In 1995, the State Service for Denominations called in and interrogated two visiting Romanian priests, Frs. Vasile Stavovci and Ion Bagea, who were conducting services at the request of the Bessarabian Metropolia. There were also unconfirmed reports that a strong supporter of the secessionist church, Fr. Anastasie Petcu, a monk from Capriana, died under suspicious circumstances in July 1995.

In September 1995, the courts ruled in favor of the secessionists, proclaiming that state interference was illegitimate and violated the constitution. However, the government intervened again and asked the Supreme Court to overturn this verdict. Members of the government were divided over the issue, but the Council of Europe, which has now extended membership to Moldova, urged the government to ensure total religious freedom for all citizens and to seek a peaceful resolution, ideally with the Orthodox Church becoming reunited. The Bessarabian Metropolia subsequently rejected a proposal that both factions should come under the Patriarchate of Constantinople. Metropolitan Vladimir warned that there would be "war ahead" and a hundred priests of the Moscow jurisdiction demonstrated outside the prime minister's residence against recognition of the Bessarabian Metropolia.

In December 1997, the Supreme Court eventually delivered a verdict against the secessionists, saying they had not appealed against the government's refusal of registration in due time. A parliamentary deputy, Vlad Cubreacov, who represented the Metropolia in court, disputed the verdict and said the case would go to the European Court for Human Rights. This is currently where the matter rests.

Orthodox believers not involved in this dispute have full religious liberty in personal terms, but minorities do not. The Catholic community of fifteen thousand is nervous of proclaiming its faith in public in the midst of an overwhelmingly Orthodox society. Among Protestants, the Baptists are the most numerous. There has been violence against them, especially when foreigners have been visiting their fellow-believers. In November 1996, an "Orthodox" demonstration interrupted a worship service of some sixty believers in the village of Gura Galbanei. In a neighboring village the Baptists hired a school hall for an evangelistic rally, but fifty demonstrators, waving Orthodox crosses, tried to prevent their entry. There was some violence but no serious bloodshed. On May 5, 1999, a mob led by seven Orthodox priests destroyed a registered Baptist church being constructed in the village of Gelo Mengir. Victor Daskaliuk,

the pastor, and several others were slightly injured. While Orthodox Church leaders have condemned such violence, they also criticize "sectarians," who enjoy little protection under the law. Despite the constitution, minority religious groups, whether registered or unregistered, face threats.

The Romanian-speaking minority in the largely Russian region is heavily persecuted, and the leader, Ilie Ilascu, has been in prison since 1992, and perhaps tortured. As a believer, he maintains a goal of uniting all Romanian-speaking people with Romania and with its patriarchate. A division of Russian troops subjugates the territory, and its president, Igor Smirnov, is an old communist. The Moscow patriarchate appointed a special Russian-speaking bishop for the territory, and he backs its Russification, even though there is no border with Russia.

Mongolia

Population	**2.4 million**
Tibetan Buddhist	**95.5%**
Muslim	**4%**
Christian	**0.3%**
Other	**0.2%**
Religious Freedom Rating	**3**

Background

China controlled this vast Central Asian region for two centuries until 1911 and again from 1919 until a Marxist revolt in 1921. The Soviet-backed Mongolian People's Revolutionary Party (MPRP) formed a communist state in 1924 following three years of nominal rule by aging Buddhist lamas. For the next sixty-five years, Mongolia was a vir-

tual republic of the Soviet Union. Pro-democracy demonstrations forced the government to resign in March 1990, and Mongolia held its first multiparty parliamentary elections. The 1992 constitution provides for a president with executive powers who is directly elected for a four-year term. The president must approve candidates for premier and can veto legislation, subject to a two-thirds parliamentary override. The constitution also created a directly elected, seventy-six-seat Great Hural and provided for private land ownership.

Mongolians face rising prices, sharp cutbacks in state benefits and industrial jobs, and other social costs of restructuring. The Asian financial crisis added to their woes by curbing foreign direct investment and slowing exports of copper and other raw materials. However, Mongolia's young democracy showed resilience as it weathered a political crisis that left the country without a government for seven months, the unsolved murder of the hero of the 1990 pro-democracy movement, and continued disillusionment over the punishing social cost of economic reform.

Mongolians can change their government democratically. The judiciary is independent. Police and prison officials occasionally beat detainees and prisoners, and prisons are severely overcrowded. In recent years dozens of prisoners have died from neglect, starvation, and illness. Scores of private newspapers represent diverse viewpoints. The state broadcast media, which include a television station and several radio stations, generally offer pluralistic views. A private television station reaches parts of the country, and foreign satellite and cable broadcasts are available.

Freedom of assembly is respected. Nongovernmental organizations (NGOs) promote human rights, child welfare, and other causes. The hardship associated with the economic restructuring has frayed traditional social support systems and, along with high rates of alcohol abuse, has apparently contributed to domestic violence. Women are often better educated than men but generally receive lower wages and are underrepresented in senior positions. Trade unions are independent, although union membership is declining as large enterprises are shut down or broken up. Due to high unemployment, employers have considerable leverage in collective bargaining. The government lacks the resources to enforce effectively laws on

child labor and working conditions. Freedom House's 1998–99 *Freedom in the World* rates Mongolia a two in political rights and a three in civil liberties.

Religious Freedom

For much of the early history of the area of Mongolia, shamanism dominated the people's religious lives. The Tibetan style of Buddhism was introduced in the sixteenth century, and many Mongolians combined it with the existing shamanist beliefs in a unique combination. Islam has been present for centuries but tends to be concentrated in the southwest among ethnic Kazakhs. Christianity has recently been reintroduced and has prospered.

The communist government of 1924–90 repressed all religious expression, including shamanism and Buddhism. Some experts estimate that the citizens are still largely atheist, but others note a very strong resurgence of Tibetan Buddhism since the lifting of religious repression. At one time there had been thousands of functioning monasteries, but in 1995 only one small Lamaist Buddhist monastery remained in Ulaanbaatar. However, by late 1998, the government acknowledged the existence of as many as 248 registered religious monasteries, as well as mosques, churches, and other religious bodies.

The democratic changes of 1990 legally restored religious freedom, but Buddhism was given a privileged position. However, other religions have not automatically been disadvantaged, and Mongolia has signed international treaties that establish the right to freedom of religion for individuals, and particularly children. A 1993 law states that Mongolia should respect religion and that the government should be separate from religion. However, despite these improvements toward religious liberty, the law also asserted the "predominant position of the Buddhist religion," forbade the "propagation of religion from outside," and banned religious activities "alien to the religion and customs of the Mongolian people." In 1994, the Supreme Court struck down several of these provisions, leaving only the provisions guaranteeing the predominance of Buddhism and the prohibition on religion "against Mongolian customs."

In 1994, a parliamentary resolution forbade religious activity that threatened "national security"—a vague term that allows for arbitrary interpretation. According to some reports, in November 1998, Mr. Badaaral from the Ministry of Foreign Affairs stated "that Christianity was a threat to the State," which seemed to be an allusion to national security grounds. Another section of the 1994 resolution made it illegal to bring religion into Mongolia "from outside." It also made it illegal for religions other than Buddhism, Shamanism, and Islam to rent state-owned rooms for meetings. As few suitable nonstate rooms were available and smaller religious groups could not afford to purchase facilities, this restriction was more formidable than it might appear.

As in other postcommunist societies, registration laws have also threatened religious liberty in Mongolia.

Some groups that have attempted to register have faced harassment or been asked by midlevel city officials to make a set "contribution" in return for securing legal status. Even after receiving official status, withdrawal of approval has threatened some groups. Those denied proper registration have experienced problems, including having their places of worship closed by the government. Generally, these problems seem to reflect local bureaucracy and corruption rather than any religious policy.

Currently, "proselytism" is tolerated and has usually been practiced by Christian groups. In general, apart from the exceptions noted, religious bodies have the right of self-government, to train and appoint clergy, carry out religious education, have contact with coreligionists overseas; and individuals have the right to adopt, leave, or change their religion. There have been occasional recent reports of nongovernmental harassment of religions regarded as foreign, but in general, the religious situation has improved since 1994. The future remains uncertain, especially if minority religions are categorized as foreign. The prospect of tighter control is possible, especially if increased proselytism is portrayed as a threat to Mongolia's religious/ethnic national identity.

Morocco

Population	**28.2 million**
Muslim (mostly Sunni)	**99.75%**
Christian (including foreigners)	**0.25%**
Small numbers of Jews and Baha'i	
Religious Freedom Rating	**4**

Background

Morocco regained independence in 1956 after forty-four years of French rule. Upon the death of his father Mohammed V in 1961, Hassan II assumed the throne and began a gradual and limited evolution of democratic institutions. Nevertheless, the king retained most power in the country. He appointed the prime minister and dissolved the legislature at his discretion. While the new bicameral legislature had greater legitimacy, it was not permitted to challenge Hassan II's core conservative policies. After his death on July 23, 1999, he was succeeded by his son Sidi Mohammed. Sidi quickly signaled a greater openness to democracy and public opinion, and former political prisoners and exiles began to return.

Morocco has close ties with Western nations, and its people have escaped both the extreme Islamist violence and severe authoritarian repression that have gripped their neighbors in the Maghreb. Islamist parties are largely proscribed but still recruit among the growing ranks of the unemployed.

An oft-delayed UN-supervised referendum on independence in the former colony of Spanish Sahara, which was occupied by Morocco in 1976, was postponed from December 1998. The territory was ravaged by a fifteen-year guerrilla war until a 1991 peace pact, and its people have suffered severe human rights violations by Moroccan security forces.

Political liberalization in Morocco gained pace in February 1998 with the election of opposition leader and former political prisoner Abderrahmane Youssouffi as prime minister. Youssouffi has pursued a reformist program that emphasizes social spending and greater respect for human rights. In June an official delegation of Amnesty International was welcomed amid pledges to end abuses. Approximately sixty political prisoners remain incarcerated, however.

Morocco's electoral process is more open today than at any time in its history. The House of Representatives was elected in largely free balloting in November 1997. The lower chamber's power is balanced by a 270-member indirectly selected Chamber of Advisors and seriously limited by the legal and de facto power of the royal palace. Judicial reform has been identified as a high priority for the new government. Courts at all levels, however, are subject to political control. Pretrial detention of one year or less is legal. Decrees demanding Interior Ministry permits for public gatherings negate constitutional protections of freedom of assembly. The government appears to tolerate small and quiet protests but not public marches.

Officially recognized human rights groups are among the numerous nongovernmental organizations that operate openly but under official scrutiny. The Moroccan League for the Defense of Human Rights has denounced many human rights abuses. Constitutional guarantees of free expression are sometimes ignored in law and practice. Broadcast media are mostly government controlled. Independent and pluralistic print media operate but are subject to official pressures and exercise self-censorship. Criticizing the king or his family or the monarchy is punishable by five to twenty years' imprisonment. Criticisms of the validity of Morocco's claim to Western Sahara and the sanctity of Islam are also prohibited.

Women face serious legal and societal discrimination and have no rights to receive property or support after a divorce. Many family-law cases are handled by special judges under the *Moudouwana*, or "Code of Personal Status." The code is based on *shari'a* law and treats women as inferior to men. In July, the government announced proposals to promote the culture of the Berbers who, activists claim, compose

60 percent of Morocco's population. Morocco's strongly unionized formal labor sector includes seventeen umbrella federations, all subject to heavy governmental pressure. The government generally respects labor rights.

Freedom House's 1998–99 *Freedom in the World* rates Morocco a five in political rights and a four in civil liberties, up from a five the previous year due to greater respect for freedom of association and expression, and improvements in the electoral sphere.

Religious Freedom

Muslim since the seventh century, Morocco has been a constitutional monarchy since becoming independent in 1956. King Hassan II maintained a reputation for religious tolerance from his accession to the throne in 1962 until his death in 1999. He relaxed discriminatory practices against the country's ancient Jewish community and also granted specific rights to the Roman Catholic Church in Morocco during Pope John Paul II's historic first visit to a Muslim country in 1985. Initial indications are that his son will continue to open up the country, though slowly.

In the revised 1992 constitution, Islam is designated as the state religion "which guarantees to all freedom of religion." The penal code makes it a punishable offense to force religious rites on anyone, to prevent the free exercise of religious rites, or to disturb religious celebrations. Officially, 99 percent of the population are Sunni Muslim. The king, who is both the political and spiritual leader, bears the title "Commander of the Faithful" and claims direct descent from the prophet Mohammed.

The Ministry of Islamic Affairs monitors the curriculum of Quranic schools and supervises the content of Friday mosque sermons to ensure the teaching of approved doctrines. Security police routinely close mosques to the public shortly after Friday services in order to prevent politically motivated gatherings. Islamist groups who restrict themselves to propagating Islam and to educational and charitable activities are largely tolerated. More radical groups that engage in violence, or question the king's religious authority, remain under tight surveillance, including the banned Justice and Charity movement. The government uses registration procedures to deny Islamist and other groups legal status and the right to meet, and such groups form a clandestine opposition. Islamist dissident Sheikh Abdessalam Yassine has remained under house arrest since 1989 for refusing to acknowledge the religious authority of the king.

Criticism of Islam remains one of the three acknowledged taboos on freedom of expression in the country. Under Article 41 of the Press Code and Article 179 of the Penal Code, it is a criminal act to criticize or insult Islam, punishable by one to five years in prison and a fine. In addition, the Interior Ministry is authorized by a 1973 amendment to the Press Code to seize or ban any publication that could "threaten the fundamental institutional policies or religion of the kingdom." It remains a criminal offense for a Muslim publicly to break the compulsory fast during the month of Ramadan.

Apart from Islam, only Judaism and Christianity are tolerated in practice. Generally they can manage their internal affairs freely, though any public manifestation is restricted. The small Jewish Sephardic community, now down to seven thousand, is occasionally the object of anti-Semitic statements by some clerics, particularly in relation to Israel, but it has maintained good relations with the king, as evidenced by his appointment of two Jewish citizens to cabinet or adviser posts in recent years. The Baha'i community of less than two hundred is regarded as heretical and, since 1983, is forbidden to meet, with some of its members subjected to foreign travel restrictions or denied passports.

The larger Christian minority, mostly Catholics, consists mainly of foreign residents, plus a growing number of Moroccans who are known to have converted from Islam to Christianity. The government publicly denies the existence of any indigenous Christians in the national population. In November 1996, authorities closed down without explanation a weekly newspaper that had printed an anonymous article entitled "I Am a Moroccan Christian."

Voluntary conversion from Islam to another faith is not a crime under the criminal or civil codes. This was corroborated in a landmark 1985 Supreme Court ruling, which declared that apostasy was not a criminal offense under Article 220 of the Penal Code. However, the same ruling upheld the legal definition of proselytism by means of seduction with the intention of turning a Muslim away from the Muslim faith as a criminal offense, punishable by three to six months in jail and a fine. Moroccans who convert from Islam to another religion are still obliged to go through the Muslim establishment to obtain their marriage licenses, permission for burial, and other civil documents.

While the Moroccan judicial system is not formally subject to Islamic law (*shari'a*), it is permeated with its traditions. Local police and judiciary continue to arrest and prosecute Moroccan nationals who have changed their religious affiliation. Muslims known to have converted to Christianity have been sentenced under the antiproselytism statutes, contrary to the state's moderate legal code. Although the harsh detention and interrogation methods to which they are subjected contradict the tolerant stance of officials in the central government and higher judicial establishment, these reported excesses have not been redressed by the Ministries of Justice and the Interior. Resident expatriates and foreign tourists are occasionally arrested and expelled on charges of proselytism, usually handled in summary trial hearings.

There are no legal restrictions on the importation and sale of Bibles in Western languages, although the required licenses are frequently obstructed by the authorities. Bibles in the Arabic language are sold legally in local bookstores and distributed by the Moroccan Bible Society. However, customs officials routinely confiscate or refuse entry to such shipments. In June 1998, a British yachtsman was arrested at the Mdiq port near Tetuoan with four other Europeans and fined forty-two thousand dollars for allegedly smuggling Arabic Bibles into the country. The government declared there was no religious issue in the case.

Namibia

Population	1.6 million
Christian	89%
Traditional	10%
Other (Muslim, Jewish, Baha'i)	1%
Religious Freedom Rating	2

Background

Namibia was seized by German imperial forces in the late 1800s. Thousands of people were massacred by German troops in efforts to crush all resistance to colonial settlement and administration. The territory became a South Africa protectorate after German forces were expelled during World War I and was ruled under the apartheid system for forty-two years after 1948. A UN-supervised 1990 democratic transition with free and fair elections followed thirteen years of bloody guerrilla war. The South West Africa People's Organization (SWAPO) scored a sweeping victory, and President Nujoma was reelected in November 1994 and in November 1999. SWAPO enjoys wide support, but has sometimes demonstrated flagrant disrespect for the rule of law.

Namibia's 1994 elections were free and fair. In 1998, the electoral commission was removed from the prime minister's office and reorganized as an independent agency. The president will still appoint commission members but only on the advice of a board that includes representatives of civil society. The ruling party's main base is the country's largest ethnic group, the Ovambo, whose prominence has evoked allegations of ethnic discrimination.

Respect for human rights in Namibia has been among the best in Africa, although reported large-scale killings on the country's northern border remain unresolved. Political discussion is generally open and vigorous. Political parties can organize and operate freely. In November 1998, the government announced plans for legislation to ban homosexuality.

Public statements by senior officials against the independent press and several direct actions against journalists have raised fears of a diminution of press freedoms. Private radio stations and critical independent newspapers usually operate without official interference. The electronic media are mostly controlled by the state but can be critical of the government. Security forces still commit abuses with impunity. In rural areas, local chiefs use traditional courts that often ignore constitutional procedures. Despite constitutional guarantees, women continue to face serious discrimination. Constitutionally guaranteed union rights are respected. Essential public sector workers do not have the right to strike. Domestic and farm laborers remain the country's most heavily exploited workers. Freedom House's 1998–99 *Freedom in the World* rates Namibia a two in political rights and a three in civil liberties.

Religious Freedom

Namibia is one of the most Christianized countries in Africa, a result of energetic missionary work and the lasting impact of European colonial rule. German Lutheran missionaries who traveled from the then-British possession of South Africa in the mid-nineteenth century opened the way for German colonizers in the 1880s. Missionaries provided schools and some health care in addition to their evangelizing and helped open the area to trade. After World War I, Namibia passed to South African control. Even after South Africans took possession of Namibia during World War I, the Lutheran church remained firmly entrenched. Nearly half of all Namibians are officially identified as Lutherans, and Catholics and other Christian groups claim as adherents most of the rest of the population. There are small groups of Muslims, Buddhists, Jews, and Baha'is.

The abetting of, or opposition to, colonial excesses and the discriminatory apartheid system by different Christian sects has been controversial and caused tensions and divisions in the churches, but religious freedom has generally been respected. Foreign missionaries have complained about difficulties obtaining work permits, but this seems to reflect a general bureaucratic problem rather than a specific religious impediment.

Since independence in 1990, the government has respected the several constitutionally guaranteed provisions regarding religious freedom. The constitution's preamble bars religious discrimination by affirming "the right of the individual to life, liberty and the pursuit of happiness, regardless of race, color, ethnic origin, sex, religion, creed or social or economic status," a right restated in Article 10. The right to religious freedom is stated affirmatively in Article 21. Article 14 provides the right to marry and found a family "without any limitation" due to religion or creed. Article 19 expressly guarantees the right to "to enjoy, practice, profess, maintain and promote any culture, language, tradition or religion." This right is restricted by being "subject to the terms of this Constitution and further subject to the condition that the rights protected by this article do not impinge upon the rights of others or the national interest." To date, there are no reports of this provision being used to restrict religious practice.

Rights to religious education are included in Article 20 (4) of the constitution, which states that "all persons shall have the right, at their own expense, to establish and to maintain private schools, or colleges or other institutions of tertiary education," provided that such institutions meet government standards and that "no restrictions of whatever nature are imposed with respect to the admission of pupils based on race, color or creed."

There is freedom to propagate one's faith, freedom of worship, and freedom to train and appoint clergy. Religious bodies have rights of self-government, of religious charitable activities, to own and acquire property, and to maintain social institutions. They can produce, import, and distribute literature, receive donations, and have contact with coreligionists, domestically and overseas. Individuals can adopt, change, or leave a religion freely, with no change of civil status.

As in many other countries, traditional beliefs have often been adapted or incorporated into religions introduced later. This is especially prevalent in independent Christian churches not accountable to external hierarchies. Many traditional spiritual and magical practices also remain current, including divination and healing ceremonies. Others are related to witchcraft and sorcery, and accusations of harmful sorcery occasionally lead to assaults, burnings, and lynchings.

Population	**24.3 million**
Hindu	**85%**
Buddhist	**10%**
Muslim	**3%**
Christian	**2%**
Religious Freedom Rating	**5**

Background

King Prithvi Narayan Shah unified this Himalayan land in 1769. In 1959, following two centuries of palace rule, the center-left Nepali Congress (NC) won the country's first elections and began initiating land reforms. In 1960, King Mahendra dissolved parliament and banned political parties. Pro-democracy demonstrations beginning in early 1990 climaxed violently in April when police fired on demonstrators in Kathmandu. King Birendra agreed to a constitution that vested executive power in the prime minister and cabinet, with a two-tier parliament.

In 1991, Nepal's first multiparty elections in thirty-two years brought the NC to power under Premier Giraja Prasid Koirala. The Koirala government began liberalizing the economy. Midterm elections in November 1994 were dominated by concerns with rising prices and the NC's factionalism and corruption. The Communist Party of Nepal (United Marxist-Leninist) (CPN-UML) won eighty-eight seats; the NC, eighty-three; the pro-monarchist National Democratic Party (RPP), twenty. The hung parliament contributed to political instability. In February 1996, the underground Communist Party of Nepal (Maoist) (CPN Maoist) launched a "People's War" in the midwestern hills, targeting government offices, landowners, and local party officials, killing more than one hundred people. In December 1998, Koirala formed a new government with the CPN-UML and pledged to hold elections in spring 1999, several months early.

Nepalese can change their government democratically, but widespread violence and other irregularities marred the 1997 local elections. Low-caste Hindus and ethnic minority groups are politically marginalized. Overall, the political system is hugely corrupt and ineffective. Because institutions are viewed as weak and corrupt, political parties often resort to mobilizing supporters in the streets. Demonstrations and strikes frequently turn violent.

The Supreme Court is independent, but politicians reportedly manipulate lower courts. The judiciary is reportedly rife with corruption. Prison conditions are life threatening. Human rights practices have improved considerably since the end of the absolute monarchy, but the rule of law is weak, and serious problems remain. Armed guerrillas have killed and tortured civilians, and security forces have responded with extrajudicial executions, arbitrary arrests, torture, and detentions. As amended in 1991, the Public Security Act (PSA) allows authorities to detain suspects for up to twelve months without charge.

The constitution restricts expression that could jeopardize national security, promote communal discord, or do harm in other broadly defined areas. The Press and Publications Act restricts reporting on the monarchy, national security, and other sensitive issues. Nevertheless, private newspapers and magazines vigorously criticize government policies. The government owns the sole television station and the influential Radio Nepal. Political coverage on the state broadcast media favors the party in power. Successive governments have restricted public criticism of China's occupation of Tibet and Indian abuses in Kashmir. Nongovernmental organizations are active and operate freely. However, both police and CPN Maoist guerrillas have reportedly harassed human rights activists over disclosures of abuses.

Property and divorce laws discriminate against women. Gangs traffic some five thousand to seven thousand women and girls to India to work in brothels each year. Nepalese jails hold women convicted of murder for abortions and infanticide as well as for acts of self-defense against men. Nepal has upwards of five million child laborers working in carpet factories, mines, and construction sites. Child marriage continues despite being outlawed. In 1997, the London-based Anti-Slavery International said that illegal, forced bonded labor takes two main forms: a feudal-based system enslaving one hundred thousand people in the lowland terai and caste-based servitude in the western hills.

Trade unions are independent but are politicized and often militant. More than 80 percent of the population is engaged in agriculture, and 45 percent live in absolute poverty. Nepal hosts some ninety thousand Bhutanese refugees. Police hand over scores of asylum seekers to Chinese authorities. Freedom House's 1998–99 *Freedom in the World* rates Nepal a three in political rights and a four in civil liberties and says the situation in the country is deteriorating due to violations by Maoist guerrillas and security forces.

Religious Freedom

Nepal sits at the crossroads of the two main races and cultures in Asia, the Aryan-Indians and the Mongolian-Chinese. Although the country has more than one hundred ethnic groups and castes, who speak more than thirty languages, Nepali-speaking Hindu high castes have used the Hindu religion and the Nepali language to control political, economic, and social life ever since King Prithvi Narayan Shah unified the land in 1769. Hinduism was the state religion under the absolute monarchy. In the mid-nineteenth century, the palace introduced caste laws that organized ethnic groups and castes into a hierarchical social order. The 1962 constitution abolished the caste laws but formally made Nepal a Hindu kingdom with Hinduism as the state religion.

The success of the pro-democracy movement in 1990 led to the emergence of political groups representing ethnic and religious minorities that challenged the political and economic power of high-caste Hindus. The focal point of debate was the proposed status of Hinduism in the new, democratic constitution. Buddhists, Muslims, Christians, and the country's powerful communist movement all called for a secular state. Adding to the debate over whether Hinduism should be the state religion was uncertainty over the religious breakdown in the country. Official figures show Buddhists, the largest religious minority, making up a small percentage of the population. However, observers say that during the 1981 census, officials in rural areas would ask residents whether they worshiped Ganesh, a Hindu deity. Those who said yes were counted as Hindus, even though many Buddhists also worship Ganesh. Some Buddhist leaders claim that Buddhists make up the majority of the population in Nepal. However, without an unbiased census, it is difficult to be sure of the numerical strengths of the various religions.

With Brahmins and Chetris in the majority in all key political institutions, the Hindu high castes were able to block calls for a secular state. Article 4 of the 1990 constitution describes Nepal as a

"Hindu and constitutional monarchical kingdom." However, unlike the constitution it replaced, the 1990 document does not establish Hinduism as the state religion. Article 11 bans discrimination on the grounds of religion, and Article 13 says no one should be imprisoned for their faith. Article 19 guarantees each person "the freedom to profess and practice his own religion." Proselytizing is banned, with up to a three-year jail penalty, but the ban is not usually enforced. People are, in principle, free to change their religion if they wish. Article 19 also says, "Each religious group will have the right, within the law, to maintain its identity; and reserve its religious rights and trust."

In practice, members of Hindu castes and religious minorities can worship freely. However, the overall status of religious freedom in Nepal must be seen in the context of the continuing control by Hindu castes over the country's political and economic affairs. Other religious and ethnic groups are cut off from the centers of society and lower caste Hindus can be excluded from Hindu temples.

Under the absolute monarchy, Christians endured the worst persecution among religious minorities. Several Christians were jailed for their beliefs. Since the advent of democratic rule, official tolerance of Christians and other minority religious groups has improved. However, Maoist guerrillas have made religious leaders one of their targets. Since there is also a view that "every Christian is rich," they have also been a target of extortion for guerrillas.

In 1994, when courts sentenced eleven Christians to two years in jail, King Birendra pardoned them after they had served three months of their sentence. Yet there are concerns that the rise to power of the Hindu nationalist Indian People's Party (BJP) in neighboring India in 1998 will foster the growth of Hindu nationalist parties and organizations in Nepal and force mainstream politicians into catering to militants. BJP offshoots have also combined with a local militant Hindu group called "Pasupati Sena" and have the sympathy of many government bureaucrats. In what was perhaps a harbinger of future developments, in December 1998, the speaker of the upper house of parliament, an NC leader, launched into a bizarre tirade accusing Christians of dispensing the wrong medicine in hospitals and other malignant acts. The remarks came at an evangelical function to which the speaker had been invited because of his ostensible support for religious freedom. In January 1998, two Christians were arrested for what the police called the "social crime" of showing a film to a religiously mixed audience, and in April three others were arrested for the same offense. All were freed on bail, but the cases are pending. In November 1998, police killed two young Christian men in custodial detention in Rukum district. In April 1999, twenty Christians were hospitalized on Good Friday after being attacked by riot police when they complained about the arbitrary banning of their worship service. On August 28, after a man claiming to be a Christian desecrated a Hindu temple in Janakpur, a mob urged on by Hindu extremists burned down the local church.

Netherlands

Population	**15.8 million**
Catholic	**35%**
Protestant	**28%**
Muslim	**3%**
Hindu	**1%**
Buddhist	**0.9%**
Jewish	**0.1%**
Other	**2%**
Unaffiliated	**30%**
Religious Freedom Rating	**1**

Background

After the Dutch won independence from Spain in the sixteenth century, the governors of the House of Orange assumed rule over the United Provinces of the Netherlands. A constitutional monarchy based on representative government emerged in the early 1800s. The bicameral States General (parliament) consists of an indirectly elected First Chamber and a larger, more powerful and directly elected Second Chamber. The Kingdom of the Netherlands consists of the Netherlands, the overseas territories of the Dutch Antilles, and the island of Aruba. These territories, which have their own constitution, are united in a federal structure and governed by the Charter of the Kingdom.

From the end of World War II until 1958, the Netherlands was governed by coalitions in which the Labor and Catholic parties predominated. From 1958 to 1994, governments were formed from center-right coalitions of Christian Democrats and Liberals. Since 1994, the Netherlands has been governed by a three-party coalition that includes Prime Minister Wim Kok's Labor Party, the Liberal Party, and the Democrats-66 party. It joined the European Monetary Union in 1999. The Netherlands' tolerant drug policy has met with growing opposition in the EU, most notably from France.

The Dutch can change their government democratically. A series of amendments to the original constitution has provided for welfare and democratic reform. A twenty-four-member Supreme Court heads the country's independent judiciary. All judicial appointments are made by the crown on the basis of nominations by the parliament. The press is free and independent, although journalists practice self-censorship when reporting on the royal family. Radio and television broadcasters operate autonomously under the supervision of the state and offer pluralistic views. Free speech is guaranteed, with the exception of promulgation of racism.

Integration of racial and ethnic minorities into the social and cultural mainstream remains a difficult domestic issue. Immigrant groups face some de facto discrimination in housing and employment. Concentrated in the larger cities, immigrants suffer from a high rate of unemployment. A new law to tighten criteria for acceptance of refugees was implemented in 1997; nevertheless, the country's asylum policies remain generous.

Membership in labor unions is open to all workers, including military, police, and civil service employees. Gender-based discrimination is prohibited. Women are well represented in government, education, and other fields. Same-sex marriages were legalized in January 1998. Freedom House's 1998–99 *Freedom in the World* rates the Netherlands a one in political rights and civil liberties.

Religious Freedom

At the turn of the sixteenth century, a number of Dutch provinces rebelled against Spanish rulers who were trying to eradicate Protestantism and impose Catholicism as the only legal religion. In 1581, they gained their independence and named themselves the Republic of the United Provinces. Calvinism was proclaimed the official religion: Catholicism was tolerated but was subject to discrimination until 1795. The territories south of the Netherlands (now Belgium, Luxembourg, and parts of northwestern France) remained under Catholic Spain and, until the beginning of the eighteenth century, non-Catholics persecuted for their religious beliefs sought refuge in the Netherlands. Hence, the traditional reputation of the Netherlands as a land of freedom of conscience, thought, and religion.

In 1795, the Republic of the United Provinces was invaded by France, and in 1796 the National Assembly granted religious freedom to all denominations. The 1798 constitution implicitly recognized the separation between church and state. This separation was not hostile: the constitution even recommended the worship of God by every citizen. In the constitutions of 1801, 1805, and 1806, the general tendency was to establish closer relations between church and state. In 1810, French legislation came into force, particularly the 1801 Concordat between Napoleon and the Holy See.

In 1813, after Napoleon's defeat in Leipzig, a new constitution was adopted. Its leading principle in religious matters was separation between church and state, but it stated that the Sovereign from the House of Orange had to profess the Reformed faith. In the 1815 constitution, made necessary by union with Catholic Belgium, religion played a significant role. References to the Reformed Church were abolished, and church autonomy was stressed more clearly. However, the church statutes of various churches were enacted by royal decree.

The constitution of 1848 was very liberal, including respecting religious freedom. Since 1848, there have been numerous revisions of the constitution that have affected religion. The revision of 1917 adopted the principle of full state funding of private (denominational) elementary education. Conscientious objection to military service was recognized in 1922. In 1983, twenty churches represented in the Inter-church Contact in Government Affairs and the government reached an agreement terminating the traditional government obligations to pay church ministers' wages.

In 1984, a parliamentary inquiry commission on cults concluded that new religious movements were no real threat to the public or to mental health. When France, Belgium, Germany, the European Parliament, and the Council of Europe started setting up inquiry commissions in the second half of the 1990s, the Dutch authorities declared that the situation had not changed in their country since 1984 and that creating such a commission again was unnecessary.

Other significant phenomena are the steady decrease of membership in the established churches since the beginning of the twentieth century, the extension of religious pluralism, and the secularization of society. According to a 1995 survey by the State Planning Bureau, the actual religious practice of the Dutch (as distinct from their claimed religious affiliation) was as follows: Roman Catholicism, about 20 percent; Protestantism, about 15 percent; Islam, about 2 percent; Hinduism, about 1 percent; Buddhism, about 0.9 percent; Judaism, about 0.2 percent;

no formal church affiliation, about 61 percent. Actual beliefs: atheists, 16 percent; agnostics, 14 percent; believers in a supernatural power, 22 percent; believers in God but with some degree of doubt, 25 percent; no faith, 24 percent. Degree of religiosity: nonreligious, 26 percent; neither religious nor nonreligious, 20 percent; a little religious, 38 percent; very religious, 17 percent.

The system of church and state relations in the Netherlands is usually characterized as a "separation," but this is not expressed in the constitution. This separation is neither total nor hostile towards religion. The main article of the constitution regarding freedom of religion and belief is Article 6, which reads: "1. Everyone shall have the right to manifest freely his religion or belief, either individually or in community with others, without prejudice to his responsibility under the law. 2. Rules concerning the exercise of this right other than in buildings and enclosed places may be laid down by Act of Parliament for the protection of health, in the interest of traffic and to combat or prevent disorders." In addition: Article 1 guarantees equal treatment in equal circumstances to all person in the Netherlands and forbids discrimination on the grounds of, among other things, religion and belief. Freedoms of religious expression and of religious association are implicitly incorporated in Article 6 but are also supported by those sections that specifically guarantee such freedoms. Article 23 guarantees freedom of (denominational) education.

These rights are fully respected. The building of new places of worship is not financed by the state, but local communities sometimes find ways of providing indirect support. The Ancient Monuments Act allows provincial authorities to provide subsidies for the maintenance and repair of monuments, including religious ones.

The 1998 Public Manifestations Act allows municipal councils to regulate the length, frequency, and volume of church bells. Concerning some street performances by evangelical groups, courts have made a distinction that a restriction of the right to amplifying equipment did not affect the freedom of expression. A small number of municipalities allow Islamic announcements. Some religious communities, often Islamic but also evangelical, sometimes use their places of worship contrary to their legally designated purpose. In most cases, local councils tolerate or ratify these situations.

In civil law, majority and minority churches are legal entities *sui generis*. The Civil Code states that legal personality shall be granted to churches, to independent units of churches, and to structures in which they are united. Centralized and decentralized church organizations and small independent churches are taken into account in an equal way. Any religious community can constitute itself as a "church" without any condition or prior government approval. Islamic, Hindu, and Buddhist legal bodies have been created as associations or foundations. The Humanist League, which describes itself as not a religious but a philosophical organization, is an association according to civil law.

The constitution guarantees the right to found and administer denominational schools, whether Christian or non-Christian. Religious schools are funded in the same way as secular ones under the condition that they fulfill the same standards of education and meet some financing conditions. The majority of elementary schools are denominational (Roman Catholic and various Protestant denominations) and are funded by the state. Educational standards for primary education must respect "in particular the freedom of private schools to choose their teaching aids and to appoint teachers as they see fit." Similar arrangements exist for other educational levels. The constitution requires secular schools to give "due respect to everyone's religion or belief"; the government provides for (optional) religious education and education in nonreligious belief in secular schools.

Charity activities may be carried out by majority and minority religions and by humanist or other associations. They can be subsidized by the state if they fulfill the necessary conditions. There is a strong political will to adjust laws so as to abolish or reduce any form of discrimination or inequality. In practice, the preexistent basic pattern had only to be extended to emerging or growing religions. Some observers have asked whether the dominance of a Christian pattern is still justifiable in a religiously pluralistic society. Legislation allows people to choose their days of rest according to their religion, but the position of Sunday as a general weekly day of rest is now being questioned. Some Collective Labor Agreements also contain provisions on non-Christian religious days. A 1994 Act prohibits dismissal on grounds of conscientious objection.

The Mass Media Act allocates broadcasting time on public TV to various mass media associations that are based on religious, political, or ideological persuasion. Each of them broadcasts a full range of programs and not only religious services. A law regulates the allotted broadcasting time according to the number of members, the focus of the programs to be broadcast, and the financial facilities. Many churches, including minority churches, enjoy broadcasting time on TV and radio. Since 1989, the Islamic Broadcasting Foundation (IOS) has been allocated broadcasting time. However, due to the lack of a general representative of the various facets of Islam, the public authority has pressed IOS to involve Islamic communities of various national backgrounds and has put the broadcasting time under the authority of the Netherlands Muslim Council (NMR). A few years ago, a Hindu broadcasting foundation (OHM) was allocated broadcasting time.

Obligatory general medical vaccination has been rejected in view of the expected conscientious objection of some minorities. Tax deductions for donations to religious and humanist associations exist in a variety of acts. The head of state does not hold a special position with regard to religion and may practice the religion of his/her choice. Members of the royal family may change religion and have done so.

Nigeria

Population	**113.8 million**
Muslim (largely Sunni)	**45%**
Christian	**40%**
Indigenous	**9%**
Other	**6%**
Religious Freedom Rating	**5**

Background

Nigeria's tumultuous 1998 ended with hopes for a peaceful transition to a genuine representative government. Army dictator Sani Abacha's mysterious death on June 8, 1998, was met by street celebrations throughout the country. The death in detention just five weeks later of Moshood K. O. Abiola, winner of the army-annulled 1993 presidential election, sparked rioting that left scores dead.

The second half of 1998 saw the lifting of most of the repression that had grown steadily worse under Abacha. Numerous political prisoners were freed, and harassment, intimidation, arrests, and assaults on journalists, trade unionists, human rights workers, and political activists nearly ceased. Political parties were registered for peaceful and largely well-run local elections that took place in December 1998. In February 1999, Olusegan Obasanju won the national election. This ex-general led a military regime from 1976 to 1979 but stepped down voluntarily. As a Christian and Yoruba, he gained southern support, but his military background also helped him gain northern support. In his maiden speech on May 29, he promised to tackle corruption and human rights violations.

These developments are cause for considerable optimism. Yet a democratic transition has just begun and faces considerable perils. Strict security laws are still in place. The stability of the military, which has ruled Nigeria for all but ten years since its independence from Britain in 1960, is far from certain.

The country's deep ethnic divides, between and among northern and southern groups, worsened under Abacha's rule and may be exacerbated if politicians emphasize ethnicity as a campaign issue. Nigeria's 106 million people include more than 250 ethnic groups. The Hausa-Fulani groups from northern Nigeria have dominated the military and the country since independence. The Yoruba and Ibo people and smaller groups of the south deeply resent this domination. Sporadic religious and ethnic strife continues in the country. Clashes among ethnic groups in the country's southeastern delta region took hundreds of lives and disrupted oil production. As Africa's most populous state, and potentially one of its wealthiest, events in Nigeria affect all of West Africa and are a bellwether for the rest of the continent.

Nigerians were denied the right to choose their representatives when Chief Moshood K. O. Abiola's 1993 election victory was quickly annulled by the military regime of General Ibrahim Babangida. General Abacha, a principal architect of previous coups, moved in November 1993 to take power himself after the high court declared an army-installed interim government illegal. A predominately military Provisional Ruling Council was appointed, and all democratic structures were dissolved and political parties banned. Chief Abiola was arrested in June 1994 after declaring himself Nigeria's rightful president.

While the first half of 1998 witnessed severe repression of civil society and increasing security force abuses, many political prisoners were freed after Abacha's death. Incarceration remains harsh and often life threatening. Nearly ten thousand prisoners are reported to have died of disease or other causes from 1990 to 1995. Media freedom has improved markedly since June 1998. Restrictive decrees remain in force, however, and press groups are opposed to new constitutional provisions that would entrench government control over media. Free trade union activities have resumed after being suppressed for several years. In Freedom House's 1998–99 *Freedom in the World*, the political rights rating changed from seven to six, and the civil liberties rating changed from six to four, due to the beginnings of democratic transition at year's end.

Religious Freedom

Nigeria's people can be divided approximately into a semifeudal, predominately Muslim north and a more entrepreneurial, mainly Christian south. There is some co-relation of religion and ethnicity. In the north, the predominate Hausa and Fulani are largely Muslim. In the east, the Ibo are largely Christian. Among the Yoruba of the southwest, there is a mixture. Consequently, religious and ethnic tensions can overlap. While, constitutionally, Nigeria is a secular state, a situation of unequal religious freedom exists. The north-south divide is territorial, ethnic, and religious, hence the predominant pattern of political and military control by the north has also meant religious dominance. Christians tend to have been marginalized in politics and the military. Traditional believers have also suffered discrimination.

Both Islam and Christianity have prominent roles in the nation's political, social, cultural, and economic life and are represented by co-coordinating bodies—the Supreme Council for Islamic Affairs and the Christian Association of Nigeria (CAN) respectively. Often their adherents overlap with traditional religious patterns.

The federal government has claimed to take an evenhanded approach toward the two main religions, and public holidays are observed for both Christian and Muslim festivals. Although both Christians and Muslims express a desire to live peacefully together, many Christians are concerned about the perceived Islamization of the country, and many feel that they are treated like second-class citizens. Muslims have complained about what they see as the permeation of Christianity in public life, with Sunday, but not Friday, as a day of rest, and the use of the cross as a symbol for medical services.

The military decree suspending the 1979 constitution has not yet been repealed, and the 1989 constitution has yet to be implemented. Pending the proclamation of the constitution written in 1995 by the Constitutional Conference, the government continues to observe some provisions of the 1979 and 1989 constitutions. Nigeria has ratified the International Covenant on Civil and Political Rights; the International Covenant on Economic, Social and Cultural Rights; and the African Charter on Human and People's Rights. Its legal system is modeled on English common law, but the *Shari'a* Court of Appeal has jurisdiction over matters of Islamic personal law. In addition, non-Muslims may apply to the *Shari'a* Court and *shari'a* law may be applicable to non-Muslims.

The secular status of Nigeria has been the subject of dispute between Christians and Muslims for a number of years. Article 11, chapter 1, of the 1989 constitution maintains, "The Government of the Federation of a state shall not adopt any religion as the State religion." Christians generally regard Nigeria as a secular state and support its secular status given the diversity of religions in

Nigeria. Many Muslims on the other hand refer to the preamble of the constitution that declares Nigeria to be a harmonious "Sovereign Nation under God" and find it unacceptable to separate state from religion. There have been increasing calls from some Muslim groups for the Islamization of Nigeria and the comprehensive implementation of *shari'a* law in the country.

On August 25, 1999, Zamfara state announced that it was an Islamic state and that implementation of *shari'a* law was underway. Four other states are considering doing so, something that the Nigerian constitution allows provided it is restricted to Muslims and to civil proceedings. Some Christian leaders and organizations expressed concerns that the situation might lead to further persecution and could possibly escalate into a religious war. In 1986, a virtual religious war almost did erupt over reports that Nigeria had secretly become a full member of the Organization of Islamic Conference (OIC). In the new year, religious violence, due to increased tensions over *shari'a*, did erupt, leaving hundreds dead in the town of Kaduna and elsewhere. Those who are not Christian or Muslim complain that both of these groups receive state privileges and accommodations denied to others and occasionally receive government funds.

Chapter IV, Article 37.1, guarantees every person "freedom of thought, conscience and religion," which includes the "freedom to change his religion as well as freedom to manifest and propagate his religion or belief in worship, teaching, practice and observance." However, the Council of Evangelical Churches of West Africa claimed in 1997 "great concern that in some states and parts of Nigeria, Christians are denied the God given rights to worship and practice their religion as they see fit." There are practical prohibitions on building new churches in some areas, especially in Kano city.

During the last ten years there have been at least eighteen recorded incidents of religious conflict between Christians and Muslims, in which many clergy and members of congregations were killed, and church buildings, and sometimes mosques, destroyed. It is estimated that thirteen thousand Nigerians, both Muslim and Christian but mainly Christian, have died as a result of religious conflicts since 1980. In May 1999, about 130 people were killed in religious conflicts in Kafanchan in the north. The Muslim and Christian leaders have denounced this violence.

While violence has been committed by all religious groups, including fights between Pentecostals, the major patterns of violence are asymmetrical. Some Muslims living in the Christian-dominated southern Nigeria have been subjected to violent religious incidents; Christians living in Muslim-dominated northern Nigeria have more often been victimized and discriminated against because of their faith. Converts to Christianity face particular threats. Because of these problems, the government has sometimes banned public religious activities, and religious activities in schools and media. But, if there are no other tensions, religious media have been allowed to operate.

In the north, Christians are frequently denied access to burial grounds, not allowed to provide Christian religious education for their children in either primary or secondary schools, denied access to the media to propagate their faith while members of other faiths have the freedom to do so without hindrance, and are discriminated against in matters of employment and recruitment to the armed forces, the police, and government agencies. Repression of Christians is most prevalent in the following states: Kaduna, Kano, Bauchi, Sokoto, Katsina, and Kebbi.

According to Chapter II, Articles 15 and 16, of the 1979 and 1989 constitutions, the Nigerian government is committed to ensure that the "composition of the Government of Federation or any of its agencies and the conduct of its affairs" shall reflect its federal character and that "there shall be no predominance of persons" from a state, ethnic, or other sectional background in "the government or any of its agencies." However, currently, Muslims from mainly Fulani and Hausa origin hold most senior government and military posts. Christians, mainly from Yoruba and Ibo ethnic background, are faced with widespread discrimination when applying for both federal and state-level government posts.

The military government has repressed militant Islamic movements, has detained Shi'a leader El-Zakzaky repeatedly, and brutally suppressed demonstrations protesting his jailing

Serious concerns have also been raised over the discriminatory policies of the country's armed forces and police, which appear to marginalize Christians. Archbishop Peter Jatau raised this issue with the government in October 1997, supporting his argument with reports of systematic discrimination based on religion. Young Christians enlisting at Zaria, the army recruitment center, have reportedly either been rejected outright or been forced to leave in the middle of their training simply because of their religion. Some Christians have reportedly changed their names to Muslim names in order to be recruited to the armed forces or gain employment in government agencies.

Chapter IV, Article 37, of the constitution maintains "no religious communities or denominations shall be prevented from providing religious instruction for pupils of that community or denomination." It also states that no person attending any place of education is required to receive religious education in a faith other than his own. Prior to 1960, most schools were operated by foreign missionary organizations. Since then the government controls the schools. Religious teaching is limited to Christianity and Islam. While state-maintained schools are meant to teach both Christian and Islamic religious education, authorities in many parts of the north prevent the teaching of Christian religious education. In mid-1999, Obasanju announced that he would return confiscated schools to religious groups, and within two months five states had done so. Since most of the schools were run by Christians, some Muslims have complained that this will leave much of the educational system, including its best institutions, in the hands of Christians.

Religious tensions have increased since Obasanju's election. Apart from the return of Christian schools, some Muslims have complained that his cabinet, ministry, and commission appointments are predominantly Christian. Muslims hold fourteen out of forty-nine ministerial posts, and commission appointments are evenly split between Christians and Muslims. Christians respond that they were marginalized under military dictators, most of whom were from the Islamic north. Obasanju has established a Panel on Human Rights Abuses to investigate the conduct of the dictators, and its mandate will included reporting on anti-Christian activity.

Norway

Population	**4.45 million**
Evangelical Lutheran	**87.8%**
Other Protestant and Catholic	**3.8%**
None	**3.2%**
Other (Orthodox, Muslim, Jewish, Buddhist, Jehovah's Witness)	**5.2%**
Religious Freedom Rating	**1**

Background

The Norwegians are primarily Germanic. For more than four hundred years, they were linked to Denmark. From 1814 until independence in 1905, they were linked to Sweden. Like the Swedes, the Norwegians are overwhelmingly Lutheran, which is the established church in all three countries. In addition to its overwhelmingly Norwegian population, there are approximately 150,000 immigrants from other countries and approximately 20,000 Lappic (Saamic) people.

The Eidvold Convention, Norway's current constitution, was adopted during a period of de facto independence immediately prior to the acceptance of the Swedish monarch as king of Norway in 1814. After the peaceful dissolution of its relationship with the Swedish crown, Norway chose a sovereign from the Danish royal house and began to function as a constitutional monarchy with a multiparty parliamentary structure.

In 1997, a centrist government took power in Norway for the first time in twenty-five years. Prime Minister Kjell Magne Bondevik leads a coalition of the Center Party, Liberal Party, and his own Christian People's Party. In August 1998, Bondevik took more than three weeks leave due to a "depressive reaction" caused by the stress of his job. The stress was induced, at least in part, by plunges in the price of oil, surges in interest rates, and depreciation of the currency. These crises led to increased support for the opposition Labor Party. However, in the 1999 elections, the Labor Party had its worst results since 1928. European Union (EU) membership, which the traditionally dominant Labor Party supports, remains a contentious political issue. In 1994, Norwegians voted against membership. However, the country enjoys nearly full access to the EU's single market through membership in the European Economic Area, and it is also a member of the Schengen countries.

Norwegians can change their government democratically. The Storting is directly elected for a four-year term by universal suffrage and proportional representation. When working on legislative issues, the Storting divides into two chambers, the Odelsting (three-quarters) and the Lapting (one-quarter). Since 1989, the approximately twenty-thousand-strong Lappic (Saamic) minority has elected an autonomous, thirty-nine-member assembly that functions as an advisory body on issues relevant to the Saami culture. In 1997, King Harald V apologized to the Saami for historic repression by the state.

The constitution guarantees freedom of peaceful assembly and association and the right to strike. Sixty percent of the workforce belongs to unions, which are free from government control. The independent judicial system is headed by a Supreme Court and operates at the local, regional, and national levels. Human rights are widely respected. The law provides for equal wages for men and women engaged in the same work activity. By law, fathers must take at least four weeks' leave from their jobs after a baby is born. Discrimination on the basis of race, gender, language, and class are prohibited by law.

Freedom of the press is constitutionally guaranteed, and many newspapers are subsidized by the state in order to promote political pluralism: although some radio and television broadcasting is funded by the state, the government does not interfere with editorial content. The File Control Board can censor blasphemous, overly violent, and pornographic films. Freedom House's 1998–99 *Freedom in the World* rates Norway a one in political rights and civil liberties.

Religious Freedom

Norway has broad freedom of religion in both law and practice. However, the Evangelical Lutheran Church is an established state church. Most of its government funding comes from local government. Lutheranism, to which approximately 94 percent of Norwegians nominally adhere, is taught in schools, but parents of other faiths may exempt their children from this instruction. By law the sovereign and at least half of the cabinet must be Lutheran. In addition, the Workers' Protection and Working Environment Act allows prospective employers in private or religious schools or day care centers to ask job applicants whether they respect Christian beliefs and principles. The Film Control Board can censor blasphemy but has not done so for twenty years.

At the same time, other faiths (even those that do not profess a religion) besides Lutheranism may receive public funding if they register with the government. This support is provided proportionally according to membership. Religious groups are not required to register with the state if they do not seek public support.

In June 1998, Norway became the first European country occupied by the Nazis to provide financial restitution to

Jewish survivors of Nazi death camps, their descendants, and Jewish organizations. In 1997, the government released a European Council Commission report that recommended that Norway take preventative action against xenophobia and anti-Semitism. As in the other Scandinavian countries, xenophobia and the pressure to conform in this extraordinarily homogeneous society are perhaps the only significant barriers to freedom of religion in the country. This, however, is a largely nonquantifiable social impediment rather than a legal restriction.

Citizens are free to worship both publicly and privately, including on nonofficial premises. They may build and maintain official premises without wrongful impediment. They may organize processions and pilgrimages, provided they register for appropriate permits, which are issued on a nondiscriminatory basis. They may choose their priests, other leaders, and personnel without government interference or discrimination. Religious leaders may perform the rites and customs of their faiths with the texts and music and in the language of their own choosing. They may also preach according to the doctrines of their faiths without threat or interference by the state. Religious leaders of all faiths enjoy access to prisons, hospitals, military installations, and other relevant bodies in order to minister to their congregants.

Communities of believers may implement their own education, institutional, and hierarchical structures. They may also designate and otherwise assign their officials and train them freely in their own institutes and other bodies. They may own and maintain buildings and other property without impediment. They may import and otherwise acquire and circulate holy books and other religious publications. They are free to print and circulate their own publications from within Norway. They enjoy access to public communication. They are free to establish and maintain relations with individuals and communities of their choosing, both within Norway and internationally. They may also solicit and receive voluntary individual and institutional financial contributions both domestically and internationally.

Citizens have access to higher education, employment, the judiciary, military service, and public office without regard to their religious faith. They also enjoy freedom of expression, movement, emigration, association, assembly, marriage, and access to information without regard to religion. Workers from minority religions may be granted leave from work to observe their religious holidays.

Pakistan

Population	146.5 million
Sunni Muslim	73%
Shi'a Muslim	20%
Ahmadiya	3%
Christian	2%
Hindu	2%
Other (Baha'i, Animist, Farsi, Buddhist)	0.1%
Religious Freedom Rating	6

Background

Pakistan was founded in 1947 as a Muslim homeland with the partition of the former British India. In 1971, Bangladesh (ex-East Pakistan) achieved independence after a nine-month civil war. The 1973 constitution (currently suspended) provides for a lower National Assembly, with 217 members (including ten seats reserved for non-Muslims) elected for a five-year term, and an 87-seat Senate appointed by the four provincial assemblies. An electoral college chooses the president for a five-year term.

Even before a military coup in October 1999, Pakistan had been under military rule for twenty-five of its fifty-one years of independence. Military governments have suspended political rights and civil liberties, crushed democratic institutions, and fostered a culture of violence. In 1985, General Zia ul-Haq amended the constitution to allow the president to dismiss elected governments. Since Zia's death in 1988, the president, premier, and army chief of staff informally shared power. Widespread disillusionment with a corrupt political elite, dominated by rural landowners and industrialists, has failed to address poverty and illiteracy. Barely 35 percent of voters turned out for the February 1997 elections. Nawaz Sharif's Pakistan Muslim League (PML) and its allies won more than 160 seats. Sharif used his parliamentary majority to consolidate his power over the president and the judiciary.

Following nuclear tests by arch rival India in early May 1998, Sharif responded to mounting political pressure and ordered Pakistan to conduct tests on May 28. The same day Sharif declared a short-lived state of emergency, preventing citizens from going to court to enforce fundamental rights. On October 30, Sharif imposed direct federal rule in Sindh province amid escalating violence.

In November the government suspended human rights guarantees in areas of Sindh where the army is deployed and ordered new military courts in Karachi to try "terrorists and criminals." The tensions underscored a national identity crisis in a society fractured by regional, ethnic, linguistic, and religious differences and where Islam has failed to serve as the anticipated unifying force.

On October 12, 1999, Army chief Pervez Musharraf, citing Sharif's corruption, usurpation of power, and failure to address Pakistan's problems, mounted a bloodless coup and suspended the constitution. He promised a civilian administration but gave no timetable for a return to democracy. Subsequently, he said that Sharif would be put on trial.

The electoral system has concentrated political power in a rural landowning elite that dominates both main parties and defeats efforts at political and economic reform. Widespread official corruption has severely undermined democratic institutions, stunted economic development, contributed to often severe civil liberties violations, and failed to provide law and order. Consequently, the relatively disciplined army was arguably the country's most respected institution.

Pakistan has not formally annexed its Northern Areas, which form part of the disputed territory of Kashmir, in order to avoid legitimizing Kashmir's de facto separation. Therefore, the million-plus residents of the Northern Areas are not represented in parliament. In the 1997 elections, tribal leaders in the Federally Administered Tribal Areas (FATA) intimidated women out of voting. According to the independent Human Rights Commission of Pakistan (HRCP), some twenty million bonded laborers cannot vote.

The Supreme Court has been independent. Lower courts are corrupt and subject to manipulation, and government officials frequently ignore court orders. By the end of 1998, military courts had sentenced several persons to death in trials that lasted just days. The police are ill-disciplined, frequently involved in crime, and subject to political manipulation. Police routinely torture detainees in order to extract confessions or bribes.

Freedom of expression is restricted by laws and constitutional provisions that cover broad subjects, including the army and Islam. Authorities occasionally detain, file false charges against, threaten, and assault journalists and attack newspaper offices. Islamic fundamentalists also frequently target journalists. Nevertheless, Pakistan's press has been among the most outspoken in South Asia. The government owns nearly all electronic media, and news coverage has favored the ruling party. Freedom of assembly has been generally respected, but police forcibly break up many demonstrations.

The 1979 Zina Ordinance introduced *shari'a* (Islamic law) into the penal code regarding sexual offenses. Courts have imprisoned many women for alleged extramarital sexual intercourse, often following false allegations by their husbands, or following rape when a victim cannot meet the strict legal requirement to prove the crime and then is charged with adultery. Lawyers for Human Rights and Legal Aid estimates that criminal gangs have trafficked some two hundred thousand Bangladeshi women to Pakistan, often with the complicity of corrupt local officials. Many are sold into prostitution and are subjected to physical abuse. Violence against women remains a serious problem.

There are perhaps eleven to twelve

million child laborers, including many bonded laborers, working in brick kilns, carpet factories, farms, and elsewhere. Politicians and landlords reportedly forcibly hold thousands of bonded laborers. Trade unions are independent, but several sectors cannot organize, and unions are prohibited in export processing zones. Freedom House's 1998–99 *Freedom in the World* rates Pakistan a four in political rights and a five in civil liberties and noted a downward trend in both.

Religious Freedom

When Pakistan was declared a homeland for Muslims in 1947, the national founder, Muhammad Ali Jinnah, pledged that Hindus, Christians, Parsees, and other religious minorities would enjoy communal equality with the Muslim majority. But when Islam was established as the state religion in the 1973 constitution, all laws were required to be "consistent with Islamic ideology." Subsequent government decrees over the past twenty-five years have conformed much of Pakistan's public life to Islamic principles and introduced Quranic standards into the judicial system of civil and criminal law. Despite the guarantees of Article 36 of the constitution, which calls for separate systems of family law for non-Muslim citizens to safeguard their rights and interests, some elements of Islamic law are imposed on religious minorities, who compose at least 4 percent of the population.

Under the provisions of Islamic law in force, the testimony of a non-Muslim in court is half the value of a Muslim's, and that of a non-Muslim woman halved yet again. A non-Muslim is required by the courts to pay a double penalty to a Muslim he has wronged, while a non-Muslim receives only half of the penalty owed him by a Muslim. In some situations neither a woman nor a non-Muslim is allowed to testify at all. The constitution prohibits discrimination in government employment, but religious minorities remain underrepresented at all levels within the civil and military services, as well as the judiciary. A Christian judge elevated to the Sindh High Court in 1997 was denied confirmation and forced to step down after eleven months; during 1998, a Hindu judge confirmed in the same court was served a petition, demanding his removal because of his religion. The right to change a religion is not guaranteed and in practice is forbidden among Muslims.

Since 1985, Pakistan's minorities have been politically marginalized by a separate electoral system that limits them to 10 reserved seats in the 237-member National Assembly, bars them from the Senate, and prevents them from voting for any Muslim candidates in general elections. Islamic studies are compulsory for all Muslims in state-run schools. Students of minority faiths are not required to participate, although they are often pressured to do so. They have no parallel studies in their own religion. The minority Christian community was stripped of their prestigious missionary schools in the Punjab and Sindh by a 1972 nationalization order. Although a 1987 Supreme Court ruling overturned the order as unconstitutional, Punjab authorities only began returning a few institutions to the owners during 1998.

The Islamization drive launched by former president Zia ul-Haq's regime imposed the controversial Hudood Ordinances of 1979 pertaining to sexual and criminal offenses. The Quranic punishments of stoning, whipping, and amputation were introduced for committing theft, armed robbery, rape, adultery and fornication, or consuming alcohol or drugs. Under the strict Islamic rules of evidence, the ordinances made a woman's testimony inadmissible in court, requiring a rape victim to find four male witnesses to support her claim. Accordingly, non-Muslim women who admit to being rape victims can rarely prove their innocence, since they must find either four Muslim men (or eight non-Muslim men) to testify on their behalf. Failure to do so leaves them culpable before the courts on adultery charges, which in principle carries the death penalty, although that has not been carried out. Private vengeance from the family is more likely.

Zia's regime also added new sections to the long-standing statutes in the penal code against blasphemy, stiffening the penalties for defiling Islam, the Quran, or the prophet Mohammed. Although Section 295 had been on the books for decades, Zia's amendments invited serious abuses of the law of non-Muslims, whose testimony in their own defense would be worthless. The vaguely worded statutes fail to define *blasphemy* and contain no safeguards against false accusations. Still in effect, these stipulations decree a ten-year prison sentence for insulting Islam—and technically the Quran (295-B), and mandatory capital punishment for blaspheming against the prophet Mohammed (295-C). Among the religious minorities, the Ahmadis and Christians have taken the brunt of intimidation and punishment fostered by these false blasphemy charges, but some Hindus and orthodox Muslims have also been threatened.

Although members of the Ahmadiya sect view themselves as Muslims, many orthodox Muslims consider them heretical. Since the Pakistan government declared Ahmadis a non-Muslim minority in 1974, their rights to profess, practice, and propagate their faith have been severely curtailed. A 1984 ruling further criminalized Ahmadis for calling themselves Muslims or using Islamic terminology, including naming their children Mohammed. Their mosques are often attacked, they are barred from being buried in Muslim graveyards or going to Mecca, and their literature is frequently seized. Some two thousand religious cases are filed against Ahmadis annually, with more than forty charged during 1998 with alleged blasphemy under Section 295-C. Ahmadi leaders say 145 Ahmadis were awaiting trial for blasphemy in late 1998. According to local human rights observers, government employees file the majority of cases against Ahmadis. In contrast to Christians, Ahmadi defendants are rarely refused bail, although both suffer severe harassment from guards and fellow prisoners while incarcerated. The Zikris in Baluchistan have also been threatened with assertions that their views are heretical.

Many Christians have been jailed on blasphemy charges since 1991. One was an illiterate eleven-year-old, Salamat Masih, who was alleged to have written blasphemy. None have been executed by the state, although four have been sentenced to death and five killed while imprisoned without bail for several years. Another five who were acquitted have fled the country to gain asylum, with or without families, and escape ongoing death threats from religious extremists. Eventual acquittal of all these defendants by the usually courageous appellate courts indicates that the cases are rooted in social hostility toward the non-Muslim minorities, compounded by issues of personal or economic rivalry. Although a 1996 administrative order had instructed magistrates to investigate blasphemy allegations before allowing formal charges to be filed, that practice has been ignored by the Sharif government.

Minority demands for repeal of the blasphemy law intensified in May 1998 when prominent Catholic Bishop John Joseph of Faisalabad died, allegedly by suicide, to protest a guilty verdict handed down against one of his parishioners. After nineteen months in jail, a Sahiwal sessions court sentenced Christian Ayub Masih to death on April 27, 1998, for alleged blasphemy against Mohammed. The bishop blamed the case on a land dispute with Muslim neighbors, who forced Masih's family and fellow Christian villagers to flee their homes after his arrest. Masih remains in jail, pending his appeal before the high court. His Muslim defense lawyers and judges involved in the case have all received death threats. Thousands of Christians marched in the streets to protest the bishop's death and oppose the blasphemy laws after his funeral, resulting in hundreds of arrests during police confrontations and two more Christians jailed on formal blasphemy charges. On May 29 and 30, 1999, two Christian brothers were jailed on blasphemy charges near Pasrun. In June 1999, the government indicated it would change the procedures of the law so that charges would need to be reviewed by a panel, including Christians, before charges are filed. General Musharraf enacted part of this change in early 2000, but then quickly withdrew it.

The country faces a serious breakdown of law and order in its major cities, especially Karachi, which has conflicts between factions of Urdu speakers from India. Sectarian violence claims an almost daily toll of lives, particularly from escalating feuds between the orthodox Sunni majority and minority Shi'ites. In the past few years, mob assassinations have even taken place inside rival mosques during prayer times. According to the provincial law minister, some 422 were killed in religiously motivated violence in the Punjab alone in the first eleven months of 1998. Other estimates put the number at one thousand. In January 1998, Sunni extremists killed twenty-five Shi'ites praying in a Lahore cemetery. In October 1999, more than twenty people, both Shi'ite and Sunni, were killed in sectarian gun attacks. Less than two months after a Muslim mob ransacked and tore down a Presbyterian church under construction in Sheikhapura, unknown attackers murdered its pastor, Rev. Noor Alam. Local authorities dismissed the incident in January 1998 as a simple robbery case that turned violent.

The culture of violence and widespread corruption in the country leaves religious minorities particularly vulnerable. The Muslim majority is fractured into more than seventy Islamic sects who oppose one another doctrinally and politically, with spiraling violence between Sunni and Shi'ite factions. The indigenous Christian population, usually descendants of converts from lower Hindu castes, are concentrated in the Punjab and are predominately rural, illiterate, and landless, with migrants to the cities employed as street sweepers, brick kiln workers, or semiliterate middle-class jobs. Their literacy rate is about 7 percent. The bulk of Hindu tribal peoples are found in the Sindh province. Christians and Hindus usually have good relations. Hindus suffered riots and arson in retaliation for the destruction of the Babri Mosque in India.

The government has made little effort to dispel a nationwide climate of religious intolerance. Fanatics who promote violence or even kill alleged blasphemers are rarely prosecuted or punished, and police complicity in such incidents is ignored. Mob action, in response to an accusation of blasphemy in

Shantinagar, in Punjab, in which a dozen Christian churches and several schools were attacked and burned and about twenty thousand left homeless, has been attributed to police instigation, in conjunction with Islamist extremists. Those responsible were only briefly suspended and never charged. Two years after a Muslim judge acquitted two Christians of blasphemy charges in a high court appeal, he was shot to death in his chambers. The kidnapping of minor girls, followed by forced marriage to their Muslim captors and conversion to Islam, is becoming more widespread in rural areas. Two poor Christian families who applied through the courts to recover their daughters last year were threatened with prosecution or punitive economic measures by landowners of the majority community.

In October 1998, the Sharif government proposed and passed through the National Assembly a fifteenth amendment to the constitution to institute full-fledged Islamic law in the country.

The measure, which has failed to pass in the Senate, would replace the civil legal system with the government's interpretation of Islamic law as "constitutionally and legally supreme." Sharif assures non-Muslim minorities that this "new Islamic order" will protect their rights. Minority leaders and moderate Muslim politicians criticized the parliament and an independent judiciary. Preliminary indications are that the new military regime will be more sensitive to religious minorities.

Although no law specifically forbids Muslims from converting to another faith, there are bars to proselytizing among Muslims. Foreign missionaries believed to have violated their vocational boundaries as medical or educational professionals are refused visa renewals for alleged involvement in proselytizing. Family reprisals against converts, such as the July 1997 murder of a young Sheikhupura woman by her brother after she had secretly undergone Christian baptism, are rarely prosecuted.

Philippines

Population	**74.7 million**
Catholic	**80%**
Protestant	**9%**
Muslim (mostly Sunni)	**8%**
Other (Buddhist, Animist,	
Nonreligious)	**3%**
Religious Freedom Rating	**3**

Background

The Spanish colonized the Philippines in 1565 and were ousted by the United States in 1898. The U.S. ruled until the Japanese occupation during World War II. After the war the Philippines achieved independence in

1946. Ferdinand Marcos, first elected as president in 1965, declared martial law in 1972 to circumvent a constitutional two-term limit. The 1986 "People Power" revolution, which saw massive street protests over a blatantly rigged election, ended Marcos's dictatorial rule. His opponent, Corazon Aquino, took office.

Aquino drew praise for her support for democracy, but her term was marked by at least six coup attempts, and she had limited success in reforming a feudal-oriented society and crony capitalist economy. Her successor, Fidel Ramos (1992–98), carried out economic liberalization that reduced the disproportionate political power of economic oligarchies and wealthy landowners. However, the reforms have widened income disparities and brought only marginal benefits to poorer Filipinos. With Ramos constitutionally barred from running for a second six-year term, Vice President Joseph Estrada won the June 1998 presidential election with 46.4 percent of the vote in an eight-way race. Estrada tried to ease fears that his administration would bring a return to crony capitalism by assembling a credible team of ministers and advisors. Yet, by the fall, allegations of cronyism had already surfaced. With the Philippines buffeted by the regional economic crisis, opponents also criticized a lack of coherence in economic policy.

In 1993, right-wing military hardliners agreed to a peace pact with the government. Since 1992, the government has held peace negotiations with a communist insurgency that began in the late 1960s. In March 1998, the government reached a human rights pact with communist leaders, but a final solution remains elusive. In 1996, the government signed a peace agreement with the Islamic separatist Moro National Liberation Front (MNLF). But two smaller groups, the Moro Islamic Liberation Front (MILF) and Abu Sayyaf, continue to wage a low-grade insurgency for an independent Islamic state.

Filipinos can change their government democratically, although outside of Manila much of the country is still largely run along feudal lines, with dominant local clans holding real power. Elections revolve around personalities rather than issues. While the presidential election appeared to be free and fair, vote buying and intimidation marred elections for parliamentary and local seats. Official corruption is widespread.

Complaints of discrimination by the country's Christian majority against the Moros, who live primarily in Mindanao, have led to insurgencies since the 1970s. In recent years skirmishes between the army and the MILF in Mindanao and nearby Basilan Island regularly displaced tens of thousands of civilians. The army bombs and shells villages during counterinsurgency operations, and soldiers loot and burn homes. The MILF and other groups often force villagers to evacuate homes and operate protection rackets and kidnapping syndicates.

Members of the army and the Philippine National Police (PNP) are also involved in kidnappings. The judiciary is independent; however, courts are heavily backlogged and are reportedly rife with corruption. In 1997, Amnesty International accused the police of torture and ill treatment of criminal suspects. Private armies are allegedly responsible for abductions and extrajudicial killings.

The private press is vigorous, although outside Manila journalists are often harassed. In the spring in Mindanao, gunmen killed two journalists who had denounced official corruption. The government sometimes restricts meetings and demonstrations on issues that might antagonize fellow Association of Southern Asian Nations countries.

Trafficking of Filipino women abroad is a serious problem, and domestic prostitution, including child prostitution, is rampant, with complicity of corrupt local officials. Unions are independent and active. The International Labor Organization has criticized labor-code provisions restricting the right to strike. Police often harass striking workers. Antiunion discrimination has prevented workers from organizing in most export processing zones (EPZ). Freedom House's 1998–99 *Freedom in the World* rates the Philippines a two in political rights and a three in civil liberties.

Religious Freedom

When the Spanish established their first permanent colony in the Philippines in 1565, Islam had already made firm inroads in the south and was beginning to establish footholds in the northern islands. Spanish colonial rule was intimately linked with spreading Roman Catholicism, but Spain neither converted nor conquered the strongly Muslim southern regions of Mindanao and the Sulu Archipelago. The United States ousted the Spanish in 1898, and ruled until the Japanese occupation during World War II.

The 1987 constitution borrows from the U.S. in its guarantees of religious freedom. Article 3, section 5, of the constitution states, "No law shall be made respecting an establishment of religion, or prohibiting the free exercise thereof. The free exercise and enjoyment of religious profession and worship, without discrimination or preference, shall forever be allowed. No religious test shall be required for the exercise of civil or political rights." The Philippines is unique in that it is the only traditionally Christian-majority country in Asia. There are no legal restrictions on religious freedom. Churches and other religious institutions are tax-exempt, and by law no public money may be spent in support of any religion. Since 1977, a Code of Muslim Personal Laws recognizes the *shari'a* as part of national law, subject to the constitution and other general laws.

Individuals have the right to freedom of religion and belief if they respect public order and morality. There is freedom to propagate one's faith, freedom of worship, and freedom to train and appoint clergy. Religious bodies have rights of self-government, of religious education, to carry out charitable activities, to own and acquire property, and to maintain social institutions. They can produce, import, and distribute literature, receive donations, and have contact with coreligionists, domestically and overseas. Individuals can adopt, change, or leave a religion freely, with no change of civil status. Religious bias in employment is illegal.

The key issue regarding religion is the status of the Moros, or Muslims. They live primarily in Mindanao and other southern islands, but some have spread out over the country and are opening mosques and schools. The five million Moros are the largest minority group. Complaints of economic and social discrimination have been one of the underlying causes of Muslim-based insurgencies since the 1970s, although more militant Muslim groups are pushing for implementation.

In 1996, the government signed a peace agreement with the separatist Moro National Liberation Front (MNLF), which had waged a twenty-four-year insurgency in Mindanao. The deal established Nur Misuari, the MNLF leader, as head of a transitional Southern Philippines Council on Peace and Development, overseeing development projects in fourteen Mindanao provinces. The accord also called for a local plebiscite in 1999 on expanding an existing autonomous region. Misuari later was elected governor of the Autonomous Region of Muslim Mindanao, which was formed in 1990 and covers areas where Muslims are a majority or a substantial minority. Misuari has since claimed that the government has not fully provided its promised financial support for the region. Religious leaders of all the main religious groups are involved in interfaith dialogue to promote cooperation.

Two smaller groups, the Moro Islamic Liberation Front (MILF) and Abu Sayyaf, are more Islamic in orientation and continue to wage a low-grade insurgency for an independent Islamic state. In mid-1999 they were both growing rapidly. Half of the population in the region are Christian and have no desire to secede. Abu Sayyaf has threatened to kidnap Catholic priests and police. The government has stepped up security at churches and provided escorts for priests in the province. A Catholic priest, Father Benedetti, was kidnapped in September 1998 by a breakaway fraction of MNLF combined with Abu Sayyaf and is still being held with demands for a $2 million ransom. In early 2000 militants took hostages from a Catholic school and tortured and murdered a priest, Father Rhoell Gallardo. In July 1997, the government had signed a cease-fire agreement with the MILF, but this has not really been honored.

The Roman Catholic Church plays an influential role in politics. Roman Catholic Cardinal Jaime Sin's encouragement persuaded people to take to the streets during the 1986 People Power revolution that led to Marcos's resignation. Since the restoration of democracy, Cardinal Sin has been outspoken on numerous political issues. There was some concern in the church about the 1992 election of Ramos, who was the country's first Protestant president. In September 1997, former president Aquino and Cardinal Sin led church groups, business representatives, students, and ordinary Filipinos in a huge rally in Manila that forced Ramos to declare that he would respect the constitutionally imposed term limit and not run for a second presidential term.

Poland

Population	38.6 million
Roman Catholic (including	96%
Greek Catholic)	(0.31%)
Orthodox	1.56%
Protestant	0.5%
Muslim	0.01%
Far Eastern Religions	0.01%
Other	1.7%
Religious Freedom Rating	2

Background

Poland was partitioned by Prussia, Russia, and Austria in the eighteenth century, reemerging as an independent republic after World War I. In 1939, it was invaded and divided by Nazi Germany and Stalinist Russia, coming under full German control after the Nazi invasion of the Soviet Union in 1941. After the war its eastern territories remained part of the Ukraine, but it acquired large tracts of eastern Prussia. The communists gained control after fraudulent elections in 1947.

Roundtable discussions between the opposition and the ruling communists ended post-war communist dominance in 1989, nine years after the Solidarity trade union first challenged communist legitimacy and eight years after authorities declared martial law. In 1992, a so-called "Little Constitution" gave considerable power to President Lech Walesa, the former Solidarity leader who had been directly elected president in 1990. A highly fragmented parliament, with some thirty parties, and a powerful president led to a series of failed governments while so-called "shock therapy" market reforms steadily improved economic conditions. In the 1997 parliamentary elections, a Solidarity-led coalition won 33.83 percent of the vote; the former communists, 27.13 percent; a pro-worker party, 13.37 percent; with the rest going to smaller parties.

In November 1998, Poland and the EU, which had in 1997 recommended Poland for eventual membership, held the inaugural meeting on the specific conditions of Poland's membership. The key issues revolved around adapting Poland's legal and administrative system to conform to the formidable body of EU laws and regulations. A controversial issue was the restructuring of local government. The government proposed reducing the number of provinces from forty-nine to twelve under a three-tiered system aimed at giving citizens greater input over the management of public finances, health care, schools, social welfare assistance, and police.

Poles have the means to change their government democratically under a multiparty system. On May 25, 1997, Polish citizens approved a new constitution by referendum. Though 53 percent supported the document, turnout was only 43 percent. The 243-article document, which replaced the 1992 "Little Constitution," confirmed civil and political rights, largely retaining the existing system while weakening some of the appointive powers of the president. It also allowed a presidential veto to be overruled by a vote of three-fifths of the members of parliament rather than two-thirds.

The constitution guarantees freedom of the press and expression, though there are laws proscribing publicly insulting or deriding the nation and its political system. More than 85 percent of the media has been privatized. There are more than 300 newspapers, 119 commercial radio stations (six national stations, five of which are state owned), as well as 10 commercial TV stations.

The law provides for freedom of assembly and the government generally respects this right in practice. Poland has a wide range of political parties estimated to total more than two hundred, but most are small or exist mainly on paper. The existing election law reduced the number of parties in parliament. Poland also has about twenty-five thousand nongovernmental organizations (NGOs), including professional, environmental, youth, sports, political, religious, cultural, women's, and democracy-building groups, as well as public policy think tanks, educational and academic associations, and charitable organizations. The constitution (Articles 12 and 57) and laws allow for the formation of independent trade unions. Under the law, ten persons may form a local union, and thirty may establish a national union. Unions must be registered with the courts. In 1997, the number of unions rose from 318 to 350.

A new Criminal Code and Code of Criminal Procedure went into effect on September 1, 1998, culminating an eight-year effort to restructure the criminal justice system. The law extends the forty-eight-hour "initial arrest" detention to seventy-two hours. Judges rule fairly in criminal and civil cases, but the courts are plagued by poor administration, lack of trained personnel, bureaucratic delays, and financial problems.

Freedom of movement is not restricted, and Poles can chose their place of residence and employment. Property rights are secure under law, though registries in land, companies, and property liens are not fully developed. In general, laws regarding the creation of new businesses are liberal and transparent.

The constitution guarantees equality of the sexes. Women are represented in government, business, and educational institutions. There are scores of women's organizations and advocacy groups concerned with issues ranging from domestic violence to women's rights. Freedom House's 1998–99 *Freedom in the World* rates Poland a one in political rights and a two in civil liberties.

Religious Freedom

Poland is predominantly Catholic: of the 92 percent of baptized Catholics, a majority attend church regularly. It has also traditionally been liberal toward other religions. Religious freedom was guaranteed to all denominations by the Warsaw Confederacy of 1573 (though only to nobility and townsfolk). Jews had found refuge in Poland (about 10% of the population), only to be almost totally exterminated during the Holocaust.

The constitution of April 2, 1997, guarantees freedom of faith and religion (Article 53). It also guarantees the freedom to profess or to accept a religion by personal choice as well as to manifest such religion, either individually or collectively, publicly or privately, by worshiping, praying, participating in ceremonies, performing of rites, or teaching. Freedom of religion also includes possession of sanctuaries and other places of worship for the satisfaction of the needs of believers, as well as the right of

individuals, wherever they may be, to benefit from religious services. Parents have the right to ensure their children a moral and religious upbringing and teaching in accordance with their convictions (with due respect to the child's degree of maturity and to his freedom of conscience, belief, and convictions).

The freedom to manifest one's religion may only be limited by statute, and that only if this is necessary for reasons of security of state, public order, health, morals, or the rights and freedoms of others. The freedom of faith and religion, instead, is an absolute right that may not be revoked even in times of martial law or state of emergency (Article 233 of the constitution).

The constitution also guarantees to all persons the freedom from being forced to participate, as well as the freedom from nonparticipation in religious practices. No person may be forced by public authorities to disclose his or her outlook, religious convictions, or faith. Data concerning religion have been classified among so-called particularly sensitive data by the 1997 Data Protection Act (this concerns data on religion disclosed in sociological surveys).

The constitution offers to all Polish citizens whose religious convictions or professed moral principles prevent them from entering military service the possibility of substitute service (Article 85.3). Both the recruits and the enrollment commissions find it difficult to define in practice the notions of "religious convictions" and "professed moral principles." The recruits tend to abuse this provision in practice, applying for substitute service; as a consequence, military authorities are reluctant in practice to grant the right to such service.

The constitution declares equal rights of churches and religious unions, as well as impartiality of public authorities in the Republic of Poland "in matters of personal conviction, whether religious or philosophical, or in relation to outlooks on life," and ensuring by those authorities "their freedom of expression within public life" (Article 25.1–2). Yet during the third term of the Sejm (Lower House of the Parliament), a deputy of the centrist-rightist coalition Solidarity Electoral Action arbitrarily put a cross up on the wall. This, however, was an isolated case of religious zealotry. Political parties do not demand that their members belong to a specific denomination or stay nonreligious.

The concordat between the Republic of Poland and the Apostolic See permits the possibility of church marriage being contracted before a Catholic priest (so-called concordat marriage). The priest is obliged to notify the births, marriages, and deaths register, and the legal effects of this kind of marriage are identical to those of a marriage contracted before an official (Article 10 of the concordat). With respect to non-Catholic religions, there is no such equalization of the church and the lay forms of marriage.

The freedom of conscience and religion is also protected by penal law (limitation of an individual's rights on account of his religion or lack thereof; disturbing the performance by a registered church of religious acts; offending religious feelings of others through defamation of their cult object or place designed for public performance of religious rites—Articles 194–196 of the Penal Code).

The religion of a church or other religious organization with a settled legal status may be taught at school; this, however, may not violate the freedom of faith and religion of others. In practice, the teachers of religion or ethics (priests, nuns, or laypersons) are paid

from the state budget and fall under provisions of the Department of Education. The Constitutional Tribunal has ruled that:

- voluntary religious instruction in schools implements the constitutionally guaranteed principle of freedom of faith and religion (judgment K. 11/90);
- placing a cross in a classroom or joint prayers do not violate the principle of freedom of faith and religion. A ban on such practices would be such a violation (judgment U.12/92);
- the requirement that programs on public radio and television respect Christian values identical with universal ethical values are consistent with the principles of a democratic state ruled by law (judgment K.17/93).

Fifteen religious groups (twelve Christian, two Muslim, and one Jewish) operate under specific agreements with the state. The remaining organizations operate under the 1989 law guaranteeing freedom of conscience and religion. This law provides for registration of churches and religious organizations. A register is kept by the Religions Department of the Ministry of Internal Affairs and Administration. In June 1999, the register listed 139 churches and religious organizations. Until 1997, this registration required submitting to the Religions Department an appropriate application (signed by fifteen persons), the organization's statute, and a summary of its religious doctrine. The statute and doctrine could not be inconsistent with national safety, public order, health, and morals; nor could they violate the fundamental rights and freedoms of others. Once a church or religious organization is registered, it may avail itself of specific tax and customs provisions, have its religion taught in schools to those who want it, build churches, own cemeteries, and complain to the Constitutional Tribunal.

The registration of churches and religious organizations proceeded undisturbed until 1996, when many demanded stricter criteria of registration. There were two reasons for this: some registered groups abused their tax provisions, and fear of dangerous sects.

In 1996, the National Security Office (an institution attached to the Office of the President) reported that among threats to national security were Satanist groups and the Scientology Church, as well as the International Krishna Awareness Society. The report reiterated popular prejudices about sects (breaking up homes, brainwashing, ruining health, forcing members to prostitution and begging, etc.).

Consequently, in 1997, the law on freedom of conscience and religion was amended. The requirements for registration were made stricter, including:

- increasing from fifteen to one hundred the required number of founding members for a religious organization;
- applications for registration can be refused when they are inconsistent with provisions protecting parental authority.

The law also introduced the possibility of removing a religious organization from the Ministry's register if "the Church or another religious organization has lost the features that condition its registration" (Article 36.1.3 of the Law).

Some reasons for refusing registration of religious organizations are actions against public morals, the use of drugs, and false or unclear doctrine. For example, the Order of Knowing Knights of the Spiral Ring Line declared that the object of its religious cult was the universe together with its mysterious energy. Yet, according to government officials, a true religion must necessarily differentiate between the *sacrum* and the *profanum*, and recognize the existence of the Supreme Being called God.

There are cases of intolerance with respect to religious organizations on part of "anti-sect" organizations. Religions that relate to Hinduism and Buddhism, such as the International Krishna Awareness Society, have been portrayed by some as "dangerous." Also, instances of vandalism against Jewish religious and cultural centers were reported in 1998. Radio Maryja, owned by the Redemptorist fathers, who are not directly under the jurisdiction of the Polish church, has aired thinly veiled anti-Semitic views by its listeners. Tensions exist between the Roman Catholic majority and the Ukrainian Catholic minority in parts of the country with a sizable Ukrainian population.

Romania

Population	**22.5 million**
Romanian Orthodox Church	**69.5%**
Nonreligious/Other	**14%**
Protestant	**8%**
Catholic	**7%**
Muslim	**1%**
Jewish	**0.1%**
Marginal	**0.4%**
Religious Freedom Rating	**3**

Background

Romania became independent following the 1878 Berlin Congress. It gained territory after World War I but lost some to the Soviet Union and Bulgaria in 1940. Soviet troops entered the country in 1944, whereupon King Michael dismissed the pro-coalition government. Ceausescu's autarkic economics and repressive governance devastated Romania during his rule from 1965 to 1988. A popular uprising and palace coup by disgruntled communists toppled Ceausescu, who was tried and executed on Christmas Day 1989. A provisional government was formed under President Iliescu, a high-ranking communist and leader of the National Salvation Front (NSF). The 1992 parliamentary elections saw the NSF split between neocommunist and more reformist members.

On March 31, 1998, after months of political wrangling that had brought economic reform to a virtual standstill, Prime Minister Victor Ciorbea resigned when the Liberals and Democrats, members of the ruling coalition led by his Democratic Convention (CDR), withdrew their support. On April 1, 1998, President Constantinescu asked Radu Vasile, a pro-reform economist, senator and general secretary of the National Peasant Party, to form a government. The new government faced major economic problems. U.S. Senator William Roth, head of the North Atlantic Assembly, said in November 1998 that Romania would not be ready for NATO membership in 1999.

Romanians can change their government democratically under a multiparty system enshrined in a 1991 post-communist constitution. The Organization for Security and Cooperation in Europe (OSCE) judged the 1996 presidential and parliamentary elections as "free and generally fair," citing such problems as incomplete voter registration rolls and irregularities in registering candidates.

The 1991 constitution enshrines freedom of expression and the press, but under Law No. 40 of the 1996 penal code, journalists face penalties of up to two years' imprisonment for libel and up to five years for disseminating false information that affects Romania's international relations and national security. Most of the diverse print media are private, while state television and radio largely dominate electronic media. The constitution also provides for freedom of assembly, and the government respects this right. There were several mass demonstrations in 1998. In May 1996, Law 27, "On Political Parties," required a political party to have at least ten thousand members before it could be registered, reducing the number of parties from two hundred to about fifty. Workers have the right to form unions and strike.

Judges are appointed, promoted, and transferred by the fifteen-member Higher Council of the Judiciary, which is elected for four-year terms by the two chambers of parliament. To diminish the politicization of the process, a 1997 revision of the law called for the Minister of Justice—not parliament—to appoint the members of the Higher Council. Judges are underpaid and generally underqualified and are subject to political pressure and bribery. The Helsinki Committee's Association for Human Rights in

Romania alleged that police routinely use cruel and abusive tactics.

Relations with the Hungarian minority remain strained over amendments to the education law and parliament's reluctance to allow for the creation of a German-Hungarian state university. Corruption is endemic in the government bureaucracy, civil service, and business. Property rights are secure, though encumbered by red tape and corruption. There are no restrictions on travel within the country. Women have equal rights with men. Freedom House's 1998–99 *Freedom in the World* rates Romania a two in political rights and in civil liberties.

Religious Freedom

Before World War II, religious minorities were more than a quarter of the population. With subsequent ethnic emigration and communist rule from 1948 to 1989, various denominational leaders and members were oppressed, persecuted, and intimidated. The officially atheist ideology coexisted with hierarchical religious systems that could be controlled or manipulated. The decade since the Romanian Revolution of 1989 has seen the coexistence of officially recognized "religious denominations" and legally weaker "religious associations and foundations." By 1999 there had been a decade of attempts to pass a new religion bill meant to supersede the current legislation, inherited from the communist period.

The 1991 constitution guarantees fundamental human rights, including freedom of religion or belief. However, it overrides international law in cases where the constitution conflicts. Article 29 of the constitution has six clauses that guarantee varieties of freedom of conscience. Notably, the Romanian Orthodox Church was not given the ti-

tle of "National Church." The post-communist government may have wanted to distance itself from the Church since many viewed it as a pawn of the Ceausescu regime. Patriarch Teoctist offered his resignation after his dubious role during the last years of the regime; however, he was re-instated amidst criticism. Through the decade of the '90s, informal alliances have continued between church and state as power struggles have persisted.

In 1999, officially recognized Protestant and Catholic denominations in Romania negotiated with the Romanian Orthodox Church over the preparation of draft religion legislation (abandoned in 2000), and some nationalist groups, currently in the opposition, wanted Romanian Orthodoxy to be the established church. Currently, 40 percent of Romanians say that they go to church a couple of times a month. While the government had involved the recognized religions in the debate on legislation, it seemed unable to take a stand or make any synthesis of the proposals.

Initially, the draft law seemed to protect the fundamental freedom of religion guaranteed in the six clauses of Article 29 of the constitution. However, there was a distinction between "religious/cult denominations" and "religious associations and foundations." The 385 "religious associations and foundations" did not enjoy the same freedoms and privileges as the fifteen "religious denominations" officially recognized and listed in Article 22 of the draft. Hence this draft law impeded freedom of religion for minority confessions. Throughout the 1990s in some regions, local civil and church officials have prematurely implemented this draft law by curbing the activities of "religious associations and foundations." Low-level government officials and Romanian Orthodox clergy impeded some efforts at proselytizing. Members of religious communities not officially recognized also accused the government of harassment.

Presently, only clergy of officially recognized "religious denominations" are eligible to receive state financial support. "Religious associations" may not build churches or other buildings designated as houses of worship and are not permitted to perform rites of baptism, marriage, or burial. Furthermore, the official registration of "religious associations" is deferred by bureaucratic delays; hence smaller religious groups have criticized the State Secretariat for Religious Affairs for obstructionist tactics in favor of the Romanian Orthodox Church.

The Orthodox Church seems still to want documented governmental status as the national church. Under the draft law, it would receive state privileges while the activities and material advantages of minority religions would be curbed. The church also insists that the government make antiproselytism provisions and tries to dominate access to mass media. The Union of the Christian Baptist Churches of Romania (UBCBR) has suggested amendments to dilute the excessive claims of the Orthodox Church. Currently many Orthodox Churches have affixed Romanian flags on the tops of their church structures, symbolizing unofficial visible "national church" status. This is prevalent in the area of Transylvania where the demarcation of Hungarian and Romanian centers of worship is most pronounced.

The bill also stated that only Romanian citizens who reside in the country can be religious leaders and church staff members. The Unitarian Church, the Evangelical Church, the Reformed Church, and the Roman Catholic Church favor a common amendment assuring that all the religious denominations may invite religious ministers from abroad.

The draft said, "Each religion is free to set its own education system and curriculum according to its own standards and to the legal provisions." The Orthodox Church does not want the state to finance educational Catholic, Reformed, Unitarian, Evangelical, and Lutheran churches. Article 77 asserted that when the parties involved cannot decide a property dispute, then the government will determine the restitution. In 1997, the Senate approved a bill to return Greek Catholic properties taken in 1948, but the bill was defeated in the Chamber of Deputies, reportedly due to opposition from the Orthodox Church. There was some improvement in returning church properties, but a 1995 law states that all buildings under the control of the Romanian Ministry of Education—including thirteen hundred confiscated Catholic and Protestant schools—will not be returned to the original owners but will remain with the Ministry. Authorities have granted exemptions from this law solely to the Romanian Orthodox Church.

In spring 1999, Pope John Paul II visited Romania, a major breakthrough in ecumenical relations. However, his travel was restricted and the event was virtually ignored by the media and greeted with mixed reactions by the population.

Russia

Population	146.5 million
Russian Orthodox	55%
Muslim	9%
Protestant (Baptist, Pentecostal)	1%
Shamanist/Animist	0.8%
Buddhist	0.6%
Roman Catholic	0.5%
New Religions (e.g., Hare Krishna)	0.5%
Jewish	0.4%
Old Believers	0.1%
Agnostics/Atheists/Other	32.1%
Religious Freedom Rating	4

Background

With the USSR's collapse in December 1991, Russia—the only constituent republic not to declare sovereignty—gained de facto independence under President Yeltsin, who had been directly elected in June 1991. In 1993, Yeltsin put down a putsch led by hardline elements in parliament, and Russians approved a constitution that established a bicameral Federal Assembly: a Federation Council (Upper House) consisting of 2 representatives from the country's 89 regions and territories, and a 450-member State Duma. In December 1995 parliament elections, the Communist Party was the largest party, with 157 seats. In the 1996 presidential vote, Yeltsin edged out Communist Party leader Gennady Zyuganov 35 to 32 percent and handily won July's runoff, 53.85 percent to 40.31 percent. His bid was supported and financed by powerful financial-industrial interests. In March 1998, an embattled President Yeltsin fired Prime Minister Viktor Chernomyrdin and his entire cabinet. The move sparked a new political crisis; the new prime minister faced Russia's most serious financial crisis since the collapse of the Soviet Union, sparked partly by the fall of oil prices and the Asian economic downturn.

In August 1998, the ruble collapsed, forcing devaluation, and the stock market nosedived, setting off a further crisis as the country faced near default on foreign and domestic debt and the possible collapse of the banking system. In response, President Yeltsin replaced Prime Minister Kiriyenko with Chernomyrdin, the man he had fired in March. In September, former foreign minister and ex-head of Russian intelligence Yevgeny Primokov was appointed as prime minister. The new government, which did not include any well-known reformers, signaled a return to greater spending and state control. In November, President Yeltsin was hospitalized with pneumonia. In August 1999, Yeltsin fired his cabinet, yet again, and appointed the former intelligence chief Vladimir Putin as prime minister. On the last day of the millennium, Yeltsin himself stepped down and appointed Putin as acting president. In the new year, Putin easily won the presidential election, and Russia had its first free transfer of power.

In other issues, on November 20, 1998, Galina Stratovoitova, a leader of the reformist party Democratic Russia in parliament, was gunned down in St. Petersburg by unknown gunmen. Her murder dramatically underscored the state of lawlessness in Russia. Several regions and localities took advantage of the turmoil in Moscow to press for greater autonomy. In November, Kalmykia threatened to secede, and several regions in Siberia used their holdover federal income to press for more control of resources.

In mid-1999, Islamic rebels seized several villages in Dagestan, just east of Chechnya. Apart from military strikes on the rebels, the Russian government accused Chechnya of supporting them and began a massive bombing campaign aimed at destroying Chechen infrastructure. Tens of thousands of refugees have fled to next-door Ingushetia. A series of bombings in Russia caused some three hundred civilian deaths, and these were blamed on Chechens, leading to widespread harassment by the authorities and ordinary Russians on anyone thought to be Chechen. The Soviet military invaded Chechnya in a brutal assault highlighted by artillery and air strikes. In the new year they had occupied most of the region but faced ongoing guerilla attacks.

In foreign affairs Russia and Japan recently signed an agreement over the disputed Kuril Islands; Russia and China settled a border dispute during a visit to Moscow by Chinese President Jiang Zemin in 1998; and the Russian parliament ratified a long-delayed friendship treaty with Ukraine. Russia and Belarus announced plans to merge into a single state under a union agreement.

Russians have the means to change their government democratically. The 1993 constitution established a strong presidency, but decentralization and institutional checks limit executive authority. The 1995 parliamentary elections and the 1996 presidential race were generally free and fair, though several regional governor's races were marred by ballot-stuffing, incomplete voter lists, and other irregularities. The 1993 constitution guarantees the freedom of mass media (Article 29) and prohibits censorship, but public officials are commonly using libel laws as a form of intimidation. Local authorities and criminal groups routinely threaten and harass journalists.

Freedoms of assembly are generally respected. In recent years, there have been many political rallies, antigovernment demonstrations, and worker protests. Political parties are allowed to organize. The Federation of Independent Unions of Russia, a successor to the Soviet-era federation, claims sixty million members (other estimates put the figure at 39 million). Newer, independent unions represent between five hundred thousand and one million workers. In March and April, several wage protests were staged by unions around the country.

The judiciary is not fully independent and is subject to political interference and corruption. Independence is also threatened by chronic underfunding and by its subordination to the executive and the legislature. The Federal Security Service (FSB), which replaced the KGB, has faced persistent allegations that its members moonlight as bodyguards, contract killers, and kidnappers. Corruption in the civil service, government, and business is pervasive. Members of the old Soviet-Communist elite used insider information, contacts, and extralegal means to obtain control of key industrial and business sectors. While the constitution explicitly protects private property, the checkered protection of these rights by parliament and the judicial system limits the protections afforded by the constitution. Citizens must register to live and work in a specific area within seven days of moving there. Women enjoy equal protections under law and are well represented in education and government, but domestic violence, discrimination, and societal norms remain serious problems.

Freedom House's 1998–99 *Freedom in the World* rates Russia as a four in civil liberties. It is also rated four in political rights, down from three in the previous year due to corruption, the assassination of Stratovoitova, and the weakening of the government.

Religious Freedom

The nine-hundred-year official Christian status of the Russian Empire was replaced in 1917 by an atheist ideology, which was not abandoned until the late 1980s, although it was enforced with varying degrees of severity. This was the first time in history that a state adopted the abolition of religion as official policy, and all the main political parties now abjure the former atheist policies.

In 1990, with a new religion law, the government of Mikhail Gorbachev established *de jure* the *de facto* religious liberty that had slowly emerged since 1986. Already at the celebration of the "Millennium of the Baptism of Rus" (June 1988), Gorbachev had personally sanctioned these new freedoms and encouraged the Russian Orthodox Church to plan public events, with full nationwide and international media coverage. Gorbachev forecast cooperation between Christians and communists as one cornerstone of the new Soviet Union.

However, when the USSR collapsed three years later, the new law on religion was only a year old. In fact, there were two laws—one for the Soviet Union as a whole and one for the RSFSR (Russia). Both had repealed Stalin's 1929 Law on Religious Associations and embraced religious liberty in a form acceptable in any Western democracy. The Soviet government sought advice from Western lawyers in drafting this law. The most significant difference between the laws was that the Russian one granted the right of teaching religion in state schools. Internal church statutes, which previously could not conflict with state atheism, were also changed to conform to the new freedom. Particularly notable was the new statute for the Russian Orthodox Church, promulgated at the "sobor" (church council) held to coincide with the millennium celebrations.

The role of religion in society changed in every essential aspect during these years. Very important was the abolition of the Council for Religious Affairs, the government body that officially acted as a "liaison" between church and state, but which in fact exercised atheist controls on religious life and took its orders from the KGB. At the same time, there were multiple incursions into Russia by all kinds of proselytizing groups. These groups included cults such as Aum Shinrikyo, implicated in nerve gas attacks in Tokyo, but also included many who sincerely wished to work with existing Russian religious groups.

The tens of thousands of now unemployed atheist lecturers and government operatives (*upolnomochennye*) throughout Russia's eighty-nine administrative divisions were discontented and soon worked to reestablish some form of government control over religion throughout the regions. They found it difficult to accept that the new Russia could permit religion to proliferate without even the requirement of registration. As early as 1993, there were discussions about establishing an "Experts' Council" on religion to investigate—not whether—but *how* the government could impose order on the apparent chaos brought about by religious freedom. Various drafts of a new law were mooted at different parliamentary levels, culminating in a long, detailed, and discriminatory new law passed in September 1997. More than twenty-five regions had earlier introduced their own local legislation, all of it variously restrictive, but with no two identical and none in complete conformity with the Duma legislation. Nor were these regional laws abolished when the federal one came into being. To add further contradictions, the new Russian Constitution of 1993 guarantees freedom of conscience to all citizens, in conformity with the international agreements to which Russia is signatory.

The imposition of the new legislation is so uneven, and sometimes ignored, that much more religious freedom exists than the letter of the law implies. In the current administrative chaos, the law in effect signals to distant officials that they have *carte blanche* to act as they wish, without laws or bodies to which they are in practice answerable. On the ground the situation is different in every one of the eighty-nine regions, varying from almost complete religious liberty in Sakha (Yakutia) to considerable controls in Moscow or Khakassia.

The Moscow Patriarchate, the administrative center of the Russian Orthodox Church, had an active hand in drafting the 1997 bill and lobbying senior government officials to pass it. Both President Clinton and Pope John Paul II intervened with President Yeltsin, who asked the drafting committee to modify it. This was not satisfactorily done, but Yeltsin received assurances that it had been and signed it anyway. All this occurred during the summer holiday period, with no discussion in the press, and no adequate consultation with the bodies most affected—the representatives of the Protestant and Catholic churches.

The purpose of the law, as stated by the Orthodox Church, is expressly to control "sectarian" groups, particularly those funded from the outside and promoted by foreign nationals. However, it can in practice be used as a tool against religion in general. If the Communist Party were reestablished and it renounced its positive view of religion, the legal tool is already at hand to begin another atheist campaign.

All religions, including the Orthodox Church, are paradoxically constrained to restrict their mission and educational work to their existing membership. By contrast, every atheist or secular group has the right to propagate its beliefs within society as a whole. There is a distinction between religious organizations (recognized churches) and "religious groups." Only the former can enjoy tax privileges, have their clergy exempt from military service, set up educational institutions, or receive state subsidies for the restoration of historic buildings.

Within the "religious groups" there is further discrimination. Those that cannot produce documentation to prove their registered existence fifteen years ago must re-register every year for fifteen years and obey every state requirement as a condition of achieving legal status eventually. This makes 1982, the end of the Brezhnev era, when religion was severely repressed, the benchmark. Some groups, such as Jehovah's Witnesses, Eastern-Rite Catholics, and Methodists (on Russian soil, not in Estonia) were completely illegal at the time; others, such as Pentecostals, Adventists, some Baptist groups, and even the mainstream Catholics, existed in a penumbra between legality and illegality, the unwritten or secret restrictions being applied in arbitrary ways in different parts of the Soviet Union. In the interim, until 2012, these groups may not own, rent, or hire property; or publish, print, import, or distribute religious literature, even for their own worship. They may not open educational institutions or make provision for training their leadership; they may not invite foreigners to preach or work alongside them or conduct services of worship or public prayer in hospitals, orphanages, prisons, or mental institutions. At the end of 1999, Putin extended the deadline for registration for one year, but threatened that those groups not registered by then would be "liquidated."

Most seriously affected by these provisions are those groups that refused cooperation with the old regime and refused to apply for registration on the grounds that this was in itself a restriction on religious liberty. Paradoxically, therefore, those that historically stood strongest for religious freedom are now the most disadvantaged by the new legislation.

In practical, as distinct from legal, terms, there is tremendous variety across Russia's vastness. In general, the gains since the Brezhnev era are immense. Teaching religion to children is possible in practice where teachers are available; most denominations—Protestant, Catholic, and Orthodox,—have their theological seminaries (in the latter case some thirty are now operative, as compared with two on Russian soil in 1980 and none for any other denomination). Printed literature is widely available, and imports continue. Churches are free to appoint their own pastors without state interference. Charitable work has developed from zero in 1980 to a nationwide network today. Much church property has been returned, and Orthodox churches are open virtually everywhere. For other groups the record is less good; for example, many Catholic churches are still in state hands, and the Orthodox Church has refused to return some churches to the Old Believers.

In law, there is theoretically less religious liberty today than in Gorbachev's heyday, but the restrictions are carried out haphazardly and they affect minority groups more than the mainstream churches. Islam and Judaism receive named protection under the law as "traditional religions."

Where there is physical violence, it is caused more by a breakdown in law and order than by state policy, as had occurred in communist days. Two respected politicians, members of the Orthodox Church, were murdered in 1995 (Vitali Savitsky) and 1998 (Galina Starovoitova), but this seemed to result from their anticorruption activities rather than action specifically connected to their faith. The 1990 murder of Fr. Alexander Men, the apostle of the new deal for religion, was apparently an isolated incident (possibly revanchism by the KGB). Sanctions against individual Orthodox clergy for their criticism of the Moscow Patriarchate are internal church matters, unconnected with state interference. There has been considerable violence against such breakaway groups as the True Orthodox Church, including accusations that their clergy have been murdered for their stance.

In Chechnya, nominally Russian but, until the latest military assault, in practice virtually independent, all Russian Orthodox priests have been kidnapped or have fled. The two pastors of the Baptist church in Grozny, the capital, have been beheaded, and their successor kidnapped, and virtually all Protestants have fled.

Muslims cannot regain their mosque in Stavropol (a unique situation in today's Russia); Jehovah's Witnesses are fighting the removal of their registration in Moscow; the Perm administration is attempting to force registration on the local Pentecostal church; the Lutheran community in Khakassia was deprived of registration in 1998; few Catholic priests are ethnic Russians (no seminary education was available in the communist period), while foreign priests are forced to leave the country every three months in order to renew their visas. In October 1998, communist lawmaker Albert Makashov blamed the country's problems on *zhidy*, a derogatory term for Jews. Anti-Semitism is growing rapidly with bombings and attempted bombings of synagogues and physical attacks on Jewish leaders. The situation is in flux and the future of religious liberty in Russia depends not only on the future of the 1997 legislation but also on the development of a democratic and peaceful society with a less corrupt administration.

Saudi Arabia

Population	**20.9 million**
(Including about 6 million expatriates)	
Sunni (Wahabi) Muslim	**86%**
Shi'ite Muslim	**10%**
Ismaili Muslim	**1%**
Other (including 600,000 Christians	
and some Hindus and Buddhists)	**3%**
Religious Freedom Rating	**7**

Background

King Abd al-Aziz Al Saud consolidated the Nejd and Hejaz regions of the Arabian peninsula into the Kingdom of Saudi Arabia in 1932. His son, King Fahd Bin Abd Al-Aziz Al Saud, ascended the throne in 1982 after a number of successions within the family. The king rules by decree and serves as prime minister, appointing all other ministers. In 1992, King Fahd appointed a consultative council, or *majlis ash-Shura*, but this is strictly advisory. Crown Prince Abdullah takes on increasing government responsibility as the king's health deteriorates.

Recent terrorist attacks and harsh government crackdowns result from growing internal dissent over widespread official corruption, fiscal mismanagement, denial of basic political rights, and the continuing security alliance with the United States. As king, Abdullah is expected to move toward greater economic diversification, less state interference in the economy, and a regional system of alliances designed to reduce dependence on the U.S. for security. Many question whether Saudi Arabia possesses the political stability to take the steps needed to move from a heavily subsidized welfare state to a market-oriented economy without sparking political unrest. A border clash broke out in July 1998 between Saudi Arabia and neighboring Yemen.

Saudi citizens cannot change their government democratically. Political parties are illegal, the king rules by decree, and there are no elections at any level. Majlis membership is not representative of the population. The judiciary is not independent of the monarchy. Under the legal system, which is based on *shari'a* (Islamic law), persons convicted of rape, murder, armed robbery, adultery, apostasy, and drug trafficking face death by beheading. Police routinely torture detainees, particularly Islamic fundamentalists and non-Western foreigners, in order to extract confessions. Defense lawyers are not permitted in the courtroom, and trials are generally closed.

Freedom of expression is severely restricted. Criticism of the government, Islam, or the ruling family is forbidden. The interior minister must approve and can remove all editors in chief. Journalists for private papers censor themselves, while the government-owned radio and television report only official views. The government tightly restricts the entry of foreign journalists into the country. In 1994, the government outlawed private ownership of satellite dishes, though they are available in markets at good prices. Government permission is required to form professional groups and associations, which must be nonpolitical.

Women are segregated in workplaces, schools, restaurants, and on public transportation; they may not drive and must wear the *abaya*, a black garment covering the head, face, and body. A woman may not travel domestically or abroad without being accompanied by a male. Foreign-born domestic workers are subject to abuse, work long hours, and are sometimes denied wages. (It appears that little advance information is given to foreigners by the Saudis, or their own governments, on what conditions they can expect.) The court system discriminates against African and Asian workers. Foreign workers constitute two-thirds of those executed in the kingdom. The government prohibits trade unions, collective bargaining, and strikes. There are no publicly active human rights groups, and the government prohibits visits by international human rights groups and independent monitors. Freedom House's 1998–99 *Freedom in the World* rates Saudi Arabia a seven in political rights and civil liberties.

Religious Freedom

Since Caliph Omar ordered the deportation of all Jews and Christians from the Arabian peninsula in the seventh century, Saudi Arabia has considered itself the guardian of Islam's two holiest sites, Mecca and Medina. The Wahhabi doctrine of Islam, which had historically linked political structures with the religious establishment, is the official creed of the Kingdom of Saudi Arabia. Wahhabism's central belief in the oneness of God is paralleled by a strong condemnation and exclusion of polytheism, broadly defined to encompass all non-Muslim rites and beliefs. But when rising oil prices brought the mid-1970s economic boom, Saudi Arabia began a large-scale importation of multinational expatriate workers.

No freedom of religion exists in Saudi Arabia. Islam is the official religion, with all citizens required to be Muslims. Any citizen who converts from Islam to another religion faces the death penalty by beheading for apostasy. The government prohibits any public practice of non-Muslim religions among the country's expatriate workforce, which constitutes a third of the population. This created great tension during the Gulf War when allied forces were pressured to hide any manifestations of non-Muslim religion among their troops.

In place of a written penal code, the Qu'ran and Sunnah (traditions) of Islam are the declared foundations of Saudi society. Islamic law (*shari'a*) is the main source of legislation, as defined by the Wahhabi sect's interpretation of the Hanbali school of Sunni Islamic jurisprudence. Judicial punishments enforced under Islamic law include public flogging, amputation, and beheading, and are applicable to all Muslims and non-Muslims residing in the kingdom.

All religious activities within the kingdom fall under the direct supervision of the Ministry of Islamic Affairs, which builds and maintains almost all mosques, sets the qualifications for imams, and pays the salaries of all mosque staff. Any clergy, even Wahhabi, who has criticized the ruling family, especially for corruption, has been silenced, dismissed, or arrested. All religious gatherings must have government permission, as must all tapes and religious books. The king lays claim to religious legitimacy for his rule as protector of the holy sites of Mecca and Medina, which usually remain off bounds for any non-Muslim, on penalty of death.

All visitors to Saudi Arabia are required to declare their religion on their visa applications. It is against the law to bring non-Muslim religious literature or religious objects and symbols into the country, even for personal use. The *muttawa*, or religious police, are the enforcing arm of the Committee for the Propagation of Virtue and Prevention of Vice, accountable directly to the Council of Ministers. Funded directly by the government, the *muttawa* monitor the strict observance of Islamic codes of conduct throughout the kingdom. If accompanied by the civil police, they are authorized to raid suspected gatherings for illegal religious worship, and to arrest and interrogate the participants for up to twenty-four hours before turning them over to the police.

The principal indigenous religious minority is Shi'ite Muslims, whom Saudi Arabia has declared to be non-Muslims located mostly in the eastern provinces, this minority is subjected to stringent government restrictions on their religious practices, although three have been appointed to the majlis since 1997, and they are allowed some family courts. This curtailment of their political, economic, social, and cultural rights has caused public expression of Shi'ite beliefs to become an act of political dissent. Since 1990, their public processions during the month of Muharram and on the Shi'ite holiday of Ashura have been allowed in designated areas of major Shi'ite cities, provided the marchers refrain from their traditional self-flagellation and display of religious banners. Shi'a clergy from abroad are forbidden, and travel to Iran for Shi'a religious training is restricted.

Although occasionally allowed to construct their own mosques, the Shi'ite minority decline to use state-built mosques since these prohibit the use of Shi'ite motifs. Practicing Shi'ites have been convicted of apostasy and sentenced to death. School textbooks denigrate Shi'ite Muslims, whom they call apostates, and who are forbidden to publish or disseminate their own religious books. The government condones private and quasi-official attempts to convert non-Muslims as well as Shi'ite Muslims to Wahhabi Islam. In 1994, some 150 dissidents, mainly Shi'ites were arrested on sedition charges. Scores more were arrested after bomb attacks on American facilities in 1995 and 1996.

Government restrictions also sharply curtail religious freedom among the millions of expatriated guest workers, who form almost a quarter of the resident population at any given time. An estimated more than half-million of these workers are Christians, many of whom attend informal private worship services held in secret. Christians from the Indian subcontinent and Southeast Asia appear to be at greater risk of arrest and ill treatment for practicing their religion than North American and European Christians. Filipino Christian Donato Lama was imprisoned for seventeen months and given seventy lashes because the religious police found a photograph of him participating in a Catholic prayer service in Riyadh. He was released in March 1997. Lama and other expatriate Christians accused of involvement in private worship services have been pressured to sign documents in the Arabic language without being informed of their contents. Their trials were held in secret, with the defendants allowed no defense counsel and the courts following summary proceedings.

A high government official stated publicly in September 1997 that the authorities would not prevent private worship services held by non-Muslims in their homes. Since that time no overt government action against private religious services has been reported. The government has cut funding for the *muttawa* and has not replaced several who have retired. However, during a sweep of arrests in Riyadh in June 1998, Saudi authorities from the Ministry of Interior arrested and eventually deported eleven expatriate (mostly Filipino) Christians accused of the illegal distribution of Christian materials in Arabic. In subsequent actions during the last half of 1998, local companies reportedly were required by Interior Ministry authorities to fire and deport at least seventeen foreign nationals known to be involved in private Christian worship activities. Several of the Filipino Christians deported in October 1998 were told they were being expelled for blaspheming against Islam. In May 1999, another Filipino resident, Romeo Macabuhay, in the country for a year, was arrested for religious activities. In July, Arsenio Enriquez Jr. was arrested after the *muttawa* found a Bible in his room. Both were deported in September, the former after the intervention of his former employer, Sheikh Abdul Aziz, a member of the royal family, who also insisted that Macabuhay receive all the financial benefits owing to him. In October two private Christian worship services were raided and forty participants detained. Most were released the same day, but thirteen were kept in custody. Raids have continued in the new year. There are small numbers of Saudis of other religions, especially Christian, but they usually remain hidden since, if discovered, they could be executed as apostates.

Singapore

Population	**4 million**
Buddhism, Taoism, Confucianism,	
Chinese Traditional Religion	**54%**
Muslim	**15%**
Protestant	**9%**
Catholic	**4%**
Hindu	**3%**
Sikh	**0.5%**
Baha'i	**0.2%**
None/Other	**14.3%**
Religious Freedom Rating	**4**

Background

Singapore's strategic location at the western entrance to the South China Sea made it the cornerstone of historical empires that flourished in Southeast Asia. Modern Singapore's history began in 1819, when Sir Thomas Stamford Raffles established a trading post on the island for the British East India Company. The British established full sovereignty in 1824 and brought in Indian convict labor and indentured Chinese workers to lay roads and railways and work on construction sites. Other Indians and Ceylonese later migrated to fill civil service positions.

Following the Japanese occupation during World War II, the city-state became self-governing in 1959, entered the Malaysian Federation in 1963, and in 1965 became fully independent under Prime Minister Lee Kuan Yew. The People's Action Party (PAP) won every seat in every contest from 1968 to 1980 before losing a 1981 by-election. Lee stepped down in 1990 in favor of his handpicked successor, Goh Chok Tong, although he still exerts considerable influence as senior minister. In 1997 elections, the PAP won eighty-one of eighty-three seats.

When financial crises hit Indonesia and Malaysia, two of Singapore's largest trading partners, it slowed exports and retail sales, and in 1998 Singapore entered into its first recession since 1985. The country also faces the question of how long its high-tech economy can thrive in an authoritarian environment.

Constitutionally, Singaporeans can change their government through elections. In practice, the PAP government has chilled free expression and political dissent through ruinous civil defamation suits, its tight control over the press, its deft use of patronage, and the use of security laws and other harassment against political opponents. In 1999, the official committee that screens political candidates approved only one of them, S. R. Nathan. Nevertheless, the PAP has considerable popular support as the architect of the country's transformation from a low-wage economy to an industrial and financial power and welfare state.

Opposition parties say they have trouble fielding viable slates for Group Representation Constituencies (GRC), or multimember electoral districts in which at least one candidate must be an ethnic minority. There are strict regulations on the constitutions and financial affairs of political parties. The government nearly bankrupted opposition Worker's Party Secretary-General J. B. Jayaretnam through a series of contro-

versial court cases, including a 1986 fraud conviction that the Privy Council in London criticized. In 1993, the National University dismissed Chee Soon Juan, an opposition Social Democratic party official, for alleged petty financial irregularities.

The judiciary is not independent, although courts have acquitted or reduced monetary damages in some cases brought by the government or PAP figures. Judges, especially Supreme Court judges, have close ties to PAP leaders. Police reportedly abuse detainees to extract confessions. Caning is used to punish approximately thirty offenses, including certain immigration violations. The Internal Security Act (ISA) permits detention without charge or trial for an unlimited number of two-year periods. Since 1990, there have been no ISA detentions. The ISA also permits the government to restrict the political and civil rights of former detainees. A 1989 constitutional amendment prohibits judicial review of the substantive grounds of detentions under the ISA and antisubversion laws and bars the judiciary from reviewing the constitutionality of such laws. There is no right to a public trial under the ISA.

Freedom of expression is restricted by broadly drawn provisions of the constitution and the ISA, and by the government's control of the media and its use of civil defamation suits. Journalists practice self-censorship. The government can legally ban the circulation of newspapers, although it has not done so in recent years, and restrict circulation of any foreign publication that it feels has published articles that interfere in domestic politics. Foreign broadcasts are available but subject to censorship.

The Societies Act requires most organizations of more than ten people to be registered and restricts political activity to political parties. There are no nongovernmental human rights organizations. Authorities must approve speakers at public functions. The police must approve any public assembly of more than five people. Race riots between Malays and the majority Chinese killed scores of people in the 1960s, and the government takes measures to ensure racial harmony and equity. Minorities are well represented in government, but Malays reportedly face unofficial discrimination. Most unions are affiliated with the pro-government National Trade Unions Congress. Freedom House's 1998–99 *Freedom in the World* rates Singapore a five in political rights and civil liberties.

Religious Freedom

Singapore's indigenous Malay population is largely Muslim though its strategic location has meant that it has always had a mixture of populations and of religions. Christianity developed under the British and the laborers they imported. The Chinese brought Buddhism, while Tamils and other mainly southern Indian workers brought Hinduism. During the nineteenth century, small numbers of Iraqi Jews migrated to Singapore and established themselves in commerce.

Singapore's constitution provides for freedom of religion, and there is no state religion. However, the government closely monitors religious as well as other groups and uses the legal system to restrict some groups. Article 15 of the 1963 constitution states, "1) Every person has the right to profess and practice his religion and to propagate it; 2) No person shall be compelled to pay any tax the proceeds of which are specially allocated in whole or in part for the purposes of religion other than his own; 3)

Every religious group has the right a) to manage its own religious affairs; b) to establish and maintain institutions for religious and charitable purposes; and c) to acquire and own property and hold and administer it in accordance with law." In day-to-day affairs these freedoms are generally respected if their practices have no public effects, subject to the exceptions noted below.

Except for Jehovah's Witnesses and the Unification Church, both of which are banned, there is broad freedom of religion. There is freedom of worship and to train and appoint clergy. Religious bodies have rights of self-government, of religious education, to carry out charitable activities, to own and acquire property, and to maintain social institutions. They can produce, import, and distribute literature, receive donations, and have contact with coreligionists, domestically and overseas. Individuals can adopt, change, or leave a religion freely, with no change of civil status.

The restrictions on religious freedom that exists are part of the authoritarian PAP government's efforts to depoliticize society and curb dissent. The 1990 Maintenance of Religious Harmony Act authorized the government to restrict the involvement of religious groups and officials in public affairs. It gives discretionary power to suppress almost any action by a group or leader and can issue restraining orders for renewable two-year terms. The Act prohibits judicial review of any possible denial of rights arising from its application or of its enforcement. A Presidential Council, mainly of religious leaders, advises on religious harmony. The president may veto appointments. The Societies Act requires most organizations of more than ten people to be registered and permits authorities to restrict or ban groups and political activity to political parties. The Act covers all religious groups and, along with the Maintenance of Religious Harmony Act, further restricts political activities by religious groups.

In 1972, the government banned the Jehovah's Witness organization (and its materials) under the Societies Act on the grounds that it opposes military service. There are some two thousand Jehovah's Witnesses in Singapore, and in 1995 authorities arrested sixty-nine suspected Jehovah's Witnesses and seized books and other religious materials. According to the United States Department of State, courts tried and convicted twenty-eight of those arrested on charges of holding a meeting of a banned society, and handed down fines of between $500 and $2,000. In 1996, courts convicted a seventy-two-year-old woman, who was also among those arrested in 1995, for possession of banned Jehovah's Witness publications. The woman refused to pay a $500 fine and was jailed for seven days. In 1998, two Witnesses were convicted for possession of unlawful materials, and one of then was jailed for a week. The Unification Church is also banned under the Societies Act, and authorities have harassed some of its members.

Although the race riots between ethnic Malays and the majority ethnic Chinese killed scores of people in the 1960s, the government makes credible efforts to promote racial harmony. While religious and ethnic lines do not coincide, and ethnic groups like the Chinese contain Christians and Buddhists, nevertheless, the strong association of Malay and Islam means that the government is also wary of religion as a source of communal conflict. It takes pains to ensure that no religious minority is particularly disadvantaged by legislation. Major Buddhist, Muslim, Hindu, and Christian holidays are public holidays. There are numerous Buddhist and Hindu temples, mosques, churches, and a synagogue, and adherents worship freely and openly. However, the PAP government also discourages debate over potentially divisive religious and ethnic issues and especially discourages people from trying to propagate their religion. Given the governments' frequent use of the legal system to stifle political debate and criticism of its policies, in practice there is limited discussion of religious affairs in the media and other forums. The Singapore Muslim Religious Council, a statutory body, standardizes Islamic practice. Since 1957, *shari'a* courts have had jurisdiction over Muslim divorce and inheritance, and since 1989, the Council has taken control over subjects taught in Islamic schools.

Religious education does not take place in the state schools. Conscientious objection to military service is not allowed.

South Africa

Population	**42.6 million**
Christian	76%
Muslim	1%
Hindu	1%
Traditional	15%
Jewish	0.5%
None/Other (Baha'i, Jain, Sikh, Zoroastrian, Buddhist, Confucian)	6.5%
Religious Freedom Rating	2

Background

Consolidation of South Africa's democratic transition continued under the new constitution that took effect in February 1997. The country's independent judiciary and other institutions that protect and promote basic rights are growing stronger. The durability of these democratic structures, however, is uncertain in a country deeply divided by ethnicity and class and plagued by rising crime and corruption. Political violence again flared in the Zulu areas of KwaZulu/Natal Province.

The 1999 polls produced a second, sweeping victory for the African National Congress, although it did not receive the two-thirds necessary to change the constitution on its own. The National Party, the longtime ruling party under apartheid, has shrunk drastically; the Zulu-based Inkatha Freedom Party joined the ANC in a governing coalition with many of its votes going to the Democratic Party, now the official opposition. Few white South Africans appear to support far-right parties or the armed resistance that is still being promoted by a few extremist groups. In October 1998, the final report of the Truth and Reconciliation Commission (TRC) detailed killings by government agents of numerous antiapartheid activists and sometimes described in ghastly detail the acts committed by perpetrators seeking amnesty. It also condemned murders and other violent acts committed by followers of Winnie Mandela and Mangosuthu Buthelezi's Inkatha Freedom Party.

The international crisis in emerging markets has hit South Africa hard, as prices of gold and other commodities that South Africa exports tumbled along with the value of the national currency. Economic liberalization is encouraging new investment, but unemployment among blacks is nearly 60 percent.

South Africans elected their government through nonracial universal suffrage for the second time in 1999, in elections generally regarded as free and fair and with less violence than many observers had expected. A constitutionally mandated Human Rights Commission is appointed by parliament to "promote the observance of, respect for, and the protection of fundamental rights" and "develop an awareness of fundamental rights among all people of the republic." The eleven-member Constitutional Court has been beyond reproach and has demonstrated strong independence. Lower courts generally respect legal provisions regarding arrest and detention, although courts remains understaffed.

Free expression in media and public discourse is respected, and new freedom of information statutes are expected to improve governmental transparency. An array of newspapers and magazines publish reportage, analysis, and opinion sharply critical of the government, political parties, and other societal actors. Concentration of media ownership is a concern. Radio broadcasting has been dramatically liberalized. The state-owned South African Broadcasting Corporation is today far more independent than during apartheid but still suffers from self-censorship. Equal rights for women are guaranteed by the constitution and promoted by a constitutionally mandated Commission on

Gender Equality. Labor rights codified under the 1995 Labor Relations Act (LRA) are respected, and there are more than 250 trade unions. The right to strike can be exercised after reconciliation efforts. More than three-quarters of South Africa's people are black, but they share less than a third of the country's total income. The white minority retains most economic power. Freedom House's 1998–99 *Freedom in the World* rates South Africa a one in political rights and a two in civil liberties.

Religious Freedom

South Africa is a predominately Christian country with a long tradition of religious tolerance but also the experience of the invocation of religion by white Reformed churches to justify extreme racial discrimination and the apartheid state. Religious freedom is written into several provisions of the country's post-apartheid constitution. While the legal effects of the new basic law are still being sorted out in enabling legislation and court challenges, in practice there is extensive religious freedom. The small Hindu community is almost entirely comprised of immigrants from South Asia, as are most Muslims. There is increasing Islamic militancy.

The Christian population is deeply divided among groups identified by racial, ethnic, and linguistic lines. Thousands of localized "African-instituted churches" operate outside the ambit of conventional religious groups and sometimes combine elements of traditional religions in their practice. About 40 percent of the African population, or nearly a third of the country's people overall, are estimated to practice indigenous traditional forms of animist and ancestral worship. As in many other countries, traditional beliefs have often been adapted or incorporated into reli-

gions introduced later. This is especially prevalent in independent Christian churches not accountable to external hierarchies. The largest Christian grouping consists of such African independent churches, and the largest single church is the (African) Zion Christian church. Many traditional spiritual and magical practices also remain. Sorcery, and accusations of harmful sorcery, occasionally leads to assaults, burnings, and lynchings, especially in rural areas.

The relationship between church and state is today being redefined under the new constitution and the majority-rule government. The Dutch Reformed Church (Nederduitse Gereformeerde Kerk, NGK), and its ecclesiastical offshoots dominated by the Afrikaner descendants of South Africa's seventeenth- and eighteenth-century Dutch and French settlers, was bedrock of the apartheid regime, citing its interpretation of Scripture to justify white supremacy. The Afrikaner's almost mystical self-description as a chosen people allowed extreme brutality and exploitation to occur with the blessing of the oppressors' religious leaders. Only in 1986 did the NGK Synod publicly state that apartheid could not be justified on theological grounds. A white extremist subsequently assassinated its leader, Johan Heyns.

Outside of the majority black churches, most other established religions took weak or no stands against apartheid, defining the issue as "political" and thus outside the scope of religious purview, until the minority regime's waning years. In November 1997, leaders of Christian, Hindu, Jewish, and Muslim groups testified before the Truth and Reconciliation Commission about their roles during the apartheid era. Each admitted to doing little to fight apartheid. Some religious communities and individual leaders were among leaders in the fight against apartheid, however, including former Anglican Archbishop of Cape Town and Nobel Peace laureate Desmond Tutu, the National Council of Churches, and the Christian Institute that is connected with Beyers Naude.

South Africa's new constitution offers not only broad protection but also promotion of religious freedoms. The constitution has been called one of the world's most sweeping in its protection of rights. However, the burdened post-apartheid state lacks the resources to make many of these a reality. The charter's Bill of Rights offers extensive safeguards. Guarantees of the freedoms of association and assembly bring broad protection to religious groups. The right of self-determination of religious communities is explicitly protected. The constitution calls for a Commission for the Promotion and Protection of the Rights of Cultural, Religious and Linguistic Communities and authorizes a Pan South African Language Board, among whose responsibilities would be promoting and ensuring respect for Arabic, Hebrew, Sanskrit, and other languages used for religious purposes.

Section 15 (1) of the constitution states, "Everyone has the right to freedom of conscience, religion, thought, belief and opinion." Section 15 (2) allows religious instruction in public institutions so long as the instruction is voluntary and equitable. Section 9 of the constitution guarantees equality before the law for all people and includes antidiscrimination clauses that demand adherence not only by the state but by all other institutions and individuals. Rights of women and homosexuals are thus created against discrimination by religious institutions. This has raised concern among many groups that they

will not be able to uphold religious teaching on homosexuality. The constitution also seems to bar religious schools from hiring only teachers who agree with their beliefs and perhaps even to forbid the Catholic Church and Islamic groups from restricting their clergy to men or even Catholics or Muslims. South Africa faces a long period of constitutional clarification of religious as well as other rights.

The constitution also provides for respect for customary practices regarding marriage, and legislation has been enacted that allows Africans to practice polygamy. Muslims may receive the same legal right. Both of these have been of concern to feminist groups. Customary practices are also being considered in new legislation concerning the rights of children, and there has been debate over whether some religious practices would be restricted to allowing children the full rights guaranteed by the constitution's bill of rights and the UN Convention of the Rights of the Child, which South Africa has ratified. The role of religion in public and private schools remains a contentious issue subject to constitutional interpretation and litigation. Here one of the concerns is whether private religious schools will be used as a cover to maintain racially segregated schools.

Apart from these concerns, there is freedom to propagate one's faith, freedom of worship, and to train and appoint clergy. Religious bodies have rights of self-government or religious education, to carry out charitable activities, to own and acquire property, and to maintain social institutions. They can produce and distribute literature, receive donations, and have contact with coreligionists, domestically and overseas. Individuals can adopt, change, or leave a religion freely, with no change of civil status.

There have been few attacks directly attributed to religious bias, although a bomb attack against a Jewish synagogue in Wynberg in December 1998 remains unresolved. People Against Gangsterism and Drugs (PAGAD), an Islamic-oriented organization that engages in acts of violence against suspected drug and gang leaders, complains that it is a victim of police brutality. PAGAD is influenced by Qibla, a group to promote an Islamic state in South Africa. However, police actions against it seem to reflect only appropriate action against vigilantes, whatever their religion.

The much clearer stand of many religious leaders against apartheid during the white minority regime's waning days has been carried over to greater involvement in promoting peace and justice in a democratic South Africa. In October 1998, religious leaders joined President Nelson Mandela in signing a code of conduct aimed at the moral renewal of South African society.

Spain

Population	**39.6 million**
Roman Catholicism	85%
Islam	1%
Protestant	0.5%
Jehovah's Witness	0.5%
Other (Mormon, Jewish,	
Secular Humanist)	13%
Religious Freedom Rating	3

Background

Spain's Basques were the first group known to have occupied the Iberian Peninsula. The country's current language, religion, and laws follow the Romans, who arrived several centuries later. The unification of present-day Spain dates to 1512. After a period of colonial influence and wealth, the country declined as a European power and was occupied by France in the early 1800s. Subsequent wars and revolts led to Spain's loss of its colonies in the Americas by century's end. Francisco Franco began a long period of nationalist rule after the 1936–39 civil war. The country became a modern industrial nation in the postwar years. Following Franco's death in 1975, the country emerged as a parliamentary democracy. It joined the European Union in 1986.

Spain's current government came to power in 1996 elections that ended fourteen years of socialist rule. At the end of 1998, the Spanish government and the Basque ETA separatist guerrilla movement, Europe's largest terrorist group, took major steps toward ending the violence that has claimed approximately eight hundred lives since 1970. They were further encouraged by the victory of moderates in Basque regional elections in October 1998. However, at the end of 1999, the ETA announced that it would end its eighteen-month cease fire since it believed that there had been little progress in negotiations.

Spanish citizens can change their government democratically. The country has seventeen autonomous regions with limited powers, including control over such areas as health, tourism, local police agencies, and instruction in regional languages. The bicameral federal legislature includes a territorially elected Senate and a Congress of Deputies based on proportional representation. A

Supreme Tribunal heads the judiciary, which includes territorial, provincial, regional, and municipal courts. Freedom of speech and a free press are guaranteed. The press has been particularly influential in setting the political agenda in recent years. The rights to freedom of association and collective bargaining are constitutionally guaranteed. The country has one of the lowest levels of trade union membership in the EU. Spain does not have antidiscrimination laws, and ethnic minorities, particularly immigrants, especially from North Africa, report bias and mistreatment. Freedom House's 1998–99 *Freedom in the World* rates Spain as one in political rights and two in civil liberties.

Religious Freedom

From the invasion of the country by the Moors in 711 until the end of the fifteenth century, Spain was partially under Muslim rule, but Christianity and Judaism maintained a presence. When Spain became independent in 1492, Ferdinand and Isabella established the Catholic Church as the state religion and expelled all Jews from the country. During the early Spanish Inquisition, the state compelled Jews and Protestants to convert or to leave. The Constitution of 1869 gave a dominant role to the Catholic Church and guaranteed a minimum of religious freedom to other faiths. The 1932 Republic disestablished the Catholic Church. General Francisco Franco's seizure of power in 1939 gave back to the Catholic Church its position of state religion whilst Protestant churches and schools were closed.

In 1945, Franco curbed his religious oppression and allowed Protestants to open places of worship, but the public manifestation of their faith remained forbidden. In 1967, the papal statement "Dignitatis Humanae" prompted his

government's Law on Religious Freedom, which said, "The profession and practice of every religion in public and in private shall be guaranteed by the State with no limitations." A democratic constitution adopted in 1978 provided for no state church and freedom for "the Catholic Church and all other religions." The specific mention of the Catholic Church in Article 16 is a constitutional recognition of its existence, its social utility, and its historical role.

The 1978 constitution in Article 14 forbids discrimination "for reasons of birth, race, sex, religion, opinion or any other personal or social condition or circumstance." Article 16 says: "§ 1. Freedom of ideology, religion and worship of individuals and communities is guaranteed without any limitation other than necessary for the maintenance of public order. § 2. No one may be obliged to make a declaration on his ideology, religion or beliefs. § 3. No religion shall have a state character. The public powers shall take into account the religious beliefs of Spanish society and maintain the appropriate relations of cooperation, with the Catholic Church and other denominations."

The 1980 Organic Law of Religious Liberty states that *religious liberty* means "to profess the religious beliefs that he freely elects or not to profess any; to change his confession or abandon the one he had; to manifest freely his religious beliefs or the absence of them; or to abstain from declaring concerning them. To practice acts or worship and receive religious ministry from his own confession; to commemorate festivities; to celebrate matrimonial rights; to receive proper burial without discrimination for religious reasons; and not to be obliged to practice acts or worship or receive religious ministry contrary to his personal convictions. To receive and impart religious teaching and information of every form, to choose for oneself and for minors and incompetents dependent on him, inside and outside the educational sphere, religious and moral education in accord with his convictions. To meet with others, publicly manifest religious purposes and associate with others to carry out religious activities." It also includes the right to "establish places of worship, to designate and prepare ministers, to divulge and propagate their creed, and to maintain relations" in the national territory or abroad."

The 1980 Religious Liberty Law distinguished several categories of religions: religious communities with historical rooting, recognized under law, with legal status and registered as Religious Entities; religious communities without historical rooting but recognized under law, with legal status and registered as Religious Entities; and religious groups without historical rooting not registered as Religious Entities but with possible legal status as private cultural associations.

The historical character of a religious community is not defined anywhere in the law.

The status of religious communities is granted to religious "families" having "historical rooting." These are non-Catholic Christianity, Islam, and Judaism. These groupings set up federations, and an official delegation represents each federation to the state. In 1990, the government annulled Ferdinand and Isabella's 1492 decree that mandated the expulsion or conversion of Spain's Jewish population.

In 1992, for the first time in Spanish history, the state signed agreements with non-Catholic communities having historical rooting: the Federation of Evangelical Religious Entities of Spain (FEREDE), the Federation of Israelite Entities of Spain (FCI), and the Commission of Islamic Entities of Spain (CIE). The agreements concerned places of worship; cemeteries; religious ministers; recognition of religious marriages; chaplaincy; education; religious classes in public schools; fiscal benefits; tax exemptions; religious festivals; dietary laws for Jews and Muslims; and historical, artistic, and cultural heritage. Agreements with "provincial" governments are also now beginning for non-Catholics. The FEREDE comprises Evangelicals and Pentecostals (about 190,000 members), Lutherans (about 10,000 members), Reformed Protestants (about 10,000 members), Adventists, Brethren, Calvinists, Anglicans, Orthodox, and others. The FCI represents most of the Spanish Jewish communities. The CIE gathers together two of the Muslim federations.

Individuals have the right to freedom of religion and belief if they respect public order. The constitution and the 1980 Law on Religious Freedom guarantee freedom of worship, but in 1996 and 1997, several Gypsy evangelical places of worship were closed by municipalities. The rights and the independence of the clergy are fully respected, as is the right to self-government by religious bodies, the freedom of religious education and instruction, and the right to carry out charitable activities.

The differing legal status of religious groups allows discrimination. Catholicism, Protestantism, Islam, and Judaism have concluded agreements with the state but are not treated the same way. The Catholic Church gets 150 million dollars yearly from the state. Half of this amount comes from 0.5239 percent of the income tax of those who choose to give that percentage to the Catholic Church, and the rest comes from the General Budget to which all the citizens contribute, whatever their faith. The three other religions are not financed by the state. The tax law allows taxpayers to deduct 10 percent of their income tax to the Catholic Church, FEREDE, the FCI, or the CIE. Estate Tax exemptions are also limited to religions having signed an agreement with the state. The other (nonhistorical) religions, which cannot sign agreements with the state, do not receive these benefits. Divorces pronounced by the courts of the Catholic Church have civil effect, but no other religion enjoys such a right.

The lack of objective criteria for entering a religious group in the official Register of Religious Entities is another source of discrimination. The General Directorate for Religious Affairs has turned down hundreds of minority religions labeled as "cults." However, the Supreme Court gave registration to the "Iglesia Cristiana de los Carmelitas de la Santa Faz," a schismatic Catholic group.

Historically rooted groups have access to public radio and television, but the Catholic Church proportionally gets more airtime. Religious and nonreligious corporations can own private media stations. Protestant radio stations experience difficulties in getting licenses. In 1998, various authorities shut down at least ten Protestant-run radio stations. One of them, Radio Genesis, had an audience of 1,800,000. Radio Amistad had nine of its sixteen stations closed. However, nonreligious groups running unlicensed stations have had few problems. Catholic stations have encountered few, if any, problems obtaining licenses. The Catholic network Voz, which began transmitting in 1995, has received more than one hundred new licenses.

In November 1998, the Ministry of Justice held a "Meeting of Christianity, Judaism and Islam" in Toledo. However, no Catholic bishop attended. Protestant, Jewish, and Muslim representatives complained about the lack of respect towards their respective religions, the lack of tolerance of the Catholic Church, and the confessional character of society.

Sri Lanka

Population	**19 million**
Buddhist	**69%**
Hindu	**15%**
Christian (mostly Catholic)	**8%**
Muslim (mostly Sunni)	**7%**
Other	**1%**
Religious Freedom Rating	**4**

Background

When the Portuguese arrived in 1505, there were three main kingdoms: the Tamil-based Jaffna kingdom in the north and the Sinhalese kingdoms based in Kandy and Kotte. The Dutch displaced the Portuguese in the mid-1600s and ruled much of the island for nearly 140 years. The British ousted the Dutch in 1796, and in 1815 became the first European power to defeat the Kandyan kingdom and control the entire island. The British promoted the use of English in commerce and administration, which tended to favor Tamils and other minorities and contributed to tensions that continued after independence.

Sri Lanka achieved independence in 1948. Political power has alternated between the conservative United National Party (UNP) and the leftist Sri Lanka Freedom Party (SLFP). The first post-independence outbreak of ethnic rioting occurred in 1956, after parliament passed an act that temporarily made Sinhala the sole official language of administration and education. Tamil claims of discrimination in education and employment opportunities and a high overall unemployment rate continued to inflame communal tensions in the early 1980s. A Tamil guerrilla attack on an army patrol and subsequent anti-Tamil riots led to civil war in 1983. By 1986, the Liberation Tigers of Tamil Eelam (LTTE), which called for an independent Tamil homeland in the north and east, controlled much of the Jaffna Peninsula in the north. In the late 1980s the Marxist, Sinhalese-based People's Liberation Front (JVP) launched an antigovernment insurgency in the south. The army and military-backed death squads crushed the JVP by 1990.

In the 1994 parliamentary elections, the People's Alliance, an SLFP-dominated coalition led by Chandrika Kumaratunga, won 105 of the 225 seats to oust the UNP after seventeen years. Kumaratunga won the presidential election held later in the year. In 1997, she formally proposed constitutional amendments that would evolve power to new regional councils in order to grant greater autonomy to Tamils and other minorities. The opposition UNP rejected the plan, saying it would lead to a separate Tamil state, as did the LTTE, which called it inadequate. With her party and allies twelve seats short of the two-thirds parliamentary majority required for constitutional amendments, Kumaratunga failed to make headway on the proposals in 1998. In December 1999 she was re-elected, but with a much smaller majority, just four days after surviving a bomb attack. The civil conflict has killed some sixty thousand people since 1983.

Sri Lankans can change their government democratically. Institutions have been severely tested by civil war, communal tensions, and partisan violence. The judiciary is independent. Courts in Jaffna have been severely disrupted due to LTTE threats against judges. Conditions in prisons and remand homes are extremely poor. In August 1997, Kumaratunga reimposed an island-wide state of emergency. The Emergency Regulations allow authorities to detain suspects for up to one year without charge and ban political meetings. The Prevention of Terrorism Act permits authorities to detain suspects for eighteen months without charge and provides broad immunity for security forces.

Government security forces, the LTTE, and state-backed Sinhalese, Muslim, and anti-LTTE Tamil "home guards" are responsible for considerable human rights abuses related to the civil war. In 1996, there were an estimated six hundred disappearances in Jaffna, often by security forces in reprisal for LTTE attacks. In a landmark judgment in July, the Colombo High Court sentenced to death five members of the security forces for murder, the first time members of the security forces had been given a heavy sentence for severe abuses. But security forces continued to be implicated in the torture and rape of civilians. The LTTE continued to be responsible for summary executions of civilians, arbitrary abductions and detentions, denial of basic rights, and forcible conscription of children. In response, authorities arbitrarily detained and sometimes tortured thousands of young Tamils in security sweeps. In the new year the LTTE won several military victories, and the situation on the ground is now roughly comparable to what it was in 1995.

Kumaratunga came to office promising to respect freedom of expression, but her government has occasionally harassed journalists and editors. Restrictive legislation chills press freedom. Women's groups report that sexual and physical abuse against women is increasing, with the number of rapes rising sharply. Sri Lanka has become a destination for foreign pedophiles. Conditions in asylums are often inhumane. Human rights and social welfare nongovernmental organizations (NGOs) are active. Partisan violence on campuses periodically leads to university closings. Trade unions are independent, and collective bargaining is practiced. Labor violations are reported on the tea plantations. Freedom House's 1998–99 *Freedom in the World* rates Sri Lanka as a three in political rights and a four in civil liberties.

Religious Freedom

Buddhism enjoys a prominent status in Sri Lanka. In 247 B.C. a disciple of Buddha introduced Buddhism. Buddhist followers eventually developed the Theravada school of Buddhism, which subsequently spread to other parts of Asia.

The majority Sinhalese are predominantly Buddhist. Most of the predominantly Hindu Tamils trace their ancestry to migrants from southern India more than a thousand years ago. They are concentrated in the north, where they form most of the population, and on the east coast. Over the centuries there has been considerable intermarriage between Sinhalese and Tamils, and it is essentially impossible to distinguish them by outward appearance. A small group of Tamils, known as plantation or hill country Tamils, are descendants of nine-

teenth-century laborers brought by the British from southern India to work on the tea plantations. In practice, the plantation Tamils are largely isolated from the more numerous "Ceylon" Tamils, and the plantation Tamils have largely kept out of the current civil conflict. Most Muslims in Sri Lanka are descendants of Portuguese-era Arab or Indian Muslim traders, although there is a smaller group of Muslim Malays. Most Christians are Roman Catholics.

Sri Lanka's 1978 constitution guarantees freedom of religion, while also giving Buddhism "the foremost place" and requiring the state to "protect and foster" it. Article 10 gives the right to freedom of thought, conscience, and religion, including the right to have or adopt a religion of one's choice and to manifest that religion in public or private. There are few direct legal restrictions on religious freedom except that foreign Jesuits have been banned from entry to the country. Newspapers are forbidden to "insult" a religion. In 1960, the government stopped funding Christian schools and brought them into the government system, where Buddhism is dominant. More recently, the churches have refused offers of state support.

Sri Lanka has a highly centralized federal structure. President Chandrika Kumaratunga has proposed constitutional changes (see above), which would grant the nine provincial governments greater powers. Authorities are generally tolerant of religious diversity and have allocated more than thirty public holidays for Buddhist, Hindu, Christian, and Muslim festivals. The respective religious groups teach religion classes in schools, and children are taught the religion of their parents. Muslims have access to their own courts in matters of marriage.

Religious bodies generally have rights of self-government, of religious education, to carry out charitable activities, to own and acquire property, and to maintain social institutions. They can produce, import, and distribute literature; receive donations; and have contact with coreligionists, both domestically and overseas. However, recent drafts for the new constitution have clauses that forbid "proselytization" and the construction of new churches. President Kumaratunga says that these clauses will be removed, but they have not been thus far.

Buddhism continues to be influential in national life. The Buddhist clergy have significant landholdings and are influential in politics. The state maintains close ties to the Buddhist clergy and occasionally adjudicates disputes among orders of monks. The various groups generally do not speak with a unified voice on policy matters. However, the Buddhist clergy has been particularly outspoken against President Kumaratunga's devolution proposals, and many have opposed anything other than a military solution to the war.

The main differences between Sinhalese and Tamils involve language and religion. Therefore, Tamil allegations of discrimination, and the country's civil war itself, implicitly have religious dimensions. Although the conflict has generally not taken on overtly religious overtones, on January 25, 1998, the LTTE exploded a bomb near Sri Lanka's most important Buddhist site, the Temple of the Tooth in Kandy. The LTTE has also harassed and expelled Muslims from areas it controls.

In recent decades Sri Lanka has experienced numerous communal riots. In the late nineteenth century the island witnessed revivalist movements in Buddhism, Hinduism, and Islam that were partly in response to the work of Christian missionaries. These revivalist movements had the effect of solidifying communal and ethnic identities, which some scholars say facilitated the ethnic conflict that followed in the ensuing decades. In the late 1800s, Buddhists and Roman Catholics clashed several times. In 1915, Sinhalese-Muslim rioting swept parts of the island. More recently, a series of Sinhalese-Tamil riots occurred between 1956 and 1983, with the last incident triggering the current civil war. The 1983 Sinhalese-Tamil riots were highly organized. Sinhalese participants used voting lists and other documentation to target Tamil homes, businesses, and shops.

Since then, there have been no widespread incidents of rioting. However, the nongovernmental Movement for Interracial Justice and Equality in Colombo has noted that private conflicts are often quickly transformed into disputes between different ethnic or religious communities. For example, in September 1998, a private conflict between a Sinhala and a Muslim in Kurunegala erupted into arson attacks on Muslim shops. In the western town of Kochchikade, a dispute between a Tamil trader and a church over the construction of a well escalated into the burning of several Tamil shops.

In another development, on New Year's Day, 1999, a mob attacked the Calvary Prayer Center in Udugampola in Gampaha district. Although the police eventually dispersed the mob, the attackers threatened to return to kill the pastor. In recent years there have been credible reports that Buddhist monks have instigated mob violence against evangelical Christians in rural areas where the Christians are treated as foreign intruders. In the last six years, the number of anti-Christian incidents has increased dramatically, often prompted by inflammatory newspaper articles. Arson and intimidation have been increasing, with twenty-one churches burned, two hundred church workers believed to have been threatened, and ninety reputed to have been assaulted. So far, the government has done little. Unless curbs are put on radical Buddhist clergy, the situation may worsen.

Sudan

Population	28.9 million
Sunni Muslim	70%
Christian	19%
Traditional	10%
Other/None	1%
Religious Freedom Rating	7

Background

Sudan, Africa's largest country, has been embroiled in devastating civil wars for thirty-two of its forty-three years as a modern state. It achieved independence in 1956 after nearly eight decades of British rule. The Anya Nya movement, representing mainly Christian and animist black Africans in southern Sudan, battled government forces from 1956 to 1972. The south gained extensive autonomy under a 1972 accord, and for the next decade an uneasy peace prevailed. In 1983, General Jafar Numeiri, who had toppled an elected government in 1969, restricted southern autonomy and introduced *shari'a* law. These actions, along with pervasive racial and religious discrimination, and fears of economic exploitation raised by government plans to pipe oil discovered in the south to northern Sudan sparked renewed civil war. Numeiri was overthrown in 1985. Civilian rule was restored in 1986, but the war continued. Lieutenant General Omar Hassan Ahmed al-Bashir ousted the freely elected government in 1989. He has ruled through a military-civilian regime strongly backed by senior Muslim clerics, including Hassan al-Turabi, who wielded considerable power as leader of the National Islamic Front (NIF—the de facto, but undeclared, ruling party) and as a speaker of the parliament. In the latter part of 1999, there was an increasing conflict between Bashir and Turabi, culminating on December 12 when Bashir declared a state of emergency and dissolved the parliament. In the early 1990s Sudan was identified as a terrorist state by the U.S. government and subject to trade and financial sanctions that were renewed in late 1999 after the State Department designated Sudan as a "country of particular concern" for its egregious record of religious persecution.

There is little cause for optimism that a solution to the bloody war will soon be found. Two million people may have been killed in fighting and famine in southern Sudan during the past fifteen years, and five million have been made internal and external refugees. Several cease-fires have collapsed. The U.S. House of Representatives and the U.S. Commission on International Religious Freedom have called the regime "genocidal." Very severe human rights abuses persist, and the Khartoum Islamist regime's forces continue slave raids in the country's south. Sudan's conflict broadly pits the country's Arab Muslim north against the black African Christian and animist south. Some pro-democratic northerners, however, have allied with southern rebels to form the National Democratic Alliance (NDA), while northern rebels of the Sudan Allied Forces have staged attacks in northeastern Sudan. Some smaller southern Sudanese groups have signed peace pacts with the government and have fought among themselves.

Both rebels and government forces launched repeated offensives during 1998 and 1999. In September 1999, an explosion damaged the government's new oil pipeline. Government aircraft have indiscriminately bombed civilian targets, including hospitals and churches, and there are indications that they have used chemical weapons. The regime's campaign against secular and democratic forces in the Arab north have continued with arrests, detention without trial, and severe pressure against media and the country's few remaining independent institutions.

The United States has identified Sudan as a sponsor of international terrorism and maintains economic sanctions against the Khartoum regime. Sudan is also under UN sanctions as punishment for official Sudanese involvement in a 1995 assassination attempt against Egyptian President Hosni Mubarak in Addis Ababa. In August 1998, the United States launched a cruise missile attack that destroyed a factory allegedly being used to manufacture chemical weapons and reportedly linked to Osama bin-Laden, the Saudi millionaire charged with planning the August bombings of the U.S. embassies in Nairobi and Dar-es-Salaam. Subsequent reports indicate that the factory was not weapons related.

Sudan's 1996 elections cannot credibly be said to have reflected the will of the Sudanese people. Sudanese are unable to choose or change their government democratically. A new constitution, adopted in July 1998, and a law regulating political associations are unlikely to bring significant change, despite paper provisions for multiparty elections, direct election of the head of state, and religious freedom. The constitution also calls for an independence referendum in south Sudan in 2002.

Under the current regime, formal guarantees of basic civil and political rights mean little. Sudan is officially an Islamic state. There is little autonomous civil society, and few independent voices in media. Trade unions were heavily suppressed after the 1989 coup and operate today under tight control by the regime. The entire judiciary and security apparatus are controlled by the NIF. Civil law has been supplanted by *shari'a* law, which discriminates against women and provides for severe punishments, including floggings, amputations, crucifixion, and death. Two Roman Catholic priests were among twenty people who faced execution by crucifixion if convicted of dubious charges of involvement in bombings in Khartoum in June. The priests refused to accept a pardon and were released by the regime in December 1999, with the charges against them still pending.

Serious human rights abuses by nearly every faction involved in the war have been reported. "Ghost houses," secret detention and torture centers, are reportedly operated by secret police in several cities. Many thousands of southern Sudanese have been enslaved after being seized in raids by Arab militias and other government forces. Relief agencies have liberated numerous captives by purchasing slaves' freedom. The government has denied and denounced the widespread slavery but has not acted to end the practice.

The war's devastation has been

compounded by famine, often politically induced, among the displaced populace. In southern Sudan, the conflict is complicated by ethnic clashes within rebel ranks. Internecine strife within rebel ranks intensified in 1998. The NDA, a broad coalition of secular and religious groups from both northern and southern Sudan, enjoys support from Ethiopia, Uganda, and, most importantly, Eritrea, where it is headquartered.

The once-vigorous print media have been steadily tamed by the closure of publications and the harassment of journalists, creating increasing self-censorship. A 1996 press law further eroded media freedom. The regime has tightened controls on international and domestic communication by confiscating fax and telex machines, typewriters, and copiers. Broadcast media are entirely state controlled. Some newspapers still test the limits of regime tolerance. Editions of two newspapers criticizing the new constitution were seized in July.

Women face extensive societal discrimination and unequal treatment as stipulated under *shari'a* law. Despite its legal prohibition, female genital mutilation is routine. Rape is reportedly routine in war zones. Freedom House's 1998–99 *Freedom in the World* rates Sudan a seven in political rights and civil liberties.

Religious Freedom

Sudan is one of the world's worst religious persecutors. It practices forced conversion, represses those who do not subscribe to its version of Islam, has applied *shari'a* law to the entire population, enslaves its opponents, and is engaged in a war that the U.S. Congress, East African Bishops Conference, the U.S. Commission on International Religious Freedom, and many other observers have explicitly labeled "genocidal."

Egyptian Christians fled to Sudan during their persecution by the Romans in the first centuries. The churches in Sudan became firmly established in Nubia (northern Sudan) in the sixth century A.D., and Christianity was adopted by the inhabitants of the Nubian kingdoms of Muqurrah, Nobatia, and Alwah. Churches flourished along the Nile until the arrival of Muslim Arabs in the seventh century. The final collapse of the Alwah kingdom in the 1500s saw the end of the predominantly Christian era. Christianity reemerged in 1848 with the arrival in the north of a group of Catholic missionaries who then traveled south. The British Closed Districts Ordinance of 1936 restricted contact between northern and southern Sudan and the Nuba Mountains. Christian missionaries were all channeled to the south.

In 1957 the missionary schools and institutions were nationalized. This left the church with only theological colleges, and these could not function properly since qualified teachers were denied the necessary visas to enter the country. In 1960, Fridays legally became a public holiday and day of rest for all, regardless of faith. The Missionary Society Act of 1962 legalized the expulsion of missionaries and placed curbs on their activities, particularly in the south. Huge numbers were expelled in the following years. Following this, many Islamic schools were established in the south, and Arabic replaced English as the medium of teaching. African languages were forbidden. Parents could no longer choose children's schools, and many were forced to send them to the local Islamic school. The same Act declared it illegal to baptize a child before age eighteen. The teaching of Islamic and Arabic history was given priority in all schools, and African, even Sudanese, history was discouraged. All Sudanese from the south who applied to study secular law were made to sit for an Islamic law exam in order to be admitted to the law faculty. It is reported that, during the Anya Nya wars of the 1960s and early '70s, Christian African Sudanese were slaughtered by the hundreds. Pastors and other leaders were specifically targeted.

Shari'a law was imposed in 1983 and was made applicable to southerners and northerners alike. The Sudan Charter of 1987 stated that the Muslim community was the majority one within Sudan. (While religious statistics for all countries must be treated with care, in the case of Sudan this is even more so because much of the country is a war zone and there has been no census for decades. Muslims appear to be about 70 percent of the population, but Christianity is growing rapidly in the south where animist views were formerly dominant.) It also gave personal, social, and family autonomy to non-Muslims. However, while a Muslim may marry a non-Muslim woman, a non-Muslim man may not marry a Muslim woman. Similarly Muslims may adopt a child of any background whereas non-Muslims are forbidden to adopt a child whose parents were Muslims or where the child was abandoned.

The 1992 National Assembly issued a document setting out fundamental rights, including a statement of respect for all "heavenly revealed religions and sacred beliefs" and prohibiting religious intolerance. Sudan's Constitutional Decree No. 7 (1993) affirms that Islam is the guiding religion for the overwhelming majority of the Sudanese people but accepts the adoption and practice of other faiths. Article 24 of the draft constitution of 1998 accords to all the freedom of creed, worship, educa-

tion, practice of ceremonies, and choice of religion. However, it is still widely held that the practice of religions other than Islam is perceived as more a privilege than a right. A new dress code was imposed on women in January 1999, requiring them to wear Islamic attire and a head scarf, irrespective of faith. Even before this, Christian women and others had been detained and whipped for not dressing according to Islamic custom.

In January 1995, Pierre Sane, Secretary General of Amnesty International, said the regime had "embarked on an armed crusade to mould its society into its own version of a radical Islamist agenda." Others have described the regime as a missionary one seeking to Islamize not only Sudan but also the whole of Africa. There are numerous calls to *jihad* against the south by government figures including Turabi and Vice President Osman Taha as well as regularly televised war footage accompanied by a stirring call to the holy struggle against the south. Nevertheless the majority of Sudanese Muslims do not share the regime's view of Islam.

The war methods adopted by the government include the bombing of civilian targets, a scorched-earth policy, looting of cattle, destruction of property, fueling of inter-ethnic and factional fighting, the arming of militias, and encouraging the taking of slaves as booty by these militias. Firsthand accounts of raids note the specific targeting of churches. The government has engaged in calculated starvation by vetoing international flights, a tactic that in 1998 brought 2.6 million to the brink of starvation. The United Nations umbrella group for delivering international relief, "Operation Lifeline Sudan" has been criticized by human rights groups for abiding by Khartoum's veto.

Islamization is accompanied by an

equal drive towards Arabization. Many women from the south in the relocation camps have been raped or forced to marry soldiers. The macabre slave trade, which reemerged in Sudan in the mid-1980s, now involves several tens of thousands of individuals, mostly women and children. Many women are raped by their "owners" and the children brought up as Muslims, given Islamic names, taught Arabic, forced to say the salat (five daily prayers), and given a Quranic education. This process destroys the ethnic and religious identity of the south.

The government's prosecution of the war was intensified in late 1999 after oil developed by the regime in partnership with Canadian, Chinese, and other foreign companies came on stream in mid-1999. The oilfields, located in the south, were subject to a scorched-earth campaign by the government in late 1999 and were the scene of many atrocities. The oil has brought substantial revenues and new international contacts for the formerly bankrupt regime.

The Lord's Resistance Army, a rebel group operating in Uganda and funded by the Sudanese government, is notorious for the abduction of civilians and children. It has been fighting since 1988 to overthrow President Museveni's secular government. UNICEF estimates that up to fifteen thousand children have been kidnapped in the past decade; many girls turned into sex slaves and boys brutalized, including being forced to drink the blood of weaker captives. In December 1999, Sudan signed an agreement with Uganda that it would stop supporting the LRA and Uganda would cease to support the Sudan People's Liberation Army (SPLA).

Churches in the north are badly overcrowded because of the government's systematic refusal of applications for repairs or new buildings. This ac-

centuates the shortages created by the demolition or confiscation of existing buildings. However, mosques and Islamic centers are freely constructed.

Church buildings are destroyed in government-held towns on the pretext that land is needed for houses and roads. However, in the same clearances mosques can be left untouched. On January 8, 1997, three churches at Thoura were razed. In December 1997, the Catholic Club (a study and recreation center for members of the Catholic church) was confiscated and subsequently occupied by the Sudan security. The influx of refugees from the south has led to new churches being established, and churches, albeit makeshift operations, do exist in many of the camps. Christians are also allowed access to prisons to pray with Christian prisoners. Government sources claim that the Catholic Church is still a major landowner in Khartoum and is free to operate unhindered. Christmas and Easter are recognized as public holidays. Muslims are given one day's holiday on December 25 in contrast to the three given to Christians. At Easter, only Christians are granted a public holiday.

A number of Christian schools operate in the north. They are primarily Roman Catholic, although evangelicals operate some. The Catholic schools (Comboni order) provide a high quality education, attracting Muslims and Christians, predominantly those from the south and Nuba Mountains. Arabic is a prerequisite for access to higher education. In the south a whole generation has been denied education as a result of the war. The church continues to try to take the lead in promoting and organizing whatever education it can.

In 1994, the present government repealed the 1962 Missionary Societies Act, which had obliged missionary groups to obtain an annual license for their activities. Many Christian groups work unhindered in Sudan, and evangelistic events, including a large rally, have been held without problems. Christian marches have also been authorized and the police have assisted by clearing the road of vehicles. Missionaries cannot work openly, and individuals have been detained in this connection. Reports suggest that others working farther south have been forcibly deported. In 1992, missionaries were expelled from South Kordofan while the mass arrests and torture of local priests and catechists were carried out. Tight limitations are placed upon church relief efforts in the north, in contrast to the privileges enjoyed by Islamic relief organizations.

Individual Christians and Muslims have been targeted by the regime in incidents that clearly relate to their beliefs. Some individuals are routinely required to report to the security forces, and most clergy face travel restrictions.

Roman Catholic Archbishop Gabriel Wako is frequently harassed by the authorities with complaints ranging from importing communion wine and hymnbooks to going outside Khartoum to visit his "flock." In July 1993, the Anglican Bishop Rt. Rev. Peter El Birish was publicly flogged for the alleged crime of adultery. Observers suggest that charges against both clergymen were contrived. Catholic Chancellor of the Archdiocese of Khartoum, Father Hilary Boma, and his colleague Father Lino Sebit were detained in late July and early August 1989 and charged with various offences relating to a bombing attack in the capital in June 1989. More than twenty others were also detained, three of whom died of torture. It is believed that Father Boma "confessed" to the crime after seeing Father Sebit tortured. They were released in December 1999 after refusing a pardon.

Other priests are believed to have been detained and tortured for their faith in prison, including some in government-held towns in the south.

Coptic Orthodox Christians, who can be found predominantly in the north, number under two hundred thousand. Following the introduction of *shari'a* law in 1983, the Copts, though not subject to the worst excesses of the new law, found their status as court witnesses reduced. Many joined a "Christian Alliance" to defend Christians and encourage secular candidates. This led to a concerted effort to encourage the Copts to leave the country. After 1989, hundreds of Copts were dismissed from the civil service and the judiciary, and their previous case of access to Sudanese nationality was undermined. Compulsory conscription has forced many to fight against fellow Christians in the south. In one case a Coptic child was flogged for failing to recite a Quranic verse. Many Coptic businessmen have fled the country as a result of more subtle harassment, such as access to licenses and inspections of properties followed by fines and/or closure of businesses on spurious grounds.

In February 1999, an exhibition put on by the Association of Christian Students at the University of Khartoum was attacked and destroyed following this incident. The Omdurman Islamic University Student Union issued a statement referring to "the suspicious movement of Christianity in Sudan" and called for stricter controls on Christian missionary work and church land and property. Threats of violence against Christians in other universities ensued.

Reports abound of incidents in which those in the so-called peace camps in the north and the Nuba Mountains refusing to convert to Islam have been denied aid. In May 1995, the

UN Rapporteur reported the execution of twelve civilians by Government of Sudan (GOS) soldiers at Lobonok because they refused to convert to Islam. Whole villages in the Nuba Mountains have been held for ransom by security forces and forced to reconvert to Islam. Christians and animists alike have been affected. Atrocities against the people of Nuba have also included the burning of a church with all the people inside and the extrajudicial killing of church pastors. Catholic Bishop Macram Gassis has been forced into exile for having testified about the atrocities in the Nuba.

Reports of persecution in areas held by the SPLA are rare but do occur. On one occasion in 1996, six missionaries who complained to the SPLA about forced recruitment of children were detained and the priest beaten by a local SPLA military intelligence officer. More recently a number of chaplains have been appointed to the SPLA.

Apostasy from Islam is punishable by death under Section 126 of the Sudan Criminal Code. Although Turabi has allegedly stated that "if a Muslim wakes up in the morning and says that he doesn't believe any more, that's his business," his views are recognized as unorthodox, and the law still exists. In 1990, a Muslim imam who had converted to Christianity was tried and sentenced to six months in prison and dismissed from work. One of the most publicized recent cases was Ali-Faki Kuku Hassan, a former Muslim sheik who converted in 1995. He was imprisoned for fourteen months before being released following a stroke.

Not only Christians have faced this charge. In 1985, Muslim scholar Mahmoud Mohammed Taha was accused of apostasy and executed. He represented a modernist Islamist group that recognized the *shari'a* as a historical interpretation of the Qur'an and the Sunna, allowing change according to circumstances. Section 126 also refers to those who give up organized religion or profess to be agnostic or atheists. Members of the Communist Party, which has now been banned, have been identified as atheists and a number detained and tortured. The Muslims in the Nuba are perceived as disloyal to the regime and have been targeted on religious grounds by the military.

Despite constitutional guarantees of nondiscrimination, Christians experience marginalization in employment. This has caused many to flee to Egypt and beyond. Non-Muslims are theoretically excluded from high-level government office, the judiciary, and the military, but some do remain in such positions. Many southerners have fled the country because of conscription requirements, which would force them to fight against their own kin. Military training includes Islamic education, regardless of the conscript's religion. Some of those conscripted have been unaccompanied minors in the capital, and non-Muslim boys in other northern cities have been picked up in sweeps by the police, subjected to the regime's version of Islamic indoctrination, and forcibly inducted into the military. Christians face problems receiving social welfare despite the fact that the tax to fund this is levied on all regardless of faith. Severe limitations exist on the time given to Christian programs on radio and TV, and the media frequently scapegoat Christians and Jews in the same breath as the West for many of Sudan's economic, social, and political problems.

Several members of an influential Muslim religious brotherhood, the Ansar sect, were arrested in June 1999, on the eve of an important Muslim festival.

Previous acts of violence against the sect had taken place in 1994 and 1997. In the latter attack, two people were killed and ten wounded when worshipers were attacked as they left a mosque. The Sudan Human Rights Organization has reported that, in April 1998, more than seventy-four children were gunned down by the NIF military as they attempted to leave a conscription camp to spend time with their families on the occasion of the Muslim Eid festival.

Sweden

Population	8.09 million
Evangelical Lutheran	90%
Roman Catholic	1.5%
Pentecostal	1%
Muslim	4%
Other (Orthodox, Protestant, Muslim, Jewish, Mormon, Buddhist)	3.5%
Religious Freedom Rating	2

Background

Sweden is a constitutional monarchy and a multiparty parliamentary democracy. After monarchical alliances with Finland, Denmark, and Norway between the eleventh and nineteenth centuries, it became a modern democracy. Although nonaligned and neutral since World War I, Sweden is now an active member of NATO's Partnership for Peace program and a member of the European Union.

In September 1998 elections, Prime Minister Goran Persson won a second term in office with his Social Democratic party gaining 36.6 percent of the vote, its worst electoral performance ever. Persson formed a coalition with the Left and Green parties, which, unlike the SDP, oppose membership in the European Monetary Union (EMU). All political parties theoretically support a national referendum on EMU, but due to adverse public opinion, no vote has been scheduled.

Swedes can change their government democratically. The 310-member, unicameral *Riksdag* (parliament) is elected every four years through universal suffrage under a proportional method. Nonnationals in residence for three years can vote in local elections. The Saami (Lappic) community elects a local parliament with significant powers over educational and cultural issues and serving as an advisory body to the government. King Carl Gustaf XVI's role is ceremonial. The country's judiciary is independent. Freedom of assembly and association is guaranteed, as are rights to strike and participate in unions. Strong, well-organized trade union federations represent 90 percent of the labor force.

The media are independent, and newspapers and periodicals are privately owned, though publicly subsidized regardless of political affiliation. In recent years new television channels and radio stations have ended the government's monopoly over broadcasting. Citizens can freely express their ideas and criticize their government. The government can prevent publication of information related to national security while a quasigovernmental body censors extremely graphic violence from film, video, and television.

International human-rights groups have criticized Sweden for its strict immigration policies. Nordic immigrants can become citizens after two years, while others must wait for five years. The country does not systematically provide asylum-seekers with adequate legal support. Dozens of violent incidents with anti-immigrant or racist overtones are reported annually.

Although the country's seventeen thousand Saami enjoy some political autonomy, Sweden was the last Nordic country to approve a parliament for its Lappic population. Reports of housing and employment discrimination against Saami continue. In August 1998, the government apologized to the Saami for abuses "carried out against them over the years."

A 1994 law requires working fathers to take at least one month of state-subsidized leave for child care or lose one month's employment benefits. In a UN study of countries' provision of equal rights for women, Sweden received the highest rating. However, in 1997, it was revealed that from 1935 to 1975, sixty-two thousand Swedes, 90 percent of whom were women, were forcibly sterilized. In August 1998, the government announced compensation for the victims. Freedom House's 1998–99 *Freedom in the World* rates Sweden a one in political rights and civil liberties.

Religious Freedom

By 1400, Sweden was united in a nominally Christian kingdom including Finland and Norway. By the 1700s, following the Reformation, Gustav Vasa began a campaign for an independent Sweden, broke with the Roman Catholic Church, and made the Evangelical Lutheran Church the country's established church. Some Swedes have become Mormons, Baptist, and adherents of other faiths. These free churches provide the voter base for the country's mi-

nority Christian Democratic Party, which holds approximately 12 percent of the seats in parliament. In addition to the country's ethnic Swedes and small Finnish and Lappic minorities, there are many smaller, non-Nordic immigrant groups. These latter have introduced Muslim, Buddhist, and other faiths into the country, but they remain largely marginalized socially. About 15–20 percent of the population is atheist, but many have not formally severed their religious ties. Church attendance is low.

Sweden generally provides for freedom of religion in both law and practice, although the Lutheran Church has been established as the state church. Until 1996, citizens were automatically made members of the church at birth. Currently the government officially appoints the bishop and the deans of cathedrals. Under a 1995 agreement between the church and the government, the church was disestablished at the beginning of 2000. At this point the church officially makes its own appointments and decrees. However, the government will still collect a church tax, although nonchurch members will be exempt from all of it (not one-fourth as now). There has been some opposition in the churches to this disestablishment, but the church will still be recognized as a "legal community," which makes it more important than a private association. As in the other Scandinavian countries, one barrier to freedom of religion in Sweden is pressure to conform in this extraordinarily homogeneous society. This, however, is a largely nonquantifiable social impediment rather than a legal restriction.

Citizens are free to worship both publicly and privately, including on nonofficial premises. They may build and maintain official premises without wrongful impediment. They may organize processions and pilgrimages, provided they register for appropriate permits, which are issued on a nondiscriminatory basis. Apart from the state church, they may choose their priests and other leaders and personnel without government interference or discrimination. Religious leaders may perform the rites and customs of their faiths with the texts and music and in the language of their own choosing. They may also preach according to the doctrines of their faiths without threat or interference by the state. Religious leaders of all faiths enjoy access to prisons, hospitals, military installations, and other relevant bodies in order to minister to their congregants.

Apart from the state church, communities of believers may implement their own institutional and hierarchical structures. They may also designate and otherwise assign their officials and train them freely in their own institutes and other bodies. They may own and maintain buildings and other property without impediment. They may also import and otherwise acquire and circulate holy books and other religious publications. They are free to print and circulate their own publications from within Sweden. They also enjoy access to public communication. They are free to establish and maintain relations with individuals and communities of their choosing, both within Sweden and internationally. They may also solicit and receive voluntary individual and institutional financial contributions, both domestically and internationally.

Citizens have access to higher education, employment, the judiciary, military service, and public office without regard to their religious faith. They en-

joy freedoms of expression, movement, emigration, association, assembly, marriage, and access to information without regard to religion. More religiously conservative priests complain, however, that the teaching in state schools, including that in religion classes, consistently undermines their own religious beliefs and morals.

One area of concern is the intrusive character of the Swedish government's social service bureaucracy. For example, Swedish law forbids corporal punishment within families, and social workers have removed children from families for parental action, which would be relatively noncontroversial elsewhere. Religiously conservative parents who have stricter views of parental discipline than the Swedish government have complained of this, and some have had children taken from them.

In 1998, a Swedish government commission on new religious movements released its report. The report, and the government itself, is more tolerant than countries such as France and Belgium, but the report still has more troubling features. It speaks of the danger of movements that "might circumscribe democratic liberties within their own ranks," though, of course, most private associations and the state church are not internal democracies. It speaks of "manipulation exceeding the bounds of free will" (both by movements and deprogrammers), and advocates setting up a "Center for the Study of Questions of Belief" ("KULT" in Swedish). The commission proposed that improper influence or "manipulation" be made a punishable offense under the penal code.

Taiwan

Population	22 million
"Chinese Religion"	
(Buddhist, Taoist, Confucian)	80%
Christianity	4%
Muslim	0.2%
Atheist	14%
Other	1.8%
Religious Freedom Rating	2

Background

Following fifty years of Japanese occupation, Taiwan returned to Chinese rule after the end of World War II. With the Communist victory over the Nationalists (KMT) on the mainland in 1949, Chiang Kai-shek reestablished the KMT's Republic of China government in Taiwan. Both Beijing and Taipei officially consider Taiwan to be a province of China, although Taipei has abandoned its long-standing claim to be the legitimate government of mainland China. Native Taiwanese make up 85 percent of the population, while mainlanders or their descendants are a minority.

After four decades of authoritarian KMT rule, Taiwan's democratic transition began with the lifting of martial law in 1987. Lee Teng-hui became the first native Taiwanese president in 1988. Since then, he has asserted native Taiwanese control of the KMT, marginalized its mainlander faction, and deemphasized the party's commitment to eventual reunification with China. On March 23, 1996, Lee won the first direct presidential election, with 54 percent of the vote. Days earlier, China had held missile tests near the island to underscore its long-standing threat to invade if Taiwan declared independence.

In the 1998 national legislative elections for an expanded 225-seat parliament, a race that was largely overshadowed by the closely followed mayoral elections, the KMT won a working majority of 123 seats, followed by the DPP with 70 seats. There were few substantive issues in the campaigns, which focused largely on personal character. Both the KMT and DPP avoided the sensitive topic of Taiwan's relations with mainland China; public opinion polls have indicated that the majority of Taiwanese oppose a formal declaration of independence, a fact widely believed to have contributed to the DPP's electoral defeats.

At a historic meeting in October 1998, Koo Chen-fu, an influential member of the KMT, met with Chinese president Jiang Zemin in Beijing, representing the highest level contact in almost fifty years. They agreed to reopen formal negotiations stalled since 1995. China has called for reunification under a "one country, two system" policy, while Taiwan insists that union would be possible only when China adopts multiparty democracy.

Taiwanese can change their government democratically, a process that was consolidated with the March 1996 presidential election. The constitution vests executive power in a president who appoints the premier without parliamentary confirmation and can dissolve the legislature. The National Assembly can amend the constitution and, until 1994, elected the president and vice president. The ruling KMT maintains political advantages through its influence over much of the broadcast media and its considerable business interests in Taiwan's industrial economy. Nevertheless, opposition parties contest elections freely, and the 1998 elections were generally regarded to have been free and fair.

Taiwan enjoys one of the most free media environments in Asia, despite some continuing legal restrictions and political pressures. Taiwanese law prohibits advocacy of formal independence from China or of communism and allows police to censor or ban publications considered seditious or treasonous. These provisions, however, are not enforced in practice.

In January 1998, provisions of the Parade and Assembly Law prohibiting demonstrations that promote communism or advocate Taiwan's separation from mainland China were ruled unconstitutional. Authorities have refused to register some nongovernmental organizations with the word *Taiwan* in their titles, although such groups operate freely. Despite constitutional protections on the formation of trade unions, a number of regulations restrict the right of association in practice.

The judiciary, which is not fully independent, is susceptible to corruption and political influence from the ruling KMT. There were a number of indictments of judges during 1998 for accepting bribes in exchange for favorable judgments. Police continue to abuse suspects, conduct personal identity and vehicle checks with widespread discretion, and obtain evidence illegally with few ramifications. Prisons are overcrowded, and conditions are harsh in detention camps for illegal immigrants. Taiwan considerably relaxed restrictions against travel by Taiwanese to the Chinese mainland in 1998, though many limits on the entry of Chinese from the mainland remain in force, ostensibly for security reasons. The country's 357,000 aboriginal descendants of Malayo-Polynesians suffer from social and economic alienation. Freedom House's 1998–99 *Freedom in the World* rates Taiwan a two in civil liberties and in political rights.

Religious Freedom

Large-scale mainland Chinese immigration to the island began with set-tlers from Fujian and Kuangtung Provinces at the end of the Ming Dynasty (1368–1644). The mainlanders brought both Buddhism and Taoism, which today are Taiwan's predominant religions. The island then came under mainland control after a period of Dutch rule from 1620 to 1662. Since the Republic of China's founding on the mainland in 1912, its leaders have promoted economic and cultural modernization. In religion, authorities favored "rationality" over "superstition." In practice, they sanctioned only organized, text-based religions, and condemned "popular" religions as superstition. As the government strengthened civil liberties protections in the 1980s, it largely ended its attempts to influence religious practices.

Taiwan's 1947 constitution guarantees freedom of religion and bars discrimination on the basis of religion. Article 7 states that "all citizens of the Republic of China, irrespective of sex, religion, ethnic origin, class, or party affiliation, shall be equal before the law." Article 13 states, "The people shall have freedom of religious belief." In practice, freedom of religion is respected. The government formally recognizes thirteen religions: Buddhism, Taoism, Catholicism, Protestantism, Sunni Islam, Hsuan-Yuan Chiao, Idam, Li-ism, Tenrikyo, Baha'i, Tien Dih Chiao, T'ien Te Chiao, and I-Kuan-Tao. There are no legal restrictions on religious practice.

Individuals have the right to freedom of religion and belief if they respect public order and morality. There is freedom to propagate one's faith, freedom of worship, and to train and appoint clergy. Religious bodies have rights of self-government, of religious education, to carry out charitable activities, to own and acquire property, and to maintain social institutions. They can produce, import, and distribute literature; receive donations; and have contact with co-religionists, domestically and overseas. Individuals can adopt, change, or leave a religion freely, without change of civil status. However, religious instruction in schools is forbidden, whether the schools are public or private. Religious studies are only allowed at the university level.

As in much of Asia, many people incorporate elements of several faiths into their religious practices, and do not consider themselves to be exclusive adherents of Buddhism, Taoism, or any other religion. Folk deities are often worshiped along with Buddhist spirits. In the 1980s, the changes brought on by rapid economic development, combined with an easing of civil liberties restrictions, contributed to the growth of popular religions, which had earlier been discouraged by the authorities. The worship of unconventional spirits, such as those of bandits and unknown corpses, often displaced worship of more traditional, community-based deities. Scholars noted that this occurred at a time when the small enterprises that spurred Taiwan's development were threatened by rising labor costs and modernization. Ordinary Chinese increasingly viewed profit as being less about hard work and sacrifice and more about luck, greed, and connections. The new deities captured this cynicism.

Taiwan's 357,000-strong Aboriginal population represents less than 2 percent of the population. The Aborigines are descendants of Malayo-Polynesians already living in Taiwan when the first Chinese settlers arrived. More than 70 percent are considered Christian, though they also practice many animistic beliefs. In 1992 and 1997, the National Assembly amended the constitution to protect Aboriginal rights and culture and improve their educational and economic opportunities. Aborigines face no official discrimination, but in general they live on the margins of Taiwanese society, face informal social and economic discrimination, and have little political influence over issues involving ancestral land rights and cultural preservation.

In June 1999, the government said it would defer the draft for citizens who cite religious reasons for refusing to perform military service. It also favored an alternative civilian service to be instituted in 2000. Currently the constitution (Article 200) states that people shall have the duty to render military service in accordance with the law. The group who would be most affected by these changes is Jehovah's Witnesses, many of whom have been jailed for refusing to serve. One Witness, Chong-Shien Wu, has served more than ten years in prison for his refusal. In October 1999, the Supreme Court ruled against his claim for conscientious exemption, with only two judges out of fifteen dissenting.

Population	31.3 million
Christian	45%
Muslim	19%
Baha'i	0.4%
Hindu	0.1%
Other	35.5%
Religious Freedom Rating	4

Background

After the country gained independence from Britain in 1961, the Party for the Revolution (CCM) dominated Tanzania's politics under President Julius Nyerere's authoritarian rule. The Zanzibar and Pemba Islands were merged with then-Tanganyika to become the Union of Tanzania, after Arab sultans were deposed in a bloody 1964 revolution. The union agreement gave the islanders, who now number more than seven hundred thousand and are 90 percent Muslim, limited autonomy. The mainland's population is mostly Christian and animist. Nyerere retained strong influence after he officially retired in 1985. Opposition parties were legalized in 1992, but the CCM continues to dominate the country's political life.

While marred by administrative chaos and irregularities, legislative and presidential elections in 1995 were the freest on mainland Tanzania since independence. The voting in Zanzibar was plainly fraudulent, but the island's High Court summarily rejected opposition demands for fresh polls. Extensive use of state broadcasting and other government resources during the campaign favored the ruling party.

Tanzania's judiciary has displayed signs of autonomy after decades of subservience to the one-party CCM regime but remains subject to considerable political influence. Laws allow rallies only by officially registered political parties, which may not be formed on religious, ethnic, or regional bases. Arrest and pretrial detention laws are often ignored. Prison conditions are harsh, and police abuses are said to be common. Many nongovernmental organizations are active, but some human rights groups have experienced difficulties.

Media freedom has expanded markedly since 1992, but instances of repression continue, especially in Zanzibar. Some private radio and television stations operate on the mainland, but state broadcasting remains predominant. Women's rights are guaranteed by the constitution and, like other laws, are not seriously protected. Workers do not have the right to organize and join trade unions freely. Essential workers are barred from striking. Approximately 85 percent of Tanzania's people survive through subsistence agriculture. Economic decline in Zanzibar continues to dim the entire country's prospects. Freedom House's 1998–99 *Freedom in the World* rates Tanzania as a five in political rights and a four in civil liberties, the latter a rise from five due to a slight relaxation in political controls.

Religious Freedom

Tanzania presents a mix of religious practices that reflects both its indigenous traditions and belief systems that arrived with traders, colonizers, and missionaries. Tanzania is inhabited principally by Bantu people whose indigenous beliefs include a range of ancestor worship and animist practices. Islam arrived mostly with traders who sought ivory and slaves from the interior and, as early as the twelfth century, colonized the Indian Ocean littoral and offshore islands, where Islam remains strongest today.

Christianity arrived with missionaries in the mid-nineteenth century. Among them was Dr. David Livingstone, arguably the best-known missionary of the modern era, who, while not lost, was famously "found" by adventurer Henry Morton Stanley on the shores of Lake Tanganyika and later buried by its shores. Early Christian missions were in part inspired by Livingstone's calls to end slavery in Central Africa by introducing commerce and a viable local economy as well as Christian teachings. Church activity expanded greatly at the end of the nineteenth century after Germany seized Tanganyika as part of "German East Africa." At the outset of World War I, British imperial forces invaded the area from their neighboring colony of Kenya and, after the German defeat in Europe, it became a British possession. Missionary activity increased, and both Catholic and various Protestant missions set up schools, hospitals, and, of course, churches. Tanzania gained independence in 1963, and both Christian and Protestant missionaries are still active in the country.

The federated isles of Zanzibar and Pemba are almost entirely Muslim, and conservative Muslim groups are increasingly active. There the Catholic Church has been invited to serve as a mediator between political factions.

Tanzania is officially a secular state. Its constitution protects freedom of worship, and this was respected even during the long period of one-party socialist rule under former president Julius Nyerere, who is also a devout Catholic. The constitution also contains provision barring the insult or ridicule of any religion. While there are no reports of any government policy restricting religious freedom, there are many complaints about the conduct of individual government officials. Religious groups may operate schools and charities, and believers may travel overseas for pilgrimages or other religious purposes. They may also run their internal affairs and import, produce, and distribute literature, and there is freedom to proselytize and change one's religion. Schools are required to provide religious education.

On the mainland, religious tensions have risen over the past few years as some Muslim groups have grown increasingly militant over what they deem discrimination against the country's Muslims. While this may be a social reality, there is no constitutional, legal, or apparent policy basis. After riots by members of an Islamic group, Khidmat Daawat Islamia, rocked the capital, Dar es Salaam, in February and March 1998, the government briefly arrested two hundred Muslims, some of whom complained of torture. The government has also warned against "slanderous preaching." Christian groups have complained that the laws are being used to stop them from doing ordinary preaching. Charges against several religious leaders were dropped as part of a plan to defuse religious strife. These prohibitions appear to have been enforced genuinely to prevent incitement and unrest and not to restrict religious practice per se. However, the government has demanded that at least twenty-two religious groups suspected of involvement with incitement to religious hatred explain why their associations should not be deregistered and effectively banned.

As in many other countries, traditional beliefs have often been adapted or incorporated into religions introduced later. This is especially prevalent in independent Christian churches not accountable to external hierarchies. Many traditional spiritual and magical practices also remain current, including divination and healing ceremonies. Others are related to witchcraft and sorcery, and accusations of harmful sorcery often lead to assaults and lynchings. Police say that 357 suspected witches were killed from January 1998 to July 1999. The Ministry of Home Affairs believes that up to five thousand were killed between 1994 and 1998.

The ethnic and historical connection between Muslims of coastal Tanzania, and especially Zanzibar and Pemba, and various Islamic groups of the Persian Gulf region continues, for good and evil. The August 1998 bombing of the United States Embassy in the capital, Dar es Salaam, has been blamed on Islamist extremists financed by the wealthy Saudi radical Osama bin-Laden. However, other foreign Islamic groups have focused on funding charities, hospitals, and religious training.

A small South Asian population is made up mostly of Muslims but also includes some Hindus, who are allowed to practice their religion freely. South Asians have been the occasional targets of political scapegoating and physical attacks but largely on an ethnic and economic basis rather than for explicitly religious reasons.

Turkey

Population	**64 million**
Sunni Muslim	**79%**
Alawi Shi'ite Muslim	**20%**
Christian	**0.2%**
Jewish (25,000)	**0.04%**
Armenian Orthodox	**0.09%**
Syrian Orthodox	**0.02%**
Other	**0.83%**
Religious Freedom Rating	**5**

Background

Mustapha Kemal Ataturk, who launched a reform program under which Turkey abandoned much of its Ottoman and Islamic heritage, proclaimed Turkey a republic in 1923. His secular, nationalistic legacy has profoundly influenced Turkish politics through most of this century, and the doctrine of "Kemalism" has been used by the military to justify three coups since 1960.

In 1995, the Islamic Refah Welfare party took advantage of discontent over corruption, high inflation, and unemployment to win 158 parliamentary seats in December elections, and its leader, Erbakan, almost immediately found himself at odds with the military-led National Security Council (NSC), which considers itself the guardian of Turkish secularism. Under intense pressure, Erbakan resigned on June 18, 1997. Misut Yilmaz was appointed prime minister two days later and assembled a ruling coalition. The constitutional court closed Refah in January 1998 for "conspiring against the secular order," and prosecutors began legal action against twelve Refah politicians.

The fourteen-year-old conflict in southeastern Turkey between the army and the Marxist Kurdistan Workers' Party (PKK) continued in 1998, often crossing over into Iraq. As the Turkish army has gained ground, the PKK has softened its rhetoric, calling for a measure of autonomy within Turkey rather than a separate state. In October, Syria expelled PKK leader Abdullah Ocalan who was subsequently captured by Turkey, put on trial, and sentenced to death on June 29, 1999. Turkey's thirty-four-year-old efforts to join the EU suffered a setback in late 1997 when the country was omitted from a short list of EU applicants.

Turkish citizens can change their government democratically, though the military wields considerable influence in political matters. The 1982 constitution provides for a Grand National Assembly that is directly elected to a five-year term. The Assembly elects the president, whose role is largely ceremonial, to a seven-year term. Along with the Refah Party, which was banned in January, the Kurdish People's Democracy Party (HADEP) suffered severe harassment at the hands of security forces in 1998.

Turkey's bleak human rights record is largely related to the PKK insurgency. Kurds, who make up some 20 percent of the population, are not recognized as a national, racial, or ethnic minority. Security forces carry out extrajudicial killings of suspected PKK terrorists and are believed to be responsible for dozens of unsolved killings and disappearances of journalists and others. Under emergency law in the southeastern provinces, the army has forcibly depopulated more than half the five thousand villages and hamlets in the region, in many cases killing and torturing villagers. The PKK and smaller Kurdish groups also commit extrajudicial killings and kidnappings.

Although the judiciary is nominally independent, the constitutional court is seen as an arm of the military. In the eighteen state security courts (SSCs), which try terrorist offenses, procedural safeguards are inadequate, and the right to appeal is limited. Prison conditions are abysmal, characterized by widespread torture, sexual abuse, and denial of medical attention to inmates. Freedom of expression in Turkey is limited by the Criminal Code, which forbids insulting state officials and incitement to racial or ethnic hatred. The Anti-Terror Law (ATL) assigns penalties for the dissemination of separatist propaganda. Writers and journalists are routinely jailed under the ATL and publications suppressed.

Authorities may restrict freedom of association and assembly on the grounds of maintaining public order. Human rights activists suffered severe harassment in 1998. Women face discrimination in family matters such as inheritance and marital rights and obligations. Laws and social norms make it difficult to prosecute rape cases. Workers, except members of security forces, may join independent trade unions. The right to strike is restricted to exclude workers engaged in the protection of life and property and those in the mining and petroleum industries, sanitation services, national defense, and education. Freedom House's 1998–99 *Freedom in the World* rates Turkey a four in political rights and a five in civil liberties.

Religious Freedom

Turkey's modern mosaic of religious and ethnic backgrounds is drawn from the historic Byzantine and Ottoman Empires that flourished within its borders in previous centuries. Due to the determination of Kemal Ataturk to forge a Turkish nation out of the fragmentation of World War I, the founder of modern Turkey started a pattern of forced assimilation of minority groups— such as the Kurds, Armenians, and other ethnic and religious heritages—into a homogenous citizenry of Turks. The miniscule Christian and Jewish minorities remain ethno-religious communities, much as they did under the Ottoman Empire's system of classification into separate "millets" or communities.

Since its founding as a secular republic seventy-five years ago, Turkey has espoused the principle of separation of religion and the state. Article 24 of the constitution strictly forbids the state to be established on religious principles. However, this form of secularism cannot be considered as religious neutrality. Rather, the state exercises careful control over all religious activity and actively discriminates in favor of what it describes as secular views.

For the country's 99 percent Muslim majority, this translates into state-controlled religion. The Religious Affairs Directorate, which is a central government agency under the Prime Ministry, supervises all activities and personnel of the Islamic religious establishment. The Muslim hierarchy of imams (prayer leaders) and hatips (preachers) are appointed and paid by the state, which also funds and administers the maintenance and construction of mosques. In August 1998, representatives of both the Ministry of Tourism and the military-dominated National Security Council were added to the Council of Religion convened by the Religious Affairs Directorate.

The constitution guarantees freedom of belief, freedom of worship, and the private dissemination of religious ideas to all citizens. However, laws restrict religious services only to designated places of worship. The right to disseminate religious propaganda without political motivation is guaranteed by Article 26 of the constitution. No law classifies purely religious propaganda as illegal, but random distribution of non-Muslim literature often results in the temporary detention of those involved, followed by the extralegal deportation of any foreigners without residence permits. Proselytism is not outlawed per se, although both activist Muslims and evangelical Christians continue to be jailed for publicly sharing their faith, on the pretext of disturbing the peace.

As an offshoot of Shi'ite Islam, the Alawite Muslim minority claims that the Sunni-dominated Religious Affairs Directorate discriminates against them by ignoring their doctrines in compulsory religion classes and classifying them as a cultural rather than religious group. Although Alawites represent at least 20 percent of the population, they have no government-salaried religious leaders. Serious outbreaks of sectarian violence continued to occur between the Alawi and Sunni factions throughout the 1990s.

Islam has become a growing political factor in the past decade, causing a growing discomfort in the state's relationship to religion. The country's first experiment with an elected Islamist-led government collapsed in June 1997, when the powerful Turkish military managed a "soft coup," forcing the resignation of the Islamist Welfare Party. Later outlawed by the Constitutional Court for illegal antisecular activity, the conservative group has been replaced by the Virtue Party, now the largest opposition bloc in Parliament. A new coalition government promptly endorsed the military's ultimatum to restrict Islamist education by requiring eight years of continuous education in state schools. Hundreds of private Muslim "imamhatip" schools, started by conservative Muslim groups, were forced by the Parliament ruling to close their middle-school grades. This new measure relegates this private Quranic teaching to weekend and summer-vacation classes.

Warning that religion was being used for political purposes, the government has set controls over Friday mosque sermons and has begun monitoring private radio and television stations to prevent "misuse of religion" to incite religious hatred or harm national integrity. Women wearing religious head scarves continue to be banned from studying on university campuses, as well as working as teachers, lawyers, civil servants, or medical professionals in some institutions. Some observers estimate that the number of women barred from university study because of headscarves is almost thirty thousand.

This banning of head scarves culminated in April 1999 when Merve Kavakci, newly elected to Parliament, was refused seating in the assembly because she wore a head scarf. Unable to find a legal reason to deny her permission to take the parliamentary oath of office, the authorities are seeking to strip her of Turkish citizenship on the grounds that she did not advise them when she took out U.S. citizenship, even though this is perfectly legal, even encouraged. In a controversial court ruling during 1998, Istanbul's popular mayor Tayyip Erdogan was sentenced to ten months in prison and banned from politics for "opposing the secular order of Turkey" because of a speech he gave in which he quoted lines from a Muslim nationalist poet. Vigorous protests against these religious restrictions have become a weekly occurrence outside Turkish mosques after Friday prayers by conservative Muslims. These are frequently brutally suppressed by riot police. Muslim leaders insist Turkey's democratization process must respect the recent grassroots revival of a traditional Islamic mindset among its people, who until this generation were only nominally religious.

Mystical Islamic orders known as "tarikats" were legally banned at the outset of the republic, although nominally tolerated by subsequent governments. After surfacing publicly during the late 1980s, they have been strictly opposed since early 1997 as part of the Turkish military's campaign against Islamist fundamentalism. Dervish practices have also been banned except for token public performances. Members of the Aczimendi Brotherhood have been arrested and prosecuted for publicly opposing the secular state. In 1999, authorities also began an investigation into Fethullah Gulen, leader of the Islamic Nurcu (light) group, and one of the most popular religious leaders in the country. The armed forces have dismissed more than 150 military officers for alleged misconduct in religious activities. The Justice Ministry began an investigation in October 1998 of forty prosecutors and judges accused of involvement in Islamist sects.

Religious instruction in public schools was made compulsory for Muslims in 1982. The law was amended in 1990 to allow members of religious minorities named in the Lausanne Treaty of 1923 (Armenian, Jewish, and Greek) to exempt their children from this Muslim instruction. Syrian Orthodox Christians were not exempted because they were not named in the Lausanne accord. The non-Muslim minorities, totaling some seventy-five thousand ethnic Christians and twenty-five thousand Jews, are mostly concentrated in Istanbul. The affairs of these Turkish citizens of Armenian, Greek, and Jewish descent are routed through the Aliens' Department of the Foreign Ministry, implying that the ethno-religious minority communities are politically suspected of giving their allegiances to Armenia, Greece, and Israel more than to their native Turkey. On this basis, government bureaucracies routinely interfere in internal church affairs. During 1998, the election of a new Armenian Patriarch was stalemated for five months, and members of the board of trustees of the Greek Orthodox seminary were summarily dismissed. Both actions contradicted

Lausanne Treaty obligations and were retracted after international pressure.

The centuries-old Syrian Orthodox community in Southeast Turkey's war zone has dwindled to less than two thousand, their exodus accelerated by the fourteen-year conflict between Kurdish separatists and the Turkish military. Some forty-five unsolved murders of Syrian Christians in the region since 1984 have further intimidated their community. In 1997 and 1998, the Mardin Governor's Office wrote to the Tur Abdin Monastery of Mor Gabriel, warning the resident bishop and his monks to stop religious instruction and classes in the Syriac language, and to stop housing visitors This, the oldest monastery in the world, is the one in which the Christian community has since the fourth century preserved the language closest to the Aramaic dialect spoken by Christ.

All of Turkey's religious minorities are steadily diminishing in numbers, making it difficult to operate their religious schools, foundations, and institutions; maintain their churches, synagogues, and cemeteries; and use their own languages. Religious property that falls into disuse legally reverts to government possession, leaving some minority communities in danger of losing some of their houses of worship. Since the trusts of the Armenian Orthodox Church are legally classified as "foreign," they are also reverting to the government. The trusts, as well as Armenian schools, are also required to pay taxes. Since the Ministry of Education typically declines to name qualified minority principals for these religious schools, as required by the Lausanne Treaty, they are often run by state-appointed Muslim vice principals.

All religious personnel are required to have Turkish citizenship and formal theological training licensed by the state. Since the historic seminaries of the Armenian and Greek Orthodox Churches have been closed by government order since 1974, these communities must send clergy abroad to meet this requirement. The Ecumenical Patriarch, the highest official in Eastern Orthodoxy, continues to push for the reopening of its Halki Seminary.

In July 1999, fifteen Americans were deported for distributing Christian literature in Izmir. In September, in the same town, Turkish police, accompanied by reporters, invaded a Protestant church service and arrested forty people, claiming that it was an "illegal" church. The local public prosecutor dismissed the charges and ordered the prisoners released. The police released them but kept the church sealed. In October security police in Istanbul raided a Protestant service and arrested most of the adult members of the congregation of sixty, claiming that it was illegal.

Periodic acts of violence or vandalism against non-Muslim institutions continue to wear on the minorities' sense of security. During 1998, the murder of an elderly Greek Orthodox sexton and a bombing attack against the Ecumenical Patriarchate in Istanbul remained unsolved. However, the courts handed down stiff sentences in 1998 against Muslim extremists who bombed an evangelical Christian bookstand at the Gaziantep fair the previous year, killing a young child.

Despite societal pressures and occasional media attacks, Turkish Muslims who convert to another religion can legally change their religious affiliation, recorded at birth on their personal identity cards. Under legal precedents set in the early 1980s, some fifteen small congregations of Christian converts and a network of Jehovah's Witness groups have rented or purchased designated "houses of prayer" for their worship services in various cities. Although their meetings are duly registered with local authorities, they have not been allowed to establish an official legal identity as yet.

A Christian radio station has been licensed to broadcast from Istanbul, and, in 1998, authorities for the first time granted permission for the opening of a new church for expatriate Christians in Ankara. The only minority representative elected to the Turkish Parliament is from the Jewish community. Jehovah's Witnesses continue to face jailing and extended harassment for their refusal on religious grounds to bear arms while fulfilling their obligatory military service.

Turkmenistan

Population	**4.8 million**
Muslim (largely Sunni)	**89%**
Eastern Orthodox	**9%**
Unknown/Other (Catholic, Protestant, Baha'i, Jehovah's Witness, Hare Krishna)	**2%**
Religious Freedom Rating	**7**

Background

Turkmenistan, the former Soviet Central Asian republic bordering Kazakhstan, Afghanistan, Iran, and the Caspian Sea, has been occupied by Turkic tribes since the tenth century and was ruled by various local leaders until the thirteenth century, when the Mongols conquered it. In 1881, Tsarist Russia seized the country. The Turkmen Soviet Socialist Republic was declared in 1924, after the Bolsheviks ousted the Khan of Merv.

Turkmenistan declared independence after a national referendum in October 1991; current president Saparmurad Niyazov then won a one-man election in December. In 1992, after the adoption of a new constitution, Niyazov was reelected, claiming 99.5 percent of the vote. The main opposition group, Agzybirlik, formed in 1989 by leading intellectuals, was banned and its leaders harassed. Niyazov is also president of the People's Council. In December 1994 parliamentary elections, only Niyazov's Democratic Party of Turkmenistan (DPT) was permitted to field candidates.

The president has extensive powers and issues edicts that have the force of law, appoints and removes all judges, and names the state prosecutor. He is also prime minister and commander in chief. Parliament has extended his term to the year 2002. He is developing a cult of personality like Lenin's.

Turkmenistan is an important possible location for the transport of oil and gas from the Caspian region and, in October 1998, it signed two oil transportation deals with several countries, including Russia and the U.S. Despite Turkmenistan's vast resources, there has been no reform of the Soviet command system, and the majority of citizens live in dire poverty. In December 1998, the National Bank suspended free currency conversion.

Citizens of Turkmenistan do not have the means to change their government democratically. Power remains concentrated in the hands of the president. The one-party elections to a rubber-stamp parliament in 1994 were undemocratic. While the constitution provides for freedom of the press and expression, the government controls and funds all electronic and print media, prohibits the media from reporting the views of opposition political leaders, and rarely allows the mildest criticism of the government. Only two newspapers, *Adalat* and *Galkynysh,* are nominally independent. The constitution allows for peaceful assembly and association, but the government restricts these rights. In 1995, authorities broke up the first peaceful demonstration in years, convicting twenty people.

The DPT is the only legal party. Opposition parties have been banned; government-controlled bodies substitute for nongovernmental organizations (NGOs). The central trade union, the Trade Union Federation of Turkmenistan, is the successor to the Soviet-era body, and there are no legal guarantees entitling workers to form or join unions. The judiciary is subservient to the regime; the president appoints all judges for a term of five years without legislative review. In April 1998, prior to Niyazov's visit to the United States, several opposition figures were released, including Durdymurat Khojamukhammed, coleader of the banned Democratic Progress Party, who had been confined in a mental hospital since 1995. Corruption is pervasive. Niyazov complains publicly about corrupt officials, but no major prosecutions occur. Citizens are required to carry internal passports, and, while residence permits are not required, place of residence is registered and noted in passports.

A Soviet-style command economy diminishes equality of opportunity and leaves citizens dependent on bureaucrats, state managers, and the government for a livelihood. Women face discrimination in education, business, and government, and social-religious norms restrict women's freedom. Freedom House's 1998–99 *Freedom in the World* rates Turkmenistan a seven in both political rights and civil liberties, its lowest possible rating.

Religious Freedom

The Turkmenistan Constitution of 1992 makes large, paper guarantees of religious freedom: Article 11 requires the state to "guarantee freedom of religions and confessions and their equality before the law. Religious organizations are to be separate from the state and may not fulfill state functions. The state educational system shall be separate from religious organizations and shall be of a secular nature." The Article further guarantees that "[e]veryone shall have the right independently to define his attitude towards religion, to profess any religion or not to profess any either individually or jointly with others, to profess and disseminate beliefs associated with his attitude to religion, and to participate in the practice of religious cults, rituals, and rites."

Article 27 grants citizens "the right to freedom of assembly, meetings, and demonstrations in the manner established by legislation." Article 17 states that "Turkmenistan shall guarantee the equality of the rights and freedoms of citizens, as well as the equality of citizens before the law irrespective of nationality, origin, property status or official position, place of residence, language, *attitude towards religion,* political beliefs, or party membership." However these guarantees are undercut by Article 19, which grants the state broad power to decide how far it will go to protect constitutionally established rights and freedoms. It states that "[t]he exercise of rights and freedoms must not violate the rights and freedoms of other persons or the requirements or morality or social order or cause damage to national security." In practice, Turkmenistan is perhaps the most repressive of the former Soviet republics in terms of religious freedom or any other human right.

The "Law on the Freedom of Conscience and Religious Organizations," amended in 1995 and again in 1996, provides for significant government control of religion. Religious congregations are required to register with the state. They must have at least five hundred members sign a registration application to be legally registered (formerly only ten members were required). Reports indicate that unregistered groups, including Baha'is, Baptists, Adventists, Jehovah's Witnesses, and Pentecostal Christians, have been harassed for holding unregistered religious gatherings. The five hundred-member restriction has caused a pattern of registration problems for most minority religious groups, which tend to be very small.

However, even those groups meeting the five hundred-member threshold have been denied registration. The government denies registration in several ways: (1) by refusing to accept registration forms because of grammatical/technical mistakes; (2) by intimidating the religious group's members who sign the registration forms, which causes many members to remove their names from the registration form; (3) by requiring that all members of the religious group submit their passports for verification, which is untenable because passports are needed in order to collect salaries; and (4) by requiring that a religious group have five hundred members in the city in which it wants to register (so that while a given religious group has more than five hundred members in the

country, the government now requires that it have five hundred members in each city in which it hopes to register). Only Orthodox Christians and Sunni Muslims have been granted registration since 1997. About 15 percent or so of the Orthodox are of Armenian descent, and they have applied for the return of their church, which was confiscated in the Soviet era.

The law also contains vague provisions strictly punishing religious groups that issue propaganda that might threaten the state or stir up religious tensions. For example, there have been recent reports that Seventh-Day Adventists are facing harassment, intimidation, and denial of their rights to religious worship, and other minority religious groups have reported similar problems. On March 25, 1998, an Adventist pastor and his fellow church worker were detained by secret police, and religious materials were confiscated. Their money was also confiscated as a fine for practicing their religion without being properly registered. In the town of Bezmein, Adventist members were warned not to have any further meetings until they are officially registered. In November 1999, officers of the National Security Committee bulldozed an Adventist church in Ashgabad (the only one in Turkmenistan).

The major religious groups, Islam and Eastern Orthodoxy, suffer fewer problems as long as they do not criticize the government. There has been a modest revival of Islam in the past few years. The government is also watchful in preventing the rise of "Islamic Fundamentalism." The government has incorporated some aspects of Muslim tradition into its efforts to define a Turkmen identity and gives some financial support to the Council on Religious Affairs, an organization intended to be an intermediary between the government bureaucracy and religious organizations.

One formidable obstacle facing those seeking democratic reform and enforcement of civil liberties in Turkmenistan is the government Committee on National Security (KNB). The KNB carries out responsibilities formerly held by the Soviet KGB (i.e., to ensure that the current regime remains in power and to discourage dissent). The Ministry of Internal Affairs directs the criminal police, which work closely with the KNB on matters of national security. Both operate without any real accountability and have been responsible for abusing the rights of individuals as well as enforcing the government's policy of repressing opposition. Their efforts have been directed at individuals and groups who attempt to exercise their right of religious freedom. Government officials routinely break up religious meetings in private residences. Members of religious groups are often taken into custody and fined for holding illegal meetings. Incidents of such government intimidation are numerous.

For example, a member of an Ashgabad religious group reports that on several occasions law enforcement officials raided the Baptist church where the group conducted meetings, confiscated religious material, and warned church authorities against permitting unregistered religious groups from meeting in its facilities. Throughout the summer of 1999, there have been several reports of raids and seizures of religious materials at Protestant churches throughout the country. In addition, churches belonging to the Union of Churches of Evangelical Christian Baptists have reported that literature from their libraries was confiscated and never returned. Members of the same church have also been arrested, taken to jail, and beaten. In May 1999, one hundred Christians were called for questioning by authorities. The Baptist congregation in Dashkhovuz was fined in March 1999 for holding unregistered religious meetings. In September 1999, a Baptist congregation in Turkmenabad was told to stop meeting and not to read the Bible or Christian literature.

While there is no law expressly forbidding religious proselytizing, such efforts, especially when done by minority religions, are subject to regulation and outright government displeasure. The government must grant permission for mass meetings that are for evangelization purposes. There have been several reports of harassment and confiscation of materials from missionaries who were attempting to promote their religion. People interrogated in June 1998 by the chairman of the Council for Religious Affairs, who is also the chief mufti (Islamic religious leader) of Turkmenistan, said he told them that New Testaments in the Turkmen language were illegal. Hare Krishnas arriving from Uzbekistan have also had their religious material confiscated. However, Islamic religious literature is distributed through the mosques, and Orthodox churches are able to offer and distribute a variety of Christian literature.

Ukraine

Population	**51 million**
Orthodox (various jurisdictions)	**55%**
Catholic (mainly Greek-Catholic)	**15%**
Protestant	**3.2%**
Jewish	**1%**
Muslim	**0.5%**
Agnostic/Atheist/Other	**25.3%**
Religious Freedom Rating	**3**

Background

Ukraine is, after Russia, the largest new state of Europe created in the wake of the disintegration of the Soviet Union in 1991. Its borders changed dramatically as a result of continuing political instability in Eastern Europe in the twentieth century. The central and eastern part of the country enjoyed three years of independence (1917–20), then became extensively sovietized under Stalin. Artificial famine was used as a political instrument to subject Kiev to Moscow in the 1930s. In 1940, Western Ukraine, with its extensive Uniate (Greek-Catholic) population, was annexed by the USSR from Poland, having been part of the Austro-Hungarian Empire up to 1917. After the German occupation, the Red Army reincorporated it into the Soviet Union, but here Ukrainian nationalism was persistent, and the language survived. Ukraine voted for independence before the collapse of the Soviet Union and achieved this at the end of 1991, when Leonid Kravchuk was elected president.

In the 1994 presidential race, Kravchuk lost to Leonid Kuchma, an industrialist and former prime minister, in a runoff. The Communist Party and its allies dominated the parliamentary elections but did not win a majority. In early 1996, Kuchma pushed a reluctant parliament into adopting a new constitution. In July 1997, Prime Minister Lazarenko, who had replaced Yevhen Marchuk a year before, resigned amid stalled economic reforms and persistent allegations of cronyism and corruption. The run-up to the March 1998 elections saw a series of charges and countercharges concerning corruption, closure of opposition newspapers, and violence, particularly in Odessa, long a hotbed of corruption and criminal activity. The Communist Party won the most seats. Political wrangling led to deadlock in choosing a parliamentary speaker, a key obstacle to IMF funding. As the crisis intensified, President Kuchma threatened to dissolve parliament and rule by decree. On July 8, after twenty attempts, parliament elected Oleksander Tkachenko from the leftist Socialist-Peasant Bloc, as speaker. On December 15, President Kuchma said he might call a referendum to extend his right to issue economic decrees for five more years. On November 1999, Kuchma was reelected in a run-off election with 59.3 percent of the vote.

Ukrainian foreign minister Borys Tarasiuk discussed ratification by the Russian parliament of a broad treaty signed by Presidents Kuchma and Yeltsin in May 1997. Ukraine's parliament ratified the treaty in early 1998. Ukrainian-Russian tensions continued over Crimea, with its ethnic Russian majority and a key Russian naval base at Sevastopol.

Ukrainians can change their government democratically. Changes in the electoral law in 1997 instituted a system where 50 percent of candidates are elected by majority vote and 50 by proportional representation. The 1998 elections were generally free and fair, though international organizations criticized the election campaign as being marred by incidents of violence, arrests, and abuse of public office. A 1991 press law purports to protect freedom of speech and press, but it only covers print media. The Constitution, the Law on Information

(1992), and the Television and Radio Broadcasting Law (1994) protect freedom of speech, but there are laws banning attacks on the president's "honor and dignity." There are private newspapers, radio and television stations. In 1998, the media faced pressure from entrenched political interests and criminal organizations, including acid and grenade attacks on journalists.

The large Russian minority enjoys full rights and protections. Hungarians in Subcarpathia continue to press for greater cultural rights. Freedom of assembly is generally respected, but organizations must apply for permission to local administrations at least ten days before a planned event. The judiciary remains subject to political interference. Corruption is pervasive at all levels of government. Bribery is common for services, education, and in the police forces. There have been no major trials or prosecutions for corruption. Law does not restrict freedom of movement within the country. However, regulations impose a nationwide requirement to register at the workplace and place of residence in order to be eligible for social benefits. The constitution and the property laws formally guarantee property rights. *De facto*, the right to private property remains ill defined. Many leading businessmen are former members of the *nomenklatura* who used contacts and lax laws to gain an advantage in the privatization of enterprises and economic sectors. Between 50 and 60 percent of GDP is believed generated by the "shadow economy" that operates outside business and tax regulations. Freedom House's 1998–99 *Freedom in the World* rates Ukraine a three in political rights and a four in civil liberties.

Religious Freedom

When it fell under Soviet domination, Ukraine was subjected to the same religious persecution as Russia, but in different ways at different times. The Orthodox Church in central and eastern areas was not only severely repressed after 1920, but the remnant was forced to repudiate Ukrainian elements and had to call itself the Russian Orthodox Church. In the West, the Catholic Church of the Eastern Rite (now calling itself Greek-Catholic) had the allegiance of the vast majority of the population and was not under Soviet domination between the wars. In 1946, the Soviets forced its incorporation into the Russian Orthodox Church and imprisoned all bishops and clergy who objected. Ukraine was also home to the highest proportion of Protestants (mainly Baptists) on Soviet soil, and some congregations firmly opposed Soviet control. They achieved considerable publicity between 1965 and the 1980s under the determined leadership of the late Pastor Georgi Vins.

As an illegal and underground church, the Eastern-Rite Catholics formed the most determined Christian opposition to communism of any group in the Soviet period, with the possible exception of the Roman Catholic Church in Lithuania. Their underground status and strong Ukrainian nationalism made them especially dangerous to communist hegemony, though propaganda concealed this from the world for many years. The release of Archbishop (later Cardinal) Slipyj from prison camp to the Vatican in 1963 first showed the reality behind the propaganda and led to intensive efforts by emigre Ukrainians, especially in Canada, to reveal the situation to international scrutiny.

By the Gorbachev period, Ukraine seethed with religious fervor. Vast crowds celebrated the "Millennium of the Baptism of Rus" in June 1988. The fact that the Russian Orthodox Church made Moscow the center of the celebrations instead of Kiev (which was the cradle of medieval Russian Christianity) made the mood more determined. However, the hierarchy of the Russian Orthodox Church under Metropolitan Filaret of Kiev, of questionable personal morality and later founder of the breakaway anti-Moscow "Kiev Patriarchate," continued its Russianizing tendencies. He survived a physical assault by unknown assailants on April 30, 1999. The Ukrainian Autocephalous Orthodox Church also reformed itself seventy years after its abolition by the communists. There are, therefore, three main Orthodox churches in schism with one another, as well as several minor breakaway groups.

Meanwhile demands, especially by laypeople, for the legalization of the Ukrainian Greek-Catholic Church became intensive. This to some extent diverted attention from the actual pastoral work that the clandestine bishops and priests were already carrying out. Continuing refusal by the authorities, backed by the Russian Orthodox Church, which could lose property, influence, and reputation, was inconsistent with Gorbachev's policy of *glasnost*. Finally, Gorbachev visited the pope in December 1989, and, as a kind of gift to the Holy See, the relegalization of the Ukrainian Greek-Catholic Church was announced the previous day. After forty-three years of repression, the Soviet Union's most persecuted large group of Christians regained their rights, and Ukraine became the last Soviet republic to gain its religious liberty. Inevitably, however, this inaugurated a lengthy and bitter dispute over the church property that had fallen into Orthodox hands in 1946. The Ukrainian Catholics regained much of what they lost, but bitterness persists.

Less than a year later the repeal of Stalin's 1929 Law on Religious Associations and the passage of the new Soviet law in September 1990 guaranteed legal religious freedom. Article 35 of the 1996 Ukrainian Constitution continued in this vein and reads: "Everyone has the right to freedom of personal philosophy and religion. The exercise of this right may be restricted by law only in the interests of protecting public order, the health and morality of the population, or protecting the rights and freedoms of other persons. The church and religious organisations in Ukraine are separated from the State, and the school from the church. In the event that the performance of military duty is contrary to the religious beliefs of a citizen, the performance of this duty shall be replaced by alternative (non-military) service." A new draft law on Freedom of Conscience and Religious Association is under consideration in 1999, the stated aim of which is to achieve conformity with European and international norms.

Therefore, Ukraine has taken a strong line to protect pacifists. In practice, however, the situation is less liberal than the law. An Amnesty International report of April 1997 said that exemption to military service may be granted only on religious grounds, so nonreligious pacifists suffer discrimination.

The requirement that religious congregations must register in order to be legal persists from the communist era. The registration process is tortuous, and rules are not published. Nonetheless seventy Christian and other religious groups now officially exist, compared to ten in the communist period. Diverse groups such as Jehovah's Witnesses, Mormons, and Muslims have had their status transformed in recent years. Foreign representatives of these groups are active, though non-Ukrainian leaders of unregistered groups may be deported. This has occurred in some instances with Polish Roman Catholic priests, despite their legal status.

Some other anomalies persist. For example, the Ukrainian Autocephalous Orthodox Church has been denied central registration, but many local congregations exist legally. The state says it is avoiding interference in the Orthodox schisms, yet there is interference at the local level. For example, in Donetsk, one parish, tired of internal disputes, left the jurisdiction of the Kiev Patriarchate and announced itself "independent" of any of the three Orthodox churches in September 1996. The local court ruled that this was equivalent to "self-liquidation" and that the congregation must lose its building. However, the wrangle is being taken to international arbitration.

Jews now have an improved opportunity to pursue their religious and cultural activities, and some have risen to prominent positions (for example, the mayors of Odessa and Vinnitsu). The government roundly condemns anti-Semitism, but incidents continue to occur. Between 1995 and 1997, some fourteen attacks on Jewish property were recorded, while in April 1999 representatives from 110 localities founded a national confederation, further heightening the profile of the Jewish community. Altogether the six hundred thousand Jews in Ukraine have some three hundred synagogues, cultural organizations, schools, and social services.

The Crimean Tatars, deported and victims of genocide under Stalin, are one of Europe's most deprived minorities. However, under their outstanding leader, Mustafa Jemilyou, who himself suffered imprisonment in the Brezhnev era, they have reestablished themselves in their homeland and set up Islamic institutions. Disputes continue over their right to repossess property from which they were evicted more than forty years ago.

Overall, Ukraine, one of the areas that suffered most from persecution in communist times, has made immense gains in terms of personal religious freedom. Evangelicals, well organized and with literature in hand, are currently the main beneficiaries of this. Schools, hospitals, orphanages, and prisons are open to religious work, as they were at the end of the Gorbachev period. Schools are open to voluntary classes of religious teaching, even during school hours. In May 1999, three pastors of the Initsiatiuniti Baptists (unregistered and persecuted in the Soviet period) were sentenced to ten days imprisonment in the Kharkiv region, the first such incident since the collapse of communism.

These gains are contested, however. The Ministry of Education is an ideological opponent and issued a report in 1996 (with no legal status, but distributed as though it were official policy) targeting foreign religious organizations. It is reminiscent of ex-Soviet antireligious propagandists: "Religious and pseudo-religious organisations [cause young people] moral and psychological harm and threaten their physical health. Their religious-ideological propaganda makes the younger generation indifferent to the fate of their own nation and state. The uncontrolled activity of foreign preachers and missionaries . . . hinders economic transformations and evokes a negative reaction from the clergy of traditional denominations and from the public." The report cites specific examples, but they are trivial. It recommends limiting the activities of the guilty parties, but nothing specific has happened, and religious activities continue as before.

United Kingdom

Population	**59.4 million**
Anglican	**55%**
Catholic	**16%**
Other Protestant	**6%**
Muslim	**2%**
Sikh	**0.9%**
Hindu	**0.8%**
Jewish	**0.6%**
Buddhist	**0.2%**
Other	**10.5%**
Unaffiliated	**5%**
Religious Freedom Rating	**2**

Background

The United Kingdom of Great Britain and Northern Ireland encompasses the two formerly separate kingdoms of England and Scotland, the ancient principality of Wales, and the six counties of the Irish province of Ulster. The British parliament has an elected House of Commons with 659 members chosen by plurality vote from single-member districts, and a House of Lords with some 1,100 hereditary and appointed members. A cabinet of ministers, appointed from the majority party, exercises executive power on behalf of the mainly ceremonial sovereign. Queen Elizabeth II nominates the party leader with the most support in the House of Commons to form a government.

Prime Minister Tony Blair's "New Labour" adopted Conservative-style positions on a number of issues and swept general elections in May 1997. The government continues to define itself as it goes along by blending traditional Labour and Conservative policies. With his sizable parliamentary majority, Blair has successfully pushed through a number of reforms. Devolution of power to Scotland and Wales began in September 1997, when each territory voted to create its own legislature. The government also made progress on reforms of the electoral system and the House of Lords.

Blair's active involvement in multi-party talks on the future of Northern Ireland helped secure an agreement on April 10, 1998. The "Good Friday Agreement" recognizes the principle that a united Ireland may not come about without the consent of a majority of people in both jurisdictions. It also creates a 108-member assembly elected by proportional representation, establishes a north-south ministerial council, and establishes a British-Irish council of British, Irish, Northern Irish, Scottish, and Welsh representatives to discuss particular policy issues. The new assembly was elected on June 25, 1998, and has spent time since battling over the composition of executive and north-south institutions and over disarmament.

Citizens of the United Kingdom can change their government democratically. Voters are registered by government survey and include both Irish and Commonwealth (former British Empire) citizens resident in Britain. British subjects abroad retain voting rights for twenty years after emigration. Welsh and Scottish legislatures have authority over matters of regional importance such as education, health, and some economic matters. The Scottish parliament has limited power to raise taxes. Northern Ireland's assembly assumed power in 1999. In June 1998, the government proposed to make the House of Lords more representative by sacking hereditary peers. A commission on electoral reform issued a report in October advocating a combination of additional-member and alternative-vote systems for the House of Commons. Analysts say that the new system would strengthen smaller parties and effectively end the current two-party system.

Britain does not have a written constitution, and civil libertarians have criticized legal attempts to combat crime and terrorism as dangerous to basic freedoms. Under the Prevention of Terrorism Act, which is renewed every two years, suspects may be detained without charge or legal representation for up to seven days. The antiterrorism laws make it possible to jail suspected terrorists on the word of a senior police officer and allow security forces to seize the property and money of known terrorists. In November 1998, the government passed the Human Rights Act of 1998, planning to incorporate articles of the European Convention on Human Rights (ECHR) into British law. It is due to come into effect in England sometime in 2000 and is already in effect in Scotland. The Act compels all public bodies to act in accordance with the convention and allows British citizens to take alleged violations of the convention to British courts.

Though uncensored and mostly private, the British press is subject to strict libel and obscenity laws. Print media are privately owned and independent. The BBC runs about half the electronic media in the country. It is funded by the government but editorially independent. British workers are free to form and join independent trade unions. Intense criticism of British procedures proliferated in 1998. Freedom House's 1998–99 *Freedom in the World* rates the United Kingdom a one in political rights and a two in civil liberties.

Religious Freedom

While about two-thirds of the British population identify themselves as Christian, only some 11 percent in England, 17 percent in Wales, and 30 percent in Scotland are active church members. In practice, about one quarter of the population is religious. Virtually all major and minor religious groupings exist in the United Kingdom.

There is full freedom of conscience and freedom of worship. All religious groups, except for the Church of England, have considerable autonomy, and there are no legal restrictions on religious bodies by specific nonneutral laws. For the Church of England, the monarch on the advice of the prime minister appoints bishops, deans, and some academic positions. However, the church receives no funding except for the preservation of historic buildings, and these provisions are available to other groups.

The Church of England is the state church in England and has a number of privileges and obligations. Twenty-four bishops of the church are represented in the House of Lords. Some older university positions are also restricted to Anglicans, largely because ecclesiastical and academic positions have been intertwined. The fact that the sovereign is also the head of the Church of England and Defender of the Faith raises difficulties if the head of the royal family does not wish to be Anglican. The sovereign currently cannot marry a Catholic. There have been calls for the disestablishment of the Church, commonly by those inside it who believe its privileged status stultifies genuine spiritual impulses. In Scotland, the Presbyterian Church is established but has had fewer political privileges. Currently, members of other religious groups are now commonly nominated as peers. In general, the remaining privileges of the established churches are largely symbolic, and other religious groups have not pushed strongly to end them.

Governmental authorities have provided accommodations for other religions, including exemption from some safety regulations for turban-wearing Sikhs and the right of non-Christian "clergy" to solemnize marriages. In schools there are still "legally required" religious assemblies, and they, like the content of religious education, must be "mainly" Christian, while required to respect other religious views. Schools are required to respect the wishes of any parent who requests that their child be exempted from religious services or classes.

Some media groups have expressed hostility to cults such as Scientologists, but there has been little open public hostility, and there have been no legal moves to suppress such bodies, as has been the case in other parts of Europe. However, in December 1999, the British Charity Commission ruled that the Church of Scientology was not eligible for charitable status, as, *inter alia*, it had not been established "for the advancement of religion." Rev. Sun Myung Moon was excluded from the United Kingdom in 1995 by an exclusion order from the Home Secretary, principally in connection with his financial dealings. The order remains in force.

One growing problem is, with the increasing secularization of society, increasing trivialization of religious beliefs in general. The manifestation of religious values is increasingly subordinated to secular and economic goals in the courts; religious manifestations are increasingly compared to social activities such as playing soccer. Muslims in particular have objected to having their religious concerns treated as ethnic traits. Especially in the past, this has sometimes been combined with discrimination in favor of Christianity.

There is generally freedom to propagate one's faith and to train and appoint clergy. Religious bodies have rights of self-government, of religious education, to carry out charitable activities, to own and acquire property, and to maintain hospitals housing services and other social institutions. They can produce, import, and distribute literature; receive donations; have tax benefits; and have contact with coreligionists domestically and overseas. Individuals can adopt, change, or leave a religion freely with, apart from the minor exceptions noted below, no change of civil status.

For example, in *Ahmed v. United Kingdom* in 1978, a Muslim was prevented from taking an hour off work on a Friday for prayers on the grounds that the United Kingdom was a Christian country and the working week was Monday to Friday. Some twenty years later in *Stedman v. United Kingdom* (1997), a Christian was lawfully dismissed for refusing to work on a Sunday after Sunday working had been introduced. The Court in the United Kingdom held that there was no jurisdiction to hear a complaint about a violation of a religious right because she had been employed for less than two years (the statutory requirement). The European Court of Human Rights held that the dismissal of an employee for church attendance did not affect her right to attend church, and thus the loss of employment was not material.

There is increasing pressure to repeal the blasphemy laws, as only the Christian religion (and the Jewish faith by implication only) is protected. The Law Commission recommended this in the 1985 Report on Offenses Against Religion and Public Worship, but so far no action has been taken. There was a successful prosecution in 1979 of *Gay News* under the blasphemy laws for a homosexual poem about fantasies with Jesus. This was the last such prosecution. In *Wingrove v. United Kingdom*, a film was banned that portrayed sexual fantasies about Christ. The Salman Rushdie affair about the publication of the book *Satanic Verses* established that the Muslim community in the United Kingdom could not take advantage of the blasphemy laws. The courts held that the blasphemy laws did not protect Islam, and the European Court upheld the position of the United Kingdom (although this case involved issues of freedom of speech).

The 1998 Human Rights Act (incorporating European Human Rights law) was received with concern by several religious organizations despite the fact that Article 9 of the European Convention protects freedom of religion. There is a concern that, under the Human Rights Act, the courts will not respect the internal workings of religious bodies, especially when the activity is not seen as purely religious but as a kind of social activity. In these instances the interests of homosexuals and alternative lifestyle groups may conflict with the housing and employment policies of religious bodies. For example, the dismissal from a Christian school of a head teacher who had become a Muslim might be held to be in breach of the Human Rights Act, and the courts would hold such a dismissal unlawful. Pressure by religious bodies in the House of Lords secured a weak amendment to the Act requiring that the courts must have a special regard to the interests of religious bodies. It remains to be seen what effect this provision will have.

British governments past and present have also forbidden religious groups to own national territorial broadcasting licenses, claiming that religion is best left in the hands of the BBC, which is regarded as "nonsectarian." The government claims that religious broadcasts by others could lead to religious tensions or manipulation of audiences. In June 1999, United Christian Broadcasters began legal action to take the government before the European Court of Human Rights on the grounds of religious discrimination.

The "Good Friday" agreement of April 10, 1998, in Northern Ireland, was the culmination of twenty-two months of talks under the chairmanship of former U.S. Senator George Mitchell. It was endorsed by 71 percent of the population of Northern Ireland in a referendum on May 22, 1998. However, in 1999, subsequent talks became bogged down over the question of the surrender of weapons by the separatist Irish Republican Army. In November 1999, this disagreement was overcome, and the different parties entered into a joint cabinet for Northern Ireland. Breakdown occurred again in early 2000 over the issue of the IRA decommissioning its weapons.

In a region where 90 percent of the population claim adherence to the Christian faith, but which has been beset by denominational strife (39% Catholic and 50.5% Protestant), the Agreement represents an aspiration for peace between two Christian communities. At 58 percent, church attendance has been the highest in the United Kingdom, and Catholics have historically suffered widespread social discrimination. The 1973 Northern Ireland Constitution Act forbids discrimination on the grounds of religious or political beliefs, the only legislation in the United Kingdom that does so. Currently the unemployment rates for Catholic men in Northern Ireland are still nearly twice that of Protestant men. Some sectarian attacks on property continue, though religiously motivated attacks on persons have declined sharply.

United States of America

Population	**270 million**
Protestant	**55%**
Catholic	**28%**
Orthodox	**1%**
Mormon	**2%**
Jewish	**2%**
Muslim	**1%**
Other/None	**11%**
Religious Freedom Rating	**1**

Background

The U.S. federal government has three branches: executive, legislative, and judicial. The American federal system gives substantial powers to state and local governments and the citizenry. The president and vice president are elected by popular vote to four-year terms. In 1996, the ticket of incumbent President Bill Clinton and Vice President Al Gore was reelected with 49 percent of the vote. The U.S. Congress is bicameral. In the 1998 midterm elections, Republicans continued their control of the House of Representatives by winning 223 seats to 211 for the Democrats, with one independent. In the midterm election, Republicans won 55 Senate seats; the Democrats 45.

Americans can change their government democratically. Elections take place for federal, state, and local offices in an almost constant round of campaigns. Voter turnout has been relatively low in recent years; in the 1998 midterm elections, it was 36 percent of the voting-age population, the lowest level since 1942. Elections are competitive, but congressional incumbents win in a majority of cases. Critics argue that contributions by business, labor unions, and other "special interests" make it practically impossible for candidates to dislodge incumbents. Today the American political system is overwhelmingly dominated by the two major parties. Various insurgent parties have had little success in recent years in electing candidates but larger success in airing issues. The two parties choose their presidential candidates through an almost yearlong process culminating during the winter and spring of election years. The nominating process has been criticized for its cost, length, and for sometimes undue influence of unrepresentative minority factions. One trend has been the increased use of initiative and referendum to determine issues of public policy, especially in California.

The American media are free and competitive. Some observers have expressed concern over the trend towards ownership by large corporate conglomerates. Another worrying trend is television news, which can be superficial and sensationalistic. Others point to the explosion of new, specialized journals as well as the Internet as novel news sources. Public and private discussions are very open in the United States. In recent years concern has been expressed over universities' restrictive codes prohibiting speech deemed insulting to women, racial minorities, or homosexuals.

The American court system is independent but increasingly controversial. Some critics accuse judges of being overly "activist" by usurping the legislative process and fear a trend towards social regulation through the courts rather than legislation. A trend towards the decrease in crime throughout the country has continued in recent years, while the prison population has increased to 1.9 million. The U.S. has freedom of association. Trade unions are free but have been in decline for some years and today represent the lowest percentage of American workers in the postwar period.

Race relations remain one of America's most serious problems. Despite progress since 1945, African-

Americans remain disproportionately poor, less likely to complete high school or college, more likely to have out-of-wedlock births, and suffer more major health problems than other groups. Affirmative action programs remain a source of friction. Voters in California overwhelmingly approved a measure outlawing the use of bilingual education for immigrant students in the public schools.

America continues to permit high levels of legal immigration, some six million every decade. At the same time, the U.S. has beefed up its patrols at the border with Mexico in an attempt to stem the flood of illegal immigrants. American Indians continue to suffer a disproportionate level of poverty and social problems, such as alcoholism. In recent years, some Indian reservations have experienced some dubious economic progress through the development of gambling casinos on Indian property. Freedom House's 1998–99 *Freedom in the World* rates the United States a one in political rights and in civil liberties.

Religious Freedom

A variety of religious beliefs existed among the original settlers of North America. When European immigration began in the fifteenth century, the United States was settled largely by Christians, often fleeing persecution or discrimination in their country of origin. Thus, religious freedom has been important to the American nation from the very beginning. Nearly all of the European settlers in what became the original thirteen colonies were Protestant (though Roman Catholics settled Maryland). Principles of ethical monotheism underlay the founding of the country. The 1776 Declaration of Independence states, "We hold these truths to be self-evident, that all men are created equal, endowed by their Creator with certain inalienable rights, and among these are life, liberty, and the pursuit of happiness."

The religious makeup of the country changed dramatically in the nineteenth century due to large-scale immigration of Catholics and, to a lesser extent, Jews. A public-school system was created, partly in order to conform these groups to a general Protestant ethos. When Catholics, in particular, sought to maintain their religious identity by developing a system of parochial schools, many states adopted "Blaine Amendments" to their state constitutions in the latter part of the century prohibiting public funding of Catholic schools. In the past half-century, there has been increasing immigration of adherents to non-Western religions (Buddhism, Islam, Hinduism, etc.).

Since the United States has a federal system of government, religious liberty issues may arise at the national, state, or local level. Soon after the Constitution was adopted in 1789, ten amendments were incorporated. The first provides that "Congress shall make no law respecting an establishment of religion, or prohibiting the free exercise thereof." This was binding only on the national government; the individual states were free to establish religions, and several did. In fact, the provision seems to have been designed, in part, to protect state religious establishments against possible federal action. The last state establishments died out in the 1830s. However, in the 1940s the Supreme Court held that, although the First Amendment refers only to the national "Congress," the Fourteenth Amendment (1868) had "incorporated" these religious liberty provisions, making them applicable to the states. The federal constitution also prohibits "religious tests" for federal offices. The constitutions of individual states often offer greater protection for religious liberty than that of the national constitution.

Though the first amendment does not refer to a "separation of church and state," the Supreme Court has borrowed the metaphor of a "wall of separation," first used by Baptist defender of religious freedom Roger Williams, a founder of Rhode Island, and later by Thomas Jefferson. Some recent scholarship, such as that underlying the exhibit "Religion and the Founding of the American Republic" at the Library of Congress in 1998, argues that "strict separation" was not envisioned by the Founding Fathers, who thought that religion was necessary for republican morality and that government could legitimately promote religion in an evenhanded (or "nonpreferentialist") manner.

Historically, the United States has afforded great latitude to citizens to worship and express their religious beliefs. Recently, however, concerns have arisen. The use of lethal force against a religious, separatist community in Waco, Texas, raises questions of disproportionate treatment of religious-based nonconformity. In 1998, the Maryland State Legislature created a task force on what it called "cults," prompting fears that it, and others, may emulate the increasing religious repression found in Europe. Likewise, recent judicial decisions permitting the use of racketeering statutes against civil disobedience at abortion clinics and a Supreme Court case invalidating a Colorado constitutional amendment concerning homosexuality raises the question whether democratic political action perceived to be religiously motivated will be subject to invalidation by the judiciary.

Americans have historically been free to worship when and where they desire, subject to ordinary zoning and other requirements. An important question concerns the constitutionality of neutral laws of general applicability that incidentally burden the free exercise of religion. In 1990, the Supreme Court, in *Employment Division v. Smith*, ruled that neutral general laws are constitutionally valid even when they incidentally burden religion and even absent a compelling state interest. This poses serious issues because of the increasing role of government in all aspects of life coupled with the notion of "strict separation." A broad coalition of secular and religious groups prevailed upon Congress to pass the Religious Freedom Restoration Act (RFRA), restoring the compelling interest standard. However, in 1997, the Supreme Court ruled that RFRA exceeded congressional power and thus could not be applied to state or local law. Currently, the Congress is considering whether, and how, to address the issue further.

Based on the free speech clause of the First Amendment, public facilities must be made available for rental use to religious organizations on the same terms as to nonreligious organizations. Nevertheless, problems continue in some states over the use of public-school facilities. The metaphor of "strict separation" has led overzealous officials to discriminate *against* religious organizations. Similar problems sometimes occur in the provision of other public spaces (such as city auditoriums) to religious organizations. Indian leaders are also trying to preserve and have access to traditional sacred sites located on lands now owned by the state and federal governments. Currently there is federal litigation with commercial rock climbers and the U.S. Park Service over the right of Indians to worship at Devil's

Tower National monument in Wyoming. This is an important test of reasonable government accommodation of religious activities on public lands.

Though clergy are generally free to preach as they see fit, hold services in conformity with the practice of their religion, and conduct chaplaincy work, problems do occasionally arise. In 1997, the armed forces attempted to restrict aspects of sermons by its Catholic chaplains and ban Jews from wearing yarmulkes. Muslims have also encountered problems with police forces that forbid officers to wear beards. Among obstacles American Indians face are laws prohibiting the use of peyote and other substances in ceremonies and dress codes in public schools, the military, prison, and other institutions prohibiting long hair, prayer bundles, and some religious attire. If the 1990 *Smith* decision is not modified by legislation, certain religious rituals, rules, and practices might be seriously limited or even effectively prohibited, albeit as an incidental effect of neutral general laws.

Religious organizations are generally free to solicit contributions, acquire property, print materials, establish subsidiary communities, and train and appoint leaders. However, there is a growing tendency in certain influential elements of society to view as "discriminatory" a requirement by a religious organization that its leaders subscribe to its profession of faith. The problem has arisen with some frequency in high schools and colleges regarding the leadership of student religious organizations. Federal antidiscrimination statutes prohibit discrimination on the basis of religion in housing, employment, and other areas. They often provide exemptions for religious organizations from antidiscrimination statutes, which would otherwise conflict with the beliefs and practices of the organization.

Although religious organizations are free to operate their own schools, there are growing problems in the area of religious education. After the Supreme Court struck down the RFRA statute, the U.S. Justice Department took the position that there is no longer a federal right for students to "opt out" of public school classes for religious reasons. This right is increasingly important in public schools as students are sometimes made to participate in classes, assemblies, or assignments that their parents believe violate their religious beliefs and values. While the Department's view is likely erroneous (given the recognized right of parents to supervise the education of their children), if it prevails, the rights of religious parents and students would be seriously infringed. (Of course, opt-out rights may exist as a matter of state law as well.) The perception by religious parents of hostility by the public schools has been a leading cause of the growth of the home-school movement.

Dissatisfaction with Supreme Court jurisprudence regarding religion in the public schools has led to efforts to amend the constitution to provide for some form of "school prayer." (The long-standing practice of having officially sanctioned prayers in public schools has been ruled unconstitutional by the Supreme Court.) In 1996, perhaps in an effort to demonstrate that no such amendment is needed, the president of the United States published guidelines (tracking current law) on religion in the public schools, declaring that schools were not meant to be "religion-free zones." The guidelines indicated that private prayer (even in groups) is permissible in schools. The Department of Education has distributed them to all school superintendents but has not taken steps to ensure that the guidelines are distributed to teachers, principles, students, and parents. Nor has it trained teachers and others regarding the guidelines. Finally, the Department has not encouraged school districts to develop district-wide policies on this issue. Access to school facilities on a nondiscriminatory basis is ensured to student "Bible clubs" by the federal 1984 Equal Access Act. Rare cases continue to arise of discriminatory treatment of such clubs.

Public schools are prohibited from providing religious education. The possibility of providing vouchers by which families could decide how to spend their "education dollars," including on religious schools, has been strenuously resisted by teachers' unions, public-school advocates, and people who favor "strict separation" doctrine. However, some experiments have begun in various states.

While cases of outright discrimination against religious believers do occur, the most common problem in public schools is a secularist viewpoint in the curriculum that masquerades as "neutrality." This view can assume a materialist worldview and inculcate an understanding based on this worldview. Children not exposed to the possibility of alternative ways of understanding the world lose the freedom to evaluate critically and to choose what belief system to adopt, and religion is intellectually and culturally marginalized.

Religious organizations are free to establish and operate hospitals, printing houses, and newspapers. Through quasigovernmental accreditation boards, some religiously based hospitals have been under pressure to alter their practices on matters such as abortion. Though federal funding has in the past been denied to charitable organizations run by religious groups in the belief that this contravened the "separation of church and state," recent "charitable choice" provisions in federal law permit states to fund religious as well as nonreligious organizations to provide social services.

Most individuals are treated without discrimination regardless of their belief or lack thereof (though, of course, pockets of bigotry do exist). Government at the federal, state, and local levels generally has statutes prohibiting such discrimination. It is unclear, however, whether the Department of Justice devotes sufficient resources to the protection of religious freedom. Critics claim that the Department treats religious freedom as a "second-class" civil right.

There is no established church in the United States. The de facto Protestant establishment, which prevailed into the twentieth century, was shattered by Catholic and Jewish immigration. Today, many denominations are divided on theological, moral, and political issues along "traditionalist" and "progressive" lines. Moral and political alliances across "denominational" lines are increasingly common. In early campaigning in the year 2000 presidential elections, the two leading candidates, George W. Bush and Vice President Al Gore, have both stressed the need for more supportive relations between the state and religious groups.

Uzbekistan

Population	**24.4 million**
Muslim (largely Sunni)	**68.2%**
Russian Orthodox	**4.4%**
Roman Catholic	**0.2%**
Protestant	**0.2%**
Jewish	**0.5%**
Other	**0.5%**
Baha'i	**0.2%**
Buddhist	**0.3%**
Nonreligious/Other	**25.5%**
Religious Freedom Rating	**6**

Background

Uzbekistan is located along ancient trade routes among the world's oldest civilized regions and became part of the Russian Empire in the nineteenth century. Separated from Turkmenia in 1924, it entered the USSR as a constituent republic in 1925. In 1929, its eastern Tajik region was detached. Following Soviet rule, Islam Karimov, former First Secretary of the Communist Party, was elected president in 1991 as head of the People's Democratic Party (PDP), formerly the Communist Party. He ostensibly received 86 percent of the vote. The largest opposition group, the nationalist *Birlik* (Unity), was barred from registering as a party, and the Islamic Renaissance Party (IRP) was banned entirely, as was the Islamic Adolat group. A February 1995 national referendum to extend Karimov's term was allegedly approved by 99 percent of voters.

In early November 1998, Tajik president Imomali Rakhmonov accused the Uzbek government of helping plot an armed uprising in Tajikistan. In February 1999, Karimov narrowly escaped a car-bomb attack. Dozens of alleged conspirators were tried and sentenced in June and July, and nearly half were sentenced to death for attempting to kill the president.

Uzbekistan is a de facto one-party state dominated by former communists. The 1994 parliamentary elections were not free and fair, and only pro-government parties took part. Most media remain controlled by the government. A new media law, signed in December 1997, purports to facilitate press freedom, but censorship and other pressures remain. Libel, public defamation of the president, and irresponsible journalism (spreading "falsehoods") are subject to possible imprisonment. Journalists have also been assaulted.

While the Uzbek Constitution guarantees freedom of assembly, authorities can suspend or ban rallies or meetings on security grounds. The constitution also contains articles that undermine the right of parties to organize. Article 62 forbids "organized activities leading . . . to participation in anti-government organizations." A 1997 law prohibits parties based on ethnic or religious lines. Opposition parties such as Erk, Birlik, the Right Path Is Justice Party, the Social Development Party, and others have been barred from registering.

A 1992 law allows for the formation of trade unions, but the Council of the Federation of Trade Unions, the successor to the Soviet-era federation, is subservient to the state. There is a small number of nongovernmental organizations whose role remains uncertain. The judiciary is subservient to the regime, with the president appointing all judges, with no mechanisms to ensure their independence. Political prisoners are estimated to be in the hundreds, including political and religious activists. Corruption in business and the civil service is pervasive.

There are no significant restrictions on freedom of movement, emigration, and choice of residence. Approximately two-thirds of the service sector has been privatized, though much is in the control of former communist-era elites. Property rights are guaranteed by the constitution, but, in the absence of a market system, citizens continue to be dependent, in large part, on the state sector. Women are underrepresented in high-level positions throughout society. Freedom House's 1998–99 *Freedom in the World* rates Uzbekistan a seven in political rights and a six in civil liberties.

Religious Freedom

Nestorian Christianity first reached the region in the fourth century. By the eighth century, an Islamic mysticism known as Sufism took root among the indigenous Uzbek and Turkic/Altaic nationalities. In the ninth century, Sunni Islam emerged as the dominant religion. Although Islam now has more cultural than religious significance for many, it remains the religion of the ethnic majority. A small Christian presence of Russian, Slavic, and other Indo-European immigrant minorities returned when the Russian Empire conquered the region in the nineteenth century. Since seventy years of enforced atheism under Soviet rule ended in 1991, all the country's religious communities have experienced a significant revival in interest. A quarter of the population still consider themselves nonreligious.

The constitution calls for a separation of religion from the state, but the government enforces strict controls over all religious activity. Religious supervision is carried out by the State Committee for Religious Affairs under the Council of Ministers, in conjunction with the Ministry of Justice. In a carryover from Soviet policy, the Muslim Religious Board remains subject to government control and funding. Hence, pro-government Islamic activities are subsidized, while other religious groups are subject to control. While the constitution guarantees religious freedom, institutionalized religion is in practice limited to Russian Orthodoxy, Judaism, and state-controlled Islam. Islamic activities that lie outside the government's religious establishment are suppressed, along with Christian ministries suspected of proselytism. Political parties with a religious agenda are banned.

Under heavy executive pressure, in May 1998, the Uzbek Parliament instituted perhaps the most repressive legislation on religion in any country of the former Soviet Union. Several parts of the law violate Uzbekistan's international commitments to religious freedom and freedom of expression. The president insists that these restrictions are necessary to prevent an overthrow of the national order by Islamic extremists linked with alleged "Wahhabi fundamentalists" from Saudi Arabia. He said (Islamic) fundamentalists should be shot.

In 1998, more than a thousand people were arrested, and several dozen were tried and sentenced for religious activities. The law requires strict registration procedures and puts restriction on religious practices, "proselytizing," and conversions. By criminalizing any unregistered religious activity, the law seriously curtails freedom of speech, conscience, and assembly. Only state-licensed religious leaders are allowed to discuss religion in public or private. Leaders of unlicensed religious observances are punished by prison sentences, fines, and confiscation of their community's assets. Religious bodies must maintain registered communities in at least eight provinces to qualify as centralized religious organizations; only the Muslim establishment and the Russian

Orthodox Church meet this standard. The Catholic Church has been able to use the diplomatic ties between the Holy See and the Uzbek government to secure registration for three of its parishes.

The government campaign against any Islamic expression outside the state-controlled Muslim establishment has resulted in a heavy-handed crackdown across the Ferghana Valley, where independent mosques have been closed down, the wearing of beards and women's head coverings banned, and religious leaders subjected to arrest or "disappearance." Religious schools have been closed, imams forced to pass state political and economic tests, and loudspeakers have been banned at mosques. Some activists were arrested in the provincial city of Namangan in the Ferghana Valley after the December 1997 killing of a policeman. Muslim religious teachers Obidkhon Nazarov, Rahim Otagulolv, and Olinjon Gloterov have been harassed, evicted, and arrested repeatedly over the last several years. Since roundups targeting pious Muslim dissidents for arrest and prosecution began in late 1997, there have been credible allegations of torture and unfair trial proceedings, and the government has not addressed them. Dozens of Muslim activists have been jailed on alleged drug charges, and several have died in custody.

By requiring a minimum one hundred adult members to register any religious body, the 1998 religion law has outlawed most small religious communities. Minority religious leaders were given details of the complicated new registration requirements too late to meet the government deadline of August 15. Although the deadline was verbally extended until the end of 1998, state authorities refused to verify this in writing. According to the government's Committee for Religious Affairs, as of August 1999, official registration had been granted to 1,566 Muslim groups, 125 Christian groups, 8 Jewish, and 2 Baha'i. While religious proselytizing and missionary activity are prohibited, neither is defined. Distribution of religious material is legal, but Bibles, Christian literature, and films in the Uzbek language continue to be confiscated on suspicion they would be used to attempt to convert members of Muslim ethnic groups to Christianity.

In 1999, government attempts to suppress minority religions increased. Government authorities fined and continued to threaten Jehovah's Witnesses, as well as several Christian groups, for continuing to hold religious services without formal government approval. In October 1997, Uzbek pastor Rashid Turibayev of the Full Gospel Church was sentenced by a court in Karakalpakstan to two years of hard labor on criminal charges of leading illegal church services. His church has been denied registration since 1995 for its missionary activities. In June 1999, he was sentenced to fifteen years on alleged drug charges, and two workers of his congregation received ten years. In June 1999, a military officer was arrested for giving out Christian literature in Karakalpakstan. In May two Jehovah's Witnesses were sentenced to fifteen days' administrative arrest. Hare Krishnas have been harassed and their literature confiscated.

In a major reversal, on August 19 the government released most of these prisoners and rapidly registered an additional twenty Christian organizations. Several observers connected this about-face to the imminent release of the U.S. State Department's survey of religious freedom in the world, and the possibility of U.S. action against Uzbekistan. Despite these releases and the proclamation of a presidential pardon for the prisoners, there were delays in the return of their documents, and legal restrictions on registration continued. On October 10, police raided a Baptist church in Karshi, several members were tortured, and two people were imprisoned for ten days.

No pattern of official discrimination has been implemented against Jews, but in September 1998, the Foreign Ministry refused without explanation to renew the visa of an American rabbi heading the Jewish community of Tashkent since 1990. Since independence, the Jewish community has immigrated steadily to Israel and the West. Meanwhile ethnic Russians, Ukrainians, and Tatars have also continued to leave, citing fears of persecution.

Vietnam

Population	78.5 million
Buddhist	60%
Catholic	8%
Protestant	1%
Cao Dai	3%
Hoa Hao	2%
Islam	3%
Other	13%
None	10%
Religious Freedom Rating	6

Background

Vietnam was colonized by France in the nineteenth century and was occupied by Japan during World War II. It gained independence in 1954 and was divided between the Republic of South Vietnam and the Communist-ruled Democratic Republic of Vietnam in the north. After years of fighting, North Vietnam overtook the United States-backed south in 1975 and reunited the country under a communist government in 1976.

In 1986, the government began decentralizing economic decision-making, encouraging small-scale private enterprise, and dismantling collectivized agriculture. The 1992 constitution codified many economic reforms, although it retained the Vietnamese Communist Party (VCP) as the sole legal party. By 1997, severe unrest had hit Vietnam's impoverished countryside. Farmers in northern Thai Binh province began demonstrations against corruption, bureaucratic abuse of authority, and falling prices for rice crops. Several thousand mainly Catholic demonstrators clashed with police in the southern Dong Nai province after authorities tried to break up protests against corruption and the confiscation of church land.

In 1998, Vietnam released several thousand prisoners in two mass amnesties. Several political and religious dissidents were among those released. No official reasons were given for the event. The Asian crisis, weak economic management, and natural disasters that have hit Vietnam in recent years are threatening to undermine, and even reverse, the country's economic progress.

In 1998, the country struggled to cope with the Asian economic crisis, which has precipitated its worst economic downturn since Vietnam's communist government launched landmark economic reforms a decade ago. Although Vietnamese officials have acknowledged the need for greater political and economic reform, real progress has been slow in coming, and in 1998, Vietnam remained one of the world's most closed and tightly controlled societies.

Vietnamese cannot change their government democratically. The VCP maintains tight control of all political, economic, religious, and social affairs. The Politburo and its five member Standing Committee decide policy and leadership issues. The Fatherland Front, a VCP mass organization, controls candidate selection for the National Assembly. The judiciary is not independent. The president appoints judges, and the VCP instructs them on rulings.

The media are state owned, and in recent years the government has shut down several newspapers for violating the narrow limits on permissible reporting. The government has announced plans to regulate local Internet use, although it remains unclear how this will be carried out in practice. Assemblies require a permit and are limited to occasional small demonstrations over nonpolitical issues.

Local authorities impose internal travel, education, and employment restrictions on ethnic minorities. Women face violence as well as social and employment discrimination. Child prostitution and international trafficking of minors are reportedly increasing. The UNDP estimates that about half the Vietnamese population lives under the poverty line. More than two million members of Vietnam's ethnic minorities live in extreme poverty, subsisting on hunting, gathering, or slash-and-burn farming methods.

All unions must belong to the state-controlled Vietnam General Confederation of Labor, and all union leaders are VCP members. The 1994 Labor Code recognizes only a limited right to strike. Freedom House's 1998–99 *Freedom in the World* rates Vietnam a seven in political rights and in civil liberties.

Religious Freedom

In this, one of Asia's most religious societies, the government has sought to eradicate all religions independent of state control. During the post-revolutionary years, it undertook a systematic campaign of repression in which religious leaders were arrested and given lengthy prison camp terms, foreign missionaries expelled, religious properties confiscated or destroyed, seminaries closed, the formation and naming of new religious leaders sharply restricted, religious education and literature virtually eliminated, and Bibles treated as contraband.

After the collapse of its patron, the Soviet Union, in 1991, and waiting to attract Western trade and capital, the regime eased religious repression while continuing control over religious activity. Now it tends to imprison, torture, and harass only believers who are outside the international spotlight such as the Hmong and other ethnic Christians from remote villages, and the Cao Dai and Hoa Hao religions that have few proponents in the West. Better connected and/or hierarchical religions, such as Catholicism, urban Protestantism, and Buddhism, suffer more sophisticated and hidden methods. These include prohibitions on printing and distributing religious literature; confiscating and controlling places of worship; refusing to grant independent churches with official legal standing; restricting seminaries, religious schools, and other institutions from propagating religious teachings; and restricting faith-based charities.

Article 4 of the constitution establishes the Communist Party as the "only force leading the society and state." Religious intolerance is thus not simply a matter of local excess, but a deliberate policy determined at the highest levels of the government.

A multilayered bureaucracy controls all religious matters. The Office of Religious Affairs makes and enforces policies at the national level. The public security police monitor individuals at the local level. The Committee on Religions, part of the Communist Party's Fatherland Front, runs religious organizations. The People's Committees, staffed by local communist party members, control activities of blacklisted clergy, monks, lay leaders, and followers. Government-controlled parallel religious groups were formed during the 1980s to compete with, divide, or simply replace independent religious organizations. The role of these organizations is to help the government enforce its religious policies.

A new Decree on Religions (26/1999/ND-CP), signed by Prime Minister Phan Van Khai on April 1999, reaffirms the strict controls on religious activity applied since the 1950s and in some cases tightens the controls. Under this decree, all religious properties confiscated by the communist authorities after 1975 become the permanent property of the state; government agencies are empowered to determine which religions are authorized, and the appointment of religious dignitaries and publication of religious materials are subjected to the prime minister's approval. Clergy and religious officials under "administrative detention" cannot exercise religious functions. All activities perceived to "oppose the State" or "go against the healthy culture of our nation" will be severely punished. The Government Board of Religious Affairs issued an ominous interpretation of the decree, containing strict instructions for its application.

Religious freedom is further restricted by laws against "endangering national security." Under Decree 31/CP on "Administrative Detention" (adopted on April 14, 1997), local police have extrajudicial powers to arrest and detain anyone suspected of "threatening national security" for six months to two years without a court order. The 1985 Criminal Code has an entire chapter of vaguely defined "national security" offenses that severely limit religious freedom, such as "sowing division between religious believers and non-believers" and "undermining national solidarity" (Article 81).

"Probational detention" (*quan che*, Article 30 of the Criminal Code) can place persons convicted of "national security" crimes "under the supervision and reeducation of the local authorities" for up to five years after completion of their prison sentence. Such persons are forbidden to leave their residence, deprived of civic rights, and are under constant police surveillance. In theory, *quan che* requires a court order, but in practice it is automatically applied to all religious prisoners after their release.

Buddhism, the most widely practiced religion, remains a special target of religious repression because of the continuing conflict between Buddhists of the independent Unified Buddhist Church of Vietnam (UBCV) and the communist authorities over religious freedom and state control of Buddhist institutions. The only officially recognized Buddhist organization is the

Vietnam Buddhist Church (VBC), established in 1981 under the control of the Communist Party's "Fatherland Front." Members of the VBC are subject to strict political control in ordination, elevation to the hierarchy, and conducting meetings and other religious activities. Since the UBCV consistently refuses to submit to these dictates, it is outlawed, and all its activities are banned. Many UBCV leaders remain in prison or under house arrest. Active UBCV supporters, both lay and clergy, are subjected to police surveillance, harassment, intimidation, and severe restrictions on their freedom. In 1998, Vietnam prevented UBCV leaders from meeting the UN Special Rapporteur on Religious Intolerance during his *in-situ* visit to Vietnam.

More recently, instead of mass arrests, the government has tried to isolate UBCV clergy and followers. Several prominent UBCV leaders were released from prison in September and October 1998, some in a government amnesty and others after completing their prison sentences. All were placed under strict police surveillance after their release, deprived of citizenship rights, refused residency permits—without which they have no legal status—and subjected to continuous harassment, interrogations, and threats. In March 1999, head of the Institute for the Propagation of the Dharma, Thich Quang Do, was arrested after he met the UBCV patriarch Thich Huyen Quang. Both monks were subjected to intensive police interrogations. On August 6, 1999, Thich Quang Do was again detained for questioning by security police after he sent a letter to ambassadors of the European Union in Hanoi calling on their support for the release of political prisoners and respect for human rights. Police accused him of *"violating national security"*—a crime

punishable by harsh prison sentences and even death. He was placed under strict police surveillance during U.S. secretary of state Madeleine Albright's visit on September 7, 1999.

Other UBCV monks and former political prisoners have also been interrogated and detained. Caught possessing press statements by the Paris-based Vietnam Committee on Human Rights commenting on the U.S. State Department's Annual Report on International Religious Freedom, Thich Khong Tanh was interrogated continuously for two days in September 1999.

The UBCV Eighth Congress in May 1999 had to be held overseas in California. Documents sent clandestinely from Vietnam by Patriarch Thich Huyen Quang and by Thich Quang Do affirmed the UBCV's determination to strengthen the Buddhist movement for religious freedom despite government repression. The government retaliated with a new wave of repression against the UBCV. Throughout July and August 1999, police and religious officials broke into VBC pagodas throughout the country and conducted midnight raids. Monks without residency permits were arrested or expelled.

Among UBCV monks currently in detention for peaceful advocacy of religious freedom are Patriarch Thich Huyen Quang, held without trial since 1982 in an isolated brick hut built specifically for his detention near Nghia Hanh village in Quang Ngai Province. The authorities deny that the eighty-one-year-old patriarch is under detention, yet they bar all visitors, including the Red Cross, from seeing him. He is in extremely poor health as a result of detention conditions. Other monks and lay leaders are serving from nineteen-year to even life sentences in reeducation camps.

Both the Cao Dai, a syncretistic faith, and Hoa Hao Buddhism are indigenous to Vietnam and have suffered some of the severest persecution. The entire Cao Dai leadership was killed after the 1975 takeover of the south, and during the 1990s more than four thousand of its members in Tay Ninh province were arrested as "reactionaries" and "counterrevolutionaries." Like other religions, the Cao Dai had its property confiscated. In 1997, the government formed a restructured Cao Dai, under a government-controlled management committee. Most traditional clergy reject the committee's edicts as unfaithful to Cao Dai principles. In late 1998, two Cao Dai provincial leaders in Kien Giang province were arrested as they attempted to meet with the UN Special Rapporteur on Religion, and they remained in prison more than a year later.

The Hoa Hao Buddhists have survived continuing government attempts to crush them. Hoa Hao Buddhism was founded in 1939 primarily for farmers, with an emphasis on home-based, rather than pagoda-centered, worship and has taken root especially around the Mekong Delta. To consolidate its control over the group, which remains fiercely independent, the government established, in May 1998, the Committee of Hoa Hao Buddhist Representatives, with Muoi Ton, a well-known communist cadre, as its head. In its first year, the Committee prohibited the celebration of major Hoa Hao holidays, barred all references to the Hoa Hao Holy Land, and banned the use of Hoa Hao religious emblems. Their religious ceremonies are prohibited, and any assembly of more than three persons is forbidden. The authorities also prohibit the distribution of the sacred scriptures of the Hoa Hao. Reportedly a number of leaders have been sentenced to death, and others have been subjected to mass arrests, with a number serving life sentences in labor camps.

The government usually seeks to undermine the Roman Catholic Church's hierarchical structure, rather than openly imprisoning clergy, though such persecution has occurred and still occurs among ethnic highland peoples and members of the popular indigenous Congregation of Mother Coredemptrix, six of whom are serving lengthy reeducation-camp terms. Coredemptrix Brother Nguyen Chau Dat, in his seventies, is halfway through a twenty-year sentence for "counterrevolutionary" activities after being caught conducting catechism classes for adults.

The government bars the appointment of new bishops and new vocations and ordinations to the priesthood. The April 1999 decree reaffirms that the appointment of bishops or apostolic administrators or the creation of cardinals must be first approved by the prime minister. All "directives" sent to bishops "from abroad" must pass through the Religious Affairs Bureau. All seminaries require the approval of the Ministry of Education. Ordinations of priests and other religious figures, or their assignment or transfer, may only take place after approval by the Provincial Committee. A special permit is required for any religious activities, except those registered in an "annual plan of activities" and taking place "inside of a Church." Consequently the majority of bishops are over seventy, and many are limited by age or illness.

The government limits the number of seminaries to six and restricts their admissions and ordinations. Seminaries can admit entrants only every two years. The regime also controls where priests can minister and where new churches can be established. Consequently there is a severe shortage of priests, although hundreds await government permission to enter seminary. In the northwest, no priests or religious leaders are allowed among the Catholic Hmong. Priests are also forbidden to visit the Montagnard and other peoples, who walk for hours in the jungle to attend Mass. In these areas, churches have been burned, and many new Catholics must pray secretly in their homes.

The government sharply curtails Catholic education for the laity and forbids most Catholic literature and publications. In the mid-1990s, the regime began to allow a limited distribution of Bibles and missals.

The government-created Catholic Patriotic Association, which functions as a church within a church, infiltrates the Catholic community, controls church matters, and monitors nonconformist priests. Its priests receive privileges unavailable to non-members, such as opportunities to travel abroad, collect donations, carry out humanitarian activities, and renovate churches.

Anticipating better trade relations with the U.S., Vietnam gradually improved religious freedom for some Protestants, including the release of long-term prisoners, building of churches, and distribution of Bibles. Recognition is granted only to the Hanoi-based Evangelical Church of Vietnam, which is under state control.

Most Protestants conduct their religious activities without legal recognition in churches, house-churches, or, for ethnic minorities in remote villages, out-of-doors. These groups are subject to police harassment, raids, and closings. Their leaders and members report arrests, imprisonment, torture, and/or steep fines for worshiping outside government control, evangelizing, or training other ministers. The Hmong, Koho, Jeh, Jerai, and other tribes suffer abuse at the hands of authorities who fear the rapid spread of Christianity far from Hanoi's control. Reportedly three evangelical churches were torn down in August 1999 in Binh Phuoc province alone. Even urban pastors continue to be sharply restricted in their activities, especially evangelizing and education. Since 1975, the regime has authorized only one class of thirteen to receive Protestant religious training. No Protestant theological establishment is authorized, while the ordination of pastors is rarely authorized.

The World Evangelical Fellowship reports that in September 1999 authorities raided a house church in Quang Nam, tied the participants together, and dragged them by their hair. One man was badly beaten and required medical attention. In October 1999, police in Viet Tri raided a Sunday service. Participants were released after interrogation, but the owner of the house, Mrs. Nguyen Thi Thuy, was placed for months in incommunicado detention awaiting charges. She was later sentenced to one year in prison for holding a baptismal service in her home. That same month, police arrested thirty house-church members meeting in Ha Long and interrogated three leaders for six days.

Protestant property has also not been returned after being confiscated by the regime.

Zimbabwe

Population	**11.2 million**
Christian	**59%**
Traditional	**35%**
Muslim	**2%**
Other/Nonreligious (Hindu,	
(Buddhist, Baha'i, Jewish)	**4%**
Religious Freedom Rating	**3**

Background

Zimbabwe gained independence in 1980 after a bloody guerrilla war against a white minority regime that had declared unilateral independence from Britain in 1965 in what was then Northern Rhodesia. From 1983 to 1987, a civil war suppressed resistance by the country's largest minority group, the Ndebele, to dominance by President Mugabe's majority ethnic Shona group. Several human rights abuses accompanied the struggle. Robert Mugabe has been president since the country's founding. He holds only a seriously tarnished electoral mandate, and there is much speculation concerning whether he will be able to serve out his term until 2002. His March 1996 presidential election victory was largely the product of state patronage and repression, including electoral laws boosting the ruling party and restrictions on free expression. The country is arguably a de facto one-party state, yet Mugabe cannot yet exercise an outright dictatorship. However, in 2000, mobs claiming to be veterans of Zimbabwe's war of independence began illegally and forcefully taking over white-owned farms, resulting in several deaths. Mugabe encouraged this, and security forces either stood by or supported the takeovers. The judiciary remains largely independent and trade unions powerful. The small, independent media report corruption among senior officials. Despite numerous obstacles, including nearly complete state dominance of media, civil society groups are seeking to organize alternatives to Mugabe and rule by his ZANU-PF party.

Zimbabwe's elections are hardly democratic. In 1998, President Mugabe won nearly 93 percent of votes cast. Less than one-third of those eligible voted in a noncompetitive contest in which the opposition had no real hope of victory. Voter registration and identification procedures and tabulation of results were highly irregular. The heavily state-controlled or influenced media offer very limited coverage of opposition viewpoints, and ZANU-PF uses state resources heavily in its campaigning.

The judiciary has repeatedly struck down or disputed government actions. Its protection of basic rights, however, has been subverted by constitutional amendments. It is a criminal offense for any individual or media to utter, publish, or distribute news deemed by the state to be subversive. Security forces, particularly the Central Intelligence Organization, often ignore basic rights regarding detention, search, and seizure. Prison conditions are harsh.

The right of free assembly is constitutionally guaranteed but generally respected only for groups that the government deems nonpolitical. Union demonstrations were banned in November. Several groups focus on human rights. Mugabe has continued his verbal attacks on homosexuality, which is illegal. The government directly controls all broadcasting and several newspapers, including all dailies; it indirectly controls most others. In December 1998, a popular talk show that voiced the public's increasing disenchantment with Mugabe was canceled. There is extensive self-censorship in government media.

Women's rights enjoy extensive legal protection. Domestic violence against women is common. The Labor Relations Act (LRA) protects private sector workers' rights, but public sector workers are barred from joining unions. Zimbabwe's economy has floundered as inflation soared to more than 40 percent and the country's fledging stock market plunged. Freedom House's 1998–99 *Freedom in the World* rates Zimbabwe a five in political rights and civil liberties.

Religious Freedom

Zimbabwe retains a strong African religious tradition and a large proportion of people who combine indigenous practices with Christian teachings. About a quarter of the country's people belong to mainstream Christian groups. Some of these groups are identified with particular regions or ethnic groups, a result of the localization of specific missions during the colonial period, due either to official geographic assignment policies or else the missions' available resources. Religion is generally not politicized, but both the colonial and current authoritarian administrations have found themselves at odds with religious groups over state violence and racial and social justice issues.

Christian missionaries began reaching the area of Central Africa that is now Zimbabwe in the late nineteenth century. Muslim traders had previously penetrated the region but left behind few local converts to Islam. Both the majority Shona and the second largest ethnic group, the Ndebele, possessed strong religious systems. Traditional priests helped lead resistance to British colonialism and were an integral part of the war against the white minority regime through the 1970s.

As in many other countries, traditional beliefs have often been adapted or incorporated into religions introduced later. This is especially prevalent in independent Christian churches not accountable to external hierarchies. The two main currents of African-instituted churches are the Apostolic and Zionist. Pentecostal churches with links to and funds from theologically conservative American groups are also gaining adherents. Many traditional spiritual and magical practices also remain current, including divination and healing ceremonies. Traditional healers are licensed and regulated by the Zimbabwe National African Healers' Association. Some other practices are related to witchcraft and sorcery, and accusations of harmful sorcery can lead to assaults, burnings, and lynchings.

Zimbabwe is officially a secular republic. Freedom of religious practice is constitutionally guaranteed, and the government generally respects this right. The constitution's Declaration of Rights includes several provisions that together enshrine broad religious freedom. These include a basic "freedom of thought, religion or belief"; the right to offer religious instruction in denominational schools; but a prohibition on coercion to receive religious instruction or to take an oath contrary to religious practice. However, these rights can be restricted "in interests of defense, public safety, public order, public morality or public health." One sect was banned under these powers because it reportedly engaged in ritual sex with minors.

Subject to restriction on anything the government finds subversive, which is a large category, there is freedom of worship, and to train and appoint clergy. Religious bodies have rights of self-government of religious education, to carry out charitable activities, to own and acquire property, and to maintain social institutions. They can produce, import, and distribute literature if the government does not find it offensive; receive donations; and have contact with coreligionists, domestically and overseas. Individuals can adopt, change, or leave a religion freely, with no change to civil status.

The government sets standards for education that denominational schools must meet, but these have not been applied to curtail religious education. The Education Act provides parental choice regarding religious education in state schools, but the Ministry of Education supplies a Religious and Morality Curriculum that is largely Christian oriented. Mission churches run much of the primary education system with government blessing and some funding. Other religious groups also run schools.

Zimbabwe's mainstream churches have clashed with authorities over human rights and justice issues and have joined with nongovernmental organizations and academics to create the country's leading human rights group, Zimrights. The Catholic Peace and Justice Commission worked against minority rule before Zimbabwe's 1980 independence and continues to denounce abuses under the current regime of President Robert Mugabe. President Mugabe, for his part, has accused churches of "double standards" and support for colonialism. A small Islamic community exists, but recent efforts at Muslim proselytizing have drawn rhetorically harsh reactions from some church leaders.

Three Americans who claimed to be missionaries were detained in March 1999 and charged with illegal possession of weapons. However, they had little or no history of missionary work and seem to be subject to the same limits on guns as other people.

APPENDIX 1:
NUMBERS AND STATISTICS

Country Population Figures

The figures given for the total population of each country are taken from the Population Reference Bureau's figures for mid-1999. It should be emphasized that, no matter what the source, population figures are not and can never be completely accurate, precise, or reliable. Some of this stems from insuperable methodological problems. Even the United States, whose constitution requires an "actual enumeration" of the population every ten years, and which devotes a great deal of resources to its census, does not know how many people live within its borders. The Census Bureau believes it may have missed several percent of the population, and the method of counting is a continuing cause of political dispute and even court action. In many other countries there has been less attention to censuses, and, in several, there has never been any census at all. Consequently these figures are likely to be even less accurate.

An even greater set of problems arises with definitions of population, that is, who is a citizen or resident of a country and who is not. For example, estimates of the population of Bhutan range from 0.6 million to 1.8 million. This partly reflects the fact that the Bhutanese government has persecuted its mostly Hindu, Nepali-speaking population and, in the 1990s, has driven tens of thousands of them out of the country, claiming that they were illegal immigrants. Since many of these refugees seem to posses valid documents of Bhutanese citizenship, there is

a question whether they should be included in the total population figures for Bhutan, even if the government disowns them. Similarly, the figure for Romania is often given as 22.5 million, but several analysts say it should be four to five million lower, since millions of Romanians left the country in the 1990s to escape dire economic conditions.

The numbers for Tibet reflect answers to the question of what actually constitutes Tibet. Tibetans live not only in the Chinese region of that name but also in the surrounding provinces of Sichuan, Gansu, Qinghai, and Yunnan, which the Chinese government administers separately. Depending on whether we define Tibet to include portions of these other regions, then the Tibetan population will be either approximately three million or six million. Similar questions of what constitutes a territory or a region affect population figures for countries as diverse as Indonesia, Pakistan, Moldova, Azerbaijan, and Israel.

Religious Adherents

When we turn our attention to statistics for the number of religious adherents within countries, we encounter similar and even greater problems. The best source for such information (www.adherents.com) lists many sources for each country, and the numbers given by these sources can vary up to 1,000 percent, even for large religious groups.

One set of difficulties simply reflects the problems noted above, which are inherent in *any* total-population figures. For example, the proportion of

Buddhists to Hindus in Nepal will reflect how we measure the total population. But there are also other difficult problems: many of these revolve around the questions of what religion is, what a particular religion is, and what a religious adherent is. Furthermore, different religions, as well as different governments and census bureaus, answer these questions differently.

There is no agreed definition on or specification of what religion is. While there is general agreement that, for example, Islam and Christianity are religions, other situations are less clear. Since Buddhism does not entail, and can deny, belief in a god or gods and is also usually accepted as a religion, then neither theism nor deism is presumably a requirement for religion. But, if so, is Confucianism then also a religion? Or Taoism? And, if they are included, then why not "secular humanism"? In this case we would be treating religion as any ultimate or basic belief or commitment, whether or not others regard it as "secular." In the United States, such a claim is often regarded as a tendentious one, often associated with the "religious right," but several Western European countries treat secular humanism as a religion or, at least, something to be recorded in listings of "religions and belief." Belgium, for example, recognizes and funds secular humanism (*la laicite*) on the same basis as it does other religions.

In this survey, religion is taken to include "religion and belief" so that, where figures and material are available, groups such as Confucians and secular humanists are included and surveyed. In other cases, where available figures on such groups usually simply list them as "nonreligious," this too is recorded. In any case, it should be clear that atheists and agnostics can be, and are, also

persecuted for their beliefs, and also need religious freedom.

These provisions do not take care of all the cases. For example, in some instances, being a Jew may be entirely disconnected from belief. There are atheist, agnostic, and believing Jews, even Buddhist Jews. Is Judaism then not a religion but an ethnicity or, rather, both? In this survey, it is taken to be both, and ethnic Jews are listed as Jews regardless of their beliefs.

We also encounter questions of what *particular* religions are. We have just noted conceptual difficulties around Judaism, but similar issues arise with most religious groups. The term *Hindu* comes from the same root as the term *India*, and both refer to the people and beliefs of the *Indus* valley. Hinduism is diverse and covers a wide range of beliefs. Should it then be regarded as referring to the whole range of beliefs that have been adopted by or spring from the people of the Indus? It is on this basis that India's nationalist BJP party claims that Hinduism is a defining characteristic of the Indian state. Many Hindus claim, with some historical justification, that Buddhism is a subgroup of Hinduism. Consequently, the Indian government has refused to recognize Buddhism, as well as Sikhism and Jainism, as separate religions from Hinduism. Many Islamic governments refuse to recognize Baha'ism as a separate religion or to recognize as valid any change of a religion from Islam. Baha'is are often persecuted on the basis that they are claimed to be heretical or apostate Muslims.

There is also the question of *who* is a member of a particular religion. In many countries, people regard themselves as adherents of more than one religion. In India there are Christians who also regard themselves as Hindus. In Japan it is very common for people to claim more than one religious adherence: the total of individually claimed religious membership is higher than the total population. In many parts of Asia and Africa, as well as Latin America, people combine Christianity with traditional beliefs. In this case, giving the number of, for example, Christians, as distinct from those who follow traditional practices, is a difficult exercise, as the two grade into one another.

Even when people are more or less involved with only one religion, there is the question of how much attachment is required to define an adherent. This is an especially acute problem in Europe, the part of the world where the division between religious practice and nominal religious identity is the greatest, although similar questions arise throughout the former Soviet Union. In Bulgaria, the 1992 census includes, apart from many Protestants, a large minority of self-defined nonreligious people as members of the Bulgarian Orthodox Church. As a result, government statistics list 85 percent of the population as "Orthodox," even though only 60 percent of the population claim any religious affiliation at all. In Scandinavian countries, membership in the Lutheran Church (usually denoting having been baptized as an infant) is usually given as 90 percent plus. However, church attendance is usually less than 10 percent of the population. Which of these figures should be used to denote the percentage of "Lutherans" in the country? It depends.

Nor are these questions simply of interest to pedants in the sociology of religion. Since, in many countries of the world, religion and political affiliation are closely related, if not identical, they are of fundamental political import. For example, in Lebanon, the distribution of high political offices is decided according to the percentage of religious groups in the population. Consequently, figures for confessional groups are highly contested and are currently ascribed according to a decades-old census.

There is no simple, noncontroversial way either of avoiding or transcending these questions. Our response simply has to be clarified, explained, and justified. There is also the additional requirement that, as this survey is also intended to be comparative, it has to consider the relative availability of statistics in different countries, and the accuracy and reliability of these statistics. Given that statistics for committed belief are rare and hard to achieve, and that statistics for nominal adherence are available for many countries on a roughly comparable basis, this survey describes religious adherents according to their formal affiliation with a religious group. Consequently, the description of someone as a Christian in the Netherlands, a Hindu in India, or a Muslim in Indonesia does not necessarily say anything about their own individual committed religious belief. It merely specifies an external religious identifier. While this is a huge distinction, it is largely in the secularized West and countries presently or formerly under communism that it makes the largest difference. In most other parts of the world, a person's nominal adherence and religious practice are much more congruent, thus the figures given for nominal adherence to a religion more closely reflect the beliefs of the populace, if not the depth of their commitment.

In any case, in this survey, the statistics for members of any particular religion reflect their nominal adherence rather than their actual participation. Where there are figures for actual attendance at religious worship or other ceremonies, or where alternative figures for religious adherence are available, usually these are noted in the text for each country.

APPENDIX 2:
CRITERIA FOR PROFILES
OF RELIGIOUS FREEDOM*

In each of the country profiles, we have sought to:

- Give a listing, with percentages, of the religious groupings within the country.
- Give a brief religious background of the country; what the major religious groups are now; what they have been historically; what changes are taking place; whether religion(s) tend to be tied to ethnicity, or to region, or to political parties; whether religious commitment is high or low, fanatic, lukewarm, or nominal.
- Mention any constitutional guarantees or restrictions on religious freedom, and other constitutional guarantees or restrictions relevant to religious freedom, and whether the guarantees are respected.
- Outline the legal framework that guarantees or restricts religious freedom, and other guarantees or restrictions relevant to religious freedom, and whether the guarantees are respected.
- Mention if the country has a federal political structure, and, if it is relevant, outline the legal framework at the provincial/state/regional level.
- Mention if religious freedom is restricted by law, outline the scope of the restrictions (e.g., what is forbidden or hampered), what the penalties for violations are, and to what degree the law is actually enforced.
- Mention if the government restricts religious freedom by extralegal means; outline the scope

of the restrictions and the penalties for violations.

- Mention any restrictions on religious freedom by "society," such as repression by family members, physical attacks, mob riots, or discrimination or exclusion in employment, housing, movement, and so forth. Here, also note the degree to which the government tries and succeeds in curbing social restrictions on religious freedom.
- Mention any restrictions on religious freedom due to warfare or terrorism and the degree to which government tries and succeeds in curbing such restrictions on religious freedom.
- Mention if other factors are helping or hindering religious freedom which are not covered by the above.
- Mention if there are noteworthy incidents in the last two years (and very noteworthy ones in the last decade). They could include important trials, imprisonment, massacres, and so forth.
- Use these criteria and the checklist to assign the country a score on a religious freedom scale of one to seven, with one being very good and seven being very bad.

The following checklist attempts to summarize the various possible dimensions of religious freedom and broadly follows the criteria given in international human rights standards. It is also derived from a similar checklist given by Willy Fautre. Many parts are repetitive: this is because it approaches the same material from different angles, such as individual freedom, self-government by religious bodies, or discriminatory treatment between religious bodies. Similarly, many boxes will be empty.

The vertical categories refer to different elements of religious freedom. The horizontal categories refer to the presence or absence of freedom, the degree of the restriction of freedom, the nature of the restriction, the intensity of the restriction, the variability of the restriction, and the agent(s) of restriction.

The first four horizontal categories are: (a) yes, (b) no, (c) yes, but, (d) no, except. The other boxes (e–p) evaluate the following aspects of each religious freedom:

e. Constitutionally guaranteed?
f. Legally guaranteed?
g. Applies to some groups, but not to others (this can then be taken up in the later section on discrimination)?
h. Suffers *de facto* or *de jure* limitation by the state?
i. Suffers *de facto* or *de jure* limitation by regional government?
j. Suffers *de facto* or *de jure* limitation by local government?
k. Suffers *de facto* or *de jure* limitation by local government agents (such as police), acting unofficially?

l. Severity of penalties applied to those who break government limits on religious freedom, e.g., fine, imprisonment, death, etc.?
m. Suffers discrimination or practical limitation through social pressure (access to employment or housing, familial violence, etc.), which the government tries to limit?
n. As m, but the government does *not* try to limit it.
o. Suffers violence or threat from radical groups, which the government tries to limit?
p. As o, but the government does *not* try to limit it.

Apart from the overall summary, each profile mentions any noteworthy incidents in the last couple of years—such as the massacre of Shi'ites in northern Afghanistan in August 1998, the apparent suicide of a Catholic bishop in Pakistan, the hanging of a Baha'i in Iran—so that we can get the flavor of the country.

Finally, depending on the size and complexity of the country, religious freedom profiles were limited to from five hundred to two thousand words.

Copies of these criteria and the accompanying checklist were sent to the writers of the country reports.

Checklist of Elements of Religious Freedom

I. Individuals' Right to Freedom of Conscience

Do citizens have the right . . .	(a) Yes	(b) No	(c) Yes, but	(d) No, except	(e)	(f)	(g)	(h)	(i)	(j)	(k)	(l)	(m)	(n)	(o)	(p)
1.1 . . . to have or not have a religion or belief of their choice?																
1.2 . . . to adopt or to abandon a religion or belief?																
1.3 . . . to change religion or belief?																
1.4 . . . to be members of religious or nonreligious communities of their choice?																
1.5 . . . to keep private their religious or nonreligious affiliation (e.g., in the case of a census)?																
1.6 . . . to manifest, to defend, to promote, and to disseminate their religious or nonreligious beliefs in private?																
1.7 . . . to manifest, to defend, to promote, and to disseminate their religious or nonreligious beliefs in public?																
1.8 . . . to manifest, to defend, to promote, and to disseminate their religious or nonreligious beliefs in the media?																
1.9 . . . to take part in worship services, processions, and pilgrimages, and to perform the rites associated with their religion or belief?																
1.10 . . . to choose not to take part in worship services and religious rites or customs that conflict with their personal beliefs?																
1.11 . . . to observe or not to observe days of rest in accordance with their religious beliefs and to celebrate festivals and ceremonies, whether secular or religious?																
1.12 . . . to make, seek out, acquire, import, export, and possess literature, audio or video cassettes, and other objects related to their religious or nonreligious beliefs?																
1.13 . . . to write, issue, and disseminate relevant publications?																
1.14 . . . to watch and listen to religious broadcasts on the radio and television?																
1.15 . . . to choose not to follow directives or to take part in official activities the aims of which conflict with their religious or nonreligious beliefs?																
1.16 . . . other?																

II. Freedom of Worship

Do communities of believers have the right . . .	(a) Yes	(b) No	(c) Yes, but	(d) No, except	(e)	(f)	(g)	(h)	(i)	(j)	(k)	(l)	(m)	(n)	(o)	(p)
2.1 . . . to have legal status?																
2.2 . . . to manifest their religious beliefs by holding private worship services?																
2.3 . . . to manifest their religious beliefs by holding public worship services?																
2.4 . . . to build, reopen, restore, and maintain religious premises and places of worship where they can hold services?																
2.5 . . . to rent premises for religious worship?																
2.6 . . . to own their religious premises and places of worship?																
2.7 . . . to claim back religious premises and places of worship that have been unfairly confiscated from them?																
2.8 . . . to make full and free use of their chosen religious premises and places of worship in order to hold meetings and to carry out religious rites or customs?																
2.9 . . . to manufacture, acquire, and use religious objects and artifacts according to their needs?																
2.10 . . . to own their religious objects and artifacts?																
2.11 . . . to hold services or meetings and to perform their rites or customs in a place other than their official premises (in open air, in cemeteries, private homes, hospitals, children's homes, prisons, army barracks)?																
2.12 . . . to have free access to places sacred to their religion or belief?																
2.13 . . . to organize processions and pilgrimages?																
2.14 . . . to celebrate religious festivals in public or in private?																
2.15 . . . to celebrate baptisms, weddings, and burials and so forth in accordance with their religious traditions?																
2.16 . . . to choose freely their religious personnel for their religious services and meetings?																
2.17 . . . other?																

III. Freedom of Clergy

Do ministers/clergy/religious leaders have the right . . .	(a) Yes	(b) No	(c) Yes, but	(d) No, except	(e)	(f)	(g)	(h)	(i)	(j)	(k)	(l)	(m)	(n)	(o)	(p)
3.1 . . . to perform the rites and customs established by their religious community using the holy books and liturgical texts of their choice and using the language, music, and songs of their choice?																
3.2 . . . to preach in conformity with the doctrine of their religious community, without threat or interference from the state?																
3.3 . . . to have access to prisons, hospitals, the armed forces, and other relevant bodies for chaplaincy work?																
3.4 . . . other?																

IV. Right to Social Participation

Do religious groups have the right . . .	(a) Yes	(b) No	(c) Yes, but	(d) No, except	(e)	(f)	(g)	(h)	(i)	(j)	(k)	(l)	(m)	(n)	(o)	(p)
4.1 . . . to establish, manage, maintain, and conduct charitable, humanitarian, medical, social, and cultural institutions and associations?																
4.2 . . . to establish and practice printing houses, publishing houses, and distribution networks?																
4.3 . . . to found and own newspapers, news agencies, radio and television stations, and other media?																
4.4 . . . to have access to means of public communication (television, radio, Internet, newspapers, magazines)?																
4.5 . . . to found political parties?																
4.6 . . . other?																

V. Freedom of Religious Education and Instruction

	(a) Yes	(b) No	(c) Yes, but	(d) No, except	(e)	(f)	(g)	(h)	(i)	(j)	(k)	(l)	(m)	(n)	(o)	(p)
5.1. Do families have the right to decide whether their children receive a religious education or not?																
5.2. Do religious communities have the authority to ensure that religious instruction is given to the children entrusted to their care?																
5.3. Do religious communities have the authority to run elementary schools, secondary schools, universities, and other institutes of higher education?																
5.4. Can religious instruction be given in teaching establishments that are not run by the religious community concerned?																
5.5. Are the religious and moral beliefs of believers' children studying in state schools truly respected?																
5.6. Are believers' children free not to participate in the activities of official organizations that have aims contrary to their religious and moral beliefs?																
5.7. Are the various teaching establishments subject to the same set of rules, regardless of their religious or nonreligious orientation?																
5.8. Other?																

VI. Right to Self-Government by Religious Bodies

Do communities of believers have the right …	(a) Yes	(b) No	(c) Yes, but	(d) No, except	(e)	(f)	(g)	(h)	(i)	(j)	(k)	(l)	(m)	(n)	(o)	(p)
6.1 … to implement their own institutional and hierarchical structures?																
6.2 … to train, appoint, elect, or designate their future officers themselves, and to train them in their own institutes?																
6.3 … to appoint, to locate, and to relocate their officers according to their needs?																
6.4 … to appoint, to elect, and to designate their own leaders?																
6.5 … to set up communities and religious orders?																
6.6 … to own possessions and to use them as they choose?																
6.7 … to build, acquire, reopen, and restore buildings and then to operate them independently?																
6.8 … to exchange, acquire, receive, import, and use holy books and other religious publications?																
6.9 … to write, print, and circulate, according to their needs, books and publications that deal with religious matters or that defend the freedom of conscience or religion?																
6.10 … to establish and maintain relationships with individuals and communities involved in religious affairs, without regard for national boundaries?																
6.11 … to solicit and receive voluntary financial and other contributions from individuals and institutions, either domestically or internationally?																
6.12 … other?																

VII. Equality/Nondiscrimination of Individuals

Do believers of different religions, different groups within religions, and atheists enjoy the same rights in the following areas?	(a) Yes	(b) No	(c) Yes, but	(d) No, except	(e)	(f)	(g)	(h)	(i)	(j)	(k)	(l)	(m)	(n)	(o)	(p)
7.1. Free to manifest their religious beliefs by holding private worship services.																
7.2. Free to manifest their religious beliefs by holding public worship services.																
7.3. The enjoyment of economic, social, and cultural rights and advantages.																
7.4. Accommodation in employment, schools, and prisons to manifest their religious belief.																
7.5. Before the courts.																
7.6. Public life; Ability to hold public office.																
7.7. Military service and conscientious objection.																
7.8. Freedom of expression.																
7.9. Freedom to seek information and to receive it from others																
7.10. Freedom of movement and of emigration.																
7.11. Freedom of association and assembly.																
7.12. Marriage or other social arrangements.																
7.13. Other.																

VIII. Equality/Nondiscrimination of Communities and Institutions

Do communities of believers, different groups within religions, atheistic groups, and institutions enjoy the same rights in the following areas?	(a) Yes	(b) No	(c) Yes, but	(d) No, except	(e)	(f)	(g)	(h)	(i)	(j)	(k)	(l)	(m)	(n)	(o)	(p)
8.1. Is there a state church or religion?																
8.2. The establishment, management, and maintenance of charitable, humanitarian, medical, social, cultural, and religious institutions and associations.																
8.3. The soliciting, receipt, and handling of voluntary contributions, financial or other, from individuals and institutions.																
8.4. The establishment and management of printing houses, publishing houses, and distribution networks.																
8.5. The founding and running of newspapers, press agencies, radio and television stations, and other media.																
8.6. Access to various public networks of social communications.																
8.7. The public sector: legal status, representation on committees, in local administrations, etc.																
8.8. The defense of their rights and denouncing of any attack on their freedom.																
8.9. Chaplaincy arrangements.																
8.10. Other.																